ENGLISH LITERATURE AND IDEAS IN THE TWENTIETH CENTURY

ENGLISH LITERATURE
AND IDEAS IN
THE TWENTIETH CENTURY

An Inquiry into Present Difficulties
and Future Prospects

by

H. V. ROUTH

M.A., D.LIT., F.R.S.L.

"That in our days a literature is alive is shown by its
submitting problems to debate."—G. BRANDES.

SECOND EDITION

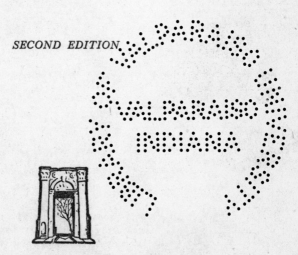

METHUEN & CO. LTD. LONDON
36 Essex Street, Strand, W.C.2

First published . *May 16th, 1946*
Second edition . . *1948*

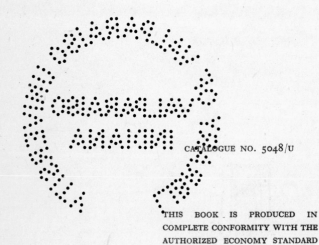

CATALOGUE NO. 5048/U

PRINTED IN GREAT BRITAIN

FOREWORD

THE purpose of this Inquiry needs a word of explanation. It does not present a record of every contemporary author worth reading. An adequate discussion of so many names would exceed the limits of any single volume, however capacious. Besides, the requisite lists and summaries can be found elsewhere, for instance, in Millett, Manley, and Rickert's *Contemporary British Literature* (3rd ed., 1935), in B. Fehr's brochures on English literature and culture (1932-4), in series *Hefte zur Englandkunde* (*ed.* H. Schöffler, Tauchnitz, Leipzig), in the appropriate volumes of B. Dobrée's *Introductions to English Literature* (1938, 1939), in Kunitz and Haycruft's *Twentieth Century Authors* (1942). Even these are not complete, for selection is unavoidable, as in the case of any other epoch. But since contemporary writers are not yet placed and labelled, some omissions are bound to be regrettable. I cannot hope to escape that criticism.

On the other hand, I believe that I have included and discussed every name which serves the spirit of twentieth-century literature. That spirit is unique. There are more brilliant periods, but none in which living was so easy (in peace time) and thinking so difficult. Our best poetry and prose have been almost overwhelmed by the impact of ideas. In fact many of the most notable achievements seem to be pointless until we realize the peculiar and by no means homogeneous atmosphere in which each was conceived. This atmosphere may be artistic, philosophical, religious, social, scientific, cynical, intuitive, or spun out of the writer's independent consciousness, but whatever its import, it is tentative and inconclusive. Perhaps that is the reason why humanism and dogma play so small a part. So I have attempted to discuss our most prominent authors in relation to the ideas which fermented in their heads, and happen to be fermenting in ours. The book is a discussion of literature linked to thought.

These authors, of course, are equally interesting when one considers the style, technique, imagery, presentment, and symbolism through which they express their ideologies; but contrary to a current opinion, they do not naturally fall into groups or schools.

In this age all good writers are free-lances. One cannot even divide or (what is worse) bisect them into prose and verse without obscuring their significance.

As already agreed, they are too recent to receive a final verdict. For that very reason I cannot resist speculating on their future places in our history of literature. There is no better way of arriving at a judgement which is dispassionate even if mistaken.

This book has been long meditated and frequently rewritten. I do not expect the reader to take it as seriously as did the author.

Whatever the outcome, I cannot end without thanking my friend Tom Stretton for the labour of revising the whole script, making valuable suggestions, and correcting an alarming accumulation of errors.

H. V. ROUTH

Verdley Edge,
September 1944

CONTENTS

vii

PART I

PRE-WAR PHASE

CHAPTER I

TRANSITION AT ABOUT 1900

FIRST SIGNS OF THE RIFT

AS far as we can judge, the period under discussion is unlike any other in the history of literature. It has arisen amid a ferment of inspiring and suggestive ideas; it has brought to the surface a surprisingly large number of really gifted writers; it has assembled an enormous reading public, only too anxious to make the fortune of any author who can hold its attention; likewise an unusually large proportion of sympathetic and discursive critics bent on teaching the reader how to appreciate a genius even before he has proved his quality. Yet somehow the authors have not lived up to their opportunities. They seem to fall short of our expectations. There is effort, experiment, adventure in plenty, with here and there a glimpse into the Unknown. But for the most part their paths divide, lost among incomplete achievements and causes which ought never to be won. It is quite possible that none of them will ever join the Brotherhood of Immortals, however great their present reputation.

Is literature, then, slowly dying out of our civilization, in which it has no longer a place; or is it entering upon a new life too big to be mastered without half a century of unsuccessful endeavour? That is the question which any history of the period ought to answer, unless the historian is content to classify his authors according to subject-matter and technique, and tell his readers what they have been told before.

The inquiry is of absorbing interest both to special students and to the general reader. The student will have a chance of studying an age of indecision, not as if it were the post-Chaucerian or pre-Shakespearean period—a museum piece, isolated in a glass case—but at first hand, a living problem, with the nexus of causes and consequences under his eyes. The general reader will be interested because this nexus is intertwined with the conditions under which we now live, and which we must hand on to the next generation. The study of twentieth-century prose and poetry is also the study of our advance into the future.

Before beginning to trace this history, we must decide where to begin. The starting point cannot definitely be fixed, because it arose not out of a manifesto, nor the inauguration of a new school of writing, but out of a change in public taste, which means a change of heart. The authors followed the lead because they were themselves part of the public. The first impulses begin to be noticeable about 1870, and become unmistakable about 1900–3. By a convenient coincidence, the death of the Queen and the defeat of De Wet opened the door to the new age which for years had been tugging at the handle.

What did these Edwardian intruders want to change? It used to be said that they were chiefly outraged by Victorian self-complacency and humbug. Such a complaint might well have been raised by social and religious reformers; and lovers of literature no doubt joined in the cry, since authors reflect the voices around them. Besides, the accusation might, as often as not, apply to their own parents and ageing relatives. But it could not be applied to the Victorian literary tradition. No one could allege that the authors of *Vanity Fair*, *David Copperfield*, *Maud*, *Past and Present*, *Bishop Blougram*, *Hard Cash*, *Culture and Anarchy*, *On Liberty*, *Short Studies on Great Subjects*, *Beauchamp's Career*, *The New Grub Street*, *Fleet Street Eclogues* were complacent. There was another deeper reason. Their idiom, their manner of presentment, the play of their imagination, even the rhythms and structure of their verse, seemed gradually to be losing the old magic. There was no obvious imperfection in either the manner or the matter; the word simply failed to evoke the spirit. Thus at first the rift was felt to be a change in literary taste.

WHY THE RIFT WAS INEVITABLE

Of course a reaction in any case was due, because art must always be renewed. Its creative influence depends on surprise. When once the freshness of the presentment has faded, the reader relapses into his daily habits. He looks for a vision and sees only phenomena. So a great book must always come with a shock of novelty, convincing the inquirer that he is only at the beginning of things, and that experiences are merely materials to play with and reconstruct into a deeper or wider perception. Had no more been needed, the literature of the last half-century would have been much greater than it is, for genius was far from dead. But at the accession of Edward VII it was not fully realized that the very materials of literature—the ideas, experiences, moods, attitudes—had changed. Freshness was lacking and could be supplied, but it must be on another level. The spirit of man may be always the same, but, like other ruminants, it has to seek new pastures.

WHY THE PASTURES NEEDED CHANGING

This failure or disintegration of values, the true cause of transition, has often been emphasized, but seldom discussed, and even then mostly with reference to the inter-war period. In reality the disillusionment began to spread twenty or thirty years earlier, but the younger generation misunderstood what was wrong, and therefore did not know how to put it right. The old values had begun to crumble before the new values began to be established.

Those who were learning to think and talk in the 'eighties and 'nineties were still being trained to enjoy the traditional culture, not without good reason; but were also training themselves to look for many things which discredited those traditions. In the first place the young were being taught by their elders to prize 'the things of the spirit' above worldly prosperity, but when they went out into the world they realized (as Gissing could show them) that the former was almost unattainable without the latter. Studious leisure, travel, and even healthy surroundings were expensive as well as necessary advantages. They had learnt to value the morals and manners of the gentleman, but social intercourse (together with Meredith's and Hardy's novels, and Wilde's comedies) soon convinced them that this cult had become a caste, and one easily to be imitated—again, by the help of money. It is true that in 1777 Dr. Johnson, possibly the best-read man of his age, could affirm [1] that opulence 'excludes but one evil—poverty'; but in 1863 Samuel Butler, ahead of his time, could write that money was like *antennae*; without it the human insect lost touch with its environment.[2] He who would acquire scholarship or gentility must first acquire cash. In order to make the best of himself, the average youth must first make money. He would have to sacrifice to possessiveness the qualities which should render possessions worth while.

His father would probably not have been so disconcerted, for many of the older generation had inherited a spiritual recess into which they could retire from the rather sordid and frequently successful battle of life. This resource did not cost money, but it cost something which money cannot buy—the contemplation of a cosmic order which transcends our limited experience, the identification with some Divine Intelligence, or Superhuman Plan which absorbs and purifies our petty egoisms, the merging of our will in a higher will. This resource was still open to those versed in the older humanisms, or indeed in modern Christianity, but was far less convincing (as George Eliot realized) when Strauss, Renan, Colenso, Schweitzer were arguing that *The Bible*, even *The New Testament*, was not the voice of God, but a corpus of myths and legends. By the same token, it was less satisfying to contemplate the sweet tranquillity of the English scene, when every glade in springtime was the centre of a savage struggle for life, as any biologist could prove and the hero of Tennyson's *Maud* had already discovered.

There was, indeed, the world of ancient erudition, classical scholarship and medieval idealism, for those who could afford to

[1] Boswell, Chap. LX.   [2] *Darwin among the Machines.*

lead a cloistered existence. Any such study contained a story of real life and convinced its votaries that it was man's function to rally the good in the depths of himself, and that he could be trusted, with the help of classical wisdom or medieval piety, to be true to his best instincts; for man is a spiritual being. But this age was realizing, every day more forcibly, that man is also a social being, and that industrial problems were already menacing the peace of Europe. Many who in an earlier age would have been content with the cult of self-perfection were now ready to accept the duty of working for others. Not a few were beginning to ponder Karl Marx, Engels, Ruskin, Morris, Henry George, and to discuss practical suggestions for the reconstruction of society. A student's career seemed to be little better than a living death when there was so much to be done.

Nor was social reform by any means the only attraction. Antiquarianism and scholarship had thrived partly on comparisons with the alleged monotony and soullessness of modern civilization. But the new age was neither soulless nor monotonous, and could well dream dreams in its own setting. For instance, there was no need to agree with Sir Richard Jebb that the *Anabasis* [1] was the most interesting book ever written, when contemporary adventurers were beginning to find their way towards the North and South Poles, and mechanization was opening voyages of discovery among the remotest peoples.

There were other and less ambitious resources, which had served the Victorians well, amongst them the sanctities of home life. But when the ideal of the gentleman declined, the sentiment for the family circle declined also. Young men and even women were no longer too genteel to earn money; besides, there were more opportunities; and having once realized the prospect of financial independence, they quickly realized the burden of parental authority and domestic narrowness—a series of irritating frustrations, misrepresented as filial duty. The sentiment of love often followed the sentiment of home. Now that young people began early to live their own lives, and consequently saw much more of each other, they responded readily to the half understood promptings of sex, gathering hints from scientific gossip. So love became much less of a romance and much more an experience.

All these are a few examples of the disintegration of values. When an author played on such sentiments as the contempt for money, divine love, natural beauty, the sanctities of home life, classical scholarship, and communion with the spirits of the Past, he ran the risk of striking a false chord. He might do well to persist in one of the familiar themes, but he would have to catch his readers in an unfamiliar mood—evoke thoughts and emotions not previously associated with the subject. The rising generation did not unlearn so much without learning something to take its place. So

---

[1] *Greek Literature*, 1877.

the literary adventurer must needs link the old idea to a new attitude ; in other words, cultivate a fresh point of view and, above all, a fresh technique.

THE POST-VICTORIAN ATTITUDE

It is of course well known that the impulse behind this iconoclasm was the impact of scientific thought, which had been gathering momentum since the Renaissance, and then, towards the end of the nineteenth century, suddenly took possession of intellectual progress. Its prevalence, in the first place, was almost irresistible, because it suited the age. The older pre-scientific culture was a laborious and privileged acquisition. It made a personal and intimate appeal to each of its votaries. The humanist had to rely on his own individual and carefully trained powers of intuition or what, in a different connexion, Newman termed the ' illative sense '. But scientific truths, when once established, are either beyond the comprehension of any laymen, or else are equally intelligible to all, and can generally be communicated in a formula. So they appeal to mass-thinking, and in an age of mass-education they win by sheer weight of numbers. In the next place these truths might seem, at a casual glance, to be foul treason to our treasured inheritance of thought and aspiration ; but nevertheless they penetrated far more deeply than Darwin, Romanes,[1] or Karl Pearson [2] imagined. They played on the feelings which had animated humanity long before science was heard of. They interested him afresh in the problems of destiny, conduct, and selfhood.

This interest caused perplexity and restlessness because it was two-sided, culminating in a paradox. On the one hand no thoughtful and imaginative reader could accept the physical and biological conclusions, so amply documented from Lyell to Huxley, without admitting that the universe looks like a colossal blunder ; that human life on our inhospitable globe is an accident, due to unknown causes which may never be repeated ; and that this accident has involved more suffering and maladjustment than any other form of evolution ; and for certain temperaments the interpretation stops there, ending in stoicism, overwhelming pity, or despair. Thomas Hardy, Mark Rutherford, A. E. Housman, and Somerset Maugham are examples. On the other hand it was equally permissible to admit that Nature was not indeed a system planned by a Divine Architect or Economist, but an experimental force, appallingly wasteful and pitiless, but infinitely resourceful and adaptable, hopelessly uneconomical, but irrepressibly progressive. Those who faced the evidence fairly and squarely, instead of losing faith in the tradition of human grandeur, might be rewarded with a new romance of self-knowledge, based on scientific truth. The materialists were perhaps not mistaken.

[1] *Thoughts on Religion*. Edited by C. Gore, 1895 posth.
[2] *The Grammar of Science*, 1st ed., 1892.

They were all the more worth attention because, in reality, they were not materialists.   Modern Europeans must have existed in their animal ancestors for at least 500,000,000 years, as submen for about 500,000 years, as men for about 20,000–50,000 years, as thinkers, each in his own civilization, for about 500 years.   Thus there must be inherited tendencies within us too elemental and mysterious to be interpreted by any of the old-fashioned schools of ethics or theology.   Human nature was both an abyss and a labyrinth, from its earliest phases the source of our deepest impulses, affinities, urges, and consequently aspirations.   Who could say whether these appetencies were good or bad ?   No man knew what secret forces permeated his system, because he had always compelled himself, or been compelled, to govern his life by his intellect worked out on a pattern.   Whereas the proper function of the humanist—especially in literature—might be to explore this labyrinth, to appreciate its elusive universality, to establish spiritual contacts and sensuous experiences by which our innermost animal selves could be brought to the surface and humanized.   As even Oscar Wilde once remarked, ' I am the only person in the world I should like to know thoroughly, but I don't see any chance of it just at present '.

Such were the new opportunities to be vigorously exploited in the twentieth century, leading some to a deeper curiosity in their lower selves, leading others to a clearer conception of a second higher nature acquired no one knew how.   We might be half animal and half god, and if so, it would rest with us to cultivate the better half.   But it was even more important to realize that man had not only gained a further insight into himself, but as if by accident an unexpected control of his destiny.   Beside the science of knowledge, there was the science of power.

Civilization (not culture) had practically resolved itself into technics, civil organization, and the arts of mechanized industry ; that is to say, the science of power.   The nineteenth century had not faced the situation philosophically.   Its poets and moralists began by celebrating the doctrine of progress, and ended by deploring the evils of industrialism.   This disillusionment reached its climax in 1860–80, when manufacture had changed into machino-facture, and had become—inevitably—a theme for protests ever since.   But neither the Victorians nor their successors have fully realized the implications of this transition.   For instance, a tunnel was driven through Mont Cenis in 1870, the telephone was invented by Gray and Bell in 1876.   In the same year the first dynamo was constructed.   In 1866 Bernard's *Médecine Expérimentale* proved that we learn from the human body how to make it stronger, healthier, and longer-lived.   In the 'seventies Pasteur was establishing the science of killing microbes and Lister was using his discoveries to ensure asepsis in operations.   Berthelot, having discovered the principles of chemical synthesis, was proclaiming that the *savant* of the future would be master of our bodies—almost of our souls. All would be explained, foreseen, prepared by science.

The trend of these achievements is most significant. Even if a humanist despaired of adapting his nature to his environment (as did Thomas Hardy), he could yet hope to adapt his environment to his nature. He was beginning to master the elements of his fate, not only those physical and metaphysical obstacles—space and time—but his most persistent and elusive enemies, disease and death. Our fathers were already beginning to enjoy a sense of security and self-rectification unknown to former ages. Men might soon realize that their only adversaries were each other, and then only if competition became too keen for compromise. Hence our newly assured attitude to ourselves—to the claims of our individuality, and to the indulgence of our own personality; hence also the increased risk of disillusionment, should these hopes prove to be premature. The paradox of the new learning should now be clear. Science, which reduced man to an animal, has nevertheless given that animal so much power that he can count himself greater than the universe out of which he evolved.

With such accessions to our resources and resourcefulness we have entered upon a phase of which everybody does not yet appreciate the responsibilities and implications. That is why the task of the twentieth-century author is so exceptionally difficult. More often than not, neither he nor his readers clearly understand what culture has lost and gained in the last half-century. Some readers and writers have been so impressed by the spectacle of mechanical power that they seem to accept technical efficiency as an object in itself, often to the exclusion of the older values. Others, alarmed at materialism, have availed themselves of its mechanical advantages but yet refused it any foothold on the ladder of culture. They seek consolation and self-expression in the ever-dwindling and over-cultivated resources of the unmechanized or pre-mechanical worlds.

And yet everyone feels, if only obscurely, that the idea of the machine is stealing over our habits of mind, bringing with it a sense of mathematical adjustment and simplicity of design. For instance, in *Le Rappel à l'Ordre* Cocteau declares, ' It is a weakness not to comprehend the beauty of a machine. The fault lies in depicting machines instead of taking from them a lesson in rhythm.' Some authors and artists were gradually to learn that lesson, trying to interweave and concentrate their feelings so as to suggest organization and one-pointedness. The elimination of the superfluous (on the model of a machine) was particularly urgent because this mechanized civilization has not only bestowed the sense of power, but has complicated that gift with a million petty obligations. One would have to spend a few days in the seventeenth or eighteenth century to realize how unavoidably we now live by the clock, applying our energies not according to mood and impulse, but according to a time scheme; how unobtrusively we are enslaved to our mechanical conveniences—tubes, escalators, suburban trains, city and country buses, water-mains, electrified cookers, circulators, registrations, government forms, the attendance of the dentist, and the treatments of the general practitioner. These and such-like services confer both freedom and enslavement, efficiency and embarrassment; more significant, they instil their own peculiar rhythm, which is symbolized as the presence of an objective world interwoven with our personal habits and inclinations, yet extraneous to our sensibilities. So there is a prospect that culture may become the study and control of these forces,[1] and that just as machinery influences the collective mind, so the collective mind may influence machinery, directing its development by the weight of public opinion or curiosity.

The twentieth-century author would have to reflect this atmosphere, and his art would certainly find but little help from the nineteenth.

THE NEW READING PUBLIC

Thus civilization would in any case have influenced the tastes of the reading public, even if that public were still as it used to be; that is to say, the cultured middle-class, not too numerous to be more or less united in tone and temper, however divided in opinion. Even in the mid-nineteenth century the right book soon fell into the right hands. But before 1900 another much wider and less accountable public had joined the patrons of the book-market: the erstwhile self-educating class now, since 1870, fully educated by the State. These newcomers perceived only too well that a world of intellectual refinement existed, just barely within their reach, and they fully realized that the readiest approach was through the literature which the Victorian middle-class had created. To facilitate this approach, the publishers of the early twentieth century began issuing whole series of cheaply reprinted classics. The proletarian enthusiasts were also in a hurry for their culture. They could not indulge in the scholar's leisurely assimilation of truth and literary taste. So the new age also brought with it a spate of extension manuals on literature, aesthetics, philosophy, and politics— short cuts to the Promised Land. A generation later they supplemented these with yet another spate of anthologies in prose and verse, and essays in science made easy. Nevertheless the newcomers were not at their ease, and with good reason. Some of the best Victorian literature and learning illustrated a stable society, meet for a governing class which had entrenched itself on the economic laws of wealth, the truth of Christianity, and the legality of the British constitution. The details might cry to Heaven for improvement, but the outlines then seemed to be fixed for ever. That is why Tennyson, Browning, Dickens, Thackeray, Trollope,

---

[1] L. Mumford, *Technics and Civilization*, 1934.

Carlyle, Macaulay, Mill, George Eliot, and Spencer write as if we must all find the expression of our best selves within the limits of the framework. We have already noticed that stability must become static even for the most favoured of the tax-paying classes, but now the normal call for movement was disconcertingly complicated by the multitudinous infiltration of the cheaply educated, who had no share in the inheritance, but very decided plans for its redistribution, together with the assertion of their own peculiar codes of moral and sexual freedom. Even those who tried to understand the wit and wisdom of the Past, could not shut their eyes to the rhythm of the machine, the all-pervading impression of flux and flight, nor hesitate to demand a culture of their own adjusted to these shifting sands.

Thus there were at least two publics, each with its own differentiations and nuances. Of course an author might be content to cultivate one single interest, in one or the other. Some were incapable of doing more—for instance, Henry James or Barry Pain (to quote extremes). But what an opportunity for the novelist, poet, or critic who could capture the whole of this million-headed and many-minded audience ! He would have more power than any crowned head, and, incidentally, nearly as big an income.

Such a possibility, however, only increased the dangers and difficulties of authorship. To think everybody else's thoughts is to distrust one's own, and savours more of a journalist's insight than a poet's perception. Says Dryden :

> Errors, like straws, upon the surface flow,
> He who would search for pearls must dive below,

and the straws might help the ambitious author more than the pearls.

There was an even more insidious temptation. These reading publics were uncertain of their ideologies and detached from their background, but desperately anxious to be impressed. They wanted to be led. So some authors could not resist trying to lead them in the quickest, easiest way, playing on their susceptibilities, and exploiting their enthusiasms. When once a style and an attitude had been established, it was not so difficult to talk them into the required point of view, by harping on the theme and reiterating examples. Thus the clever writer might end as the prophet of a school in which he did not believe. Often, no doubt, the magician fell a victim to his own incantations. We shall meet many examples of that likelihood.

But whatever the author's intention, his chief care was to increase his circulation. Few people are averse to making a reputation, and money.

B

LITERATURE UNCERTAIN OF ITS DESTINY

To appreciate these difficulties one must bear in mind the function of literature. It creates intellectual and emotional pleasure out of experiences from within. At the same time it has to suggest this pleasure through experiences from outside. So an imaginative author has to know how people are living and thinking; their habits as well as their feelings. He has, of course, to find the centre of common interest, which will appeal to as many readers as possible, and consequently he invents what critics of this century are fond of terming symbols, myths, life-forms, ideas, allegories ; or, as Oscar Wilde would say, ' Man is least himself when he talks in his own person. Give him a mask and he will tell the truth.' Needless to add, this objectification is not solely ideological or even factual. Its effect largely depends on presentation. Style and technique supply half the pleasure, since they enable us to see farther than our own eyes can see.

Now it will be noted that in the great periods of literature, the author and his public were more or less at one. His genius might temporarily dazzle and thereby darken the eyes of his readers or listeners ; but his means of communication, what one might almost call his code-words and code-figures, were such as everyone could quickly recognize and apply to experience. In the twentieth century our authors had and have no such advantages. They are not so easily at home in either their material or their audience.

This disability began to be felt towards the close of last century, and a large group of literary men, born and bred in the old familiar world, were tempted to despair of the new spirit and to cultivate another atmosphere of their own, expressive of their disillusionment. Hence the stoic bitterness of the neo-realists, the dreamy remoteness of the symbolists, the discontent and superficiality of the decadents ; and in all these the negation of hope and the play on sensibility at the cost of sense. Max Nordau even went so far in *Entartung* (1892–3) as to diagnose the whole *fin de siècle* attitude as so many symptoms of degeneration and hysteria. In his judgement it all savoured of a hospital. The age was exhausted by two or threee generations of change, alarm, and surprise, and the troubled atmosphere favoured the seeds of insanity lurking in us all. Such pessimistic conclusions could not have been reached without the help of clinical research and the study of psycho-neurosis, and, in fact, *Entartung* is based on the best scientific authorities then available. A generation later the historians of civilization began to corroborate the neuro-psychologists. For instance, W. Rathenau in *Zur Kritike der Zeit* (1912) and O. Spengler in *Untergang des Abendlandes* (1918) prophesied that Western culture had completed its cycle of progress and would therefore inevitably, by the law of periodicity, decline into exhaustion ; and G. Ferrero in *La Vecchia Europa e la Nuova* (1918) was to proclaim that the new monstrous gods of machinofacture were imposing on the modern world the worship of pleasure and power.

This anti-humanism was the work of foreigners, but their warnings lingered in the memory of Englishmen because they confirmed certain suspicions of our own. So the dawn of the twentieth century brought with it a spirit of regression as well as of progress. It was difficult not to lament the passing of the old values, and some groups of writers, as we shall see, were to create ample scope for their genius out of the prevailing nostalgia. A few were utterly to despair of the future, and others were to revert to an artificial primitivism, either in sentiment, or style and diction, as the one hope of a recovery. If such were the only or the dominating tendency of our era, a history would hardly be worth writing. But every reaction in a healthy community provokes a counter-reaction. Nor was help lacking. Nietzsche had already proclaimed the irrepressible energy of man, and Teilhard de Chardin and Alfred Loisy were both affirming their faith in humanity as well as in the far-off divine event to which creation moves, and both were insisting that its consummation depended on working not for oneself but for one's fellow-creatures. So we have to record spirited and sometimes aggressive attempts to retain or revitalize old values in a new setting, or if the old eluded our grasp, to create new values to take their place.

Out of these tensions a unique literature has arisen, abnormally difficult to assess, irresistibly fascinating to study. Will it prove to be merely the record of unco-ordinated efforts? Not unless we expect a conventional progress along academic lines, easily divisible into types and schools. Instead of such conformity we shall find guesses, adventures, experiments which seem at first to be irresponsible, but gradually acquire a common spirit of discovery peculiar to the age. By following these clues we shall perceive an undercurrent which is directing the future of letters. That is why the study of twentieth-century literature is inseparable from the study of ideas.

CHAPTER II

THE PIONEERS OF THE TWENTIETH CENTURY

IN the last chapter we reviewed the influences which induced our nation to begin changing its mind, and consequently its literature. We saw that the transition involved something deeper and wider than the gulf which always severs youth from age; but that the younger generation, not altogether unaccompanied by its elders, was committed to a pilgrimage without signposts. We have now to consider the first stage of its orientation. It is characterized by a number of highly gifted and industrious writers who learnt all they could from nineteenth-century culture, but were caught up into the newly declared spirit of progress and followed that lead, feigning more assurance than they felt, and adapting their technique to their material because they could not do otherwise.

These authors cannot satisfactorily be classified and discussed according to their subject, and *genre*. They prevailed by their attitude and personality, and should be interpreted as individuals.

RUDYARD KIPLING (1865–1930)

To be consulted : A. M. Weygandt, *Kipling's Reading*, 1939; E. Shanks, *Rudyard Kipling*, 1940; T. S. Eliot, *A Choice of Kipling's Verse*, 1941 ; *Definite Edition of Kipling's Verse*, Hodder & Stoughton, 1940; H. Brown, *R. Kipling: A New Appreciation*, 1945.

[*Son of professor of archaeological sculpture, connected with one of the most cultured and artistic circles of his time. Born in Bombay. Educated at the United Services College. When offered the choice of studying at the University, he preferred to return to India. 1882–7, assistant editor of* Civil and Military Gazette *at Lahore, and during this apprenticeship produced nothing better than local satires and society verse. 1887–9, travelled through India, China, Japan, and America to settle in England. 1891, travelled through S. America, Ceylon, Australia, and New Zealand. 1892, settled in Vermont, U.S.A. 1896, returned to England, henceforth his home, except for frequent world voyages. His work as an imperialist and poet of action begins about 1890 and begins to discontinue soon after the end of the Boer War. Thereafter he devoted himself chiefly to the arts of recapturing the sentiment of Old England and the continuity of her culture. Accepted many literary and academic honours (e.g., Nobel Prize, 1907 ; Fellowship at Magdalene, Cambridge, 1932, Rectorship of St. Andrews, 1922–5), but no public appointments or titles. Claimed to write only when in the mood, at the instigation of his ' daemon '. If* Something of Myself *is a faithful record, the hardships of his childhood explain much in his character which is otherwise inexplicable.*]

LITERARY AND IDEOLOGICAL BACKGROUND

For the average reader Kipling's name still suggests all that one would like to read in all the newspapers at their best. Moreover he generally writes with studied carelessness, his prose full of colloquialisms, his verse adapted to recitation. He is, in fact, one of our first artists in illiteracy. So to many the bulk of his work hardly seems to rise above inspired 'journalese'.

We might have expected something quite different. His family connexions brought him into touch with the Pre-Raphaelite movement; his father was an archaeologist; his childhood was passed in India, where he must have imbibed some tincture of the primitive mysterious East; at any rate he never outgrew the consciousness of the spirit world with its magic and mythology. He spent his boyhood in England, but if *Stalky and Co.* is in any sense autobiographical, he must have lived or relived the life of an inventive barbarian of the Bronze Age. Though he also acquired the habits of an omnivorous reader, he did not acquire the mentality of a modern scholar. His taste was old-fashioned. The authors he knew best belonged to the Middle Ages, Renaissance, and the seventeenth century, especially the Bible and *Pilgrim's Progress*. To the end of his career he took little interest in poets and novelists younger than Browning and Dickens. His earliest experiments in original writing mostly amounted to light society verses, mere journalistic flutters (republished in *Departmental Ditties* (1886)). If his genius appears at all at this period (1882–7), it is in the conception of such stories as *The Man who would be King* and *The Mark of the Beast*; that is, he was still fascinated by primitive, adventurous men, or by our ghostly enemies and black magic. Out of the whole range of English poetry he most admired one passage in *Kubla Khan* and one in *Ode to a Nightingale*.

As he 'heard the East a calling' he refused Oxford or Cambridge, returned to India at the age of seventeen and served 'seven years' hard' at an editorial office in the torrid zone. He owns to have acquired 'some sort of workshop facility'. As a matter of fact this journalistic training awoke his genius for 'rapportage', and to that extent influenced his style and perceptivity.

He was still an unsophisticated and far from prosaic observer, inexperienced in Western manners and morals, when he left India in 1887 and travelled for two years all over the world, on his way to England, and his experiences changed the whole bent of his development. He met everywhere a civilization based on a new religion,[1] the worship of power. Men of science and enterprise had evoked strange gods out of the forces of nature and the world's mineral wealth, deities who dwelt in temples made with hands and known as factories, banks, shipyards, and mining installations, who bestowed on their worshippers the joys of life, especially that god-like joy of

---

[1] *Ante*, pp. 6 ff.

ruling not obeying nature, and thereby mastering other people as good as themselves.

This arrogance and insolence were particularly to be noted in national ambitions. Since about 1860 all more or less civilized countries had entered upon a new phase in the struggle for life, or rather the pomps and vanities of life. Civilization now supplied the necessities, so everyone hankered after the luxuries. As a result, enterprising men spread all over the world in search of its riches; national boundaries were effaced in the sense that cities and settlers' areas had become cosmopolitan; enterprise was international. But the spirit of it was not international; the tendency had degenerated into a scramble; and finally the nations had begun to think like individuals. They were all afraid that other folk would grab what they themselves wanted.

Such was the state of affairs when Kipling entered upon his first grand tour. As he was at heart a primitive, unfamiliar with the great centres of world activity, he saw and noted it for the first time. His mind was like a tablet with no writing on it. As his genius for observation had been trained, he saw more than his contemporaries. As he had been gifted with a creative imagination, he discerned in the Evil the possibility of Good, as a poet should.

A glimpse of this possibility was bound to bring back his thoughts to the posture of his own country, for, like all Englishmen who live abroad—however dreamy or remote their preoccupations—he could not help regarding himself as to some degree the representative and supporter of the British Empire. The prospect was enough to obsess any Anglo-Indian not lost to all sense of public responsibility. The reader has only to recall the Irish insurrection of 1879, the revolt of the Boers in 1880, the death of Gordon in 1885, Russia's threat to India which in the same year came to a head over the Afghan boundary, the young Kaiser's policy of aggression and bid for naval supremacy, openly avowed in 1890. Besides, ever since 1867 the Japanese government, while suppressing the old Shinto religion, had officially diverted all that enthusiasm into a passion for nationality, and had made its first appearance as a world conqueror by declaring war on China in 1895.

Meanwhile England, which ' seemed, as it were, to have conquered and peopled half the world in a fit of absence of mind ', had at last realized that it does not pay to be absent-minded. Imperialism began to be taken seriously. J. R. Green's *A Short History of the English People* appeared in 1874, and his *The Making of England* in 1881; Tennyson's *Ballads* appeared in 1880; Sir W. Hunter's *England's Work in India* in 1881; and Sir J. Seeley's *The Expansion of England* in 1883. The Imperial Federal League was founded in 1884, J. A. Froude published *Oceana, or England and her Colonies* in 1886. The Queen's two jubilees in 1887 and 1897, and her funeral (*un jubilé en deuil*) in 1901, blended imperialism with the British love of pageantry.

Never was there a greater need of a poet who could discern the inner meaning of England's destiny, could raise it above the jingoism and vulgarity of music-hall and newspaper publicity, and wake the national consciousness to its grandeur and responsibilities. So it came about that a 'smart young Anglo-Indian storyteller' (as Le Gallienne described him), an unmistakable master of words, with a weird imagination and uncanny insight into the spirit world, yet started to write about ships' boilers, screw steamers, turbines, cranks, gunrooms, the army canteen, colonial wars, gentlemen rankers, and the Flag of England.

KIPLING'S IMPERIALISM

It was no small feat to introduce literature to the world of technology, trade routes, colonial administration, military tactics, and economic forces. For others the Empire was a framework, but Kipling peopled it with individualities. His heroes were miners, engineers, merchant seamen, prospectors, planters, railway officials, agents, inventors, civil servants, soldiers, mostly inconspicuous folk, common or eccentric, generally modest, always unconscious of their own significance;—so unconscious, that their creator had to emphasize the poetry, humour, and prowess immanent in the mechanized job. So he created the romance of practical life.

The interconnexion between the man and his job involved an artistic problem of no small difficulty. If the world's workers were to reveal their souls, they must talk in character, use the language of their trade—slangy, colloquial, reeking of machine oil, the odours of the fo'c'sle, or the illiteracy of the self-made man. This inartistic artistry had the spice of novelty. It interested the experts and exquisites of the 'nineties as a fresh departure in realism. Something similar was to be exploited by Masefield in another ten years or so. Kipling, they said, was demonstrating that an artist's personality could render any theme worth reading; but not, they would add, worth calling great prose, much less great poetry. Since his characterizations reeked of commonness and philistinism, they were too lowly for the epic spirit. They needed raising, and since they were scattered among short stories and occasional verse, they lacked a central idea. Kipling felt able to overcome this difficulty because he was not only a story-teller. He was sufficiently a puritan to preach the war-like morality of the Bible, to fight the good fight, and beat down Satan under our feet. But in conceiving the epic of British civilization, he rightly understood that the antagonist is a negative power : the taint of moral laxity, the spirit which leaves things undone. This taint of obtusity and obstructiveness, inherent in 'the lesser breeds', can be visualized only if the reader understands what they obstruct. So he invented 'The Law'. E. Shanks has admirably explained this idea. The Law stands for the progress of civilization, the enforcement of an orderly world, armed everywhere against famine, disease, wastefulness, and sensuality, and also against the powers of barbarism which might oppose its march. Thus Kipling presented the British Empire as the minister of peace and prosperity, conquering the world to set it free.

It was a profitable and attractive theme, and certainly inspired some of his most arresting stories, for example, those in *Mine own People* (1891) and *The Day's Work* (1898); and some of his most spirited verse, for example, 'The Ballad of East and West' (1889), 'A Song of the English' (1893), 'The Native Born' (1894), 'A Hymn before Action' (1896), 'The Recessional' (1897), 'The White Man's Burden' (1899), 'The Islanders' (1902). In his prose he developed a casual but concentrated style, presenting his narrative in vivid, unpretentious scenes. In his verse he often struck that note of spontaneity at which the twentieth century was to aim. And yet at this period his writing leaves us unsatisfied. We learn much about other people, little about ourselves. He inspires patriotism but not contemplation. No wonder; he had lost faith in his cause. Ill fares the poet who entrusts his ideals to everyday human agents, necessarily limited by their vanity, factiousness, and self-interest. Sooner or later Kipling was doomed to convince himself if not others that the most insidious enemies of 'The Law' were neither the 'lesser breeds' nor even the remittance men, but the imperial people itself and their party-ridden bureaucrats. That is why we frequently catch him relying on mechanical rhythms, dialogues made to order, and tricks of style. His heart was not in his theme.

HIS SECOND PHASE. KIPLING CHANGES BECAUSE HE REMAINS TRUE TO HIMSELF

His disillusionment reached its climax during the Boer War. Thereafter his tone changes, and so did the tastes of the reading public. In any case a reaction was overdue. The nation had had enough of imperial expansion, and began to concern itself with standards of living and the redistribution of wealth. H. G. Wells and Bernard Shaw became its popular gods, and professional men of letters began to look for models among the Russians and French. War literature rang false when confronted with the muddles and miscalculations of real war, including dysentery. Contemporaries frequently remarked that Kipling, being a journalist, was quick to note the turn of the tide and steered his boat accordingly.

We can now see that he changed because he remained the same. Being quite sincere in his self-appointed office, he did not turn from the imperial democracy, nor its tenacious, elderly, governing class. But he now wrote of them as censoriously as Milton wrote of the fallen angels, or Swift wrote of Lilliput and Brobdingnag. By contrast, he dwelt even more sympathetically on the unconscious heroism and single-heartedness of the artisan, engineer, or colonist, or on the fascination of machinery; for instance, 'The Settler' (1903), 'The Sons of Martha' (1907), *Letters to the Family* (1908). But having also the true instincts of a poet, he returned to the broader more human issues which really lay nearer his heart.   These he rehandled, drawing on his stores of experience, probing them (as it were) for more significant experiments in manhood, such as his country needed.   What he accomplished is most remarkable.   He would have accomplished yet more if his genius had not lost its fire, too embittered by the world to rise above it.   Besides, he kept to his old style, acquired in the 'nineties.

KIPLING'S LAST PHASE.   HE ENDS AS HE SHOULD HAVE BEGUN

One is tempted to forget that Kipling could handle two or more themes at the same time with equal thoroughness.   For instance, everyone was still discussing *Barrack-Room Ballads* (book form 1892) when *The Jungle Book* (1894) and *The Second Jungle Book* (1895) appeared.   These fantasies, something between Aesop and the mysteries of the tropical rain forest, create the dream of a new spiritual order, in which children should learn to trust animals and profit by their sagacity.   Similarly, people were still enjoying *Soldiers Three* (1888), *Wee Willie Winkie* (1889), *The Ballad of the Seven Seas* (1896), when *Captains Courageous* was published in 1897 to teach a pampered youth, and us, the meaning of elemental life amid the hardships and dangers of the Grand Banks.   Two years later, *Stalky and Co.* (1899) demonstrated that the education of a future soldier or Anglo-Indian journalist is not acquired even in the best-regulated classrooms.   Kipling's admirers had hardly got used to these new settings, and temporarily forgotten the Orient, when he published *Kim* (1901), the panorama of India with its suggestion of all a boy may learn and become, if he can acquire ' the common touch ' and meet all human beings in the primitive spirit of fellowship and adventure—a foretaste of Baden Powellism.

These studies in childhood and school-boyhood might be mistaken for technical devices, mere backgrounds to fiction, till one remembers that such was the education which Kipling had tried to give himself. He had come to understand that the surest way to master our new world was to start from the beginning, in the spirit of the Bronze Age ; to recover our early ancestors' mother-wit, inventiveness, unanimism, their sense of kinship with beast and clod, their aptitude for arts and crafts, their genius for mystery and symbolism.   Experience ought to be somewhat like folk-lore applied to life.   Some of his most artless and intimate ' yarns ' are treatises on education. *Stalky and Co.* actually arose out of a discussion on that subject.

These ideas were running in his head at the height of his imperialism ; and they were his chief resource when he began to despair of England's future.   So he surprised his less discerning readers with yet another theme, first developed in magazines and then published in book form as *Puck of Pook's Hill* (1906) and *Rewards and Fairies* (1910).   Yet the appearance might have been expected ; it is foreshadowed in ' Sussex ' (1902) and ' An Habitation Enforced ' with its admirable appendage ' The Recall' (reprinted in *Actions and Reactions* (1909)).

Having spent his manhood absorbing the world, Kipling was almost sure to end by absorbing England. Since her sons are now scattered over the world, he would write about their forbears who found more than enough to do within her shores. History in verse and fiction was to be expected and the implications of racial continuity. But, to his admirers' surprise, he had something more to contribute : what one might call archaic regionalism. Regionalism is the cult of a certain district which has helped the poet to realize himself. Kipling realizes in the countryside, not always in ' Wessex ', the human interest, fortitude, and efficiency he so often missed in the modern world, but evokes out of past records, in glimpses of the dead whose virtues survive in tradition. Thus he impressed his personality on the scene, without talking about himself. Very skilfully he lets the garment of the Present fade away, as if of its own accord, uncovering the romance which in his portraiture seems so real, and true to common sense. The Roman Wall is the most memorable evocation; but often a single oaktree, the traces of some ancient trench or mound, even a flake of pottery, is enough to remind him of the piety, prowess, and passion of those who went before, not forgetting Hobden.

So he completed his chronicle of the English race, working backward. He began with Anglo-India society in Simla, and ended with the God Whelan and the spirit of the thorn bush.

HIS PLACE IN TWENTIETH-CENTURY LITERATURE

Sooner or later his position will be established as one of the first few adventurers who reconciled the individual to modern civilization, and thereby to himself. While the contemporaries of Kipling's youth were still fretting because man was too big for this world, Kipling persuaded them that the world was big enough for the greatest and smallest man. The destiny of England gave authority and one-pointedness to his message.

It was essentially a ' message ', very dear to him, because he loved England and loved writing like a Hebrew prophet. And yet this seemingly spacious theme gave little scope to what was deepest and most distinctive in his nature. Too often it imposed the qualities of sameness, superficiality, and rhetoric. Now and then he escaped from his task into himself, and we see his true significance.

His significance has often been overlooked because the critics are slightly puzzled by the workings of his mind, and so turn more readily to points of style and composition. There is a mystery about Kipling's approach to the world he studied so widely and closely. He might be described as an aboriginal, a survivor from some period of prehistoric civilization, innocent of the mists of modern culture, and for that very reason clear-sighted enough to assess the values around us; especially the underlying continuity of human nature, and the permanent outlines of character, however twisted and disguised by modern requirements. His imperialism, though undoubtedly sincere, was an accident, an opportune but inelastic medium for his talents unfortunately trained to super-journalism, also accidentally. It was his genius to read the human soul by a natural cunning and craftiness—one might almost say primitive guile—which reveals itself in flashes of mother-wit, primitive sympathy, and an instinct for the unending shallowness of man when he tries to use his reason.

If and when this unique quality is appreciated, his lapses in literary taste, his jingoism, prolixity, and inconsequence of treatment will be overlooked. On the other hand, it will not be overlooked that he introduced us to our own cosmopolitan civilization with the freshness and curiosity of a newcomer.

JOSEPH CONRAD (1857–1924)

To be consulted : G. Morf, *The Polish Heritage of Joseph Conrad*, 1930 ; R. L. Mègroz, *Joseph Conrad : Mind and Method*, 1931 ; E Garnett, *Conrad's Prefaces to his Works*, With an Introductory Essay, 1937. G. Jean-Aubry, *Vie de Conrad. Sagesse de Conrad* (Textes choisis) 1947.

[*Joseph Konrad Theodore Korzeniowski, born in the Ukraine. Though the orphan son of distinguished and well-connected parents, and destined for the university, he insisted on becoming an ordinary seaman at the age of sixteen or seventeen, apparently convinced that there was more freedom within the confines of a ship than in a Polish city riddled with German spies. He did not set foot in England nor speak a word of English till 1878, nor become a master mariner in the British Merchant Service till 1884. In 1893 he first met Galsworthy at Adelaide, on whom he exercised an unmistakable influence for thirty-nine years. In 1894 he left the Merchant Service and settled in the south of England, often changing his residence, but always within sight of the sea. Almayer's Folly (on which he had laboured intermittently since 1889) was published in 1895, on the advice of Edward Garnett, reader to Fisher Unwin. Garnett also persuaded him to continue at his new vocation instead of returning to sea. In* The Nigger of the Narcissus (1898) *he discovered the natural bent of his genius, and though a slow and laborious writer, he followed it with* Lord Jim (1900), Youth (1902), Typhoon (1902), Nostromo (1904), Mirror of the Sea (1906). *Thereafter his work becomes, not less powerful, but less confident, and less inspired by the sea—e.g.,* The Secret Agent (1907), Under Western Eyes (1911), Chance (1914) (*which first won him popular recognition*), Victory (1915). *The Four Years War, and possibly the sweets of success, seem to have impaired his genius, and, although he published six more volumes, only* The Rover (1923) *is to be compared with his pre-war novels.*]

LITERARY AND IDEOLOGICAL BACKGROUND

Conrad's career is one of those many paradoxes which render the study of literature so fascinating. Nature had gifted him with an abounding love for his fellow-creatures, and therewith an unusual insight into all that they might accomplish and enjoy. Fate compelled him to denationalize himself, though a wholehearted patriot; to become a citizen of the world, spending the best years of his manhood in no other home than the ship in which he happened to serve, or the port at which she happened to call. These twenty years of strenuous life revealed to him the central problem of human nature—that is, the tension between our higher and lower selves; but the training also brought with it the excessive consciousness of his own lower nature, together with the memory of mistakes, humiliations, and corrections under authority. Hence one reason for his almost morbid interest in lamed and harassed souls.

Moreover, the sailor's life is a one-sided experience. A mariner has no special opportunities of studying the natives and Europeans who live up-country in outlandish places—outcasts, adventurers, bandits—who are the story-teller's best material. He usually learns their histories at second hand, in hotels, clubs, and smoking-saloons. That may be the reason why Conrad so often developed his plots through a third person as if in a conversation, the voice and personality of the narrator being ' extremely suggestive quite apart from the story he was telling me '. No doubt he was confirmed in this device by the example of Nikolai Leskov, who had already forty years earlier introduced into Russian literature the *skaz*—' a stylized spoken tale . . . told in such a way that the accent and inflexion of the narrator himself are perfectly preserved '.[1]

What inspiration he derived from his professional life is supposed to be revealed in *The Mirror of the Sea* (1906). If so, the revelation is disappointing. Apart from the fascinations of seamanship, so vividly presented, he seems to have learnt only to measure life by the norm of the ' ship-shape '. But when this sailor meditates on the psychology of sea-life his manner becomes most unshipshape. In fact the Merchant Service seems to have given Conrad an attitude to life, but only a limited knowledge of men. This latter he had to learn elsewhere, and it is to be noticed that most of his best characters are only accidentally connected with the sea.

In middle life, at the ' dangerous age ', the artistic instinct asserted itself and Conrad became an author. He made England his home because it is the country ' where men and the sea interpenetrate ', as he afterwards declared in *Youth* (1902). Falling in love with the people, he fell in love with their language. It filled him with enthusiasm and a sense of discovery. Its idioms seemed to create his thoughts for him. Though a prose-writer, he is one of the first modern poets to use words as guides more than servants.

[1] J. Lavrin, *An Introduction to the Russian Novel*, 1942.

It is now clear that Conrad might have been expected to write in much the same kind of vein as Kipling. Both had acquired the twentieth-century cosmopolitan touch ; both were experts in the romance of adventure. Neither was a home-bred Englander ; both adored England and dreamt of her destiny. Yet the two authors are only so far alike in that both breathed the atmosphere of the age in which they lived.

This paradox brings us to the last element in Conrad's background : the authors who influenced him most. He admired the artistic rectitude and probing subtlety of Henry James and Proust. He professed to model his style and treatment on Flaubert and de Maupassant, apparently impressed by their Olympian detachment and discerning study of environment, though he rarely mastered their genius for economy of effect. Most significant of all, he followed Turgenev, to whom Garnett introduced him, and Dostoevsky, whom he affected to despise. Both these Russians have widely influenced the Georgian and the interwar novel because they had outgrown the cult of nationalism, had celebrated the pan-humanity and ' togetherness ' (Katherine Mansfield's phrase) of all Europeans, and, moreover, portrayed characters strong or weak enough to live by impulse, not by law. What most fascinated Conrad was their complete portraiture of incomplete characters ; men and women at war with themselves, thwarted by their own passions and impulses—introverts who either missed their life purpose, through lack of self-direction, or found their only outlet in crime.

It was unfortunate that Conrad's masters fitted some of their most telling characters onto a background of big city life ; they were mostly temperaments imprisoned in sedentary habits, minds narrowed to the streets which fretted their energies—whereas Conrad proved the mettle of his heroes often far beyond the bounds of civilization.

Thus when Conrad began to learn from others, he added yet one more complication to his own spiritual history. As if it were not enough to change his nationality and language, to devote the prime of his manhood to a restless and exigent profession, rich in glimpses, but blank to every intimacy, he now sought counsel from artists who knew nothing about the lives his characters had led, nor the scenes in which they must play their part. Probably no man in this adventurous century has tried to store so much of the multitudinous modern world within the compass of his head, and give it back to us impressed with his single personality.

CONRAD'S IDEA OF THE SCOPE AND METHOD OF THE NOVEL

Being a cosmopolitan settler, he and his public lacked a common meeting-ground, unless it were the sense of humanity and the consciousness of a destiny surrounding all our lives, even the most prosaic. Out of the wealth of his experiences he could recall a procession of figures sufficiently unaccountable and suggestive to interest us in all that human beings could become; some few utterly and restlessly bad—'the incarnation of everything vile and base that lurks in the world we love '—some very few serenely good because masters of themselves; the majority oscillating between the two poles.

But unlike Henry James, Flaubert, or Turgenev, he had neither the experience nor the opportunity to examine them as social types or psychological puzzles. His imagination thrived on glimpses which suggested a mystery; for instance, Almayer, who was always expecting something better; Lord Jim, who seemed to feel himself under a cloud; Nostromo, a vile little creature who nevertheless committed a stupendous crime and openly boasted of it. Always the disinterested human observer, he set himself to create the explanation, to complete their inner history as revealed in their outward behaviour, generally.' the passions of men short-sighted in good and evil '.

In fact, when Conrad was in the mood to write, he acted on a hint from outside and then descended into the depths of himself, wherein our stored impressions of others blend with what we have ourselves enjoyed, suffered, and above all condemned. What he found there he refashioned, and transposed into these figures, originally viewed at a distance. So he preserved his air of aloofness and objectivity.

How, then, was he to make his externalizations seem real to his reader? By surrounding them with the scenery to which they belonged, on a background of the same tone and colour, in tune with their behaviourism. This expressive environment is varied— sometimes a city or the countryside, not seldom a ship on the high seas—but the most memorable scenery is something new to the English literary imagination: rivers running up into uncleared country, the air laden with the acrid smell of decaying vegetation, or the hot, gloomy forest path ' overgrown and strangled in the fierce life of the jungle '. Such were the ' telling, representative facts, helpful to carrying on the idea '. He confessed that he used the Malay Archipelago so often, not because he was specially familiar with the country, but because it served his artistic purposes.

The *psychology of scene* (Edward Garnett) laid a heavy strain on the author's powers of description. His visions of tropical forests, sea-storms, docks, streets, natives, and Europeans gone native, are not romantic touches, but half the power of his realism. He was well aware that he aimed at the highest. In fact he took his art as seriously as he took his seamanship, and in his prefaces he has often explained his ideal. He termed it the ' conscientious render- ing of truth in thought and fact—or truth disclosed in a moment of illusion '. He dived down into his heart, and when he at last succeeded in putting all he found there into the heart of some figure glimpsed in passing, he had found the truth, as his predecessors hoped to find it, first in religion and then, centuries later, in lyric poetry.

Thus his themes transcended temporary and material interests. He scorned to expose social abuses, or laugh at social prejudices, however intellectually, or even to experiment in psychological finesse, though some of the best Victorian and Edwardian novelists had set those fashions. He lived on his past, but only after the lapse of years, evoked as an opportunity for the author's nobler qualities, especially his capacity for intellectual sympathy and single-heartedness. In this clear, revealing light he felt that he was true to himself and to the characters he created.

CONRAD'S ACHIEVEMENT

If Conrad had fully realized his ideal he would have become as great as the greatest poets and story-tellers. His first three novels (1895–8) do not differ in tone from the work of any contemporary continental realist, except in their exotic scenery. Our author seems unwilling to portray any human virtue, lest he be accused of sentiment; or as if he must first settle his account with Evil before turning to what might spring to Good. But his masterpieces— *The Nigger of the Narcissus* (1898), *Lord Jim* (1900), *Typhoon* (1902), *Nostromo* (1904)—are such as only Conrad could have written. The series covers an immense range of human activity, from man's conflict with the eternal sea to the revolutionary and avaricious passions raging round the fabulous wealth of the San Tomé mine, and so on to official life in a southern roadstead, and tribal wars between remote savages. Yet such is the real life going on around us. It seems strange because its interest is both exotic and cosmopolitan, and the tastes of the average novel reader are insular. But the scenes are described by one who knows how things happen in the big modern world, and his actuality makes the characters seem actual.

These characters are a literary type of their own. There is, or rather was, a convention that men of action have plenty of resourcefulness, but no nerves,—certainly no cerebration. Conrad's heroes (if they can be so designated) have enough, or more than enough of both. They are not, for the most part, refined or fashionable people such as Conrad must now and then have met on liners and private yachts but did not easily understand. They are men who may or may not have once been like those others, but have lost their acquired habits in the struggle for life. They have changed their hearts with their skies. These decivilized civilians gradually return to their natural selves under pressure of their wildly natural environment, but they do not therefore become beasts, maniacs, or saints. They become slaves to their peculiar idiosyncrasy—some secret cowardice, infidelity, strain of egoism, or touch of vanity, such as (according to Conrad) haunts every human being, and we watch them transform the impulse into an obsession or action. So some become criminals and some heroes, without knowing why, deceiving themselves and the undiscerning reader,

Since Conrad generally met the living human material more than half-way through their transformation, he preferred to present his reincarnations at the same stage. Besides, it was more artistic to plunge his reader into the middle of the plot. So he was forced to reckon with the psychological axiom that there are no dead selves. A man's past is telescoped into his present. That is why it was futile to ask Lord Jim for facts (as did the court of inquiry) until you knew his whole life.

Yet his studies frequently arouse without satisfying the readers. Critics, for instance Garnett, insist on his ' uncompromising sardonic perception of the human drama '. Ironical interpretation is not the quality of the greatest artists, nor was it Conrad's aim. He attempted to engage and satisfy what one might term the religion of human sympathy and insight. But since our sympathies must not darken our insight, his mood was judicial, so free from illusions that he sometimes appears to be disillusioned. If he relapsed into irony it was as a last resource, because even his best characters disappointed him. He felt he had not succeeded in rendering them worthy of his own sympathy, nor of ours.

That is why Conrad could seldom stop at the right place. His characters have tormented souls, and he laboured on them, till he tormented himself. He was so afraid of missing a single trait either in the complexities of the man or of the encompassing scenery, that his visions often become an embarrassment of impressions. They leave the reader no opportunity of contributing his share to the spiritual effect. His use of the third-person narrative and ' the time-shift ' is equally prolix and perplexing. Once he achieved simplicity and acumination : in *The Secret Agent* (1907). Both plot and characters are as clear cut as in the best French novel. But he was then working on a lower level ; the personages are types and the background is merely a setting.

He achieved everything except his artistic ideal.

HIS POSITION IN OUR LITERATURE

As psycho-analysis, the Russian novel, and travel in distant countries are certain more and more to become commonplaces in English thought, the educated reader will be able to follow his ideas more easily. It will then be understood that his novels are a world of their own, not likely to be replaced. While Kipling demonstrated that cosmopolitan civilization breeds its own epic heroes, Conrad demonstrated that those heroes often border on tragedy. If his inspiration sometimes outran his technique, he has at least left us some descriptive passages seldom if ever surpassed. Only Milton and very rarely De Quincey can make us see the unseen as this author can. He never wrote down to his public, in fact he assumed that it was living up to his ideal of the English temperament—its impartiality, practical wisdom, sense of fitness, and freedom from sentimentality.   To admire Conrad is to live up to his standard.   So his place is assured.

HERBERT GEORGE WELLS (1866–1946)

To be consulted : H. G. Wells, *Experiment in Autobiography,* 1934.

[*Born in Bromley ; his father an under-gardener, then a small retailer in hardware who earned the family income as a cricket professional ; his mother a lady's maid.   The future novelist, after a good primary education at Midhurst Grammar School, was apprenticed to a linen draper at 13 years of age.   Three years later he cancelled his articles, became an usher at his old school, then in 1884 a student at the Normal School of Science (Royal College of Science).   1887–93 supported himself by teaching and journalism, though suffering from ill health.   1895 published* The Time Machine *and* The Wonderful Visit.   *Thereafter his career was assured and may be divided (despite overlapping) into four periods : 1895–1908, scientific romances ; 1905– 10, social and humorous studies ; 1911–18, novels of political reform and intellectual direction ; 1919–32, summary and reinterpretation of historical, scientific, and economic principles.   Since then he has been retracing his steps.*]

LITERARY AND IDEOLOGICAL BACKGROUND

Whereas Kipling and Conrad were citizens of the world before they were men, Wells was born and bred a provincial.   Till he was over thirty, his experience was confined to West Sussex and London lodgings as known to a poor man who often fell ill.   Yet his thought became just as progressive, and his sympathies even more cosmopolitan.

He achieved his emancipation partly because he was class conscious.   His mind began to grow when [1] Darwin, Huxley, Haeckel, Lister, Berthelot, Pasteur, Ruskin, Morris, Marx, Engels, Hyndman, Henry George, H. C. Hinton, and the technologists were making much stir in the world, but had as yet produced surprisingly little effect on the traditional humanism of the upper class. All the more reason why ardent and intellectual youngsters of the lower class should embrace the ' new learning ' which held out such hopes for the future.   Some even felt obscurely that the taint of capitalism clung to the study of Greek drama, medieval art, and Anglicanism ; and condemned, without understanding, the culture from which they imagined themselves to be excluded.   The age of introductory text-books and extension lectures had dawned, so their nimble, eager minds could make short cuts to science and socialism, and then dream of reconstructing England.

Wells made himself the prophet of this class.   He was not really gifted with the scientific temperament.   He was a rather super-

[1] *Ante,* pp. 8 ff.

C

ficial, inaccurate thinker, a man of impulse and imagination, a humorous observer of his fellow-men. But he had a constructive, experimental mind, impatient of any complication, and science set it free. Take, for instance, the theory of evolution. It addressed no flattering appeals to your sensibilities, it chose the most direct path to the fundamental mysteries of existence. It demonstrated that life might lead anywhere—to the liver-fluke, the skunk, or the microbes that batten on disease, and also to the inventive genius of the human species. ' Life was a various and splendid disorder of forces that the spirit of man set itself to tame.' [1] In the light of this truth science supplied means and motives for bettering our fellow-creatures. It rationalized, as it were, the sources of Good and Evil. Wells knew at first hand—none better—that the primary obstacle to progress was the muddle and stagnation of lower-class life, and then the vested interests and ignorance of the well-to-do. The knowledge which helped him to expose this passive resistance also helped him to reckon with his own instincts and appetencies ' those living, writhing, warm and thrilling organs ' [2]—all that submerged self which religionists tried to suppress and humanists passed over in silence. Hence his advocacy of free love.

WELLS TURNS SCIENCE INTO ROMANCE, AND THEREBY FINDS HIS BENT

His development as an author is most significant. He began by manufacturing ' pot-boilers', apparently acting on a hint from Barrie's *When a Man's Single* (1888), and in order to sell what interested others, he soon concentrated on what interested himself— that is, the probable and possible applications of science to civilization. Jules Verne had shown the way, but Wells writes as if he had also absorbed C. H. Hinton's *Scientific Romances* (1st series, 1884).

In other words, he took his data seriously. Each story was based (more or less) on a current theory or practice, the property of specialists, but recently made public and of possible importance to the whole world. For instance: in 1893 Schiaparelli propounded the theory that the long straight markings on Mars were ' canals '. In 1894 Percival Lowell founded an observatory in Arizona to study this phenomenon, and opined that they were the work of intelligent beings, threatened with drought. Wells adopted the idea and produced *The War of the Worlds* (1898). In 1905 Wilbur and Orville Wright succeeded in flying thirty-six miles, and aeronautics became a practical proposition. Only two years later and one year before Blériot crossed the Channel, Wells published *The War in the Air* (1908). Perhaps the most remarkable of all his ventures is his first: *The Time Machine* (1895). The hypothesis of the fourth dimension had filtered down to the educated public. When C. H. Hinton published *Scientific Romances*, the volume contained,

[1] *The New Macchiavelli*, 1911.   [2] *First and Last Things*, 1908.

among other essays, 'What is the Fourth Dimension?', 'A Plane World', and 'Many Dimensions'. With a flash of genius, Wells saw that the idea might be used to show how human beings could, just possibly, travel forward in time. The time-traveller has fascinating experiences. But he also finds the law of evolution working itself out to the logical conclusion. Nor is the speculation a dream of progress.

These are three examples out of more than nine stories, all suggested by current science. Of course the data are not always reliable. For example, *The First Men in the Moon* (1901) might more appropriately have been entitled *The Last Men*, since on that planet there is no air to breathe. In *The Food of the Gods* (1904) those who partook could not grow into giants; 'boom-food' was too extra nutritious to be digested. Still the fiction is surprisingly and ingeniously realistic; nothing so speciously convincing had appeared before; and it must have reflected adult public taste, for the fantasies were an immediate and immense success. Incidentally Wells helped to educate our imagination.

Yet the stories, though written to please, are by no means messages of hope. He does not hint that research may be leading us towards the hydro-electric age of plenty; or indeed that mankind has any collective capacity for progress. For instance, in *The Island of Dr. Moreau* (1896) the arts of healing are exercised to outrage nature. The earlier fantasies end in melodrama, the later ones invite us to contemplate society disintegrating under the impact of scientific progress. His tone, always inclined to irony, becomes pessimistic and occasionally cynical. In his first attempts this tendency may have been due to the requirements of the book-market: the public likes its meals served hot. But as soon as he felt at home in his material, he began to realize that he was playing not with dreams but with possibilities, some extravagantly remote, but others alarmingly imminent. He was already conscious that laboratory research takes its direction from public opinion. Inventors try to supply what their generation asks for. But at this period the public was not asking for anything at all. It was all unconscious of the superhuman forces threatening the routine of its petty life. So the inventors were left to themselves—to satisfy their curiosity. There was no co-ordination, much less leadership. The knowledge which should humanize nature might well be let loose to destroy human beings. It should not be forgotten that Wells foresaw the principle of poison gas, and the actual practice of aerial warfare, as well as the developments of motor-traffic and the fitments of utility houses.

In any case he had begun to realize that science was not the all-sufficient life-guide he had once hoped. Under the influence of Huxley and Haeckel it meant the observation and comparison of facts—'systematic classification'—and our powers of observation overlooked the deepest truths in human nature.

HIS SECOND PHASE: SOCIAL AND POLITICAL NOVELS

Vision had been effaced by foresight, and the consequent dis-illusionment hampered his creativeness; within ten years he had exhausted his stock of scientific gadgets with cosmic consequences. But he was now something more than a publicist with an imagination. His ideas were concentrated into a life-purpose both profitable and public-spirited, ahead of his age; and his next task was to show why his contemporaries were like travellers who had lost sight of their destination. For this reason he turned to examine the nature of man, beginning with himself. He was already familiar with the mystery of his own body, known to him through impulses and desires, which he durst not suppress, but must perforce dominate by that something termed personality, and must direct towards the enjoyment of beauty and power. But what was true of himself was equally true of everybody else. We are all actuated by the same needs, dependent on each other. In fact we are so inextricably implicated that we can only move forward altogether, not only thinking alike, but feeling alike.

This social philosophy, propounded in *First and Last Things* (1909), is simply an old-fashioned doctrine brought up to date. Mass-education is to overshadow the individual's private quest of self-culture. But Wells's presentment is original. He commits himself to a series of realistic novels in which the hero, sometimes himself as he might have remained, sometimes himself as he actually was, sometimes himself as he would have wished to be, an inventor or public reformer—but always himself—is let loose, with all his ideas and ideals, on the most typical phases of contemporary English life. In every scene he becomes the victim not of organized opposition, but of ill-instructed individualism. Both the stupid and the clever are wrapped up in their personal associations; they cannot think beyond themselves or their class. But whatever the embarrassments of the intellectual intruder, Wells never loses his sense of humour. He is one of the very few reformers who can see the comic side of reforms, including his own.

His technique is almost primitive. He had learnt in his scientific romances how to combine episodes and link them together in the experiences of one or more lightly sketched figures. He had also learnt how to sustain interest by suggesting the approach of a climax without suggesting what the climax would be; so skilfully, that the reader can live in the plot without the help of a central character. While Conrad and others were leaving the Victorian novel far behind, Wells was demonstrating that the ancient art of story-telling was still potent if it could awake curiosity, as of old. So with his social novels. A central character (himself) was indeed in-dispensable, but chiefly as a thread on which to hang his theories and illustrations. The real interest centres in the sequence of episodes, one event leading unexpectedly but inevitably to the next.

The method is still as unsophisticated as in the days of Chaucer or Herodotus, and the novelist still appeals to his readers' curiosity; but this time it is the new middle- and lower-class willingness to learn how and by whom their lives should be regulated, and the author is the most inquisitive of them all.

The conversations and self-examinations are so ideological that the atmosphere often reminds one of an un-Platonic dialogue. Now and then it leads to the creation of a genuine character which lives in its own right, illuminated by that quality of indulgent middle-class humour which can be denoted 'Wellsian'. The Ponderevo circle in *Tono-Bungay* (1909) is a good example; but the best are the lovably and pathetically comic Art. Kipps and Mr. Polly. The two novels (*Kipps*, 1905, and *The History of Mr. Polly*, 1910) which immortalize these square pegs in round holes, come nearest to 'jesting with serious thoughts behind', for they reveal how human nature is being wasted. The more ambitious volumes interest only so far as they discuss current topics. Perhaps the most spacious is *The New Macchiavelli* (1911). The most stimulating and best constructed is *Tono-Bungay*, a vivid exposure of commercial capitalism, with its huge and insecure fortunes extracted out of public stupidity, the arts of advertisement and the fluctuations of the Stock Exchange, by which money is made and lost without being earned. There is just a glimpse of how this muddled haphazard system can be turned to the use of an inventive genius.

Early in his career Wells started to write on the sexual, rather than the inventive man. *Love and Mr. Lewisham* (1900) was the first and most searching enquiry. As a student of science he had learnt to consider passion as an expression of the life-force, and the more he rose in reputation, the more he harped upon the instinctiveness of love, insisting that we could enrich our hold on life if we relaxed the ties of wedlock. There is nothing prurient, much less sentimental, in his advocacy; it is mere importunity; he never tired of this preachment, though many of his admirers tired of it.

Wells's other pre-war and post-war novels add little to our idea of his art and mentality; though *Mr. Britling Sees it Through* (1916) should be remembered for its impression of our first 'Home Front'; *Joan and Peter* (1918) for its study of educational experiments, which are still a subject for research and controversy; *Christina Alberta's Father* (1925) and *The World of William Clissold* (1926) because they photograph interwar society.

HIS INTERWAR PHASE: THE EDUCATION OF MANKIND

His heart was elsewhere. The Great War of 1914 seemed then to have fulfilled his gloomiest anticipations, and it needed no very far-sighted prophet to perceive that the disaster might well be followed by another. Pamphleteers and propagandists (including Dean Inge) were busy by the hundred at enlightening society and reforming its administration. But in Wells's opinion they began at the wrong end, proclaiming how well the world would go if such and such adaptations were effected. This partisan advocacy would always encounter prejudice and vested interests because the rising generation, like its predecessor, was not of one mind. It had not the basic knowledge to see its way. Wells was only proceeding to another stage of his life purpose when he constructed *The Outline of History* (1919–20), *The Science of Life* (1929–31, in collaboration with Julian Huxley), and *The Work, Wealth, and Happiness of Mankind* (1932). The aim of these three surveys is to reconstruct knowledge so that we can reconstruct civilization. The trilogy are a contribution towards the humanism of the future and a warning that democracy, without education, cannot survive.

He bases his teaching on history, because history reveals, or ought to reveal, tendencies rather than accomplishments. So he sketches the origins of man as a single species, a tentative adventure in an inhospitable world. He explains how this new-comer gradually established his right to exist and then to rule creation by his inventive intelligence, and then lost his way, divided into envious and antagonized communities, because he misunderstood his destiny—mistook his struggle against nature for an internal struggle with his own species—witness the Great War, in which the nations tried to exterminate each other with forces produced by international collaboration.

The Science of Life begins with the carbon atom and its combinations, possibly two thousand million years ago, and with admirable lucidity traces the experiments of evolution, first in the sea, then on the land, from microbes to megatheria, culminating in *homo sapiens*, our latest phase, hardly fifty thousand years old. This biped mammal carries in his system all nature's mistakes as well as successes. His physiology is a complex and ill-balanced mechanism, his social sense is rudimentary, his spiritual experiences are illusive, since he is only an animal which has acquired the faculty of speech and consequently of thought. The review covers an immense range of biological knowledge, and yet tells us so much about the common interests of life that one almost loses sight of the moral. It demonstrates that we hold on to the precarious thread of life at the cost of infinite labour and ingenuity ; and that our greatest victories are won over our environment and by obscure heroes, such as the men who discovered the causes of malaria.

We have considered Kipling's and Conrad's reactions to the machine ; they were interested in the individuals who served it. We have also seen that Wells in his youth was more interested in the machine itself, not as it is, but as it might become. *The Work, Wealth, and Happiness of Mankind* differs from all these points of view. The author inquires how far we have adapted the resources of the world to our use—machinofactures, exploitations, and distribution—in a word, our ' economic citizenship '. He unfolds a fascinating tale of adventures, experiments, and accomplishments, but dwells even more on their incompleteness. Modern industry, he repeats, is a vast cosmopolitan collaboration ; anyone can see that the separate countries depend on each other, just like individuals in a single country. Yet in both cases the producer measures his usefulness by his own narrow idea of what is good for himself. He still cultivates the ' enlightened self-interest ', which may or may not have insured progress in the eighteenth century, but certainly spells failure in the twentieth.

Therefore the most-needed reform in our time is a reform of education. We must impress historical, biological, and economic facts on the public intelligence in such a way that everyone is eager to co-operate in the world's affairs. ' The motive of service must replace the motives of profit and privilege altogether.' In so doing, we shall be following the course of our human nature. Once upon a time, somewhere between the Neolithic and Bronze Ages, man entered upon his first epoch of inventions. Somewhere within the seventeenth and nineteenth centuries he has stumbled upon fresh sources of power and, without knowing it, entered upon his second epoch. These discoveries have transformed not only his social habits, but also his instincts, emotions, and ideas. As such, he must now live in a different way.

The idea of the world state is, of course, far from original. It was mooted by Adam Müller in 1816, Carlyle in 1832, Emerson in 1856, J. A. Froude in 1870. Yet Wells's three surveys are a new departure. He has retained all his accustomed literary skill and zest, but turns his back on the culture from which these arts were once derived. His ' thought pattern ' (as he calls it) seems to be completed out of psycho-analysis and socialism, and his religion rooted in the quest of power multiplied by the participation of the whole species.

HIS CHANCES OF IMMORTALITY

In the first place, Wells deserves to be remembered as a man with a style. Though seemingly a rather slovenly writer, he can make any subject interesting, even the deficiencies of his mother. He will also be entitled to a modest niche in history as a humorist who illuminated the soul of the lower middle class without emphasis or sentiment. These, however, are feats which clever men can accomplish in any age, thereby effacing their predecessors. Wells is much more notable as a thinker of other men's thoughts, one who could grasp the ideas floating in the atmosphere and switch them on to the passing show after the manner of a spotlight. Thus illumined, he is the first social commentator who not only knows his own mind, but claims to know the minds of all his contemporaries all over the world ; and he has arrived at his conclusions by a series of popular works which present (not without lapses) a progressive and consistent scheme, beginning with dreams of scientific possibilities, continuing with exposures of social realities, and ending with a vision of the path which civilization (not culture) must take.

Unfortunately for his reputation, knowledge moves so rapidly and forgetfully, and events are so unpredictable, that his influence may well be effaced, and others will revive his principles believing them to be their own. If so, he will barely survive as an entertainer, intermittently in demand at lending libraries.

GEORGE BERNARD SHAW (1856–   )

To be consulted : G. B. Shaw, *Prefaces*, 1934 ; E. Strauss, *Bernard Shaw*, 1943.

[*Born in Dublin of a well-established Protestant Irish family, not wealthy, but bred to habits of wealth. Educated to be a gentleman without the means to live as such.* 1871–9 *earned his living as clerk in land-agent's office (Ireland), and after migration to London (*1876*) in Edison's Telephone Company.* 1879–91, *devoted himself to novel-writing and higher journalism. During this period formed his ideas on philosophy, politics, socialism (Fabian* 1884*), and the arts of success in modern England.* 1892–1902, *produced ten comedies, including* Arms and the Man (1894), Candida (1895), Caesar and Cleopatra (1899), Captain Brassbound's Conversion (1900). *In these comedies he achieved mastery of his special technique, adjusting social and political discussion to clearly drawn, humorous characters, and a fairly well designed plot. In spite of lavish self-advertisement, he was still little more than the idol of a coterie, though already known on the continent, his work mostly produced at suburban or provincial theatres, or by the Stage Society and the Court Theatre.* 1903, *attracts attention by publication of* Man and Superman (*produced Court, May* 1905). 1904, *won popular success with* John Bull's Other Island (Court, *November*). *Thereafter he became a celebrity. At the same time his comedies, for the most part, became more controversial or speculative, the characters tend more towards symbolism, and the plots are lacking in design, but with the exception of* Heartbreak House (1921), *and* Back to Methuselah (*published* 1921, *performed* 1923), *his sense of the stage never fails him. Perhaps the best are* The Doctor's Dilemma (1906), Androcles and the Lion (1913), Saint Joan (1923). *Throughout his life he has also been an active and pungent pamphleteer and journalist. He is an inveterate propagandist, but whether he writes for the Stage or the Press, his most ill-considered polemics abound in humanity and good humour, and he often seems superficial because his style is always lucid and his thought as clear-cut as a Greek statue.*]

LITERARY AND IDEOLOGICAL BACKGROUND

Shaw is rightly coupled with Wells as another of the school of Rousseau, which believes in man's progress up to the point of perfection. Otherwise he is quite different ; by temperament a shy and whimsical dreamer, searching for Platonic realities in art, philosophy, and literature.

He woke out of his dreams between 1876 and 1892, when he convinced himself that scientific industrialism had gone awry because ill distributed. Its benefits were controlled by a handful of egoists with a capacity for business and for nothing else ; meanwhile the vast majority of mankind were missing all that civilization had to offer. So, under the influence of Morris and Marx, he came to the conclusion that the only hope for the future was a planned and classless society, and set about devising means to that end. Unlike his two masters, he disbelieved in revolution, and in 1884 joined the Fabian Society, so called because in the Second Punic War Fabius fought Hannibal by avoiding battle. On the same principle, the complete socialist should prepare the way for his reforms, and not force them.

Shaw might have thought less of discussion and persuasion if he had also thought less of human nature. His favourite authors were Bunyan, Goethe, Blake, and Shelley, all idealists who believed that there was something in man which reached upwards towards God. His idea of God was much influenced by the late nineteenth-century reaction against Darwinism. He learnt from Samuel Butler that evolution was the achievement of racial purpose and memory, the primordial will to become better and stronger, and that our chief obstruction was society's perverted institutions, due to ignorance of this tendency. Butler may also have convinced him that industrial civilization could and should mark a fresh stage in evolution. It grafted immense energies and appliances onto our puny organs, completing the development which nature had denied. Therefore money was the greatest of blessings, since it paid the way to this extension of human power. Shaw must also have been influenced by Nietzsche, who condemned Christianity because (he argued) its deity became man in order to impose the slave's morality ; whereas the god of the future must be the unrepressed human being, the more-than-man, afraid of nothing, least of all of himself, so free and self-reliant that he could trust his deepest and most dangerous instincts to keep pace with his noblest aspirations. Shaw must also have been moved by Nietzsche's protests against the emasculating influence of the herd-instinct, which leads to the cult of incompetence and mediocrity.

This defiantly optimistic humanism may also have been confirmed by Bergson's *Évolution Créatrice* (1907). The definition of the *élan vital* as ' a jet unceasingly creating something out of nothing ' (*un jaillissement ininterrompu de nouveautés*) was much to the taste of our author, in his mature revolutionary period.

From 1886–1905 Shaw tried his hand at novels which have lively situations and cardboard characters. But at the same time he was a music and dramatic critic and more than sufficiently alive to perceive the new and amazing importance of the stage. The English theatre, once the best and then the worst in Europe, had revived and become the talk of London in the 'nineties. Above all it demonstrated that the theatre was the best medium for social satire ; that we need the actual exhibition of wrong-headed but well-mannered types—the tone of voice, the personal appearance, the revealing gesture—if we are to understand how and why our friends are not what they should be.   However, English comedy, according to Shaw, failed in this its proper function because it diverted attention to 'footlight sensations', and mirrored the lives of the governing class which wanted to change nothing but the government.   These perversions would have to be reformed, and meanwhile a Norwegian dramatist was proving that the reformation could be effected, and if so, the theatre might become the most inspiring moral force of the age.

Ibsen's realistic dramas (those produced 1877–90) are based on the conviction that every human being has a certain peculiar nature which needs a certain peculiar outlet, but generally misses it, because the conventions of religion and society stand in the way, and seem to be as tyrannous as fate.   In fact his dramatic situations imply the tragedy of character pitted against destiny.

This conflict had often been dramatized before, but not in some petty provincial scene, generally the family circle.   These homely surroundings were unequal to the weight of old-fashioned tragedy, so he created a technique of his own.   He kept attention fixed on the inner history of his characters, marking each new situation by a change in the emotional undercurrent.   Thus he accustomed his audiences to look for his ideas within the heads of his personages.

Shaw must also have been encouraged by some of the more controversial and progressive French *pièces à thèse*, especially *Blanchette* (1892), *Les Bienfaiteurs* (1896), *Le Berceau* (1898), *La Robe Rouge* (1900), *Les Remplaçants* (1901), which study the practical problems of social life, and not seldom sacrifice dramatic emotion to a lesson on morality.   But Ibsen was his master, partly because he turned on the footlights to illuminate our personal private problems, and partly because he championed them in the name of the new religion, an assertion of the rights of man.

Nevertheless Shaw did not forget that his audiences would be neither French nor Norwegian, but drawn from an undercurrent of intelligent London observers, just below the surface of West End society, ready to be interested in economic and moral reform, not in family horrors.   Though wise enough to learn from continental technique, he cultivated the emotional steadiness of the English.   If he were to establish himself in the theatre, it would be as the 'laughing philosopher'.

HOW SHAW CAPTURED THE LONDON PUBLIC

It is obvious that he would not quickly rise to fame, because theatre-goers were unprepared for what he had to give them.   They expected actor-managers dominating the footlights with their theatrical personalities, whereas the Shavian comedy would be centred in an idea, not seldom a controversy, and his cast would have to forget themselves in order to serve his purpose. Besides, he relied less on action than on intellectual laughter (like Meredith, another author with a limited circulation), and a play rarely holds the stage unless something is always happening, or about to happen. Nor could he easily find actors capable of interpreting an invisible plot. By practice and experiment he gradually overcame these disabilities and at the same time succeeded in advertising himself.

Like Ben Jonson (another ' high-brow ', and therefore unpopular), he took the bold course of publishing the plays which were so difficult to produce, and thus gave himself the opportunity of describing his personages and their backgrounds as both ought to be presented. In fact, his character sketches are among the best in our language. He added brilliant and paradoxical introductions which explained and emphasized the thought behind the comedies, and included cognate ideas for which there was no room in the plot. These amplifications should be enough for the public which buys books, but not for those who buy theatre tickets. The latter want something new to talk about and laugh over. So he enlivened his plays. however serious the issue, with the kind of topic exploited in a newspaper paragraph ; for instance, the then newly invented motor-car, the newly instituted women's clubs in Dover Street, or the problem of proselytizing suburbia. And finally, since his plots were thin, he varied the movement with incidental and neatly introduced reversals. For instance, in *Arms and the Man*, Bluntschli, fleeing for his life, is unexpectedly revealed fast asleep on Raina's virtuous couch.

These expedients, together with his talent for personal publicity, helped to make his reputation, even before they made his income. When at last his plays began to attract frequent if select audiences, his following was delighted to find the essential pleasure of comedy distilled for them in an unexpected way. That pleasure is, of course, the sense of incongruity : the contrast between a character's real self and imagined self. The masters of the Old Comedy took good care that their audiences perceived the contrast from the start, and enjoyed the joke. Shaw often ventures to postpone that enjoyment. He throws dust into the spectators' eyes, leads them on to the wrong impression, and then suddenly wakes them up to the truth. For instance, the audience at *Candida* begins by believing that Marchbanks is an irresponsible dreamer, at *Man and Superman* that Anne is no better than she should be. In both cases it is suddenly undeceived by a turn of the handle. Thus the dramatist disposes of the spectator's immemorial right to omniscience in the theatre. But the shock of surprise puts him in a good humour. Besides, the Englishman enjoys laughing at himself, as much as he resents being laughed at.

Shaw was sufficiently confident and sufficiently a humorist to venture on another familiarity with his audience. He pretended to be an anti-sentimentalist who saw things as they really are, like a man with a perfectly normal eye. Under this fiction he introduces us to the wildest of romances, a world in which contemporary habits are simplified into transparency. Molière was the first modern who completely succeeded in this art, and Shaw must have learnt much from his audacities. Both ridicule current poses and prejudices, both take almost ludicrous liberties in their presentment of characters and situations. But whereas the seventeenth-century Frenchman was lucky enough to operate on psychological aberrations —the miser, the misanthrope, the valetudinarian—as old as humanity, the twentieth-century Anglo-Irishman had to work with material which changes its aspect from age to age.

THE VALUES OF SHAVIANISM

Shavianism, then, can be defined as the comedy of humours complicated by socialism and one's duty towards one's neighbour ; and it needed a very clear thinker to do justice to all three aspects at one and the same time. Nor does Shaw always succeed.

His first three comedies (published as *Plays Unpleasant*, 1898) are staged pamphlets. They expose the wolves who wear sheep's clothing because capitalism has made such clothes fashionable ; though there is the promise of better things in the character of Miss Vivie, the first sketch of the ' new woman '. His genius first began to appear when he dramatized ' romantic follies and the struggles of individuals against these follies '. Act I of *Arms and the Man*, with its surprises, suspense, and touches of poetry, constitutes one of the best ' expositions ' in the modern theatre. *Caesar and Cleopatra* and *Captain Brassbound* present his first portrait of the superman and the superwoman, at any rate so histrionically alive that Forbes Robertson in *Caesar* and Ellen Terry in *Brassbound* could do full justice to the characters. *Candida* is his first master-piece. While the unsuspecting audience awaits the outcome of the usual sex-triangle, the dramatist introduces them to his second study of the superwoman. Candida discovers how to be happy, though childless. She adopts her husband as a grown-up baby. Family life, however, may be impossible unless that baby unlearns the habit of taking himself for granted, and in the intimate and sensitive complications which ensue, Shaw himself discovers that a ludicrous figure is generally pathetic. We ought to feel pity as well as amuse-ment. As Marchbanks exclaims, ' Do you think that the things people make fools of themselves about are less real and true than the things they behave sensibly about ? ' With those words Shaw found his special place in the history of English drama.

But it was not easy to keep that place ; it was much easier to keep his name before the public. *Man and Superman*, with its voluminous introduction, tries to persuade us that we shall be much nearer the superman of the future if we discredit marriages of convenience and face the mysterious necessities of sex-attraction. The complications are as amusing as ever, but we are not so ready to feel pity because the characters are caricatured. *John Bull's Other Island* ought to have penetrated the problem of spiritual self-fulfilment, confronted either by false sentiment or false strenuousness ; but the author could not resist the temptation to mishandle the Irish Question, just then acute ; and thereby enjoyed his first big financial success. *The Doctor's Dilemma*, the best and worst of his plays, borders on the tragedy of untimely death, of jealousy, and the quest of beauty in an age of false values. Moreover, it contains his third guess at the perfect woman, the sketch of a pure and etherial spirit, illumined with the touches of Celtic fantasy. But he half missed his opportunity in order to caricature the medical profession, because operations for appendicitis had become a town topic.

In these and other plays, produced 1900–14, he was obviously insisting too much on socialism, as if economic reorganization would somehow simplify the management of oneself. If so, the Four Years War blighted his hopes. As if to reassert his philosophy, he committed himself to a series of dramatized pamphlets, of which *Heartbreak House* (first composed 1913, revised and produced 1917) dwells on the spiritual death of those living material lives ; and *Back to Methuselah* (1921) expounds ' vitalism ' with fallacious lucidity. This laboured and loquacious propaganda exhausted the author, likewise his admirers. Once more he returned to his proper province—that is, the comedy of situation and the inexhaustible problem of living for other people, without forgetting oneself. With advancing years he lost little of his verve though much of his grasp on actuality ; but not before he produced *Saint Joan* (1923), his fourth and last portrait of the superwoman, and dramatization of her fate, if she appears before the age is ready for her.

SHAW'S FAILURE IN SUCCESS

Up till the Four Years War our author exercised a very real influence, which gradually spread over the civilized world. In fact he was known and admired on the continent long before he became a household word in England,—but nowhere in the way he hoped. He made his public think, and then they applauded him as a disillusionist, not as a constructive thinker.

There are good reasons for this anti-climax. Like John Mill, he believed that the best way to prove the truth is to disprove error ; and so he laboured at exposing abuses till iconoclasm became a habit, almost an obsession. Like Captain Shotover, he dreaded more than old age ' the happiness of yielding and dreaming instead of resisting and doing '. As a reward he lost his sense of proportion and power of self-criticism. He also lost influence because he frequently failed to strike the balance between propaganda and pleasantry. He used the stage as a looking-glass in which conventional people could catch sight of their real selves and realize how they appeared to their fellows. Consequently he had to make them talk in an apparently offhand manner, their language unimpressive, their thoughts inconsequential. Thus their muddle-headedness came to the surface. The audience, however, must not be muddle-headed, and if its thoughtful attention was to be held, it must also be amused. So he became disconcertingly clever at introducing farcical and often irrelevant paradoxes, jests-in-action, anything to raise a hearty laugh, and he succeeded with such theatrical effect that many supposed him to be posing as a dramaturgic clown. They forgot that he was also trying to bring philosophy into the picture of morals and manners.

And what is his philosophy worth? We do not know, nor does Shaw. He gloried in the splendour and dignity of man, and on the strength of that enthusiasm he proclaimed that there runs through human nature not only the urge-to-live, but the will-to-live; and not only the will-to-live, but the will to consummate our being in art, intellect, and humanitarianism, and that this conscious teleology will find its goal, as soon as we have the sense to give it the chance. But he offered no arguments to prove that such really is the prospect, nor did he explain how and why it should culminate in equalitarian socialism. His preachments aroused scepticism or perplexity in the mind of some admirers, otherwise ready to enjoy his common sense, artistry, and insight into our human failings.

HIS FUTURE

In the history of the stage his name is likely to survive. Theatre audiences will become more and more interested in the working of their inner selves, their efforts at self-assertion, their sense of contacts, and the friction between impulse and habit, and they will not forget to thank Shaw for enlivening this self-examination with the contagious laughter of the auditorium. He has, in fact, externalized the ' internal monologue ' [1] before it was invented. So he will be remembered as yet another pioneer in the technique of stagecraft. Amongst other innovations, he abolished the ' curtain ', the ' aside ', and the ' one-man play ', and if he also abolished the opportunity for imaginative acting, he introduced the arts of conversational argument, and elocution disguised as self-control.

His theatrical reputation ought to keep alive his literary fame. His propaganda will be taken for granted as a relic of the Past, and book-lovers no longer irritated by its irresponsibility, will be free to appreciate his essential ' sweet reasonableness '—a return to the classical ' know thyself ' in order to guide thyself. Probably the historical plays will be the favourites, because his practical wisdom is more effectively illustrated when disentangled from modern associations. Future generations will be more indulgent than usual because his mature work has the imperfect charm of eternal youth : its enthusiasm, over-simplification, and what Aristotle termed ' educated insolence '.

[1] See *post*, p. 176.

ENOCH ARNOLD BENNETT (1867–1931)

To be consulted : G. Lafourcade, *Arnold Bennett. A Study,* 1939.

[*Son of a solicitor, born in ' The Potteries '. Received a middle-class education, devoid of culture, but full of nonconformist instruction and discipline.* 1889–92, *earned his living and acquired experience as office clerk, journalist, reader to* Pearson's, *sub-editor and then editor* (1896–1900) *of* Woman. 1900, *resigns journalism for literary profession. Resides in country till* 1903, *then takes bachelor flat in Paris, producing all varieties of marketable reading material.* 1907–12, *marries ; settles at Fontainebleau. Produces among other books :* The Old Wives' Tale (1908) ; Clayhanger (1910) ; Hilda Lessways (1911) ; Milestones (1912) (*with* E. Knoblock). 1912, *after American tour returns to England, continues his prolific output. During the Four Years War employed as Director of British propaganda in France and becomes a public character.* 1918–22, *enjoys his wealth and reputation amid the excitements and extravagance of inter-war society. Publishes* Riceyman Steps (1923) ; Lord Raingo (1926) ; Imperial Palace (1930). *His dozens of other novels are negligible ; so are his writings on ethics and literary criticism. His* Journal *is only of biographical interest. Yet his career and achievement will always command their full share of attention. In half-a-dozen masterpieces he has equalled the best work of his contemporaries. He has surpassed them all in the sheer volume of inferior fiction. Yet he appears always to have laboured with the same conscientiousness on good and bad alike.*]

LITERARY AND IDEOLOGICAL BACKGROUND

Bennett dabbled, from time to time, in many subjects, including history, Latin, and philosophy ; but he was not a man of culture. The only literature that he knew well was that of the great French and Russian novelists of the nineteenth century.

He preferred Balzac because his *Comédie Humaine* embraced every aspect of the modern zest-to-live, Flaubert because he exhausted the resources of art to produce the impression of reality, de Maupassant because he does not search for ' slices of life ' beyond the requirements of his plot, and knows how to convince with the fewest possible touches. He cultivated Turgenev and Dostoevsky because, though interested in perverts and irresponsibles, they colour their portraits with the insight which breeds sympathy. Some critics detect the influence of Daudet, and even of Huysmans. He cared little for the school of minute documentation—for instance, Zola, the de Goncourts, and George Moore (in his early phase).

In the light of these examples, he convinced himself that all aspects of society are interesting and therefore legitimate themes for literature, provided that your narrative is not only an organization of data, but a ' composition '. By ' composition ' he meant a narrative constructed so as to interpret not only the facts, but the author's personality. Any experience might suggest a theme, and each detail of the background should be conscientiously verified, but the presentment must evolve out of the artist's tastes and convictions.

Such was Bennett's idea of realism. But it was also his idea of making a fortune. With that other end in view, he had to study the tastes and curiosities of the biggest possible number of people—that is to say, swim on the surface of twentieth-century society, a troubled expanse much shallower and more treacherous than the Victorian stretches. Bennett was caught and carried along in the current, fascinated by the movement and multitudinousness. Now and then his feet felt the bottom, and he became master of himself and his material.

WHY BENNETT SO OFTEN CHOSE SUBJECTS UNSUITED TO HIS GENIUS

He was a provincial who had fled from the provinces. As such, he became what Barrès would call a *déraciné*, an artist uprooted from the soil in which his spirit ought to thrive. Modern culture, with its disturbing questions and encouraging vistas, had naturally turned him against the stagnation of his own unintellectual world in the Midlands; so, having left his native home in disgust, he began by under-valuing the old life, and much over-valuing the new. But every artist has to learn sooner or later that his creativeness has little to do with his acquired tastes and habits of life. It generally works on a plane of its own based on early experiences among which his mind took shape and which can be viewed from the distance objectively, a part of himself as he would now wish to be. So it came about that while Bennett was seeking artistic self-expression in metropolitan and cosmopolitan society, he found his opportunity where he at first scorned to look for it : in ' The Five Towns ', or among narrow and unadventurous people such as that society might have produced. His genius was most at home among self-impeded or commercially minded characters, that is to say in *The Old Wives' Tale* (1908), *Clayhanger* (1910), *Hilda Lessways* (1911), *Milestones* (1912), *These Twain* (1916), *Riceyman Steps* (1923). This half-dozen, with perhaps *The Pretty Lady*, are the only efforts worth considering out of eighty volumes.

HIS PHILOSOPHY AND ITS EXPRESSION IN ART

In 1913 Bennett wrote in his *Journal :* ' Idiocy of loathing or scorning a different kind of existence from your own '. In this spirit he realized the haphazard maldistribution of this world's goods, which sanctions the vices of the lucky, and discredits the virtues of the unlucky. He perceived no less clearly than did Goethe that life is a game of cards, but that in the twentieth century character depends more on the ' hand ' dealt out than on the skill or unskilfulness with which we play. If we have a *real self* it is expressed either in some half-realized affinity—for instance, the sense of beauty, or in moments of detached and generous insight, when we perceive the futilities of existence and rise above their influence, as did Sophie Baines, contemplating the aged and desiccated corpse of her erstwhile betrayer, in *The Old Wives' Tale*.

These moments are few. For the most part we microcosms are alive because life must and will reproduce itself, and die because we are not able even to preserve our health. Bennett is almost morbidly interested in influenza, bronchitis, catarrh, paralysis, and softening of the brain. He is not only an expert in the sudden collapses of the physical machine, but in the normal passage of time which leads us downward into what Gide has termed ' the sinister degradation of old age '. Besides the two classic examples in *The Old Wives' Tale*, the reader should remember all the subtle changes through which Edwin Clayhanger passes between the unforgettable scene on the viaduct, and his parting with Hilda towards the end of *These Twain*. This industrious technician, bred among money-makers, who sometimes himself realized over £16,000 in a single year, and then luxuriated in extravagance, eagerly absorbing the surface of life, nevertheless, in his best work, has convinced us that youth and manhood are a fight against illness which every day leads us nearer to the grave. Such is our destiny.

Yet he is not a depressing writer. He had his own ' Consolations of Philosophy ' expressed in art. In the first place, he seems always to be in search of beauty ; and since his really inspired themes are drab or even sordid (witness *Riceyman Steps* (1923)), he has to look for it in the occasional effects of cloud and sunshine, sudden perspectives over the roofs of houses or over stretches of country at first glance defaced by industrialism, sometimes in artistic interiors, though more often in the criticism of interiors which might be more artistic. He is most effective when he recognizes the beauty of character—glimpses under the surface of minds which are wistfully seeking a better, fuller life, and therefore are at war with themselves. In the next place, it should be noted, that though the individual's only progress is from the cradle to the grave, yet society can unite these scattered and erratic journeys in order to assure its own steady advance. The most felicitous example is the comedy *Milestones*, in which, with the help of Edward Knoblock, he shows us how enterprising business men degenerate and decay under the strain of existence, but their achievement continues, each accomplishment handed on to the next generation, as material for a further advance. This suggestion of collective progress out of individual retrogression was new to the drama of 1912, and rendered the Royalty Theatre so popular that it had to sanction standing-room for those who could not get seats. Thirdly, Bennett took immense pains with the style and construction of his novels. He laboured to describe even the commonest scenes as if beholding them for the first time ; in his portraiture he did his best to ' get near to ' the presence of his characters, and then leave the reader to enjoy the

D

effect without any comment of his own. He was so careful not to mix himself with his descriptions that he sometimes feared lest they might be ' a shade too stiff, too severe as a narrative '. The death of Edward Povey in *The Old Wives' Tale* is a striking example. Thus Bennett sometimes fulfilled his ideal. He ' composed ' certain narratives so as to express his sense of form, and his reasoned attitude to life. Such was the ' personality ' he did not impose, but infused. Thanks to this classic objectivity, the reader is able to view the passing show in the same spirit of judicial detachment. It was not for nothing that Bennett would sometimes go into a picture-gallery ' to get into a frame of mind sufficiently large and expansive for the creation of the central idea '. [1]

HIS FATAL FLUENCY

He would have succeeded more often, except for another less desirable ingredient of that ' personality ' of his. He schooled himself to write regularly and rapidly. Self-direction and brain-control became one of his proudest boasts. Soon it became a part of his artistic consciousness. A book by Arnold Bennett was not self-expressive unless it were written quickly and methodically, and, as he verged towards middle age, he began to take an almost childish pleasure in his productivity. Efficiency was for him a necessary condition of excellence. Thanks to his own cult of self-discipline, he was able to sit down, day after day, and write vividly, honestly, and entertainingly, often producing two or three thousand words between morning and evening. As his novels are always well constructed, and the characters can be seen and their presence felt, the public asked for nothing better, and bought his publications as fast and as often as he could school himself to produce them. He saw no reason to wait for those hard-won moments of inspiration and insight which dawn on the author after agonizing hesitations and revisions. So again and again he missed his opportunities.

HIS PLACE IN LITERATURE

At the moment of writing, many consider him to be our representative realist; not without reason. He brings home to our intellects the familiar friction of modern life, without the least distortion or partiality. He is so completely at one with his subject, that he can make the facts speak for themselves. As such, he will surely enjoy an academic immortality; he will be a name in bibliographies, and in histories of the novel the subject of a paragraph or two, which the student will read and take on faith. It is doubtful whether he will really live in the hearts of future generations. Even his best characters have neither length nor breadth. They lack, for instance, the wild depths of Emma Bovary, the lovable frailties of Tom Jones, the cool and yet good-natured un-

[1] *Journal*, 25 March, 1904.

scrupulousness of Gil Blas, the exuberant naïvety of Mr. Micawber or Mrs. Gamp. We have nothing by which to remember them.

JOHN GALSWORTHY (1867–1933)

To be consulted : H. V. Marrot, *The Life and Letters of John Galsworthy,* 1935.

[*Of an old Devonshire family. Enjoyed the advantages of the Victorian upper middle class, including its expensive pleasures. Educated at Harrow and New College, Oxford. As his father was a prosperous solicitor, the son was called to the Bar in 1890 ; never practised ; but for the next four years travelled much, especially in America and colonies, ostensibly on his father's business. In Adelaide in 1893 formed friendship with Conrad which lasted thirty-nine years and influenced his work. Had no genuine object in life till Ada Galsworthy (then wife of his first cousin and married by the author in 1904 after ten years' attachment) suggested in 1895 that he ought ' to write'. After eight years' apprenticeship, he found his vein in* The Island Pharisees *(1904), which he wrote three times. During the next six years produced his best work. In 1910, owing to his advocacy of prison reform, he was brought into touch with leading politicians, and became more or less a public figure. 1914–17, continued to write industriously but with less artistic effect and more insistence on humanitarianism. Refused knighthood in New Year's honours for 1919. In 1918 suddenly inspired to continue the history of the Forsyte family (inaugurated in* The Man of Property *(1906)), down to the Four Years War. This series, republished as* The Forsyte Saga *in omnibus volume (1922), rendered its author a popular celebrity, partly because of its appeal to the spirit of transition. 1924–9, continued* The Forsyte Saga *in yet another series of four volumes which enjoyed an equal vogue as portraiture of contemporary post-war society. Produced in all twenty-six plays, of which only* The Eldest Son *(1912),* The Skin Game *(1920),* Loyalties *(1922),* Escape *(1926) appealed widely to the general public. 1929, awarded the O.M. and in 1932 the Nobel Prize. His prominence was partly due to his personality and partly to his interest in social reform and international culture (President of P.E.N.), though he always claimed that his humanitarianism was incidental to his art.*]

LITERARY AND IDEOLOGICAL BACKGROUND

In his earliest attempts (about 1895–9) Galsworthy imitated Kipling ; he did not begin to master his material till he was drawn to de Maupassant and Turgenev. Both novelists at once gave him ' real artistic excitement and an insight into proportion of theme and economy of words '. Like any other would-be novelist, he had to begin by looking into his own mind. There he found certain moral problems and sensibilities, essentially a part of himself, because also a part of his epoch, and especially of his class. This atmosphere, now a thing of the past, has coloured all his work with a peculiar, almost unique interest. Hence his claim on our attention.

We are now considering the 'eighties and 'nineties, when the Victorian middle-class was at the height of its social prestige, but was already beginning to relax its hold on the national income. It had become a caste, and that spirit could be summed up in the one word *gentleman*, which Amiel in 1866 termed ' *le schibboleth de l'Angleterre* '.

What is a gentleman? [1] The word has never been adequately defined, but when Galsworthy was growing up, it implied the obligation to give every man his due, especially oneself. A gentleman took no liberties with others, not even in thought, but he must be so trained and placed that nobody else was inclined to take liberties with him. The note was prestige defended by self-respect. Galsworthy was born and bred in this atmosphere, and seems to have thoroughly enjoyed the life as schoolboy, undergraduate and young man about Town.

As his manhood matured, he realized that the gentleman was at a moral disadvantage because his pre-eminence depended on his income. Possessiveness was the condition of their class survival ; and as fortunes have to be defended as well as inherited, it was easy to feel jealous of one's equals, difficult to think kindly of the labouring classes hidden away in factories, basements, and mean streets. The gentleman was also at a disadvantage because of his acquired refinement. He had become skin sensitive to what one might call the crudities of living cheaply. Between the rich and the poor there was now yet another gulf fixed : the five senses, especially the sense of smell. Consequently this well-groomed upper middle class, who seemed to possess the earth, hardly possessed themselves. They had no insight into life outside their pale.

Even within their own exclusive circle it was difficult to be openhearted. The gentleman had to be too careful of himself, too meticulously learned in the arts of apparently effortless and unconscious superiority. These accomplishments isolated the well-bred human being and rendered him a lonely and loveless pilgrim in a world of material comfort and superficial friendliness ; so much on his guard that he hardly durst indulge his own personality. His classic example is Hilary Dallison (*Fraternity*).

Galsworthy might perhaps never have realized the tameness of his fashionable existence if he had not, between 1893 and 1904, passed through a period of acute emotional stress, which in various ways aroused his latent capacity for literary self-expression, and gradually opened his eyes to all that he and his class were missing. As a gentleman he perceived that he was living in a prison, as an

[1] For further discussion of the word see H. V. Routh, *Money, Morals, and Manners*, 1935.

author he had to find the way out. Two courses were open. He could either follow the leaders of moral propaganda, a school much in fashion, thanks to the prominence of Kipling, Wells, and Shaw ; or he could follow the French and Russian realists, together with Henry James and Conrad, and reproduce the surface of society so artistically that he also revealed its human depths. Under the influence of his friends he chose the latter course, which also suited the dignity of an amateur. Yet the spirit of the age often beguiled him into the ranks of the propagandists. Conrad was right : he was always in danger of becoming an ' humanitarian moralist '.

Whether as artist or preacher, his sense of human contacts is unique.

HIS PERIOD OF ARTISTIC ACHIEVEMENT

To know Galsworthy at his best we must turn at once to his fifth novel, *The Man of Property* (1906), not only because he toiled over it for years, but because he wrote it with his blood. In fact this book is really a confession. He put into it all he had himself suffered from his own ego-centricity and the suffocating atmosphere of his class, and especially from the clannishness of his family. Above all, he put into it the memory of those ten years of ' ecstasy and torture ', during which he had to conceal his intercourse with the lady he finally married in 1904. Yet the whole drama of self-discovery and self-illumination is transposed into the impersonal, objective realm of art. There is not a hint of spite or even resentment, such as falsifies the satire in Butler's *The Way of all Flesh*, nor of the ' simmering revolt against the shibboleths of my home, school, and college '. The deep personal emotion can be detected only in the uncanny indirectness by which he depicts vivid personalities through their chance conversations and almost unconscious actions. The character of Soames is generally considered his masterpiece, yet it is surprising how little we know of that figure apart from the effect on the other personages ; nor should we forget that the senior and therefore authoritative members of the group are portrayed with rare tolerance and understanding, and as a reward he has been able to add just the touches which render them unforgettable. The passion so powerfully and unobtrusively condensed in the Irene episode unifies the many threads of the story and weaves them together under the haunting presence of Fate, in a way almost worthy of a Greek tragedy. Even when the climax, or rather, the intentional anticlimax, is reached, the reader is left with something to think about : the impression that he who has strength to carry property is not strong enough to realize that he stoops under the weight.

The Man of Property was the author's own favourite, and certainly the three which followed it are second bests. Galsworthy tried to visualize his own trials and troubles inside the spacious mansions of the landed gentry and hereditary peerage, *The Country House* (1907), *The Patrician* (1911), or among those who are not indeed content with the property and self-importance they enjoy, but busy themselves with what they read in books or discuss with social workers (*Fraternity* (1909)). As these circles were outside his spiritual experience, he had to import representatives from his own set, and then imagine how they would react to the environment for which they were not fitted. The effort at intuition is stimulating, but too obviously an effort; nor do the plots move inevitably; and when events fail him, he begins to rely on sentiment. Nevertheless, apart from their psychological insight, these four novels prove that their author had made his style: a serene and rhythmic prose, urbane yet touched with emotion, illuminated by a sense of outward things, especially the breath of spring. They also prove that he had ideals, though he rarely trusted his characters with them.

Galsworthy, then, like Conrad, believed that the novel should be objective. That is one reason why he could not resist the lure of the footlights. The theatre-goer is necessarily a detached observer, not in a fireside mood; theatrical technique is adapted to the art of drawing contrasts, and to the illumination of personality by inter-play; above all, the stage lends itself to characters which are ready made, only waiting for an opportunity to betray their wrongheaded-ness, and ours. So he created three dramatic situations which should appeal at once to that 'sense of other people' which the gentleman should, but generally does not, possess. In *The Silver Box* (1906) and *Justice* (1910) we see how the majesty of the Law may end in a horrible human mistake, because social thinking does not allow for individual circumstances. *Strife* (1909) leaves the logic of facts to convince us that fanaticism and inflexibility alike overreach themselves in a society which ought to thrive on mutual understanding; especially in trade disputes.

These three plays would lead us to suppose that their author was a born dramatist. They are full of action; each story contrasts two sets of lives, two civilizations antagonized in the same social system. Above all, he developed the dramatic possibilities of undramatic facts. The pregnant moments are reached in a police court, a court of justice, and a company board-room—places in which every tragic suggestion is suppressed by routine—and these scenes are effective in so far as they are free from over-emphasis. Altogether our author upholds the naturalism [1] of the twentieth-century theatre, and yet rouses his audiences to a 'mental and moral ferment, whereby vision may be enlarged, and understanding promoted'.

Yet he did not surpass nor equal this achievement, either in the twenty-three plays or the thirteen novels yet to be written. Con-trary to appearances, he had exhausted the themes, and was soon to outlive the atmosphere, which gave his talents scope.

HIS LAPSE INTO HUMANITARIANISM

These four novels and three plays helped to demonstrate that the well-to-do cannot keep their affairs to themselves. Modern capital-

[1] See *post*, pp. 92 ff.

ism brings the rich and poor together, and at the same time keeps them at loggerheads. So we are all less humane and sympathetic than we should be, and consequently less happy. In order to transform this idea into art, he had to show what poverty really means, its sorrows and resentments, and soon found himself unable to portray grievances without insisting that they should be righted. In 1908 he drew up a long list of abuses, and after 1910 he devoted much time and money pleading for them to be reformed.

But the more he served his fellow-creatures, the less he served his own talents. All the novels and plays produced between 1911 and 1918 mark a decline. Even the best (for instance, *The Eldest Son* (1912) and *The Dark Flower* (1913)) lack the touch of the artist creating what is part of himself. In the rest he merely searches for what concerns others and should be presented for their edification.

HIS PERIOD OF POPULAR SUCCESS

The Forsyte Saga (1922) brought him universal recognition and world-wide sales. There are several reasons for this suddenly acquired popularity. The British public nearly always pays homage to a sustained work completed in a series of volumes. The consummation seems to impress the collective imagination. Moreover, this sequence exactly reflected the anti-Victorian mood, during which England shed her insularity, accepted labour as a political power, and renounced, in word if not in deed, the mammonism and caste-spirit which were now regarded as the besetting sins of the nineteenth century. Thus the saga of the Forsyte family became the saga of national transition—the first vivid, sympathetic and sustained narrative recording the moral evolution of the new world, just dawning on the post-war consciousness. The reading public was at his feet.

Yet the volumes published in and after 1924 may have added to his income, but not to his posthumous fame. The explanation is simple. Galsworthy had made his mark by fighting his own life-battle in other people, extending the gentleman's loyalties far beyond his class. He made of himself a ' sculptor ' of men and women frozen in prosperity and an impressionist advocate of those other human beings frozen in adversity. His talent throve on opposition, and the battle was won. Possessiveness was unfashionable because possessions were insecure, and our humanitarian moralist could complain only that the rising generation was all too human. Even the word *gentleman* had ceased to be the ' shibboleth of England '. So his inspiration flagged while his facility increased.

There was another reason for his decline. Although apparently so self-contained and defensive, he was somewhat an extrovert. He was content to approve himself when others approved him. So now, when his novels were bought up and translated as soon as published, he was too ready to mistake applause for the hallmark of excellence. He followed the popular taste he was supposed to lead.

Now and then there are touches of his old self (for instance, Fleur's ' exquisite buoyancy ' and Jon's ' shy grace '), but for the most part he is content to satisfy middle-class curiosity in the manners of the smart set. Nor does he always take the trouble to verify his facts.

It is also noteworthy that, amid this success and publicity, he produced no less than fifteen more plays after 1917, none of them really artistic successes, all of them financial failures, except *The Skin Game* (1920).

WILL HIS PLACE BE PERMANENT?

Galsworthy ought to be remembered in histories of the modern drama because, like Shaw, he showed how to abolish ' footlight sensations ' and made it necessary for his actors to exercise their art in team-work. Like Shaw, he also reminded his audiences that a good play should appeal not only to their sympathies and imagination, but also to their moral sense, and proved that this impression is most effectively conveyed by atmosphere, not by exposition. He surpassed Shaw, in that his plots were generally more closely knit, more deeply charged with the drama of destiny,— and led to a more sudden and decisive climax. At the same time he succeeded in demonstrating that the most poignant emotions can be suggested in the fewest words, often an apparently irrelevant ejaculation. So he is one of our leaders in the cult of studied understatement. Nevertheless many will forget these services, because he was often careless or misinformed about details intended to be realistic, and not infrequently lapsed into sentimentality.

His novels are more popular than his plays, and yet their future is even less certain. He may be referred to as the authority on the age of Victorian and Edwardian opulence, and on the idea of the gentleman. But if future students go farther, and read him for his portraits of English nationhood, as foreigners do now, they will frequently be disappointed. His characters are less representative of his class than of his own circle. If society continues to tend toward equalitarian citizenship, he may be remembered as one of the first novelists who helped to bridge the gulf between what Disraeli called ' the Two Nations '. Apart from these and other such adventitious interests, his memory will probably fade. Unlike Trollope or Meredith (with whom he is often compared), he is not sufficiently expert in human nature to earn a recurring revival. He sacrificed too much to the manners and moods of his own time.

WALTER DE LA MARE (1873–   )

To be consulted : R. L. Mégroz, *Walter de la Mare, a Biographical and Critical Study*, 1923 ; Forrest Reid, *Walter de la Mare, a Critical Study*, 1929.

[*Descendant of an old Huguenot family. Attended St. Paul's Cathedral Choir School, in 1890 entered the city office of the Anglo-*

American Oil Company, and in his spare time contributed to magazines and published his first novel (Henry Brocken) *in 1904 and first volume of verse* (Poems) *1906. Did not resign his clerkship (Department of Statistics) till guaranteed a permanent income by grant of a Civil Pension in 1908. For the rest of his life has resided quietly in or near London, publishing poems, short stories, novels, selections, reviewing and occasionally delivering public lectures. Though shrinking from self-advertisement, he became, about 1920, one of the best-known and certainly the most acceptable character in literary and artistic circles. His popularity is largely due to the charm of his personality.*]

LITERARY AND IDEOLOGICAL BACKGROUND

De la Mare has been compared with Swift, Blake, Coleridge, Poe, Hawthorne, Christina Rossetti, even Lewis Carroll. His verse forms, and his harmonious and rhythmic prose sometimes recall the seventeenth century, especially Vaughan, Traherne, Herrick, and Sir Thomas Browne. His technique and perceptiveness occasionally remind the reader of Shelley, Keats, and Tennyson. In fact he is a very well read and cultivated author. But unlike most writers of this period, his mind owes very little to influences, schools of thought, traditions, and the atmosphere of the age. He looked inside himself for his inspiration, and there he found an intense and ever-widening curiosity about the spiritual significance of what he could observe or imagine, first outside, and then within himself. His genius found its scope in trying to give literary expression to this curiosity. Thus the whole career of this sedentary artist was a voyage of discovery, or rather, of experiments.

HIS FIRST PHASE : FROM CHILDHOOD TO MANHOOD

De la Mare took a very old path in order to reach something new. He began as a writer for and about children. Such is *Songs of Childhood* (1902). Such also is *Henry Brocken* (1904), a boy's evocation of certain immortal characters (amongst others Electra, Bottom, Gulliver, and Lucy Grey) ; and their portraiture is dream-burdened and remote in comparison with the originals, as Francis Thompson observed.[1] Such again is *Poems* (1906), though there is less of childhood's exuberance, and more of childhood's boredom. Lastly, there is *The Three Mulla-Mulgars* (1910), a romance concerning a family of royal monkeys. It has plenty of fun, fantasy, and poetic feeling ; but there is a fatal facility about animal heroes. They are too lovably perfect to represent human beings.

He was trying to see life from within, with the eyes of a child. Had he persisted, he would have ended, like so many others, by seeing childhood with the eyes of middle age, his vision clouded by nostalgia. Besides, the intimations of early youth are not easily crystallized in the language of adults. But we can now understand

[1] *The Academy*, 26 March, 1904.

that he was only taking his first look at the world, seeking for the best point of vantage, and he felt instinctively that for him child-like intuition was the most clear-sighted, exquisite, and comprehensive because the least contaminated. But he was also a practical business man, with a Huguenot's awareness of life, a student of character, keenly interested in the activities and oddities of those around him. He was also realizing, again instinctively, that childhood's wisdom loses half its value unless it illuminates the prison-house of manhood.

Some years later [1] he explained the artistic principle underlying his (at this period) studied artlessness. All poets, he said, resemble children or boys. By *children* he meant the introverts, who create their own ideas out of themselves—for instance, Vaughan, Blake, Freeman. By *boys* he meant the extroverts, who learn from outside —for example, Browning. In that psychological sense De la Mare might be said to create after the manner of a child, but eventually to range over the experiences of a full-grown man.

MATURITY

He achieved this synthesis of ' childhood ' and ' boyhood ' in *The Return* (1910). He may have taken a hint from *Dr. Jekyll and Mr. Hyde*, from James's *The Turn of the Screw*, from Le Fanu's *Green Tea*, or from Morton Prince's *The Dissociation of a Personality*, which explains how ' Miss B.' came to develop two personalities, organized round two sides of her nature, which had long been in conflict. Or again, he may have had in mind R. H. Benson's *The Necromancers* (1909), a really powerful novel, relating how a disappointed lover dabbled in spiritualism and thereby laid his soul open to the influence of evil spirits. Such ideas were in the air. Kipling had suggested that an animal's spirit might enter a man (' The Mark of the Beast ' in *Life's Handicap*, 1891), and that a ghost could tamper with the morse code (' Wireless ' in *Traffics and Discoveries*, 1904) ; Chesterton was to produce *Magic* in 1913. But it is more likely that, in this atmosphere, the idea would come of its own accord. De la Mare, with the impulse of childhood, was always inclined to fasten on to some fantasy which might mean more than appears, and then let his adult imagination hunt down the reality behind it. Not seldom his search led him farther than experience can go. In this case he posed the question : what would happen if your or my face suddenly changed into that of a stranger ?—and his speculations carried him away into the mysteries of spiritualism and split per-sonalities.

Most authors would have worked up the situation into ' a chapter of accidents ' ending in a tragedy (as in Wells's *The Invisible Man*). De la Mare created a problem of moral conduct and spiritual illumina-tion. Arthur Lawford falls asleep by an eighteenth-century grave,

[1] *Rupert Brooke and the Intellectual Imagination*, 1919. Reprinted in *Pleasures and Speculations*, 1940.

and from underneath, the fiery spirit of a suicide, yearning for a second lease of life, enters into him, and imposes his features on the sleeping victim. Lawford returns to his friends and family, unaware that he is masked, and henceforth the ghost-story becomes also a realistic study of social relationships and human contacts. A lesser artist would have tried his hand on a psychic or at least hypersensitive youth. But De la Mare makes Lawford an uninteresting, middle-aged stockbroker, so that his spirit, starved from boyhood, can at last come to life, assert itself against the spell, and gather strength to rescue the consciousness of his identity. The narrative style is worthy of this experiment in spiritual tension. As Reid says : ' the mind of the reader responds to every subtlest vibration in the mind behind the work '.

Like his prose, his prosody was becoming more significant and expressive. At first glance *The Listeners* (1912) and *Peacock Pie* (1913) seem to share the inspiration of his earlier volumes. The dream-like quality is still there, only it implies much more. Some of the lyrics really seem to be free of the waking consciousness, and to reach us through the mysterious, yet lucid veil of sleep ; inspired by longing, not thought ; but not the longing of a child. Each symbol suggests the deeper emotions of one who has lost more than he has gained out of life. In some poems the effect is almost surrealistic, at any rate so uncanny that one doubts whether it arises from the rhythmic schemes and melody appealing to the ear, or the neatness and concentrated simplicity of the diction, appealing to the thought.

In *The Veil and Other Poems* (1921) these qualities reached their con-summation. There is still something of the old shrinking from the facts of life, but there is also the courage to face them, and therewith to create fine poetry. De la Mare sings of thwarted effort (' The Imp Within '), loneliness, disillusionment, sin, misery (for instance ' The Dock ', ' Drugged '), of shipwreck and again and again of death (especially ' The Hospital ') as though he could now trust his soul to the terrors of his imagination, because, at the utmost limit, he found a sense of beauty, a thrill of disciplined creative-ness, which raises him—and us—above the frustrations of daily life.

In 1921 De la Mare published his longest and most popular novel, *The Memoirs of a Midget*. The idea has a very superficial relation to Gulliver's experiences in Brobdingnag, but is redolent of the modern sense of spiritual isolation familiar to readers of Shelley and Arnold. For the ' Midget ' is a mature and profoundly sensitive human being condemned by Fate never to know the equalities of comradeship. The author, always on the look-out for a freakish paradox, instead of creating another Faust or scholar gipsy, asked himself what would be the experiences of a human being otherwise normal except that she is a dwarf twenty-two inches high. That possible improbability granted, the situation develops into a realistic novel, with no more romance than is implied in the author's insatiable love of nature and sense of night's mysteries. The reader will look in vain for the ghostly enemies and spiritual struggles which thrill even if they do not convince in *The Return*. The ' Midget ' is but a human curiosity, who attracts an assortment of normally statured people, themselves curiosities, if only they knew it. Their predilections and impertinences are viewed through the dwarf's vigilant eyes which catch the giants off their guard. In other respects we should expect her miniature life to be passive, but with remarkable skill the novelist manages to involve his pigmy in quite credible adventures. However, the chief value of the book is to be found neither in its conception nor structure, but in its tone. Rarely has an author proved it possible to be so disillusioned yet unembittered, and to have given shape to so many shapeless characters in such soft outlines.

De la Mare has produced one more novel (*At First Sight* (1928)), several volumes of verse, eleven more books for children, five studies in criticism, half a dozen collections of short stories (including experiments in crime, especially *Missing*), and *Ding Dong Bell* (1924), a suite of epitaphs in a prose setting, faintly reminiscent of the eighteenth-century ' Churchyard School ', not altogether out of touch with E. L. Master's *Spoon River Anthology* (1915), but unique in its life-giving humour, kindliness, and charm of style. His latest poem, *The Traveller*, tells us most about himself and about your and my destiny.

HIS FUTURE INFLUENCE

De la Mare will be studied by our children and grandchildren because he asks no more of life than it can give, and proves that little to be enough, since whatever the world refuses can be found in poetry. This cheering and intimate companionship has not been established without exquisite craftsmanship, and De la Mare will also be remembered as an artist in language, all the more so because he occupies a peculiar place in the history of prosody. He is a traditionalist in that he pins down the reader to the poet's thought and mood, and generally employs the accepted verse-forms with which to lay bare his heart. Yet within these limits his haunting rhythms and studied felicities suggest so much that there is space for our undisciplined modern consciousness. He is somewhat a mediator between the old and new schools.

He should also be remembered as the prose-writer who gave direction to the modern fairy-tale. A fabulist tells a fairy-tale as often as he tames the spirit-world—that is to say, brings it down to earth, mixes it with our daily experiences, and shows how humans can equal superhumans. So does De la Mare. Obviously he must not deal in elves, giants, or other such stark impossibilities ; but in hypotheses, not too fantastic to be adjusted to modern habits of thought ; and therefore to be taken seriously. Their verisimilitude kindles the imagination and encourages us to view our familiar contacts in an unfamiliar setting. As our lives become more and more a part of machinery and civic administration, we shall feel the full value of these stimulating paradoxes.

In English literature even a work of art rarely survives many generations unless its import is moral, or can be construed as such. De la Mare, however, has sometimes been classed as a dreamer, interested in nothing but self-discovery leading to self-expression. We have already seen that these dreams, if they are no more, have also led him face to face with reality. It should now be noted that in searching

> . . . The long road bleak and bare that fades away in Time,

he has learnt a philosophy, one of the oldest in the history of culture. Fanciful as it may sound, he is a modern *manichee*. He believes that there is a power of Evil as well as of Good. Both are hidden beneath appearances, and man in quest of the one must run the risk of meeting the other. If he lets his imagination roam too far, beyond the sweet and gracious presences, he may, at his peril, penetrate to the lurking forms of terror, despair, crime, and madness. This conviction need not be an avowed article of the poet's faith, but such is the effect of his poetry. Our author is not altogether unlike Pilgrim groping through the Valley of the Shadow of Death, though his vision of Heaven is much clearer, more sensuous, and easier to pursue.

Before 1914, or even up to 1921, such a view would have been pardoned as an extravagance, merely a picturesque experiment in demonology. Since then, history has taught us more about ourselves, and humanism has learnt humility. It is not at all unlikely that many people will feel less confident about human all-sufficiency. If so, De la Mare's sense of spiritual danger will mean more than it does now.[1]

JOHN MASEFIELD (1878–   )

To be consulted : W. H. Hamilton, *John Masefield : a critical study*, 1922 ; G. O. Thomas, *John Masefield*, 1932.

[*Son of a lawyer, born at Ledbury, but orphaned early in life. The adventures of his youth are still obscure, but certainly included many experiences at sea (possibly before the mast) and in America (as farmhand, millhand, and possibly as a potman in New York). The passion to write, especially poetry, soon asserted itself, encouraged by casual readings in older literature, and in 1897 he returned to England, and came under the influence of Synge and Yeats. Worked for six months on the* Manchester Guardian. *Produced his first volume in 1902 (Salt-water Ballads). During the next eight years he attracted attention by six more experiments in verse, prose, and drama, all too*

[1] See *post*, pp. 140 ff.

personal and distinctive to be ignored. In 1911 *he became the most discussed writer of the day, because* The Everlasting Mercy (*published in* The English Review) *challenged, in fact insulted, every other tradition of English poetry, except faith in man and a sense of outward things. Making the most of his opportunity, he produced three more narrative poems in much the same strain within two years, also published in* The English Review. *Thus Masefield's reputation was made and twentieth-century poetry accepted a new influence. Having inaugurated or asserted the spirit of revolt, he has himself reverted to tradition, producing many works of varying merit, but all unmistakably vigorous and vivid, whether dramas, poems, or novels.*

Thanks to his common sense and firm but unobtrusive personality, he has played no unimportant part in the direction of literary life, and as befits an author capable of becoming a public figure, he has received many honours, notably the laureateship (1930) *and O.M.* (1935).

He has accomplished more by example than by actual execution.]

LITERARY AND IDEOLOGICAL BACKGROUND

Many authors have been mooted as influences on Masefield, of whom Kipling and Chesterton are certainly to be felt in his earlier work, and Chaucer in the structure and spirit of his middle and later period. He also appears to have learnt from Synge and Yeats. But these and other such influences are only skin-deep; mere preliminaries. The real impulse behind his work is to be traced to the spirit of his contemporaries.

What the age needed, amongst other things, was a new tone.[1] The younger poets were afraid to trust their impulses, lest they should not be taken seriously as poets. It was wiser to belong to a school and convince the reader that their taste was as cultured as his. So they were not free to create beauty out of any bare skeleton, clothing it with their own flesh and blood, and not even suggesting the influence of an acknowledged master, dead and buried in the nineteenth century. They were waiting for someone to show them, first how it could be done, and secondly how to win thereby enough public approval for the work to be recognized as literature.

Masefield did not of set purpose contribute towards their leadership, otherwise he could more conveniently have been discussed in a later section.[2] He is all the more significant because he had no such pretensions, but felt the need for freedom more intensely than any, and took the shortest way, guided by instinct. He described his mood in *In The Mill* (1941): ' the seeker for truth goes into the *desert*, or wherever there is nothing, to correct his sense of values '. The values which he brought back amounted to an attitude, welcome to his age, but heavy with responsibilities. His own works illustrate their defects as well as qualities.

---

[1] *Post*, pp. 104 ff.   [2] See *post*, pp. 111 ff.

HOW MASEFIELD FREED HIMSELF AND OTHERS

Like Keats, Masefield declared himself unable to live without poetry. Thus all day long he had to create something unusual out of the most usual experiences, were it only the suggestion of poetic form and fitness. If the material was in itself uninspiring, so much greater the reward; the recollection of the rough conquered and made smooth. This principle is noticeable in his earliest tentative verses, for instance in ' Cape Horn, Gospel II ' (*Salt-water Ballads*, 1902) and much more in *The Tragedy of Nan* (1909). Despite its inconsequential plot, it sheds an air of strangeness over a miserable set of facts, all too possible in themselves, and leaves the spectators with the feeling that they have been ' cleansed ' in their pity, if not fear. Two years later he submitted his idea to a final and supreme test : *The Everlasting Mercy*.

The theme of its poetry is at least as old as the romantic movement : the sweet mystery and tranquil charm of the countryside at night time. Out of this dreamy impressionism there emerges a burlesque epic of poaching and tavern orgies, through which Saul Kane, the village jail-bird, realizes his manhood, hears the call of God, and ends as a religionist. This kind of story is also old ; something like it has inspired many pious tracts ; not so the drunken escapades which doubtless originated in personal reminiscences. Yet the resulting harmonization comes as a complete surprise. Regionalism, revivalism, and blackguardism are blended into a single poetic effect.

Masefield has succeeded, because contact with these wasters puts us off our guard. For the moment we shed our scholarly respectability. In this unbookish mood the night scenery penetrates our senses as deeply and freshly as it penetrates the poet. Being well under the spell, these thieves and drunkards cease to be police-court specimens ; they become outgrowths of the mysterious background, seething with wild life. The spirits of the earth claim them ; and all because the author has tricked us out of the library atmosphere.

One cannot decide how far this poetic conjuror was also influenced by the very human desire to attract attention. Authors naturally want to be read. But he has certainly grasped the inspiration which the decadents missed, and which Housman half concealed. Whatever the technical faults of the poem—its slovenliness, the artificiality of its blackguardism, its artistic bad taste—it has intensity, rhythm, and vivid phraseology. These qualities, together with a *succès de scandale*, went far to liberate and license the profession of poetry.

HIS BLACKGUARD PERIOD

The tendency sketched in *Nan* and consummated in *The Everlasting Mercy* was continued in his next three narrative poems. Masefield was determined to strike while the iron was hot. All are inferior to their predecessor. *Dauber* (1913) is the best, because it aims the highest. Yet it just misses the poignancy of great poetry, because we gain no deep insight into the mind of the artist-shiphand. *The Widow in the Bye-Street* (1912) and *Daffodil Fields* (1913) are grimly realistic, but without enthusiasm. Yet all have that intense feeling for a locality in the open air, akin to regionalism, of which Masefield is unquestionably a master. The ' sea-pieces ' in *Dauber* are justly celebrated.

All have another claim on our attention. Masefield, like Hardy, understood that character is destiny ; a man, like an animal, has instincts which he is forced to follow. Unlike animals, however, a man can think about what he wants to do and when thwarted always suffers intensely and sometimes acts wildly. Hardy's victims are generally resigned and contemplative figures rooted in the soil. Masefield's characters are mostly Celts or Iberians, men of passion and adventure. In the Heroic Age they would have been kings of men. Unfortunately they are born to the twentieth century, in some remote district, where the call of nature is just as strong, but the sanctions of civilization much stronger. So they do nothing heroic. They take to drink, quarrel, break their mothers' hearts, break their own necks, commit adultery, commit murder, and, whatever their end, suffer more than their fair share.

These tales are not intended to depress or scandalize, but to elevate. If their author claims freedom, he does so in order to serve his art. In his essay *Shakespeare* (1911) he lets us see that the greatest English poet was already teaching him to understand ' villains ', and those tragic figures whom we account failures ' because they do not conform to a type lower than themselves ' ; and, moreover, how to portray their villainies or misfortunes in all the naked horror, without degrading his poetry or the sympathy which poetry should always inspire.

HIS GENTLEMAN PERIOD

Low life had no inherent attraction for Masefield. Once assured of his freedom, he used it to seek inspiration elsewhere. He wrote novels of purposeful middle-class life, of which the best is *Multitude and Solitude* (1909), the story of a medical expedition, deriving from a youthful ambition of his own, and the most complex is *The Street of To-day* (1911), because it deals with the moral problems of city life. He has composed thirteen dramas ; amongst them the noble tale of Japanese devotion published and occasionally produced as *The Faithful* (1915). Yet he rarely chose a subject which suited his talent. He was at his best only in a narrative so vivid and breathless that thought is merged in action, on a background of nature's grandeur or charm ; and only then, if the subject seems on the surface to be unpoetical. As his reputation and income had grown, and he now moved in a gentler, more refined circle, this double opportunity was not easily found. He had his chance in the thrilling yet restrained war-piece *Gallipoli* (1916) followed by *The Battle of the*

Somme (1919), though neither was a sufficient challenge to his inventiveness. At last, having searched in imagination over half the world, he found what his genius needed in the home counties,—which had already served him well.

The result was *Reynard the Fox* (1919). Masefield had often been impressed by the picturesque quality of a ' field ' in which the local gentry, in all their trappings, mix with their more sober-suited followers and tenants, all alike ' riding to hounds '. The theme had not been handled with a poet's insight and zest-to-live, so his imagination caught fire ; with such effect that his Chaucerian epic is as big a surprise as *The Everlasting Mercy*, of which it is the belated counterpart. As before, the poet's background is ' the earth of England ', with its intimate sights and scents (as if there had never been a world war), and the mother of men of spirit. But this time, the inhabitants are not wasters, but gentlemen and yeomen who have taken kindly to our civilization. Some of them may have travelled as far as the bounds of the British Empire, but they are all a part of the home landscape, products of its traditions and continuity. Yet the fascination of wild life has not been forgotten. If there is a Saul Kane, it is now the fox, an irreconcilable by birthright, no unworthy protagonist in the adventure, compact of cunning, speed, and endurance, through which he survives the ordeal, by the law of poetic justice.

Reynard, with its predecessor *Lollingdon Downs* (1917), marks a fresh and final phase in Masefield's development. During the next seven or eight years he kept to the same method, trying, through verse tales of action, to catch his own genius ' in places where the will to live clothes itself in lovely shapes '. All are well told, with rapid movement in loose-flowing verse, the suspense sustained to the last moment. But none realizes that peculiar blend of composition and transfiguration which characterizes his best work. His second best is *Right Royal* (1920), the romance of a steeplechase in which the horse and the rider are two heroes in one.

MASEFIELD'S PLACE IN HISTORY

He is a born story-teller, but his novels are not sufficiently distinctive to survive. They lack insight into the subtleties of character and the fascination of individuality. In histories of literature he ought to be remembered because he demonstrated so vigorously that the subject of a poem has nothing whatever to do with its quality, a truism previously discredited by generations of cultured poets.

As he did not otherwise tamper with tradition, his lesson was soon learnt, and his influence is now forgotten. Will posterity revive him for his own sake ? It cannot be denied that he wrote too much, and had little instinct for the perfect expression. Moreover, he lacked artistic refinement so unmistakably that he could not always discriminate between significance and sentiment, or even between

E

sentiment and sentimentality. But future readers will forgive much, first, because he has achieved simplicity both in thought and style ; and secondly, because he reminds them that poetry can still be well realized in action, and that without the praise of courage action is not poetical.

EDWARD MORGAN FORSTER (1879-   )

To be consulted : R. Macaulay, *The Writings of E. M. Forster*, 1938 ; L. Trilling, *E. M. Forster*, 1944.

[*Educated at Tonbridge and King's College, Cambridge, where he studied Classics and History, and developed into a humanist in search of Truth. 1900–11, applied the lesson learnt at Cambridge to middle-class society in four scholarly novels (of which* Howard's End (1910) *is generally considered the best), and a number of playful fantasies (re-published in* The Celestial Omnibus (1911)*), and enlarged his ideas on English life, character, and polity, by comparison with those of other countries, travelling extensively in the South and East. 1912–14, he seems to have passed through a period of indecision and unfulfilled development, visiting India with G. Lowes Dickinson, drafting two novels, laying them aside, and writing on occasional topics. After the Four Years War (spent on duty at Alexandria), he revisited India (1920–1), resumed, completed, and published* A Passage to India (1924)*, which brought his name prominently before the public, and readers began again to inquire into his earlier work. Since then his reputation has steadily grown, though he has since produced little to enhance it.*]

LITERARY AND IDEOLOGICAL BACKGROUND

Forster is one of the few novelists influenced by University life. He came up to Cambridge in 1898 at one of the most interesting stages of its history, when the traditions of the Victorian era seemed ready to blend with the dawn of the twentieth century. The Classics were still believed to be the gentleman's straightest and broadest pathway to the problems of modern culture, partly because the ancient world could face the essential aspects of human nature in a simpler, clearer light than in our crowded, confused civilization, and partly because the study of Greek and Latin developed an unique insight into the value of words, and ' the meaning of meaning '. So Forster was encouraged to outline his ideas before he put them to the test.

In this atmosphere he learnt something else equally characteristic of Cambridge and essential to his own temperament and development : the value of intellectual conversation. On this plane two or more minds can start by pursuing the knowledge of ideas, and end with a knowledge of each other, and therefore of themselves. Undergraduates have the leisure ' to digest their own souls '. Thus Forster acquired a very keen sense of spiritual contacts, first with the wise and brave of ancient days, then with his contemporaries. From both he learnt that thought, which seems so personal, depends on a co-operation; that we define our own identity by sharing it with kindred spirits.   If we are not fortunate in our friends, and therefore cannot construct an attitude out of the friction and inter-change of opinions, we must rely on the forms and formalities current in our class, behaving as if they were our own.   Forster, however, was fortunate.   Amongst his friends he claimed G. Lowes Dickinson, one of the first internationally minded scholars, whose *The Greek View of Life* (1896) was to be followed by *A Modern Symposium* (1905) and *European Anarchy* (1916).

Dickinson's influence was particularly valuable because culture had crept into social education, bringing with it a pseudo-culture which the conventionally minded can acquire.   Many a young man and woman was beginning life like supers on the stage, and they had to spend the rest of their existence trying to find out what was really in themselves; Forster, no doubt, amongst others.   This is what he means by the search for *reality* or *truth*.   The problem would be a suitable theme for a dissertation or dialogue, but since he had a novelist's eye for character and comedy, he projected his inquiry into imaginary people, keeping himself severely aloof, so that he, and we, can enjoy the comic side of their adventures.

The novelists whom he most admired were Defoe, Richardson, Sterne, Miss Austen, White Melville, Emily Brontë, Tolstoi, James, Proust, and Lawrence.   All these writers, it will be noticed, were fundamentally interested in the secret workings of the mind, and collectively explored the never-ending conflict between class-think-ing and individual self-expression.

THE PROGRESS OF HIS EXPERIMENTS WITH THE NOVEL

It was Forster's intention to combine what is best in nineteenth-century thought and style with what is most fascinating in twentieth-century mentality.   He succeeded very rarely.   As Oliver Edwards said, ' cheerfulness was always breaking in '.

His first serious attempt was *Where Angels Fear to Tread* (1905). The plot has just that touch of facetious inventiveness of which he was master, and he throws his problem of spiritual misunderstanding into the boldest relief.   He takes an impulsive, and only half-conventionalized English woman out of a priggish, conventional circle, wafts her away to an even more provincial townlet in Italy, marries her to an irresponsible and mercenary Italian, full of sex appeal, and, to complete the anomaly, presents them with a son and heir.   The situation is almost too good to be true, and all the time our humorist is aiming at something fundamentally human : the continuation of life as symbolized by their child, who dies within a year, and the mother, who dies a few days later.   This significance is obscured by the complexities of the story, with its serio-comic episodes, unexpected and inevitable ; our admiration is too often diverted to a scholar's and poet's impression of Italy—a dream of classic beauty and grandeur; we content ourselves with the subsidiary moral that the English and Italian temperaments, the extreme poles of unreason, are not yet ripe for mutual understanding, not even through the mysteries of life and death.

The novel lacks intimacy, as Forster must have realized, for his next study, *The Longest Journey* (1907), is simply a ' human document ' transposed into a novel. One half suspects that the author is speculating on his own probable fate, if Nature had given him less, and he himself had made a certain irreparable mistake. He projects a quiescent and impressionable youth of moderate attainments and exquisite sensibilities, who goes to Cambridge, begins to realize his true self in the genial warmth of undergraduate friendship, and then, in an evil hour, marries, or rather is married by, the wrong woman; and he gradually loses sight of his own dreams, and with them the sympathy to see into the dreams of others. He becomes like his associates, ' the Sawston set '. Such is ' Rickie ' Elliott's longest journey (Shelley's name for married life), and one would expect its narrow, monotonous course to bring the author's idea to a point. So indeed it does as far as concerns our understanding of ' Rickie's ' character, but not of his destiny. Too many things happen, which are excellent comedy, but do not prove that the issue is inevitable in its tragic gloom.

Again Forster tried to simplify his plot. He resumed an idea drafted as early as 1903, completed the scheme and published it in 1908 as *A Room with a View*. The focus is certainly concentrated. He brings together in a Florentine boarding-house a group of British middle-class specimens, and, in his own inimitable way, divides them into two factions : those who believe in the value of human choices and relationships, and those who ' follow neither the heart nor the brain, and march to their destiny by catch-words '. And yet, in the end, though we understand and enjoy the half comic relationships between these particular individuals, and chuckle over their vagaries (not forgetting the nudists in the woodland pool), we feel that this laughing philosopher is still laughing at too many things. The values have a bright surface but are not clear as crystal.

The explanation is simple, if one remembers the author's intention. He is trying to catch and focus one glimpse of the twentieth-century ideal; nothing transcendental or impracticable ; merely the habit of feeling one's own way out among other people's thoughts. The author follows the gleam where it ought to burn brightly, and finds that it is burnt out. Other people are all too preoccupied to think for themselves, so he and his hero or heroine spend their time looking for what cannot be found. Forster laughs off his disappointment and contempt with inimitable grace and facetiousness, but the result is negative. Could he not give human nature a better chance ? The answer is *Howard's End* (1910). In this

novel his sense of humour is as neat as ever, and the minor characters (especially the unforgettable Bast *ménage*) at any rate serve as
an amusing contrast to the protagonists. These, of course, are the
Schlegels, a family of German extraction (because the Germans of
the old school inherited an aptitude for culture), and he gave them
a comfortable fortune, quite enough to ensure self-development.
The Schlegels are essentially in and of the twentieth century; that
is to say, they have discarded the old idea of permanence through
property. On the other hand, they are always in pursuit of intellectual pleasures—concerts, literary dinners, art-societies—because
these avocations lead to that other sense of permanence: contact
with the best in human nature. The two sisters, full of their
ideologies, art-criticism and poetry, encounter the Wilcox family,
that domineering, hard-headed business group, whom the Schlegels
half conquer by their sheer humanity, and by whom they are themselves half conquered because efficiency and will-power are not to
be acquired through culture. The Schlegels are sufficiently civilized
to appreciate something they have not got. Such is surely the
impression with which we should close the book.

We cannot be sure of this interpretation, since, as before, our
novelist is too objective. He does not tell us enough about what
takes place within the minds of his characters; we do not know
their spiritual history; only the words and the actions by which
they are supposed to betray themselves. The reader is not allowed
to satisfy himself that the heart has its reasons which the reason
cannot comprehend. Hence, though *Howard's End* is admirably
detailed, we feel a looseness in the texture, and here and there an
unaccountable twist in the plot which the reader is left to explain
as best he can.

Such are the defects of his qualities, all the more because he
chose aspects and situations so familiar that the reader expects to
be admitted behind the scenes. Though the pattern of his mind
was fixed, he had not yet devised the most effective framework.
Fourteen years later, after much artistic meditation and cosmopolitan experience, he ventured on another and more remarkable
experiment. *A Passage to India* (1924) may be just as arbitrary
and psychologically cryptic as his previous novels, but it is much
more in tune with the new twentieth-century spirit, because England
is left behind, an island on the western coast of Europe, and Englishmen are tested by their attitude to the rest of the world. Under
strange skies Forster's mind worked freely. The human background is far more vivid and varied than before; the visions of
scenery and climate are unforgettable; the character studies are
more succinct and satisfying, notably that of Aziz the Mohammedan
(possibly the best modern portraiture of one nationality by another)
and of Fielding, the typically level-headed Britisher. These two
carry the story on their shoulders, and the contributory figures are
skilfully grouped round their presence. Furthermore all English-

men capable of appreciating Forster's humour enjoy the unique privilege of viewing their compatriots through the eyes of a foreigner —eyes sharpened by a sense of political inferiority and national pride.

HIS FUTURE REPUTATION

Forster is one of the very few contemporary authors who have not written more than they were able to write well. In return, he will be remembered as an expert in the dialogue which reveals, and a creator of personalities, whose presence can be felt. It will also be recognized that few have managed to manoeuvre the details of their plots so effectively that every little meanness, insincerity, and interference should meet the appropriate discomfiture, comic and poetically just. This humorous sequence of episodes and en-counters is presented in a classic prose-style, together with occasional touches of genuine poetry, and underneath the wit and satire there runs a current of moral earnestness. So even if he sometimes scamped an important turning point in his plots, he will be remembered for what he did not scamp.

His position in the history of the novel is of special interest. Ostensibly he is a traditionalist—that is to say, he keeps to the principle of an organic, consequential plot, and of one or more central characters, who are possessed by a certain motive, generally some particular virtue or vice, which shapes their destiny. The treatment is ' dramatic ' in that the personages appear to reach their appointed end without the interference of the author. Forster writes as if such was his idea of the novel, but in reality he has outgrown this older method. Being in touch with the twentieth century, he does not believe in character or destiny ; he believes in accidents. His personages are very ordinary people, neither vice-ridden nor virtue-ridden ; they are more or less free to choose their own course ; and they do not know what to choose. As they cannot see themselves reflected in the comments and counsels of discerning friends, they take the wrong course, well intentioned but misguided, until their suppressed subconscious nature asserts itself, again due to some accident. Fortunately they are well-to-do and well educated, so the result is more often comic than tragic. They are in search of a more satisfying life, so his novels beguile you into a foretaste of a brighter world, by showing you those who happened to miss it.

This kind of story cannot well be told in the old ' dramatic ' way. It needs an inward as well as an outward plot, a psychic as well as a circumstantial atmosphere, a more prying curiosity in human behaviourism. Forster's technique was out of date for such guesswork. That is why his position is almost unique. He stands between two schools, so good a master of the nineteenth-century technique that he cannot do full justice to twentieth-century material.

WILLIAM BUTLER YEATS (1865-1939)

To be consulted : J. M. Hone, *W. B. Yeats,* 1940 ; L. Macneice, *The Poetry of W. B. Yeats,* 1941 ; V. K. Narayana Menon, *The Development of W. B. Yeats,* 1942 ; C. M. Bowra, *The Heritage of Symbolism,* 1943; P. Ure, *Towards a Myth,* 1946.

[*Yeats was born into an artistic and literary family near Dublin ; spent his boyhood attending school in London and holidays at County Sligo ;* 1880, *returned with family to Ireland ;* 1883, *began studying art and Indian theosophy ;* 1886, *began to devote himself to literature ;* 1887, *returned with his father to London ;* 1889, *began to find his place among the rising generation of English writers (partly thanks to* Oisin). 1891, *joined the Rhymers' Club. From the middle nineties onward began writing for the Irish stage ;* 1899, *joined in the founding of the Irish Literary Theatre, afterwards known as the Abbey Theatre, of which he became in* 1904 *a director with Lady Gregory and J. M. Synge. Lived or travelled in Ireland, London, and Paris. Helped to found secret and hermetic societies, played no small part as an 'underground' collaborator of Irish nationalism, prominently in* 1916. *Senator of the Irish Free State,* 1922-8. *Nobel Prize,* 1923. *Detested science and positive philosophy, yet devoted his genius to solving the same problems through intuition, folklore, and contemplation. ' As he grew older his music grew younger.'*]

LITERARY AND IDEOLOGICAL BACKGROUND

Yeats stands out as a dominant figure, because (it is claimed) he taught younger poets how to write. Whether or no posterity will agree, he certainly had to begin by teaching himself, and the circumstances of his life and his unique temperament led him through all the movements and influences of his age, from the decadent 'nineties, almost to the catastrophic 'forties. Though centred in himself, in search of his artistic personality, he became a part of all he saw and felt. Hence his importance.

He was a Celt never reconciled to Anglo-Norman habits and way of thinking; something of an artistic bohemian, not even well read in the best literature, steeped in prejudice and vanity. So although England (which, unlike Shaw, he hated) was to offer the best scope for his genius, he rarely felt in the mood to merge himself in the stream of its life. This abstention suited his temperament. He was at heart a dreamer, a visionary fascinated by folk-lore, balladry, and the superstitions of the Irish peasantry. Like them he believed in fairies, gnomes, and demons, in the truth of dreams, and in personal immortality. Like Shelley he believed that experience was restricted to a succession of appearances, and that death would reveal reality. Quite early in life he cherished the fancy that verses should be spoken to the notes of a harp, if not sung.

Such a man could not help feeling strange in a world of scientific facts and mechanical appliances, in which truth was tested by logic and the evidence of the senses. So he convinced himself and set out to convince others that modern civilization effaces our fundamental consciousness of ourselves. Learning, like wealth, isolates human beings, pinning them down to man-made theories and personal affairs, entangling each in the surface complexities of existence. Even literature was divided among sectional aspects of experience, and thus played upon the sense of human differences. Rarely did a novelist or even a poet strike to the common root of human nature. They were all too intent on the matters which their minds had been trained to consider. As Blake had said, reason divides, but imagination unites.

Yeats trusted to his imagination, and however uncritical his method, it certainly carried him deeper and farther than the range of folk-lore and mythology with which he began. Through ' the passions and beliefs of ancient times ' he got near to the primitive but perennial throb of life which civilization had tamed. Others were on the same track. Meredith had warned his generation that man is possessed by a ' triad '—blood, brain, and spirit—and that all three elements must be equally balanced if the human being is to be complete. Nietzsche had dwelt on the chaos of urges and energies in primitive man—the Dionysian impulse—still surviving under civilization, and symbolized in national legendry. Samuel Butler, especially in *Life and Habit* and *God the Known and Unknown*, had argued that our will-to-live is a single vital tendency, like an unconscious and hereditary memory, which pervades the whole race, as the sap pervades all the branches of a tree. Lastly, Andrew Lang, Sir James Frazer, Edward Carpenter, and others [1] were beginning to interpret prehistoric civilization by the light of ethnology, folk-lore, comparative religion, mythology, and even biology. The ' Return to Nature ' was very much in the air.

These pioneers, for the most part, were steady men of research, more or less scientifically minded. Yeats was an obstinate anti-rationalist. Yet intuition brought him just as near to what thinkers now call depth-psychology. For instance, he writes in *The Autumn of the Body* (1895), ' Our thoughts and emotions are often but spray flung up from the hidden tides that follow a moon no eye can see '.

The moon is not merely a figure of speech. Its influence had been recognized from time immemorial. Yeats took it as a symbol of life's mystery ; and he believed in magic. That is to say, he persuaded himself that primitive folk were not mistaken : occult influences could penetrate our spirits, now as then, sharpening our senses with an uncanny prescience or awareness. So he dabbled in theosophy and hypnotism as a ' revolt of the soul against the intellect ' in the hope to acquire ' a more conscious exercise of the

[1] For the significance of this movement see *post*, pp. 120 ff.

human faculties '. By the same token he believed in the magic power of words, not of course the hocus-pocus of a conjuror, but the phrases and terms which appeal to our common humanity. Once upon a time, a single magical symbol meant the same to emperor and clown; so now the modern magician, in the guise of poet, painter, or priest, could touch our hidden selves through notions born of sensation and traditional memory, awakening man's deepest and oldest consciousness of love and death, or his impulse towards adventure and self-fulfilment. Roused to impatience with the disunion and ineffectiveness of modern culture, Yeats went so far as to assert that this ancient universal artistry literally amounted to spells and incantations. He only half believed in what he said, and his claims must certainly be accepted in the spirit of a poet; and yet they suggest the conclusion at which sober-minded humanists arrive—for instance, I. A. Richards in *Principles of Literary Criticism*.[1]

It is obvious that Yeats was inclined towards symbolism, in the very modern sense of the word, and he has sometimes been hailed as our English-speaking representative of the school.[2] He certainly needed some such escape in the early 'nineties when he was contributing to *The Yellow Book* and *The National Observer*, and was ill at ease in the sophisticated atmosphere of the London decadents. So he was all the more ready to follow A. Symons's lead and study Verlaine, de l'Isle-Adam, and Mallarmé.

These verbal wizards were to beguile not a few of subsequent verse-writers,[3] but Yeats got no farther than the fringe of their mysteries. They confirmed his belief that a symbol should be more than ' a representation which does not aim at being a reproduction ' (A. Symons), and that rhythms, combinations of sounds, and fragments of imagery, which mean little to the intellect, may mean much to the soul. But these Frenchmen lived obscure lives, indifferent to everything but friendship and esoteric contemplation, whereas the Irishman was a man of action, always trying to manage his fellow-creatures; the director of a theatre, a patriot, almost a conspirator; at one period a public man who imagined that he could rule. It was not enough for him to seek transcendental treasures, hid behind shadowy doors. He had to fight many battles with other people, and consequently with himself, before his imagination had free play.

HIS APPRENTICESHIP

Yeats, then, came forward as the reformer of poetry by breaking not with the Past but with the Present. We must revive the simplicity and ' altogetherness ' of the first ages blended with our modern ideas of good and evil. The only true singer is he who tells the most ancient story so that it applies to the people of to-day. He

[1] *Post*, pp. 138 ff.
[2] E.g., C. M. Bowra, *The Heritage of Symbolism*, 1943.
[3] *Post*, p. 113.

first catches sight of his idea on his third attempt, *The Wanderings of Oisin* (1889), the long narrative poem in the form of a dialogue, not uninfluenced by Ossian, the spirit of it chilled by the laboured simplicity of the style. There is more warmth and pointedness in *The Countess Cathleen* (1892) and *The Land of Heart's Desire* (1894), but Yeats had not yet succeeded in isolating and expressing his own deepest idealisms in the naïve outlines of a primitive tale. He made a marked but inconclusive step forward in the spirit of the symbolists; their vague imagery seemed to stimulate his own dreams; and as his imagination began to work freely his expressions become more vivid and his presentment more forceful. *The Shadowy Waters* (1900) and *The Wind Among the Reeds* (1899) record the climax of this phase, but one still feels that the author, like his readers, does not yet really know what he can hope to find deep down in himself. Beneath those ' wavering, meditative organic rhythms ', like glimpses of an Irish landscape bathed in mist, this impressionist seems to be seeking wisdom in reveries, as if illumination, as uncontrolled as a dream, would come of its own accord.

HIS ADVENTURES IN DRAMA

By the turn of the century the decadent atmosphere was dissipated, as he himself described in *The Tragic Generation*. Like so many of his contemporaries, and with more reason than some, he began to feel strongly the call to action. He realized that his head was confused with images which effaced each other; he repeated to himself ' hammer your thoughts into unity '; he had come to know Lady Gregory, Masefield, Miss Horniman, Rothenstein, and especially J. M. Synge, who smacked of ' all that has edge, all that is salt in the mouth, all that is rough to the hand, all that heightens the emotions by contest '. So he flung himself with ardour into the projects of the Abbey Theatre, and the intrigues for the nationalization of Ireland. Thanks to these ambitions, enterprises, and the quarrels which accompanied them, he learnt that his opinions were really desires, not convictions, and that when thwarted they seemed to kindle his imagination and intensify his artistry. So his inspiration began to thrive on human contacts and on the rough and smooth of life rather than on moods. Besides, as the characters were created with a definite view to the stage, they had to be presented as human beings, not dramatic projections. They were still statuesque and mythological and their speeches were to be pronounced with a severe and symbolic intensity (if it were practicable), to the accompaniment of slow music, and they were designed to imply a more than human significance; but their grandeur arose out of a tension. As the old peasant declared, ' God possesses the Heavens, but he covets the earth '. *The Pot of Broth* (1904), *The King's Threshold* (1904), and *On Bailey's Strand* (1904) are representative of this phase. All lack the actuality of the stage. His improved precision of imagery and restrained intensity of feeling are much better illustrated in *The Green Helmet* (1910) and, above all, in *Responsibilities* (1914). These short lyrics enshrine either fables or personal experiences. All are realistic, yet most of them suggest a moral which the reader can keep in his memory and meditate as often as the mood comes over him.

To this phase belong the essays in which he explained his attitude with much repetition, but in singularly lucid and lively prose. *Ideas of Good and Evil* (1903), *Discoveries* (1907), and *The Cutting of an Agate* (1912) are not judicially critical, but every sentence throbs with his earnestness and enthusiasm. His talent for controversy, his mastery of rhythmic prose, and his pungent phraseology would have been more fully recognized if he had not written so much verse.

THE CONSUMMATION OF HIS CAREER

The Four Years War and its peace-time consequences only changed Yeats to complete him. He continued to study spiritualism, and in 1916 married a lady who was a medium. He became deeply interested in the mysticism of Plotinus, and was fascinated by Croce's [1] theory of 'the General Will', and by Gentile's assertion that 'the external world is so improbable that we go along touching it with our hands to convince ourselves that it exists';[2] and he expounded his philosophy in *A Vision* (finally published 1925). On the other hand, he was deeply moved by the European struggle, and even more by the Irish disturbances, especially the Easter rebellion of 1916, with its tale of hatreds, and the maddening memory of mistakes. His subsequent career as a public man had also its own disturbing lessons. These conflicts with men and manners did not efface his dreams, but gave them a more realistic direction. They turned his eyes away from mythology into his own soul, divided between earthly passions and unearthly visions, and at last he realized that poetry must be achieved through the mastery and fusion of both. As usual, the synthesis began as a speculation : this theory of the *Self* and the *Anti-self*, an hypothesis authorized by Boehme and Blake, and tested only too effectively in his inward and outward experiences. As expounded in *Per Amica Silentia Lunae* (1918), the *Anti-self* is a soaring spirit fretting against bondage to our mental habits and associations.

The philosopher becomes conscious of the *Anti-self* through the study of psychic phenomena ; the poet must give it a shape. Here again, Yeats founded his practice on a theory. 'Give a man a mask,' said Wilde, ' and he will speak the truth.' Yeats convinced himself that the artist must have two : the *Mask* (through which we externalize our acquired character) and the *Anti-mask*, ' streaked with gold ', by which we should figure the aspirations of the innermost spirit. Yeats wears both.

As a result his once dream-burdened will worked with more

[1] *Post*, pp. 124 ff.   [2] Quoted in letter to G. E. Sturge Moore.

freedom. He still occasionally wrote plays, but with a different purpose. Instead of dreaming ' wonderful and rather mournful things ' about his characters apart from what they say on the stage, he now encouraged a popular theatre for ' the making articulate of all dumb classes each with its own knowledge of the world, its own dignity, but all objective ', as he wrote to Lady Gregory in 1919. His own best contribution was *The Player Queen*, a clear-cut study of temperamental contrasts and conflicts (though full of psychic implications), at which he worked for half a lifetime, and produced in 1922.

As before, his lyrics are his best expression, and of these *The Wild Swans at Coole* (1917), *The Tower* (1928), and *The Winding Stair* (1929) are the most effective. He has taught himself ' to hit the reader hard with a carefully poised word '. The younger generation praise his ' hardness ' and ' dryness ' and, one might add, the metallic glint of his style ; and there can be no doubt that he had at last arrived at a more or less satisfying presentment of the wholeness of man—the *Self* so far subdued (not effaced) in the *Anti-self* that you feel its presence in the discipline and restraint of his manner. The workmanship is proof of passion overcome, ' of something to batter down and get our power from this fighting ', as he wrote to Lady Dorothy Wellesley.

HIS FUTURE REPUTATION

Yeats will be remembered as a personality as much as a poet. His influence is due, in the first place, to his long life. For half a century he has continued to convince the world of his utter sincerity and his commanding streak of genius. In the next place, he has always insisted that this genius recognizes no law but itself, even in the teeth of civilization's acquired tyranny. Thirdly, though not a typical symbolist, he reminded his age that poetry depends on symbolism.

In his early and middle career he relied on folk-lore, real or imitated, for his symbols. Latterly he agreed that one need not brush aside the accidents of daily life which are for the uninitiated the only reality. The poet could draw on his own personal experiences, provided that he also presented their implications without apology or explanation. Finally he demonstrated that the most convincing and inexhaustible symbol is oneself.

Seldom, if ever, has a poet externalized more clearly and consecutively the experiments by which temperament is translated into art. The whole *Corpus* of his work might be classified by slightly changing the sub-title which served *The Prelude* : the growth of a poet's faculty (not mind).

It will probably not be remembered that Yeats was also one of the first and most imaginative pioneers, in the twentieth-century rediscovery of man through folk-lore, anthropology, and unanimism.[1]

[1] *Post*, p. 120.

CHAPTER III

HUMANISTS WHO ACCOMPANIED THE LEADERS, BUT WOULD NEITHER LEAD NOR BE LED

KIPLING, Conrad, Wells, Shaw, Bennett, de La Mare, Masefield, Forster, Yeats stand in the forefront of Edwardian literature because they showed the educated reader how to think out his own immediate affairs in terms of other people. Each writer adopted one aspect of our secret selves and gave it currency. Of course they did not solve our difficulties, whether social, political, or introspective; but they helped us to view them impersonally and yet practically, under the influence of contemporary ideas. So they broke new ground.

In another sense these writers continued in the old tradition. There is nothing esoteric about them; the reader does not require a special initiation; none of them founded a school. They kept to nineteenth-century methods. They were well advised to do so, because behind and around them there was a body of traditionalists, less inspired or less creative, but nevertheless sufficiently influential to sustain public opinion. Some of these must now be noted. As they were more interested in humanity than in human beings, in culture than in conditions, despite some appearances to the contrary, they can best be discussed as humanists.

SIR MAX BEERBOHM (1872–   )

This individualist, besides other paradoxical peculiarities, marks the transition from the Victorian era by persisting in the tradition of its culture.

Having grown up in the atmosphere of the Beardsley period, he believed in leisure to make the best of ourselves and in genius to see where the best lay. In the 'eighties and 'nineties it lay, or seemed to lie, in the refinement of the intellect and sensibilities. At that period commodities, even luxuries, were cheap; human services were cheaper; so any well-educated member of society with a moderate income might feel entitled to spend it on his own mental and artistic development, secure against the vulgar struggle for life. Such was the mood of the time, such its opportunities. 'As for living—our servants will do that for us,' said de l'Isle Adam. 'Life is ritual,' said Lionel Johnson. So our author might well write: 'You must care greatly for the little things that only civilization, as we know it, can give'. Consequently, he was content to master life by mastering himself. He became a dandy who pursued a self-centred, unadventurous existence, with a keen eye for the fitness and unfitness of his environment.

Before long that keen eye had to become abnormally vigilant. The decadents hoped to maintain their artistic integrity, partly by ridiculing the philistines, and partly by idealizing the enjoyments which those same philistines helped to circulate. But, unhappily, few of the aesthetes could keep their balance and remain aesthetes. The more distinguished—for instance, Wilde, Beardsley, and Dowson —like *The Yellow Book* ended badly, and their place was taken by a host of quacks and imitators, either irresponsible youths, or older men eaten up with vanity. So the tradition of the 'nineties degenerated into a pose and nothing more. The genuine inheritors could continue the legacy only by ridiculing the fakes.

Of these Beerbohm was the most conspicuous. He employed the art and wit of the 'nineties to celebrate its decline and fall. Even so self-contained an artist could not always suppress a playful insolence which borders on silliness. But in his best fantasies and portraits—for instance, *The Happy Hypocrite* (1897), *Zuleika Dobson* (1911), *A Christmas Garland* (1912), and especially ' Enoch Soames ' (in *Seven Men*, 1919) the reader will find inventiveness, sustained interest, clear outlines, olympic detachment, an impeccable style, and serious thoughts lurking beneath the extravaganza.

GILBERT KEITH CHESTERTON (1874–1936)

His chief virtue can be summed up as humility, or the art of realizing cosmic immensities, by also realizing that we ourselves are of no size at all. So he went through life with the eyes of a child. His early essays in criticism and biography—e.g., *Browning* (1903), *Dickens* and *Shaw* (1909)—reveal more than a critic's insight into what genius can do with material at everyone's disposal. His exuberant excursions into the monotony of London streets, and the routine of urban administration—especially *The Napoleon of Notting Hill* (1904), *The Club of Queer Trades* (1905), *The Man who was Thursday* (1908)—demonstrated the artistic pleasures of playing with experience. His ethical treatises also began well. For instance, in *Heretics* (1905) he meets the sceptics and immoralists with the indulgent criticisms of a philosopher, too clear-sighted to be controversial. In *Orthodoxy* (1908) he insists that we can worship God as devoutly as did our forefathers, without sacrificing our intellectual independence. To that extent he was a pioneer in the religious revival which begins to be felt in the Inter-war Period.[1] Unfortunately, this sage and genial moralist was not only an author, but a journalist. As such, he had to cultivate a style on which to rely whenever his inspiration flagged. This style was aphoristic. So Chesterton gradually became an expert in surprises rather than in arguments. As he grew older, and the sombre problems of his overcrowded, under-educated, and plutocratic age began to obsess

[1] *Post*, p. 140.

him, he took refuge in this fatal facility. The less he retained of his glad confidence, the more he trusted to wit. Consequently his later volumes lack insight and vision.

None of them lacks the Chestertonian quirks and whimzies. In 1911 he invented Father Brown, a simple cleric practising God's will in an atmosphere of Scotland Yard and crossword puzzles ; wise as a serpent because harmless as a dove. This series of murder mysteries lasting, at intervals, till 1926, fascinates the average novel reader, but only as *Sherlock Holmes* fascinated their fathers. In 1911 Chesterton also clinched his reputation as a spirited verse-writer with *The Ballad of the White Horse*. This narrative poem, together with his other ballads (notably *Lepanto*) and his occasional and meditative pieces (notably ' The Donkey '), are all touched with their author's originality of style ; but they are touched with little else. The fixed metrical systems in which he composed, as did Kipling and Newbolt, are vigorous but too uniformly rhythmic to induce contemplation or even a sense of intimacy, except in *The Rolling English Road*, *The Silent Men*, and *The Song of the Dog Quoodle*.

JOSEPH HILAIRE PIERRE BELLOC (1870–)

A friend, almost a fellow-worker with Chesterton, has expressed himself with no less versatility ; and if he lacks the other's genius for eccentric phraseology, he is his equal in lucidity of thought and in the guardianship of public morals. As a catholic, Fabian,[1] and professed historian, he has produced serious though readable books, all coloured by his controversial point of view. *The Servile State* (1912), in which he contends that slavery, the natural condition of social coexistence, can be eliminated only by christianity, is his ablest but most questionable work. *The Path to Rome* (1902) is the most vivid, observant, and vigorous of his travel books. His originality has freest play in his essays in inspired nonsense, for instance, *Caliban's Guide to Letters* (1903), and his fantastically satirical stories, for instance, *A Change in the Cabinet* (1909).

Belloc and Chesterton would, in any case, be worth mentioning because both illustrate the change which was passing over literary life. They belonged by rights to the great age of periodical literature which began with Addison's *Spectator* and ended with the *Edinburgh Review* of Macaulay. Under those happier auspices their versatility would have been disciplined, and their ideas would have found the shortest passage to those who ought to read them. As it was, they never mastered their literary selves or their public, because they never understood the public they were trying to master. However, they became a centre and an example for those who loved England but hated what England was trying to become, and still believed that most evil things could be proved to be silly.

[1] For Fabian, see *ante*, p. 33.

SIR EDMUND GOSSE (1849-1928)

This scholar, and book-man, librarian to the House of Lords, belongs in spirit to the same group. He began his career as a poet and dramatist and then became known to academic circles as an authority on Scandinavian languages, and as a rather whimsical inquirer into the less-known literature of the seventeenth and eighteenth centuries. But in 1907 the whole reading public was intrigued by an anonymous autobiography of childhood (soon traced to Sir Edmund) entitled *Father and Son : A Study of Two Temperaments*. It should have been designated a study of two ages, or even two civilizations. The protagonist, Philip Henry Gosse (1810-88), a capable zoologist, a sufficiently industrious popularizer to be noticed by Huxley as ' one of the hod carriers of science ', was yet so enslaved to the fetishes and taboos of a primitive sect, that he expressed his horror of evil by throwing Christmas puddings into the dustbin, and his dream of beatitude by punctilious observance of a ritual, quite unauthorized by any established Church. This austere father, with the best intentions, tried to relive his own asceticism in the religious education of his son. The lonely and sensitive child endured the domestic discipline till he gradually discovered (God knows how) that he had a will and personality of his own, and belonged to an age which could prove all things.

Many contemporaries of Philip Henry Gosse had declared that religion need not imply ritualism ; amongst others, Carlyle, Froude, Ruskin, Mill, W. H. White (Mark Rutherford), George Eliot, Arnold, and Seeley. *Father and Son* owes little or nothing to any of them. It is free from resentment, satire, or documentation ; no more than a narrative conspicuous for its ' economy of implication ', with refined touches of humour and an unexpressed appeal to the reader's sense of fitness and of the rights of youth. There could be no more convincing proof that Victorianism was dead, slain by good temper, and the comic spirit. Incidentally, this book, like Butler's *Way of All Flesh* (1900), helped to encourage the growing reaction against parental authority.

WILLIAM HENRY HUDSON (1841-1922)

Though not among the conspicuous figures, Hudson is one of the most significant. He began writing in the 'eighties, mostly about the wild life, including human beings, he had known on the South American pampas, where he was born and lived till 1874. These earlier essays and tales (though he lacked the novelist's talent) dwell with an almost epic gusto on what is strong, strange, and primitive. His genius found its true scope before the turn of the century, when he began to discover and describe the more subtle and intimate secrets of the English landscape, beginning with the trees in London.

Like Stevenson in *Travels with a Donkey* (1879), he succeeds in giving interest to his most ordinary experiences; and the classic simplicity of his style almost escapes notice, because he seems to let his subject speak for itself. Conrad could never understand how he 'got his effects'. But his originality and significance are to be found in his attitude to nature. He claims to investigate with 'the eyes of a naturalist curiously observing the demeanour of all beings around me'; and his mood is certainly scientific, one might say Darwinian. In *The Land's End* (1908) he speaks of 'this dreadful unintelligible and unintelligent power that made us, in which we live and move and have our being'. Thus he has his full share of twentieth-century freedom from sentiment.

He was equally free from the kind of pessimism in which Hardy indulged. While recording as accurately and objectively as possible the facts of life, he also recorded the facts of the human spirit, what he himself described as 'the mind's projection of itself into nature'. He had the skill to temper perceptions with conceptions, without distorting either. In this whole-hearted mood, the facts of science gave ample opportunity for his sense of wonder, his consciousness of the variety and vigour of creation, even an intimation of brother-hood—he called it *commensalism*—with lower animals. Thus we could satisfy our spiritual needs, perhaps reconcile ourselves to the thought of death and frustration, while enjoying the eternal youth of nature. What he actually found on the English downs or the American pampas might be summarized as vitality expressed in beauty.

As he put his whole life into what he wrote, he matured early, and his literary output does not reveal the usual stages of development. Possibly *Nature in Downland* (1900), *Hampshire Days* (1903), *Green Mansions*, *A Romance of the Tropical Forest* (1904), *A Shepherd's Life* (1910), *A Traveller in Little Things* (1921) are the most satisfy-ing. Even these are not likely ever to be appreciated by a wide public because Hudson lacks human sympathy. He claimed to be an observer of all life from Cabinet Ministers to the prismatic hues of insects, but he is rarely interested in men except as animals, or as those concerned with animals, such as shepherds and bird-catchers. In fact, till close on death, he was better known as an ornithologist and advocate of bird-sanctuaries than as a prose poet who sought full scope for the human spirit in scientific observation.

ROBERT BONTINE CUNNINGHAME GRAHAM (1852–1936)

Resembled Hudson in that he was an intense individualist, prizing self-expression above the sale of books. But he had too many other interests, including socialism, politics (1886–92), and the love of adventure which lured him into all sorts of dangers over the sea and in the desert; in Africa, South America, and Spain. He seems to have written only when the mood was on him: biographies of memorable men of action who had been forgotten, some vivid travel-

F

books, and unforgettable tales, or rather studies, charged with irony, and sometimes burning with indignation. *Thirteen Stories* (1900) and *Scottish Stories* (1914) are his most characteristic. Much of his best work has been reissued by E. Garnett in *Thirty Tales and Sketches* (1929). Had he devoted himself wholeheartedly to literature, his sincerity and pungent rhetoric—above all, his sympathy with reckless, thwarted characters—would have gained for him something more than the title of 'hidalgo'.

SIR HENRY JOHN NEWBOLT (1862–1938)

He had much in common with Cunninghame, Hudson and Doughty,[1] but Fate gave him a different part to play. He went to a public school (Clifton) and the university (Corpus, Oxford), and, thanks to a peculiar trait in his character, became one of the very few writers who caught and interpreted their spirit. But that spirit is essentially a call to action—to public services, loyalties to mankind, and the expenditure of personal influence. So much of his energy was not dissipated, but diffused among social and political activities. The average reader remembers him chiefly as the author of much spirited and patriotic verse, or as an anthologist, popularizer, and commentator on English literature, notably with *A New Study of English Poetry* (1917) and *New Paths on Helicon* (1927).

Yet there was more in Newbolt. The traditions of England had sunk so deep into his spirit that he could dream of dead personalities as still alive, the Past separated from the Present only by an illusion. 'At one time we see them and hear them, at another they are invisible and inaudible', like figures on a tapestry, unconscious of each other's presence; not really separated, since collectively they make up the Absolute, the *anima mundi*; a spiritual contiguity of which we can become aware through love. That being so, the Real Universe (as his friend the metaphysician J. E. McTaggart also believed) must consist of persons, ancient and modern, and their interrelationships; and a human being, who happened to be alive, should nevertheless be able to change his point of time and associate with characters and communities supposedly vanished. All men and women are contemporaries, since eternity is an instant. Such were the sanctions for Newbolt's patriotism, and he would as soon have killed a man as change the traditional name of a place. This conviction of contemporaneousness is implicit in his best verse, though he lacked the technical skill to give it expression. He tried twice to put it into prose, and thereby, like Wells in *The Time Machine*, enlarged the scope of the novel, the second pioneer in an interesting interwar development.[2] But, though *The Old Country* (1906) enjoyed an unmistakable success, and *The New June* (1909) a warm but more qualified reception, neither romance has the power to convince.

[1] *Post*, pp. 105 ff.   [2] *Ante*, p. 26, *post*, p. 143.

The dream comes nearest to effective expression in his memoirs,[1] which also contain delightful examples of how a letter should be written, besides a fascinating record of social and political contacts and of the relaxations of busy men.

[1] *My World as in my Time*, 1932; *The Later Life and Letters of Sir Henry Newbolt*, edited by Margaret Newbolt, 1942.

CHAPTER IV

POETS WHO TRIED TO POUR NEW WINE INTO OLD BOTTLES

IT is characteristic of this age that many writers were *bilingual* in the sense that they expressed themselves equally in verse and prose ; and amongst them some of the most progressive and adventurous. They seemed to be so full of ideas that they could hardly decide on the best way of presentment. At the same time there were yet others who had no hesitation about the choice, and trusted to verse-forms to open a passage to thought. They relied on the nineteenth-century tradition, reserving, of course, the right to eschew sententious-ness, verbosity, and imperialism. One cannot add that they found ' the fair guerdon ' and ' burst out into sudden blaze '—not in the setting they chose.

THOMAS HARDY (1840-1928)

He ceased writing prose before Victoria died, and it is no reflection on his skilful construction, technically effective characterization, and unforgettable tones and tints, to say that his novels are Victorian in spirit as well as in period.

Meanwhile he had been composing verses since the 'sixties, and not infrequently borrowed scenes and situations from this source to enliven his novels. He found no publisher for the poems till 1898, but thereafter produced no less than ten volumes containing in all 850 pieces. These effusions belong equally to the nineteenth and twentieth centuries. On the one hand there is the old-fashioned sense of form. His best poems are classic in their condensation, slimmed down to the neatest and most epigrammatic expressions, purged even of legitimate ornamentation ; the poet's sensibility symbolized or dramatized in a situation. He experiments in rhythms and measures, not always successfully, but always seeking the right music to suggest his mood. He considered ' A Tramp-woman's Tragedy '—*Time's Laughing-stocks* (1909)—to be his best.

On the other hand, his mood is not that of the nineteenth century. Hardy has ideas—the sense of justice, of mortality, of poetic and scientific truth, of humanity sensitized by misfortune—and he ' applies them to life ', but not (to quote Matthew Arnold's *dictum*) so as to ' form, sustain and delight us '. As if in reaction from Arnold's morality, he takes a rather perverse pleasure in dwelling on man's helplessness, his self-inflicted misery, and the irony of his fate. Nor do his meditations suggest an outlet in action. He has the very modern conviction that our being is rooted in pity and revolt, not, as a Victorian would hope, in the effort to live well. Poetry, then, should also spring from these same roots, not transforming, much less hiding its dark origin, but taking the artist's only revenge : an escape through the fascination of words ; satire transferred from personalities to circumstance.

In this novel and sardonic atmosphere Hardy's achievement is considerable. He might easily have relapsed into the self-importance of the decadents, harping on his own disappointments, as did Edward Dowson. But he did not keep his pity for himself. Occasionally his wry humour betrays him into sheer paradox and ' crooked thoughts '. Sometimes, again, one suspects that he is only playing with a conceit, fixing a passing fancy for the sake of effect, as in ' The Strange House '—*Late Lyrics and Earlier* (1922). But at his best, he succeeds in depersonalizing the sorrow of life, merely posing a situation, and leaving the reader to supply the comment, as in ' Unrealized ' —*Pieces Occasional and Various* (1909)— and ' Ah, are you digging on my grave ? '—*Lyrics and Reveries* (1914). In these and other such moments reticence is more suggestive than eloquence. Similarly ' An August Midnight '—*Miscellaneous Poems* (1902)—actually says no more than any amateur naturalist might say. Yet the style and turn of phrase forecast a second rebirth of wonder arising from common observation.

Hardy certainly believed that the best way to know things was to experience their meaning, and therefore cultivated an awareness so intense and single-minded that every impression could be crystallized for its own sake in poetic forms, purged of poetic formulas. But he lacked the enthusiasm and constructive power to deduce a philosophy. The attitude sketched in ' Hap '—*Wessex Poems* (1898)—and in ' The Rambler '—*Pieces Occasional and Various* (1908)—remained with him to the end.

The Dynasts (1903–6–8) is no exception. The theory of unanimism is a mere scaffolding, detailed with far-fetched phantasmagorias, bird's-eye views of battles, together with dramatically appropriate episodes and duologues—an effort at artistic realization, admirably sustained and documented, but in the nineteenth-century manner. The poet is again most himself when he forgets history and remembers his touches of human nature.

ALFRED EDWARD HOUSMAN (1859–1936)

The influence of atmosphere must indeed be strong, for Hardy and Housman have much in common, though no two authors could have lived more different lives. The London Latinist was already known in university circles for his emendations of classical texts, his acrid criticisms of fellow scholars, and his insight into the spirit of Latin poetry. Housman, however, needed something more than an academic reputation ; he yearned for eminence ; and once, while experimenting in English verse as a relaxation, he discovered in his compositions a quality which might win fame. Such was the 'continuous excitement', under which *A Shropshire Lad* (1896) was rapidly created. He might well be excited. Like Hardy, he was possessed by the anti-Victorian mood, depressed by the disappointments of life, the presence of death, the complications of sex, the futility of our pursuits, the transience of nature's charm. He was well versed in the decadent attitude, a contributor to *The Yellow Book*, yet, again like Hardy, he was too original an artist to be contented with the cult of self-pity. Much as Theocritus and Virgil had made their own rather commonplace sentiments sound new in the mouths of shepherds and tillers, so Housman relieved his spirit through a parody of pastoralism. He chose Shropshire (for no apparent reason), and wandered through the county, whether on his feet or in his imagination, seeking parables in which to externalize his melancholy. As a result, his 'lad' enjoys neither the modern literary consolations of contact with nature, nor feels the unliterary primitive companionship of the seasons and the soil. He has a heart restless with cultured discontent, like a young man bred on the land and unsettled by a board-school education—one who knows that he is worth little, and will never be worth more, who expects to die early having never lived, who foresees his sweetheart in the embraces of his best friend, who knows the inside of the county gaol, who is bored at Ludlow fair, who is bored with everything except football and beer.

The reader would also soon have been bored, except for the polished workmanship of the verses, especially the economy of effect, and the colloquial commonplaces, as unrhetorical as conversation. Housman cultivates the simplest prosody, modelled on the Border Ballads, Shakespeare's songs, and Heine's *Lieder*, though the classical student will frequently be reminded of Martial's epigrammatic neatness of thought. Contemporary critics rightly admired his escape from sentimental luxuriance, his lucidity, his unerring instinct for the essential and suggestive. During the Edwardian era he became more influential than Hardy, because he imposed his melancholy on such unmanageable material, re-experiencing and redefining his mood again and again, and not attempting to impair the artistic effect with thoughts on God or destiny. If an idea transpires, it emanates from the *still*-birth not the *re*-birth of wonder. So the reader is left free to contemplate and absorb the expression of an acrid, stoic, uncompromising personality. *Last Poems* (1922) still play on the old mood, ringing changes, with surprising variety, on the ever-recurring note; except for the *Epitaph on a Mercenary Army*, which will live as a triumph in intensity through understatement.

WILFRED WILSON GIBSON (1878–   )

His best poem is his life, from which he learnt to understand the poor and therefore unconsciously heroic, as have few others.   As a collaborator with Abercrombie and Rupert Brooke in *New Numbers*, and through the sheer bulk and sustained continuity of his publications, he has become a recognized figure in Georgian poetry, but his performance lacks the touch of genius, and his style is too reminiscent of Wordsworth, Tennyson, and Rossetti.   Despite his long life and conscientious labour, he has not improved on *Stonefolds* (1907), *Daily Bread* (1910), *Fires* (1912), but sincerity and single-heartedness shine through all he wrote.

WILLIAM HENRY DAVIES (1871–1940)

Until thirty years old, our poet was a vagrant, hobo-ing in the States and dossing in the slums of London, if we are to believe *The Soul's Destroyer and other Poems* (1904) and *The Autobiography of a Super Tramp* (1906).   Both volumes attracted attention, and discerning critics recognized that this half-educated wanderer had somewhere and somehow acquired a sensitive awareness of outward things, including his fellow paupers, together with insight into his own moods.   Admirers have traced the influence of Campion and of Wordsworth on his style, but its directness and simplicity are his own, the result of concentrating his whole being on what he sees. So he seldom penetrates beyond aspects which lie within reach of the senses ; he does not reveal the hiddenness of spiritual things. Now and then he flames at some social wrong or muddle, but for the most part the charm of his poetry abides in his child-like vision. His best work can be found in *Collected Poems 1916* and *Collected Poems 1928*.

EDWARD THOMAS (1878–1917)

He made his living as an hack-writer, publishing very little verse (under the name of Easterway) till the year of his death in France. His *Collected Poems* did not appear till 1922.   In a sense he belongs to no school, for he appears to be quite unconscious of Victorian technique, and at the same time equally unconscious of the experiments being made around him.   He wrote in running verses, innocent of emphasis, beat, or rhythm, recording his daily experiences, nearly always in the country ; yet suggesting the charm of England with unusual insight, as if he could not help doing so.

JAMES ELROY FLECKER (1884–1915)

If Thomas knew too little about his art, Flecker knew too much. He was academic to the backbone, and retained through all his career as a foreign consul and a poet the passion for traditional culture. Such being his discipleship, he was zealous to hand on the torch brighter and clearer for his transmission, and like Hardy and Housman, aimed at simplicity of outline and an economy of words. The great masters needed trimming. Being a doctrinaire, that is, more in love with authority than adventure, he believed that his generation needed a definite theory on which to work, so he fixed on the principles of the so-called French Parnassians.

There was once in Paris a group of young poets (mostly born in the 'forties) and more accurately termed ' les epigones ', which became loosely known as ' les Parnassiens ', because their publisher, Lemerre, established his house in 1866 under the title *Parnasse Contemporain*. This group cultivated the style and attitude of Baudelaire, Gautier, de l'Isle Adam, and Banville (the Tetrarchs). They tried to write as if no experience was worth recording for its own sake, but only as a means to artistic expression. Ideas were dreams unless the poet could merge his egoism in his technique. He must take his craft, but not himself, seriously. The Parnassians did not believe that a poet should be raised above himself by inspiration, and feel more than he could see and express through some clear-cut object.

It is doubtful whether Flecker understood the Parnassians. His favourite poets—de Regnier, Moréas, Samain—were not pure Parnassian. But he was well advised to cultivate the Parnassian discipline. There was a streak of southern gorgeousness in his imagination ; a love of colours, precious metals, majestic and radiant perspectives ; and this luxuriance was not discouraged by his Eastern experiences in the consular service. So he needed some authoritative and restraining influence. As it was, he went some way towards reforming English poetry, especially his own. By 1910, in *The Golden Journey to Samarkand*, he had achieved mastery of his technique—clarity, compactness, haunting rhythms, and the perception of beauty as in an entaglio.

It remained to discover the deeper, more universal implications to be revealed in experience. But though he unlearned the love of himself he had not time to learn the love of humanity. It is significant that some of his most accomplished pieces are translations. Of the others, *Hassan* (completed 1913, performed 1923) reveals a promising sense of the stage, a remarkable skill in the contrivance of episodes, and the unmistakable intention to symbolize a life-philosophy within the limit of an Arabian night's entertainment. The climax of the drama is the power of love, which compels poor Hassan to behave like a fool, and condemns Pervaneh and Rafi to a cruel death. The dramatic production was an immediate success, but short lived. Theatre-goers soon felt that the symbolism obscured the thought. The taste of the theatre demanded realism, and realistic scenery confines the imagination to the footlights. In any case the drama's fatalism, hard as polished steel, boded ill for his future development. But, then, Flecker died at the age of thirty-one.

THOMAS STURGE MOORE (1870–1944)

This man of many accomplishments—a poet, artist, essayist, and aesthete—ploughed a lonely furrow within the limits of tradition. Arnold, Rossetti, Swinburne, and Hebbel have been suggested as influences, because his imagination was opulent and romantic, and his thought was austere, sometimes profound. Whatever the impulse, he has produced poetic dramas with Hellenic or Biblical backgrounds, unsuited to the stage, but a joy to the dramatic imagination—for instance, *Tragic Mothers* (1920); and much poetry which is always impressive except when too crowded with ideas, or too uncompromisingly sincere to be self-critical. *A Sicilian Idyll* (1911) and *The Unknown Known* (1939) are perhaps his best volumes, but his work is often difficult to read. A critic has called him ' a knotty poet ' and another has spoken of ' the stubborn severity of his outlines '. His name deserves to live because he has searched so far and wide for the material which should best serve a single purpose—the quest of beauty—and because he not seldom attained to it. To some extent he has explained his theory of art in *Armour for Aphrodité* (1929).

GORDON BOTTOMLEY (1874–   )

Few traditionalists have made a more interesting attempt to put new wine into old bottles so that both are preserved. He has written many volumes of verse, especially *Chambers of Imagery* (1907), but will be chiefly remembered because he was a dramatist, who aimed at renovating the old tragic spirit and settings in the cold, clear light of modern realism. He drew from many sources, including ancient Greek, Celtic, and Germanic, possibly not uninfluenced by Yeats, but his most memorable adventures were pitched in the world of Shakespeare. In *King Lear's Wife* (1915) and *Gruach* (1921) he recalls to life the fond, impetuous King of Britain, and the ambitious, passionate murderer of Duncan, but while they were still young men, unconscious of the seeds of disaster within their souls.

It was a fascinating experiment. Unlike Shaw in *Caesar and Cleopatra* or St. John Ervine in *The Lady of Belmont* (1923), he does not misrepresent their personalities in favour of modern humanism. He realizes that Shakespearean character is destiny, and displays no little insight into psychology, and cleverness in the contrivance of events. But in order to revive the bracing intensity of the old art—its crude realism and reckless passions—he resorts to the kind of horrors which were nearly as artificial then as now. Instead of tragedy we have the ' tragedy of blood ', a literary interest doing duty for inspiration.

RUPERT BROOKE (1887–1915)

The Fellow of King's College, Cambridge, is a complete contrast, being the last poet of Victorian prosperity expressed with neo-Georgian freshness. From boyhood at Rugby he had been a social, athletic, and intellectual success, the centre of admiring and devoted friends. After graduation he travelled widely, and in 1911 settled at Grantchester, near enough to play a part in the publishing of contemporary verse and the revival of student dramas at Cambridge. Such was life as he knew it.

In this tranquil atmosphere he composed verses conspicuous for their clearness, simplicity, good taste, humour, and a verbal felicity which is often unmistakably individual. Furthermore, they have a high moral tone, the sense of what he called ' goodness ', the disposition to appreciate ' the extraordinary value and importance ' of everybody and everything he met. In fact, if Brooke is the representative of pre-war culture, his experiences will show the post-war generation how select and generous that culture used to be.

On the other hand, his experiences may also show that this atmosphere does not hold the secret of modern poetry. His range is astonishingly restricted. Here and there the reader notes some touch of mysticism, a sense of the vivid strangeness lurking in the commonplace, but for the most part he is content with creature comforts and homely unfailing pleasures, such as would satisfy any grown-up child with the heart of a poet. We have seen that Hardy and Housman had lost the taste for these simple joys, because they could not replace some more spiritual comfort which was lost. One imagines that Gibson, Davies, Thomas, or Flecker had resigned themselves to the consolations of nature and craftsmanship for the same reason. But Brooke has culture, and wants nothing more. He is no scholar gipsy. For instance, his thoughts on love, death, beauty, or sadness are mere commonplaces, untouched by vision or even restlessness, only enlivened by his graceful style. Witness ' The Great Lover ', perhaps his best poem, or ' The Funeral of Youth '.

As he died from blood-poisoning on active service, at the age of twenty-eight, we shall never know how he would have developed, if at all. His slim volumes represent Georgian poetry in its resignation to little things. G. Keynes collected and edited his work in 1946.

LASCELLES ABERCROMBIE (1881–1938)

Brooke was born with a silver spoon in his mouth, while Fate offered Abercrombie only the prospect of a business career. He preferred the precarious independence of poverty, and after a year's journalism at Liverpool, retired into the depths of the country, resolved to live on poetry such as only cultivated people can appreciate. Quite early in his career he outgrew the ego-centricities of youth, and began to pierce the surface of life in search of other people's tragedies and aspirations. It may have been for this reason that he admired Hardy so intensely.

As a poet, however, he betrays a certain kinship with Tennyson and Browning in choice and treatment of theme ; and here and there one notices touches of the mysticism congenial to Meredith. Above all, he loved the vividness, splendour, and impetuosity of the seventeenth century, especially Shakespeare and the metaphysical school, and the eloquence and insight with which the poets dramatized the passions of their age, even ' the grand emotional impulse driving all existence '. It became the wish of his heart to write poetic drama and monologue worthy of their spirit.

Almost at once he found his style. It consisted, for the most part, in following the traditional verse forms, but not the traditional rhythms and phraseology. He ventured upon daring and sometimes sinister imagery, and upon exquisite variations in melody and musical emphasis. Without such innovations, he could not have expressed himself, nor the modern consciousness to which he appealed, nor, indeed, the kind of half-scientific mysticism implied in, for instance, ' A Fear ' and ' Ceremonial Ode ' (*Interludes and Poems*, 1908). So he became modern as well as academic, sometimes cultivating the dreamy, antiquarian symbolism of Yeats's early period, sometimes the crude, coarse-mouthed phraseology of Masefield, or the aesthetic impressionism of Bridges.

Had he fully succeeded in fusing the old and the new, Abercrombie would have achieved more than any poet of his age. But he was too completely dominated by the passionate urgency of his seventeenth-century models, and tried to create conflicts as deep as theirs. He searched far and wide for subjects which might give his imagination scope, and found what he wanted sometimes in classical mythology, sometimes in medieval lore, sometimes in the lonely lives and self-communings of his fellow-craftsmen, and yet again sometimes among the obscure tragedies and comedies of the underworld. In every situation, we are invited to sympathize with the cravings of the infinite soul imprisoned and individualized among the instincts of each healthy human body—art (he would say) thrives on the undecided tension between the physical and the metaphysical—and only death can resolve the tangle. Such themes obviously lend themselves to dramatic representation, and Abercrombie has achieved some notable exercises in *Blind* (1908), *Deborah* (1913), and *The Sale of Saint Thomas* (part 1911, complete 1930), thus following the best traditions of the Renaissance and at the same time symbolizing his own emotional experience. Would that he had attempted no more ; but he became so oppressed by our spiritual and carnal entanglements, that he writes as if he were himself a tortured soul caught in a trap. There is something overwrought in these conflicts. Through his devotion to the great masters, he cultivated their inspiration without acquiring their spontaneity ; or, in Gibbon's phrase, ' he expressed the enthusiasm of poetry, rather than the feelings of nature '.

Whether he was beginning to despair of perfection, or of public recognition, he gradually relinquished creative work after 1914, and took to criticism. The poet who in 1912 suggested that for sheer impressiveness of personality Christopher Sly is on a level with a university professor,[1] eventually became one himself. As such he has made some spirited contributions to poetic theory and technique. *An Essay towards a Theory of Art* (1922), *The Idea of Great Poetry* (1925), and *Romanticism* (1926) are his best.

[1] ' The Function of Poetry in the Drama', *The Poetry Review*, 1912.

CHAPTER V

NOVELISTS WHO HELD BACK AND DRAMATISTS WHO PRESSED FORWARD

THE novel was by now firmly established as the dominant literary type. But it had not, with very few exceptions, made the most of its opportunities. It had worked its way into the centre of civilization, but not into the heart of culture. At least, such was the defect of the best-known and most-admired authors. They dwelt on the things before their eyes, as if afraid or ignorant of what they could not see. They left untouched the intimations, intuitions, and intellectual refinements without which the most cultured minds do not fully possess themselves. De la Mare may seem to be a brilliant exception, but his speculations in *Memoirs of a Midget*, and even in *The Return*, are confined to two narrow middle-class circles. Kipling was manifestly restive within the limitations, and so was Conrad, but neither would have made much progress without the actualities of politics, machinery, money affairs, or navigation. The others seemed satisfied that experience held no secrets beyond the range of their workmanship.

It was easier, and more profitable, to study man as a social animal trying or failing to adjust himself to the claims of the family or the community. This theme gave ample scope as long as the public believed that society spelt progress. But the age was already disillusioned. In these Isles money, morals and manners were beginning to thwart character.[1] After the war novelists were to seek a more spacious hunting-ground,[2] but, for the moment, even the most adventurous hardly dared to transgress the accustomed limits. But a few were already insisting on a spiritual secret to be appreciated behind the veil of routine, and their names must be noted because some of them may outlive their more conspicuous contemporaries.

HENRY JAMES (1843–1916)

At first sight, this American Londoner might seem out of place in any survey of twentieth-century literature. He was born in New York, and in 1875 migrated to Europe, avowedly to live by literature. He first tried Paris, but within a year settled in our capital because at that time it seemed to realize the cultured American's dream of upper-class refinement and gentlemanly leisure. In this environment he set himself to perfect the novel of conversation; that is, to create problems or situations which involve the essential realities of life, but can be developed through a series of dialogues and contacts on a background of West-End politeness and easy circumstances. His first masterpiece was *The Portrait of a Lady* (1881).

---

[1] *Ante*, pp. 3–5, *post*, pp. 91, 137, 149.   [2] *Post*, pp. 149 ff.

Then, after several lapses and many experiments, he again made his mark with *The Tragic Muse* (1890). His insight into society becomes more sombre and searching with *The Spoils of Poynton* and *What Maisy Knew*, both in 1897; and he began to realize his final manner in *The Awkward Age* (1899). It depicts a ' set ' of attractive and idle-rich Londoners who enjoy nothing so much as detecting one another's hidden thoughts and secret impulses, beneath the flow of trivial if vivacious conversation. He struck more deeply into the drama of life in his last and accredited masterpieces, *The Wings of the Dove* (1902), *The Ambassadors* (1903), *The Golden Bowl* (1904). But though he now perceived and portrayed the vices which underlay the polished surface, he still kept to the refinements sanctioned by three centuries of culture and conventionality—contacts without conflicts. He did not allow himself to plunge his characters into some broad field of action, nor even to investigate individuality among the unsatisfied aspirations of the age of restlessness. Moreover, the types which played their part in his social comedy were about to make their exits.

The insistence on a static society with its expensive toys and pastimes discouraged the general reader. So James might have been dismissed as irredeemably Victorian, in tone as well as in theme, except for the enthusiasts. These more careful readers of his own and of our age noticed that his apparently trivial and purposeless episodes nevertheless lingered in the memory, linked to the progress of the narrative; in fact each novel with its drawing-room scenes was methodically organizing a personality, concentrating the light on a central figure which finally emerged as a human quality, distilled drop by drop. This quality was a revelation to twentieth-century students of the novel. It suggested a human being's individual sensitiveness to right and wrong, a consciousness of human dignity sanctioned by self-respect, and James was demonstrating how such a vision of the ' finer decencies ', peculiar to the personage and his circumstances, could gradually be woven into the texture of latter-day civilization. Such an adaptation could not be worked through passion, sentiment, impulse, instinct, or the pressure of social conditions. Yet it sprang from a motive : the exercise of intelligence, first on the part of the character—that is to say, of the author—and then necessarily of the reader. James was recreating his own impression of life through the sensibilities of a character, bent on realizing his inner self, amid people and things outwardly favourable to the cult of integrity.

It mattered little that these moral and spiritual problems were out of fashion; the treatment opened a new possibility to the novel. The artist had first to originate a dilemma which put someone's will-power to the test. It must involve the qualities which are the crown of European culture. The motive must pervade the structure of the novel, adjusting each line and contour to its development, preserving verisimilitude, eliminating every unnecessary circumstance, and producing an atmosphere of inward excitement. James himself declared that he had achieved a new aspect of beauty ; it was more like a new aspect of human experience, social and psychological—a susceptibility to the more intimate values, such as poets allude to and philosophers infer, but no one else had first analysed and then translated into continuous lines of conduct.

Unfortunately James's intricate and baffling style, his insistence on composition at the expense of representation, his process of ' saturation ', make no small demand on the patience and sympathy of the reader, unless he is teaching himself how to write novels. F. O. Matthiessen in *Henry James: The Major Phase* (1946) will make his task easier.

GEORGE MOORE (1852–1933)

This Irishman, educated in a well-to-do but unprogressive family, went off to Paris, at the age of eighteen, to study art. He fell under the influence of the Impressionist painters, especially Manet, Monet, Renoir, Degas, and Pisarro, and soon transferred their principles to the business of writing novels. Lest he should lose command of his own language, he migrated to London, resolved to introduce the new technique into English circles and figure as its most eminent exponent. Between 1883 and 1890 he produced seven novels, of which *A Mummer's Wife* (1885) is remarkable for its skilfully connected sequence of ignoble episodes, and *Esther Waters* (1894), even better documented, adds a note of unheroic heroism which ensured popularity.

These achievements in Victorian realism were a good beginning. Besides, Moore seemed able to give life and truth to events beyond the range of his own subjective self. But by the time he had published *Evelyn Innes* (1898) and *Sister Teresa* (1901 ; rewritten 1909), critics began to wonder whether his development would fulfil its promise. Superficially, both books are influenced by Balzac ; in reality they are even more influenced by the author's craving to express his whole unexpurgated personality. He had yielded to the neo-realist's persuasion that truth to life must involve truth to one's lower nature. Moore had forgotten that he was irreclaimably an artist, not, like Zola (who influenced his early work), a social naturalist ; much less an introvert, like D. H. Lawrence. It was his function to express the sense of rhythm, composition, colour, fitness, and human dignity in print, as some others do in paint.

This specialization begins to be noticeable in *The Lake* (1905), even more in *Memoirs of My Dead Life* (1906) and *Hail and Farewell* (1911–12–14). Such reminiscences, so apparently callous and self-centred, are really an escape from self. He was learning how to objectify his past experiences, however unedifying, so as to express his incomparable sense of style, serene and olympic, indifferent to every consideration, except the arts of presentment.

He nearly arrived at complete detachment in *The Brook Kerith* (1916), *Héloise and Abelard* (1921), and *Aphrodite in Aulis* (1930). Just as Peter Paul Veronese used the ' Marriage Feast of Cana in Galilee ' in order to express his genius for grouping, colour, calm, and masculine perfection, so Moore used a biblical, a medieval, and a Periclean theme in order to express three narrative fugues, presenting his idea of how certain personalities (not types) ought to have lived down their past, and thus fulfilled themselves. He chose periods in which humanity was not yet complicated by modern civilization, and could be represented as near to primitive habits of mind. Even these masterpieces fall short of perfection because they are tainted with disillusionment, sadism, and sensual curiosity. Yet he spiritualized the novel in so far as he obeyed nature to rule her ; or, in his own words, ' art is a rethinking of life from end to end '. The unobtrusive skill by which he produced these effects can only be felt, not described. He might almost be said to live in the failure of his imitators.

ARTHUR MACHEN (1863–1947)

The author of *The Great God Pan* (1894), *Hieroglyphics* (1902), *The Hill of Dreams* (1907), and *The London Adventure* (1924) should be read in order to appreciate George Moore. Machen was a voluminous writer ; he once worked in a publishing house and on *The London Evening News* ; he was a student of metropolitan life, but was rarely able to see it with the eyes of his contemporaries. There was some ghostly presence at the bottom of human nature such as materialists could not see, and which he groped for and tried to symbolize. Some others felt as he did, and at one time he became the centre of a cult. But not for long. Machen's intuitions do not give us the feeling that human nature is, or could be, subject to the primitive supernatural. His style lacks the mystic touch. He could only conjure with the pseudo-mysticism of demonology, magic, and occultism. His romances do not imply certainty, but the escape from certitude.

ALGERNON BLACKWOOD (1869–   )

The son of Sir Arthur Blackwood, K.C.B., gentleman-usher to Queen Victoria, and educated at Wellington College and Edinburgh, began his career by losing touch with the social and professional activities for which his birth and training had prepared him, and ended by losing touch with the culture of his age. Like so many of the next generation, he was possessed by ' the roving spirit '. He set out to find himself in America, and learnt how to fail as a rancher, a hotel-keeper, and a reporter on the *New York Sun* and the *New York Times*. In these ventures he experienced all there is to know about the struggle for life—its obscure virtues and blatant

villainies—but earned only the freedom to starve. He has told the
story of this apprenticeship in the unforgettable *Episodes before
Thirty* (1923).

For it was an apprenticeship. Thanks to this life of hardship
he acquired an uncanny sense of spiritual contacts; or, it may be,
he recaptured some primitive instinct for personalities destined to
be linked to his and to create a mutual dependency either for happiness or suffering. To him, these affinities seemed to partake of
the spirit of the universe; ' a spell that invades the heart and brain
like a drenching sea '. Nor could he cease dreaming about ' the
eternal scheme ' as revealed in the wonders of creation, especially
in the night sky full of stars.

In 1906 he started to live by his pen. He could not resign
himself to the routine of current fiction; and he could not keep
himself from dabbling in nearly every kind of fictional eccentricity.
But he failed to make his mark except when he concentrated his
visions and intimations on the metaphysics of reincarnation and
personal immortality, as in *The Wave* (1916), *The Garden of Survival*
(1918), *The Wolves of God* (1921). His spiritualism is quite different
from the virtuosity of Le Fanu's *Green Tea* or Montagu James's
Ghost Stories of an Antiquary. Blackwood feels in his bones that
we now know too much to content ourselves with modern positivism,
and he harks back to the whispers and intuitions of ancient wisdom.
It is easy to see that his imagination had roamed so far into the
heart of things that he often lost his bearings. He can communicate
the artist's sense of scenery, especially that of Cornwall, Devonshire,
and the Lake District. Yet the historian should note that he was
less than a generation ahead of his time; others were to roam in
the same direction.

SIR HUGH SEYMOUR WALPOLE (1884–1941)

This name recalls a long and imposing list of novels, once
deservedly popular. The author knows how to manage a progressive plot, full of interesting and sometimes surprising situations;
his characters are so clear-cut that the reader can feel their presence.
Moreover, he continues the authentic tradition. Hawthorne,
Thackeray and Trollope can be recognized as his models, and
some critics have suggested Meredith. His well-sustained narratives
are enlivened with touches of humour, and he writes nothing that
lacks a moral interest. Yet the lending library will be the end of
his fame.

He began well with *The Wooden Horse* (1909), the story of a
provincial community, divided between the progressives and ob-
structionists; *Maradick at Forty* (1910), in which a conventional
theme is handled with originality, and realism is blended with
romance; *Mr. Perrin and Mr. Traill* (1911), nearly a masterpiece,
a school novel from the masters' point of view. Their dreary pros-

G

pects and the daily friction of their common-room are exposed so vividly that one forgets to criticize the fantastic ferment in Mr. Perrin's breast. So with *Fortitude* (1913). The idea of anarchist outrages organized in a London bookshop hardly recommends itself. But there was a genuinely psychological significance in the character of Peter Wescott, the youth who completed his character by conquering his past. Thus in one way or another Walpole was firmly established in the public consciousness before the outbreak of the Four Years War.

Since then his imagination has travelled far and wide, through the Russian Red Cross Service, the sordid respectability and more sordid underworld of Cathedral towns, the social struggle in Mayfair, the sinister machinations of submen, and child life in the nursery. His creative energy culminated in *The Herries Chronicle* (1930–33), a 'saga' such as Galsworthy had rendered fashionable, symbolizing the rise of the modern English spirit, with the refining of its manners and the softening of its cruelty.

These workmanlike novels are cast in the old mould, but conceived in the new mood. Walpole's heroes are not amiable individualists trying to find their niche in the social scheme. They are, indeed, normal characters, but rendered abnormally sensitive because of the powers of Evil. Evil is a convergence of tendencies, each in itself negligible, but combining to produce stagnation, meanness, and stupidity, or any other spiritual or moral perversion which thwarts the men of goodwill. The central character is generally a young man wandering among the impalpable perils of comfortable, middle-class society, floundering in a Slough of Despond, amid scenery which Walpole loves as only a prose-poet can. The result is unconvincing—length and breadth without depth.

Superficiality was inevitable because the novelist was fishing in waters too deep for him. His early manhood was a succession of failures as a lay missionary, a private tutor, and a schoolmaster. Then he turned author, and quickly rose to fame and fortune. Through the long period of prosperity he tried to tell the story of his own unhappiness, externalizing his conflicts, as a craftman should, confronting his characters with some impersonation of the Evil which haunted his imagination. So he conjured up human spectres. As Clemence Dane says, ' He could not find what he sought, so he put something else in its place '. The casual reader thoroughly enjoys bad men and women when contemplated behind the barrier of 60–100,000 words ; but the thoughtful reader knows that Evil is an abstraction, only to be suggested to his thoughtfulness.

HENRY MAJOR TOMLINSON (1873–   )

In general terms, one might say that James, Moore, Blackwood, and Walpole were seeking some intimate and impalpable quality which influences our lives, but which, as it turns out, can only be sensed and suggested. Meanwhile the cult of direct impressions and contacts continued to thrive. A striking example will be found in the work of Tomlinson, a journalist and war-correspondent, who knew the sea first as a landsman in Poplar, close to the traffic of the Thames. Yet he developed into one of our most effective author-travellers. In *The African Coast* (1907), recording a Mediterranean voyage, he gives an unforgettable impression of the force and confusion of a storm. His masterpiece is *The Sea and the Jungle* (1912), the story of a voyage up the Amazon and the Madeira, fired with ' the force of a personality formed but not yet too mature to feel wonder and to respond to it '.[1] *Tidemarks* (1924), the journey to Singapore and through Indonesia, is more finished and pictorial, but the wild sea and wilder land no longer wake the almost boyish delight in romance and exploration. The war had already left its mark on his mind ; and henceforth he grows over-careful to note the encroachments of our mechanical civilization, with its vulgarity and platitudes, and more and more to regret the effacement of old-world habits and adventurous personalities. In *Gifts of Fortune* (1926) he returns to memories of his seafaring life and of the great travel-books which have pervaded his imagination, and meditates on man's spirit confronting the Ocean. But he cannot for long help thinking of the disintegration of society, the tyranny of privilege, and the abuses which call for reform, or at least for protest, as in *The Wind is Rising* (1941).

Dickens (especially in *American Notes*), Thoreau, and, of course, Conrad and Melville are the masters who inspired him. But it is significant that he cannot escape the gloom of the Interwar Period. It is more significant that he joins or anticipates those authors [2]—for instance, Stevenson, Cunninghame Graham, E. M. Forster, D. H. Lawrence, Somerset Maugham—who seem to write most freely and imaginatively when they have escaped from England.

LITERATURE AND THE THEATRES

The drama depends on so many conditions outside the world of books that its progress may have nothing to do with the progress of literature. Such, however, was not the case at the dawn of the twentieth century.

Its decadence since 1777 was largely due to circumstances. London was becoming every year more densely populated, not with leisured and thoughtful people, but with business men jaded in office routine, and women jaded in family routine. Whereas two or three theatres were all that the eighteenth-century metropolis could claim, the Theatre Regulation Act in 1843 (legalizing all play-houses) multiplied that number ten times over by 1900 ; since ground rents increased as fast as the population, these resorts had

[1] E. C. Bolles, *The Literature of Sea Travel*, 1943.   [2] *Post*, p. 149.

to attract large audiences and rely on long runs. As the fashionable dinner hour was postponed to the end of the day, performances became a night entertainment, and the evening is the time for relaxation.

So the English drama had degenerated into a many-sided industry of which the actor-manager was the centre. The business of the playwright was to keep himself out of the picture—to contrive situations, to project character-types, to invent phrases with which the leading performers could conjure. He wrote for the actor, not the audience. Hence the success of pieces, otherwise so different, as *The Bells* and *Charley's Aunt*, *Trilby* and *The Importance of Being Earnest*.

Even so, the nineteenth-century theatre was far from negligible. It produced a generation of expert and resourceful dramatists, thoroughly experienced in the technique of their craft, and two generations of magnetic actors and actresses, who were sufficiently masters of their art to make you believe in the unbelievable, at least while they were on the boards. The performance might be enlivened by romance or ridicule, and was not devoid of ideas, but in any case, both actors and authors left you with the impression that the scheme of life behind the show was good enough for the best. The audience need not be perplexed with the dread of social change—not in the theatre.

This standard of entertainment suited the middle-class majority, but not the unclassed minority, which had no interest in society as it is, nor in the stock Victorian types—women with a past, professional men with a present, youths and maidens with a future, stage Irishmen, and comic clergymen. The Unclassed wanted dramatists to write for the audience rather than for the actor, to tell them about the changes creeping over the world, and about the obscure folks, hidden in the nooks and corners of society, who had not even heard of the Leicester Lounge, the Albany or the Beef Steak Club. They wanted the spirit of literature to be made flesh behind the footlights.

THE NEW THEATRE

The movement is supposed to have begun with the introduction of Ibsen to the British public. The Norwegian was certainly influential ; we have already seen how Shaw welcomed that influence ; [1] so did Gosse, William Archer, Pinero, and H. A. Jones. Janet Achurch, Herbert Waring, and Tree brilliantly interpreted some of his parts. But we have also seen that Shaw valued him as a whetstone on which to sharpen his own blade, and so did the others. Ibsen was accepted as a fellow-worker who knew how to make a drama as searching as a French and Russian novel combined. If he was ahead of England, it was because, in his own country, he had

[1] *Ante*, p. 34.

both actors and audiences adapted to his method. We must do likewise.

So between 1891 and 1910 societies and repertory companies were formed all over the country ; notably the Stage Society (1899); and various managements rented London houses every year for a ' season ' with short runs, generally in cycles. These ventures aimed at the simplification which denotes good literature. Henry James, the conscientious artist, had written by 1907, ' No character in a play (any play not a mere monologue) has, for the right expression of the thing, a *usurping* consciousness ; the consciousness of others is exhibited in exactly the same way as that of the " hero " '.[1] Such was to be the artistic ideal of the new theatre. Ideas were to be more important than ' idols ' ; the players were to serve the play rather than their own artistic personalities ; the public were to think more of the plot than of the scenery. They could not do so, unless the presentment also was untheatrical. It should follow the apparent inconsequence of real life, each episode beginning and ending as if by accident, and the characters attracting attention by their conversation as much as by their presence. So the ' curtain ' and the ' aside ' were always, and the monologue was frequently, abolished.

We have already seen that Shaw and Galsworthy made full use of the new tendencies and enlarged their scope. So did Yeats, whose *The Land of Heart's Desire* was produced in London in 1894 and *The Countess Cathleen* in Dublin in 1899. But he did better service as a leader of the Irish National Theatre Society. This movement affected the English drama, for the most part, by showing how French naturalism and Ibsenite thoughtfulness could be expressed in local Irish colour and character ; for instance, W. Boyle's *The Mineral Workers*, T. C. Murray's *Birthright*, and especially Lady Gregory's neat little sketches and quaint dramatized anecdotes —each and all isolating some primitive human trait elsewhere perverted by civilization. John Millington Synge had something more to show. After he ceased brooding on Parisian modernism and went back to the Aran Isles to study not literary defects but tinkers, topers, farmers, fishermen, beggars, and innkeepers, he taught his contemporaries that you can find material for the liveliest comedies and the darkest tragedies, among folk who had altogether escaped modern civilization. You could faithfully portray the primitive human being, without the primitive grossness. Above all, you could dramatize in the simplest outlines the immemorial pathos of man always missing the happiness he always dreams to be just within reach.

The importance of the Irish movement can easily be overrated. Its range was hopelessly limited. On the other hand, it demonstrated that a door is never locked till you have tried the handle. And lest any critic should object that its choice of characters gave little opportunity for the best acting, Sarah Allgood, J. M. Kerrigan, Arthur Sinclair, and Fred O'Donovan, in their London seasons,

[1] Pref. to *The Tragic Muse* (N.Y. Ed. of Works).

proved that the most talented could rely for their effects on the cadences and imagery of the spoken lines, and merge their personal identity in the interpretation of their parts. Moreover, their local colour was an encouragement. Dramatists awoke to the freedom as well as the artistry which novelists enjoyed. Why should not playwrights capture the spirit of the age where and how they chose to find it—like the Irish players?

There was even the prospect of developing the deeper and higher truths of poetic drama. It will be remembered that not only Yeats, but Bridges, Masefield, Bottomley, Sturge-Moore, George Moore, Flecker, Abercrombie, and even Chesterton (though only in his prose fantasy *Magic*), created plays more or less designed for the theatre, and also for the lovers of drama in the grand style. Shakespeare was, of course, at the back of their minds. It was argued that the lavishly realistic productions of Tree, Irving, Forbes Robertson, Hackett, and in a lesser degree of Benson and Ben Greet, all distracted the attention of the audience, dwarfed the actors, and failed to create the tragic atmosphere. As Maeterlinck declared, ' The efforts of the poet to create above all a superior existence, a life closer to the soul, has been nullified by the introduction of an enemy substance '.[1] In poetic drama the visual effects ought to suggest the presence of the invisible. Edward Gordon Craig championed this spiritualization in *On the Art of the Theatre* (1911), *Towards a New Theatre* (1913), *The Theatre— Advancing* (1917), maintaining that scenery could and should be symbolic. He advocated bold and simple outlines, colour-tones contrived by drapery and screens, the distribution of lighting and shadow, the imaginative arrangement of the perpendicular and horizontal, suggesting far-flung perspectives and towering portals, or, contrariwise, low-lying roofs and interiors seemingly contracted, because the lines converged. At about the same time Max Reinhardt at the Berlin *Deutsches Theater*, and even more at his *Kammerspielhaus*, and yet again in his productions of *The Miracle* and *Oedipus* at the London *Olympia*, exhausted every device to bring the play-goers as near as possible to the play, even mingling the performance with the audience. In his American production of *Samurûm*, he presented a drama in which costume, music, lighting, and decoration carried the play. Both Craig and Reinhardt believed that masks could effectively be worn by the actors, as in the old Athenian and Roman theatres, and that such was the importance of atmosphere that the characters might function best as marionettes.[2] Both went too far in their impressionism, but both enforced the conviction that a poet's vision can be enjoyed in the theatre more spaciously and intensely than we thought possible, but not through scrupulously accurate realism.

[1] Pref. to *Pélleas and Mélisande* (N.Y. ed., 1911).
[2] See also A. B. Walkley, *Drama and Life*, 1918; *Pastiche and Prejudice*, 1921.

This movement towards literary ideas presented in front of simplified and symbolic scenery, means a return to the *spoken word*. We have already noted the tendency in Yeats's love of recitation and Shaw's and Galsworthy's use of actors and actresses to express their views. It was felt that literature should be more of a human contact than an author's self-revelation in print. But it was also soon to be realized that the drama could thrive only on a spacious stage, with the prospect of many full houses in a centre of multitudinous activity. Provincial managements and amateur societies relied on London as their guarantee of success and hallmark of merit. St. John Ervine and Dunsany soon drifted thither, Shaw, Galsworthy, Barrie, and Granville Barker seldom left it. As soon as the drama of ideas began to be tested in this atmosphere, before a miscellaneous audience, an unforeseen problem arose. The innovators expected that all spectators would take themselves and the play as seriously as did the author. They forgot that literature could not be made dramatic unless it obeyed the laws of the drama. They thought it could be presented as easily as a book.

A book accomplishes its purpose if it produces its full effect on the single reader, then passing on to a second, and a third, and so on. A play must produce its effect on an assembly of ill-assorted auditors, comprehensively, in a flash. The spectators must be unified at a stroke, and unless they suddenly become aware of the generous contagion and give it back across the footlights, the dramatist's utterances have not come to life. A stage-performance is a triple collaboration between the author, his interpreters, and his audience, all three under the spell of mass psychology. That is why phrases which seem colourless when read as literature, sometimes assume an overwhelming significance when diffused among the rows of eager upturned faces, radiant with laughter or tense with expectation. The auditorium contributes at least a third of the author's meaning and more than half of his wit or pathos. The new school of dramatists frequently sacrificed these necessary effects to ideas. They were too engrossed in their situations to cultivate their stage-sense.

ITS PRACTITIONERS

Such is the risk of discarding the one-man-play led by a genius for impersonation—a risk that even Shakespeare did not often run. We must now consider some dramatists who endeavoured to overcome the disability. They are men of ideas who collaborate with actors, electricians, stage-carpenters, the management, and the audience. As far as they succeed, they produce literature.

SIR JAMES MATTHEW BARRIE (1860–1937)

The future dramatist who left Kirriemuir and Edinburgh to become a journalist, eventually on the *St. James's Gazette* (in 1884), first made his mark by unpretentious stories of bachelor life in London and village life in Scotland. These experiments initiate the reader into the kindly and sympathetic study of human nature at its simplest, but despite their individuality of tone, they are too superficial to survive in their own right. The author was not expressing himself. He was an eccentric, impulsive, and rather ill-balanced personality, not easily at peace with himself and the society in which he was to carve an unusually comfortable niche. In self-defence he had captured and treasured a child's dream of what life ought to be, and can be, if only we see it in the searching light of innocence, and show ourselves the truth by showing it to other people. So all through life he searched for the child's ideal, and thereby developed an unusually keen eye for the vices and vanities of grown-up people.

He did not find his characteristic and original note till he had completed *The Admirable Crichton* (1902). It begins as a drawing-room comedy somewhat in the manner of Pinero, Jones, or Alfred Sutro's *Walls of Jericho* (which was to appear in 1904), except that Barrie discovers a hero where the world-worn humorist had seen only the snobbish and obsequious tyrant on the wrong side of the baize door—in the heart of the family butler. The events which waft him and the family he serves onto a *Swiss Family Robinson* island develop into a schoolboy's dream of natural life, and culminate in a joyous and innocent orgy killed by the report of a gun fired from an approaching ship. So we awake from romance and return to the day-to-day comedy of London life, having learnt to know what each character really is worth, by the simple process of renewing our youth in the theatre. The excursion seems to be convincing not because it is probable, but because the improbabilities are adjusted to the realism of the stage.

So with *Peter Pan* (1904) 'the masque of adventurous childhood'. Young people enjoy the rapid succession of story-book characters come to life, even those youngsters who would be puzzled by *The Blue Bird* and vote *The Golden Age* as dull as lead. Old people enjoy being implored to believe in fairies. Neither class spares a thought for the dramatist because he has hit upon just those episodes which the stage can present with the reality of dreams and memories.

For the next few years Barrie seems to have lost his knack of testing human contacts by the wisdom and innocence of childhood. He made a half-way return to his peculiar art in *What Every Woman Knows* (1908), *The Twelve Pound Look* (1910) and *The Will* (1913).

In 1916 Barrie completely regained his earlier manner with *A Kiss for Cinderella*. The fantasy is sometimes dismissed as sentimental; it should be accepted as sadder, if not wiser. The author has now realized that childhood's desires can become more real to the child than actual experiences, and if not effaced by adolescence, may develop into obsessions. Owing to the cheap fooling with Mr. Brodie and the policeman, one is apt to overlook some other fooling which is not cheap. For instance, ' Celeste et Cie—The Penny Friend ' may be a fantastic whimsy, but out of it emerges ' Cinders ', a sublime if ludicrously imperfect figure, the soul of human goodness disguised as a kitchenmaid in a serio-comic pantomime. If Saintsbury is right and humour is ' jesting with serious thoughts behind ', this modern interpretation of Perrault's fairy-tale is Barrie's best effort in dramatic humour.

Unless that achievement was reserved for *Dear Brutus* (1917). The underlying idea is not impressive. It assumes that character is destiny, not only in Shakespeare, but in the prosaic dealings of the twentieth century ; and the characters are as commonplace as the idea they exemplify. But they reveal their petty idiosyncrasies with such comic artlessness, and their creator manages his stage effects so cunningly, that the plot dawns upon the audience as an illumination, refreshed with humour. Few dramatists have succeeded so well in prolonging our sense of expectancy till the end of the last act ; none, since the Elizabethan era, have so effectively suggested the proximity of fairyland.

Barrie never surpassed these achievements, not even in *The Boy David* (1936), his last and most ambitious drama. His theme is the candid soul of boyhood, as the grown man would wish it to be, this time not only dreaming of action, but suddenly brought to the threshold of great deeds. As we would wish, David's soul is divided between diffidence and aspiration, and he wins all hearts, even that of Saul. The dramatist's problem consists in interweaving and contrasting this future champion, the Lord's Anointed, with the comedy of domestic life and the perils of a public career. Unfortunately, the element of surprise (always one of Barrie's best effects) is weakened because the story is too well known; and the ' suspension of disbelief ' (his other principal resource) cannot be replaced by the imagined presence of God, and the visualization of his prophet. Nor does scenic art seem equal to the dream visions and the symbolism of battle. For the first and last time Barrie's imagination transcended his means.

In fact, he was a skilled technician, who kept his head in an age of experiments. At a time when advanced drama threatened to degenerate into talk, he never allowed his plots to stand still. His episodes grow out of each other with refreshing unexpectedness, yielding to crisp dialogue and contrasts of character. Actors and actresses can always do justice to his situations, however fantastic or sentimental, because they are in reality true to life. With rare insight he discovered that theatre-goers, like himself, wanted the sincerities of childhood in an age of adult affectations. So he showed them, more intelligibly and sympathetically than Proust, how to start on *la recherche du temps perdu*. That is his title to literature.

EDWARD J. M. D. PLUNKETT, LORD DUNSANY (1878–   )

If Barrie tried to make romance realistic, Dunsany could not help making realism romantic. He could gaze on the mud flats of the Thames wondering what diaphanous sprite of beauty or quaintness might rise from that slimy bed, or draw inspiration from S. H. Sime's Japanese-like schemes and harmonies, without knowing what the designs meant. He could also (like Stevenson) gaze on predatory adventurers, outlaws by instinct, all too ready to feel cramped in the routine of civilization ; nor could he help noting how inevitably society revenged itself on these irreconcilables.

His early work attracted little attention ; nor did he care. He was himself something of an adventurer, an amateur scribbling for his own satisfaction, merely because visions would keep rising from the depths within himself. So he might well have left nothing but a few whimsical trifles, for instance some experiments in 250-word tales, such as the unique *The Assignation*, some dramatic sketches like the unforgettable *Bureau de Change*, and some autobiographical facts and fancies, like those breathing the joys of health and hunting in *The Curse of the Wise Woman* (1933). Such is the memory he leaves behind in *Patches of Sunlight* (1938).

However, at Yeats's suggestion he composed for The Abbey Theatre *The Glittering Gate* (1909). The theme was not wholly to his taste because it was not wholly his own. But the effort imposed on his manner a steadiness of outline and the art of following other people's imagination, that is, concentrating dramatic interest on some symbol which could be kept before the eyes of the audience. So much he learnt from Yeats, but he did not drop into Yeats's habit of exploring the twists and turns of thought—by which the characters reached their consummation, while the plot stands still. Dunsany devised dynamic figures, too simple to be explored, and plunged them into the situation which tested their mettle. His first complete realization of the technique was *King Argimenes and the Unknown Warrior* (1911). It will not be forgotten that the slave-king unearths a sword which becomes the symbol of conquest and reconquest.

Since Dunsany economized his plots, simplified his characterization, and relied on suspense to emphasize his climax, he stands apart from any modern movement, more in sympathy with the classical school. But where was he to find the naked, typical humanity of the story-teller's art which he hoped to intensify by stage-effects ? Rarely by the reproduction of modern life, which is ' thickly veiled and cloaked with puzzles and conventions' and labours ' in the agonies of self-consciousness ', as he confessed in *Romance and the Stage*. So, like Yeats, he created a world of his own, independent of time and place, with a preference for Oriental colour and mysterious magic, because he could not repress his imagination. He had no intimate knowledge of the East till 1913. Having alluded to himself as a romantic dramatist, he has been taken at his own valuation.

He has also published fifteen volumes of stories, of which *A Dreamer's Tales* (1910) and *Tales of Wonder* (1916) are amongst the best, though it is doubtful whether they imply enough to be honoured as literature. Nor is he likely to live in the history of the stage. Though he knew far more than Barrie about the depth and power of human nature, he knew far less about the mannerisms by which human nature can be revealed. Despite the classical regularity and romantic unexpectedness of his plots, he frequently created situations in which his actors could merely recite their lines, and though Yeats would have approved, the audiences remain cold.

And yet it is his dramas, at their best, which have given us literature. Now and then he has done justice to the stark truth underlying his exotic settings or paradoxical conclusions; notably in *King Argimenes* (1911), *The Gods of the Mountain* (1911), *The Tents of the Arabs* (1914), *A Night at an Inn* (1916), *If* (1921). In these and such-like pieces the author's quizzical, ironic imagination jolts the reader out of his settled habits; he feels a sense of awe, wonder, suspense and moral illumination; and fantasy compels him to accept what he would shrink from in fact.

HARLEY GRANVILLE-BARKER (1877–1946)

Few craftmen of the theatre followed Barrie's or Dunsany's lead. Most tried to inspire thoughtfulness within the limits of common experience. They aimed high, yet often without much financial or artistic success. Granville-Barker is a case in point. No one has done more for the establishment and organization of repertory companies, the encouragement of 'little theatres', and the cult of small audiences. It is claimed that he is the most capable stage trainer in the English-speaking world. During his long and intensely active career, he has produced some of the greatest masterpieces from Euripides to his own time. He has not only produced but composed at least five plays which command attention and stimulate discussion.

He aimed at creating what should rank with the best literature of the printed page—that is to say scenes and situations which compel the audience to revise their values, and order their lives more wisely. Having studied Ibsen and Shaw, and having at least heard much about Nietzsche, he felt more deeply than a Victorian could, that society was depressing or perverting the life-force, a vital urge more essential than any sanction or tradition, however venerable. He was not primarily concerned with class distinctions and economic readjustments, like Shaw, nor extreme cases of domestic and social injustice, like Ibsen or Galsworthy, thereby running the risk of oversimplification. His chosen theme was the study of individualism

and the now recognized right of self-direction in normal healthy personages, who owe a duty to society, or at any rate to their own circle, as well as to themselves.

This special emphasis was unfamiliar to the theatre, and so was his method. He elaborated something like the 'atmosphere play'. The projected environment gathers like a mist, developing tone and colour. Then it forms into figures which detach themselves from the background ; one or two assume marked firmness of outline, and stand forth as the protagonists. The misty background clings to their movements and they seem to be resisting it. In this resistance we soon discern some personal problem sufficiently ambiguous to exercise our moral sense, and convince us that conduct in our century is an intellectual more than a religious puzzle. Besides, these characters, though seldom to be met in a novel or a play, are often to be met in life ; or so it seems, because they are consistent and presented with animation and humour. Moreover they say many unexpected and memorable things. But being devoted to self-revelation, they say too much and do too little. They lose themselves and us in discussions by no means so simple as the issues which Shaw managed so deftly. Out of the atmosphere grow the characters, out of the characters an idea which monopolizes attention.

For instance, in *The Marrying of Ann Leete* (1901) the intention is clear-cut, but the domestic environment is indistinct. In *Waste* (1907), his most ambitious drama, Trebell breaks his heart, because he cannot live his own ideal. The climax might have been worthy of the *Ajax* of Sophocles, but the author cannot keep the others from discussing his fate. *The Madras House* (1910) is a well-informed and otherwise enjoyable exposure of suburban and commercial life, both domestic and professional. The revelations of character are as striking as ever. Unhappily Barker tries to cover the whole field, which is too vast and varied for a single play. It would need a Ben Jonson with his comedy of humours.

In fact our dramatist who had handled so many classic plays was himself too modern to observe classic restraint and artistic economy. Witness the success of *The Voysey Inheritance* (1905). It contains no moral lesson which is not obvious ; and for that very reason the dramatist is able to concentrate his plot in a few tense scenes so full of humour, characterization, and actuality that the public forgives its inconclusiveness. It is also noticeable that in collaboration his work becomes less distinctive but more convincing ; for instance *Prunella* (with L. Housman in 1906), *Amatol* (from A. Schnitzler in 1911), *The Harlequinade* (with D. C. Calthrop in 1918). But when he set himself between 1919 and 1922 to create another drama single-handed, *The Secret Life*, the wave of post-war disenchantment engulfed him.

So Granville-Barker is one of the few stage experts who often failed when he wrote for the stage. Yet his failure is most instructive to the student of literature. He dramatized the individual who cannot easily adjust his inner self to his outward life—surely a time-honoured theme for the drama as for the novel. This individual encounters no barriers nor pitfalls worth conquering, but on the other hand no encouraging opportunities for his better self; merely a spiritual void. So he cannot focus his own needs. The more successful writers of the period had felt this atmosphere somewhat vaguely and had pitched upon some accessory grievance—notably Wells and Shaw— or had taken refuge in sheer art—for instance, Conrad and de la Mare—both classes avoiding moral issues, because they could find no reflexion in the manners and modes of their time. Granville-Barker was one of the first of this age to study spiritual aimlessness for its own sake; hence his claim on our attention. The next generation was to give definite outlines to the picture.

ST. JOHN E. C. HANKIN (1860–1909)

If Granville-Barker was ahead of his time, he nevertheless introduced to the public an older man who knew better how to temper his ideas to the conditions of the theatre. Fashionable audiences were indulgent, because on first nights Hankin seemed to be continuing the society drama of Pinero, H. A. Jones, and H. H. Davies. In reality he renovated the late Victorian themes by introducing Edwardian disillusionment, criticism, and impatience with moneyed folk who got more out of life than they put into it. Hence his characters are more distinct, more temperamental, more ignobly revealing than those of the older school; and having brought them to some crisis in their rather fussy, futile lives, in each case he works it out to a logical conclusion, when possible avoiding a happy ending, or at any rate, a conventional ending. Though dialogue is his inevitable organ of exposition, he rarely allows himself to be caught in a static conversation. Even when two or more personages are simply talking, the plot continues to twist and turn.

Of his four plays, *The Return of the Prodigal* (1905) is the most amusingly cynical, *The Charity that Began at Home* (1906) the most original, *The Cassilis Engagement* (1907) the best constructed and sustained, *The Last of the De Mullins* (1908) the only one which helps the old world to move forward. But all persuade the spectator or reader that the new world should not tread in the steps of its predecessor.

STANLEY HOUGHTON (1881–1913)

Theatre audiences are often surprised into thought if the picture is a remote reflection of themselves, a parable not a reproduction. So Miss Horniman did well to stage Houghton's early one-act plays at her repertory theatre in Manchester, and thereby encouraged his talent for the local colour of the Midlands. Thanks to this training he won a considerable success with *The Younger Generation* (1910), which interested the London public in the folk of the Lancashire cotton-mills, especially their attitude to the humours of parental control, a situation as ancient as Plautus in the history of comedy. So he prepared the way for *Hindle Wakes* (1912). This drama is memorable because of what William Archer describes as ' that strain of suspense, that throb of emotion, which was, is, and ever shall be the central secret of the drama '. [1] It is even more noteworthy for the climax in which Fanny Hawthorn surprises the audience and epitomizes the new womanhood, likewise the spirit of the new generation, merely by refusing to marry for the sake of the proprieties, however advantageous the match.

The situation is not of wide application, but Houghton raised an essentially human issue, without Shavian dialectic.

ST. JOHN G. ERVINE (1883–   )

This earnest and rather over-sensitized Irishman attempted to create tragedy, where Houghton created comedy ; and did so out of everyday life such as he himself had experienced or observed. He discovered in family circles that the man, having grown old and lost zest in his small battle of life, often hardened into a monomaniac, clinging instinctively to some religious or social dogma, his only hope of self-assertion in the presence of the rising generation ; whereas the woman, thanks to the instinct of motherhood, and long experience in the exigencies of rearing a brood of children, retained her humanity and even-mindedness. The tension between these two attitudes might well develop into a tragedy.

Ervine served his apprenticeship in the Irish National Theatre, and his first notable attempt, *The Magnanimous Lover* (written 1909, produced 1912), is a comedy morally akin to *Hindle Wakes*, *The Last of the De Mullins*, or even Galsworthy's *Eldest Son*, except that the repentant seducer is a formalist, superficially comic, but charged with ominous perversity, a victim of his own virtue. This effort is a curtain-raiser. *Mixed Marriage* is a four-act tragedy, presenting an Orangeman's hatred of papists, complicated by industrial unrest, and crossed by his Presbyterian son's love for a Catholic sweetheart. John Rainey sacrifices his humanity and peace to his convictions, and his heroic wife, with her practical motherly wisdom, is not only a well-executed foil to his character, but an example of high thinking in low life.

By this time the Irish movement had spent its force ; Synge died in 1909 ; and Ervine was looking to the London stage. *Jane Clegg* (1913), a dramatically expert study of English lower middle-class life devoid of tragic horrors, is memorable for the narrow but indomitable womanhood of his heroine. His masterpiece is *John Fergusson* (1915). The scene is once more in Ulster, and this time a narrow-minded, bigoted Protestant, the head of a well-conducted

[1] *The Old Drama and the New*, 1923.

household, is plunged by coincidence and the vileness of one or more rather stagey villains into every calamity within reach of his homestead, and yet preserves his faith and integrity to the last.

Ervine wrote little more that can reasonably be ranked as literature. The subject nearest his heart was the man of divided impulse, a theme as ancient as Sophocles, Shakespeare, and Racine, but obscured among the distractions of the multitudinous modern world, in need of a new setting. Ervine revived the type among his own people, in the backwaters of Ireland and then among uninteresting people in England—one more sign that the static, fashionable classes had lost value in a fluid society, except as a subject for satire.

CHAPTER VI

THE CRISIS IN POETRY AND ITS WOULD-BE REFORMERS

THERE can be no doubt that the literature of this period was full of life, nor that its vitality was most marked in prose. The Edwardians and neo-Georgians enjoyed looking at themselves in the guise of somebody else; they realized that an indirect mirror was the most serviceable; in other words: novels, plays, essays. At the same time poetry was by no means neglected; there were poets in plenty, but for the most part they were inclined to use the direct mirror; we have already seen that Kipling, de la Mare, and Masefield were exceptions; but the majority wrote of themselves subjectively; and on the whole the result was disappointing.

This situation is significant. If we take thirty as the age at which a poet usually begins to master himself and his material (whatever the accidents of publication) we find that of all the verse-writers then living or just dead, Doughty, Dobson, Hopkins, and Bridges matured in the 'seventies, Watson and Housman in the 'eighties, Trench, Kipling, and Binyon (born 1869) in the 'nineties, and then de la Mare, Sturge Moore, Davies, Hodgson, Bottomley, Chesterton, Gibson, Masefield, Thomas, and Monro in the first decade of the twentieth century, and Abercrombie, Flecker, and Brooke early in the second decade. The first ten or fifteen years of our era produced at least twice as many as did the preceding thirty years. This short period was also the time when the new unclassified reading public,[1] born of the Education Act of 1870, also began to mature and make its influence felt. The middle class was no longer the one voice of culture, as in Arnold's and Trollope's day; and the intrusion of this multitudinous presence was bound, of itself, to confuse the stream of culture, and may, perhaps, eventually dominate its course. Under this influence, we should have expected these younger poets to be erratic, if not iconoclastic, but those already discussed [2]—the majority—kept to the old tradition. They presented their reactions either to everyday experience (for instance, the sights, sounds, and characters of country life), or their reactions to the themes and sentiments already celebrated in great poetry. Their conservatism may be partly due to the fact that they were still self-trained in the world of books, but they must also have been satisfied with their material. In any case, they unquestionably fell short of the best.

Their prevailing defect is fairly obvious: they were too self-conscious. They had the talent to express *their* moods, not the

[1] *Ante*, pp. 8 ff.   [2] *Ante*, p. 54.

genius to express *ours*. Poetry had become a cult, and, like all cults, needed leadership. Neither Kipling, de la Mare, nor Masefield, however outstanding, had the qualities they needed.

How was poetry to regain its old power, and make the reader feel the same delight as the poet felt, or tried to feel? Not merely by widening its view, for all eternity can be focused in a raindrop. It is diction and prosody which release and direct the spirit. The poet can feel and express everything, and the reader will respond, if only the *word* kindles the thought and carries him along, inspiring insight through artistry. 'Literature is immortal through style.' By such means the great masters had worked their way into the hearts of their readers, but magic seldom travels the same road twice. New spells and incantations were needed;—so said the self-appointed guardians of art, when they contemplated the correctness and conformity around them.

One would expect the very young poets to lead the way. It is more accurate to say that they eagerly followed, even in defiance of well-tried standards. The first attempt was made by certain of their predecessors, already middle-aged, one already dead, because they belonged to the older culture which was fading away, and were quick to save the relics. The reform of poetry, they said, must begin with the reform of diction, and instead of breaking with the Past, they searched its storehouse for half-forgotten words and rhythms. Innovation was to be achieved by renovation.

CHARLES MONTAGU DOUGHTY (1843-1926)

He would seem to be out of place in a history of twentieth-century literature, till one remembers that in his old age he was as full of protest and experiment as were his youngest contemporaries. From the dawn of manhood he was possessed by the desire to reform his countrymen by reforming their language, reviving the toughness and straightforwardness of pre-Renaissance England by reviving its idioms and diction. His first opportunity came in 1876, when he started on his two years' pilgrimage through and around the Arabian Peninsula. These experiences called for some literary record which might, he felt, also serve as a first step towards his self-appointed mission. So, after ten years of incessant labour, he published *Arabia Deserta* in 1888.

This classic is inspired by the ambition utterly to discredit the superficiality and emotionalism of late Victorian culture. Doughty eschews the kind of graces which, for instance, adorn A. W. Kinglake's *Eöthen*, likewise the Biblical interest emphasized, for instance, in E. H. Palmer's *The Desert of the Exodus* and Sir R. F. Burton's *A Pilgrimage to El Medinal and Mecca*. His purpose is to bring before the reader his contacts and encounters with primitive personalities so vividly and directly that you can hear the tone of voice and see the play of feature. In order to produce these graphic

H

effects he wrote after the manner of *Hakluyt's Voyages*, in which travellers do not try to suggest their own susceptibilities, but only what they see and hear. As far as possible he confined his vocabulary to words current in Middle English. For instance, he would say 'hot-hearted' instead of 'passionate'. Despite these rather pedantic and eccentric mannerisms, he has described the East as never before, except in *The Old Testament*.

Thus he prepared himself and (as he hoped) his readers for his volumes of poetry, especially *The Dawn in Britain* (1906), *Adam Cast Forth* (1908), *The Cliffs* (1909), *The Clouds* (1912), *The Titans* (1916), *Mansoul* (1920). He lacked neither sensibility nor a sense of beauty and grandeur, and his responsiveness sometimes finds expression in the felicities of genuine poetry. He had more than his fair share of what Longinus and Arnold called 'high serious- ness'. At the same time he can write imaginatively about games and earth-born fairies in *The Cliffs*; and in *The Clouds* he foresees the part to be played by aeroplanes and even radio in modern war. He describes the forces of the physical universe as if he were a con- temporary of the ancient *Eddas*, yet he adds a background of science, in order to indue his mythology with a touch of the twentieth cen- tury. In fact his scheme and scope are as vast as any in literature.

He might have been a force. But he missed his chance, because he was more bent on purifying our vocabulary than our hearts, not realizing that language has its own destiny independent of those who use it. Instead of the intellect dancing among words and casting images on the visual imagination, we meet, too often, a linguist manipulating an archaic diction. The poet even allows himself the licence to suppress particles and auxiliaries, forgetting that ellipsis is permissible only in the spoken word. He intended to reinstate a tradition which had declined—in his judgement—ever since Shakespeare showed posterity how to play with language as with toys, thus inducing anarchy. We must, he implies, return to the phraseology which seemed fresh and vigorous when Chaucer and Langland were fusing Anglo-Saxon with Norman French.

GERARD MANLY HOPKINS (1844–89)

This artist, musician, scholar, thinker, Jesuit, and poet, dead eleven years before our era opens, is nevertheless more a part of the twentieth century than Doughty is. During his brilliant career at Oxford he was much impressed by Jowett, Arnold, Pater, and Wilde. After his conversion (1868) he abjured all his other en- thusiasms, and did not even write poetry for the next seven years. Gradually, however, the spiritual exercises of his order recalled him to himself. The Rule of St. Ignatius (the Jesuit discipline) enjoins that the votary in all his thoughts and actions should yearn towards identification with Jesus. So Hopkins learnt not to eschew outward and sensuous experiences, but enjoy them sacramentally as intimations of Divine Presence. A priest could live in and for God, and still be a poet.[1]

With this high purpose, he resumed writing. A flower, a sward, or the view of Oxford, now stirred his poetic sense more than ever. He could perceive God in so far as he could perceive in any object its distinctive virtue of design or pattern, the inner kernel of its being as expressed by its outer form—the soul peculiar to each manifestation of beauty. He borrowed from Dun Scotus the term *inscape* to denote this immanent quality. For instance, in writing of the bluebell : ' its inscape is mixed strength and grace '.

Such intuitions could hardly be conveyed through the rhetoric of Victorian verse. Not only trees, grass, and prospects, but each human spirit had its personal inscape, a mystic creative force which shapes the mind and must express itself in an ' individual distinctive beauty of style'. Thus the poet was most likely to find his proper diction among words and phrases originating in Anglo-Saxon or folk-lore, and preserved in the parlance of common people who spoke from the heart. So also with prosody. Quantitative metres, every syllable counted as in Latin, were (in his opinion) imported conventions. In conversation we stress significant words and syllables, with so much emphasis that accompanying syllables and words are left to take care of themselves. Such should be the scheme of living, spoken verse : a system of beats and stresses, as in Old and Middle English.

But there was this difference. The modern mind works on two planes. The poet can perceive the beauty around him, in a moment of heightened mental acuteness, and reproduce his impression in the best words ; that was the lower intellectual level. At the same time he can also be raised above himself by the inspiration which comes from God, and on this higher level *create* what is beyond the range of human observation. The two impulses work side by side, and the interplay should be suggested by the manipulation of rhythms ; by interweaving an under-current with an over-current, one melody added as accompaniment to the other, like musical counterpoint, thus producing *counterpoint rhythm*, which Herbert Read defines as ' rhythm pointed counter to the proper flow '.[2] This effect was generally produced by ringing changes on the beats and stresses, inducing the metre to run back on itself; sometimes making a second line reverse the movement of the one before ; sometimes in the same line confronting a metric foot by its opposite, for instance, an iambic followed by a trochee. As these variations produced the momentary effect of a break or split, Hopkins borrowed a nautical expression (e.g., *spring a butt*) and called the device *sprung rhythm*. There are striking examples in ' God's Grandeur '. Sometimes he added ' slack syllables', as in ' Felix Randal'; again and again he experimented in alliteration and assonance.

[1] J. Pick, *G. M. Hopkins. Priest and Poet*, 1942.
[2] ' G. M. Hopkins ' in *Collected Essays in Literary Criticism*, 1938.

There may be a profound justification for these technical experiments. R. W. Dixon described his quality as 'a right temper which goes to the point of the terrible, the terrible crystal'; and it may be that through his religious discipline acting on his unique genius he had gained insight into what Father Lahey called 'the bleak heights of spiritual night with God'; and if so, his apparently freakish diction and fantastic symbolism may be the only means of suggesting the initiation. There certainly runs through his verse an emotionalism which he described as 'poised but on the quiver', as if he had seen more than a mortal ought to see and was at times struck down by 'a horror of height' ('The Windhover') or sunk in 'the swoon of a heart' (ibid.), and was then trying to fill the spiritual void with what others call the simple beauty of nature, and love for the virtues of common folk. Under such pressure a poet would have to originate his own methods. He might rely on Old English phraseology and prosody, thus apparently reviving tradition, but if his work was to be truly an illumination, he would have to let it create itself; 'each poem growing according to the laws of its own nature, but in a line which is more often the irregular though entirely natural shape of a tree'.[1]

So indeed he did, and he certainly revived the poet's divine right to mean more than he can say. But he did not often compass the poet's duty to say what would help others towards his meaning. Some few of his lyrics are sublime, but the majority are vexatiously obscure. His mind lacked the ordinary man's perspective, and his failing health no doubt intensified the difficulties of self-expression. Very few pieces were published during his lifetime. His friends, especially Dixon, Patmore, and Bridges, criticized and encouraged his efforts, privately circulated, and now and then slipped a little masterpiece into an anthology. His *Poetical Works* did not appear till 1918, and a second edition was not called for till 1930. His correspondence and literary remains and life history were not published till 1935 and 1938 by E. E. Abbott. His style and expressiveness have been exhaustively analysed by W. H. Gardner in *Gerard Manly Hopkins. A Study of Poetic Idiosyncrasy in Relation to Poetic Tradition*, which appeared in 1944. A new biography by E. Ruggles was published in 1946.

His present vogue, apart from his intense personality, is largely due to his theories. Yet they are not new. All the great masters have exemplified *sprung rhythm*, especially Milton, all divined *inscape*, though they did not think of the word. Hopkins gave a nomenclature to the intuitions of his predecessors; that is what the twentieth century needed; hence one reason for his influence.

[1] Edith Sitwell, *Aspects of Modern Poetry*, 1934.

ROBERT SEYMOUR BRIDGES (1844-1930)

The poet who first recognized Hopkins's genius—more or less—and rescued something from his broken career, lived an almost ideal life. After an enviably wide training as a classical scholar, a traveller, and a hospital physician, studying man's battle against our heritage of suffering, he retired from professional life at the age of thirty-seven, and devoted the next half-century to the interests of culture—pure English, phonetic spelling, the split infinitive, art, hymn-singing, Milton's reputation as our greatest verse-technician, and, above all, the creation of poetry.

His own output was sustained and prolific, his first volume appearing in 1873 and his last in 1929. During this long, laborious period, he produced almost every type of poem, from dramas to quantitative hexameters, but the most notable is his immense body of odes and lyrics. From first to last he experimented in the choice of words and the techniques of versification, including 'neo-Miltonic-syllabics' which were published in *October and other Poems* (1920). No contemporary humanist was more convinced that to reform the poet, you must reform his prosody.

The reader will at once appreciate the impeccably good taste, the sensitive and scholarly handling of words, the chastened pleasure in Nature's everyday beauty, and sometimes what Hopkins called 'the manly tenderness and flowing, never-failing music'; the quality which Charles Williams has termed 'beauty in restraint'. Edward Thompson, in *Robert Bridges 1844-1930* (1944), has depicted the old-world, scholarly atmosphere in which the poet lived, and makes much of this middle period of lyrics devoted to 'the growth of love' and the study of Nature's charm. Yet this sometimes rather superficial faultlessness was not the goal of his career. It was a preliminary. Even his most felicitous lyrics—for instance, 'London Snow' and 'Asian Birds'—despite their 'assured quietness' and 'more certain knowledge', are exercises; mere glimpses of a much wider synthesis. Bridges had grasped the varied and apparently conflicting essentials of scientific and artistic culture, and then, as he wrote to Henry Bradley in 1901, 'beyond that, stretching out to infinity, the realm of the imagination'. Since the vision, after ranging over humanism and science, found its spiritual focus in the necessity for what is fair and lovely, he entitled his exposition *The Testament of Beauty* (1929).

This long, elaborate poem, the climax of his life, is one of the most revealing and characteristic documents of the twentieth century. Many poets have felt, consciously or subconsciously, that a sense of beauty is the crown of culture, even the blessedness of religion. Bridges differs from all of them in that he is an inveterate teacher and tries to convince as well as persuade. He invokes modern science and scholarship, not stopping short of the most recent and disputed theories,[1] to establish and amplify what his predecessors knew by instinct or intuition.

Like any physicist, he agrees that man in his origin is a mere combine and complex of atoms and electrons, pervaded by 'the spontaneous functions and motions of life', and in that sense a part of the lower creation around us. Like any psychologist, he further agrees that as we ascended the scale of evolution, we became conscious that we are distinct from our environment, we learn to live a life of our own, to indulge the impulse towards self-assertion, and sex (which Bridges terms *breed*). In a word, we acquire selfhood, but with it a certain distrust of Nature's influences. So we turn our thoughts inward, towards our own species and its works, as if we were an existence apart, the masters, not the product, of our environment. While this estrangement endures, our selfhood is incomplete. Since we have passed through the lower stages of creation, we are still under its laws; and since these laws have helped to raise us above our original selves, they must be good. The proof is, that primitive peoples and children look out on the world not only with interest and wonder, but also with love.

The mature and civilized man must recognize the secret of this attraction: it is like tending to like. The rhythms, harmonies, outlines, and gracious schemes which charm us in Nature are part of ourselves. Our lives are penetrated by 'eternal Essences which exist in themselves', and since we have shouldered the responsibilities of self-direction, we must voluntarily lend ourselves to their magic. We can do more. These vital influences do not only refine our senses, they inspire us with Nature's own creativeness, so that we can second the spirit of her design, and give her back her own idea, humanized and embellished for our proper use. Such is the only guise in which Truth is revealed to us, and under its spell we can perfect our selfhood, and attain to the wisdom we call the knowledge of God.

The Testament of Beauty is chiefly important because the poet writes with the exaltation of a mystic, and is yet in sympathy with D'Arcy Thompson and A. N. Whitehead, who maintain that the structure of matter corresponds to the morphology of art, and with Santayana, the materialist who accepts super-material values, a believer in 'the realm of essences'. Bridges must also have known S. Alexander's *Space, Time and Deity* (1920), R. W. Sellar's *Evolutionary Naturalism* (1922), and C. L. Morgan's *Emergent Evolution* (1923), which examine in what senses evolution creates new powers out of its ascending line of development, even a *nisus* towards deity. It is also noteworthy that to a certain degree he anticipates Herbert Read's definition of art as 'mankind's effort to achieve integration with the basic forms of the physical universe and the organic rhythms of life'.[2] If the poem should be compared to any other work, it should not be to Lucretius' *De Rerum Natura*, nor to Words-

[1] *Post*, pp. 136 ff.   [2] *Education through Art*, 1943.

worth's *Prelude*, but to J. B. Haldane's *The Philosophy of a Biologist* (1935), which asserts on scientific principles that God is the will to perfection, evoked in us by sorrow, sin, and perversity, and consummated in art and aspiration. However, Haldane wrote in prose.

Some critics wish that Bridges had done likewise. The discipline of prose might have saved him from distracting digressions and discontinuities ; whereas he wrote in ' loose alexandrines ', in which he expected his argument to move freely. It moves so freely that he now and then rambles with an almost senile freakishness, and he still believes that good verse is made better by antiquated words and fancy spelling.

T. E. HULME (1883–1917)

If Bridges relied on the sense of beauty, this restless, rather reckless thinker went back to the history of man's idea of himself ; and came to the conclusion that the decay of poetry was due to the decay of spiritual humility, which began with the humanism of the Renaissance. In that age poets and philosophers made too little of God and too much of themselves. Montaigne set the example, and the climax was reached in the Romantic Movement. Hulme sees hope only in our return to the pre-Renaissance belief in a power, influence, or standard infinitely higher than ourselves and independent of our existence, by which ' man himself is judged to be essentially limited and imperfect '. To clinch his idea he revived the doctrine of original sin. ' We may define Romantics ', he declared in the preface to his translation of Sorel's *Reflections on Violence*, ' as all those who do not believe in the Fall of Man.' This contention seems more revolutionary than it really is. In deprecating classical humanism, the would-be innovator is amply forestalled by, for instance, Milton.[1] He was original only so far as he applied to modern literature what the seventeenth-century poet applied to Greek.

Our decline has been mirrored in our poetry, and it is through poetry that the decline must be arrested. Hulme had already perceived, more than a decade before *Principles of Literary Criticism*[2] appeared, that verse has a psychological power penetrating to our nerve-centres, unobtrusively pervading the reactions of our whole being. So verse must keep to the limitations of that being. Since we are incapable of perfection, it is futile to dream about it, or aspire to the Absolute. Our consciousness is confined to what we can see and feel, and the same should apply to our imaginative literature. It should eschew intuitions and find expression only in pictures. If the poet could keep to a succession of images following one another in the prism of the mind, we might *perceive* all the truth that he can reveal, and all the truth that we could safely know, without transgressing the limits of our humanity.

[1] *Paradise Regained*, IV, 285 ff.   [2] *Post*, p. 138.

In compensation, words would mean much more than they do now. At present they are handled like algebraical signs to indicate abstractions which cannot be seen or felt. So the average person is like a vain babbler. But if he could *see* the thought as a visual presentment, he would *perceive* it with all the nerves of his being—with his *eidetic* self—that is, see it freshly, with surprise ; ' see each word with an image sticking on to it, never as a flat word passed over a board like a counter '.

This is much what D. H. Lawrence meant when he wrote of a ' stark, bare, rocky directness of statement ', and T. S. Eliot of ' poetry so transparent that we should not see the poetry '—both after the Four Years War. Hulme himself summed up his doctrine in the formula, ' poetry should be dry and hard '. Yeats, in his old age, would agree.

Hulme's theories were not published till 1924,[1] seven years after the author's death at the Front. But they were freely ventilated in London in 1908–12, among all those dissatisfied with poetry as it then was. He himself produced only five short specimens to illustrate his idea. Nevertheless, his insistence on visualization continues to influence poets, while his anti-romanticism and anti-humanism continue to disunite critics, and group them in opposing camps.[2]

THE IMAGISTS

In 1909 Hulme's disciples referred to themselves as the School of Images ; in 1912 Ezra Pound, in his preface to *Ripostes*, christened the movement Imagisme, and the practitioners Imagistes. Their efforts appeared sporadically till *The Egoist*, founded in 1914, became their organ. In 1914 Pound brought out the first anthology : *Des Imagistes*, with eleven contributors. Thereafter Amy Lowell, with her purse and personality, captured the leadership and brought out *Some Imagist Poets* in 1915–16–17. A final *Imagist Anthology* appeared almost apologetically in 1930, for the movement provoked much opposition and had died a natural death at the end of the Four Years War.

Yet it survived as a ghost. The Imagists insisted on turning word-pictures into entaglios, and this cult of precision has continued to inspire and chasten subsequent verse-writers. But its influence as an avowed cult was restrictive. It distorted self-expression, and confined adventures in thought. Meanwhile its erstwhile practitioners were realizing that even if twentieth-century civilization discredited the old values (as Hulme and others maintained), it also involved moral and social responsibilities, and, above all, a vague expectation that unexplored feelings and unfamiliar emotions were almost within reach. There is nothing so interesting as a wall behind which something is happening. So it is not surprising that the best-known contributors—for instance, James Joyce,

---

[1] *Speculations*, edited by Herbert Read.   [2] *Post*, pp. 139 ff.

D. H. Lawrence, T. S. Eliot, Hilda Doolittle, R. Aldington, Ford Maddox Hueffer, and Ezra Pound himself—soon went their own way. All wanted release from the older forms of verse; none wanted a control not of their own choosing. So they tended to subdivide into sects—vorticism, cubism, dadoism, unanimism, fantasism, surrealism—seeking freedom and a following under the dignity of a label. While all the time what they really sought was ready to hand under the capacious term—*prose*.

Prose-writers had always been libertarians, whereas poetry was so ancient and sacred a trust that its morphology had gradually governed its subject-matter. For instance, the sentiment appropriate to an ode could not adequately be developed in a sonnet. Yet Conrad or de la Mare could put all they thought and felt into this or that chapter of a novel, contriving their own opportunities. Why should not the poet of the present or future be equally free? 'In poetry', says Herbert Read in *English Prose Style* (1928), 'the words are born or reborn in the act of thinking.' So, between them, the poets connected with Imagism tried to blend the subtleties of verse with the elasticity of prose, and thereby established *Free Verse*.

FREE VERSE

The hint came to them from the French innovators of the 'eighties, not only Jules Laforgue and Gustave Kahn. These poets and their school had recognized that prose could and often did reveal a content that was nothing less than poetry. In fact Mallarmé asserted that there was no such category as prose: only the alphabet and then verse, more or less compact or diffuse.[1] It was termed prose when the object was lucidity, and poetry when the object was spiritual revelation. In these heightened moments, language acquired a music of its own; not the music associated with verse-forms, based on the rhythm of metrical feet; but cadence which was bound to no counted syllables or even lines, but rose and fell with the emotions, and the flow of the words. Within its own law of cadence, this way of writing had no absolute rules, otherwise free verse would not be free.

Our poets need not have waited for the example of the French. Every lover of English literature knew that certain passages in Sir Thomas Browne, Jeremy Taylor, Johnson (though few are aware of it), Ruskin and Meredith have an emotional and imaginative power which the most studied poetry cannot surpass, and that certain passages in Langland, Shakespeare, Webster, and Milton carry their intense meaning all the more effectively because they can be read as impassioned prose. But it needed the French to demonstrate that prose-poetry is more recognizable if not written as prose or poetry. The clauses should have their own special alignment, tempered to the cadence, the words patterned so as to

[1] 'Enquête sur l'Evolution Littéraire,' *Echo de Paris*, 14 March, 1891.

suggest their proper harmony to the eye as well as the ear, and also to mark the progress of the thought, thus rendering the intention visible as well as visual.   Readers could then again encounter Sheridan's neat rivulet of text meandering through a meadow of margin, except that the rivulet is seldom neat, and often broken into weirs and stretches.

Thus *Free Verse* is not so much free, as freed from the restrictions peculiar to formal verse, while the unexpectedness of the composition suggests spontaneous growth : something that is immediate and instinctive.   As D. H. Lawrence asserted in his preface to *New Poems* (1920, American edition), ' In free verse we look for the insurgent naked throb of the instant moment '.   On the other hand, these impulsive gestures often take not only the reader, but the author by surprise ; the latter not always foreseeing whither his cadenced clauses were leading him ; hence obscurity and disconcertingly abrupt transitions.   There was another cause.   Poetry must, of course, always be approached in a mood of sympathetic understanding, and in the old days metric form usually served the purpose.   The *verslibristes*, having discarded those accustomed aids, were tempted to resort to ' enchanted difficulty '—that is to say, some artistically designed inconsequence or paradox which focused attention, and when the enigma was solved, came with an illuminating shock.

Up to the present, the illumination has frequently failed, because Free-verse, a dangerously difficult art, appears to be even more dangerously easy.   Yet that is not the principal reason why it has almost certainly come to stay.   Though a seemingly irreverent innovation, it is really very old.   A ninth-century author of the *Life of St. Wulfram* notes that prose tends towards the cadence of verse, *ad quamdam tinnuli rhythmi similitudinem* ; and so it used to do.   There seems little doubt that language evolved out of a series of connected sounds, which conveyed a rudimentary emotion or thought, with the help of gestures and facial expression.   Even now one gathers the gist of a spoken sentence more by the rhythm and emphasis than by the words, of which one catches only a few distinctly.   It was first the art of writing, then much more the art of printing, which introduced the insistence on verbal precision, as if a continuous flow was not enough, as if meaning could best be conveyed by the notation of nouns, verbs, and suffixes.   The transition can be appreciated by comparing the opening lines of *The Canterbury Tales* with those of *The Vision concerning Piers the Plowman* ; or *Beowulf*, with any of the famous romantic odes in which every epithet has special significance.   Free-verse is an attempt to recapture the old abandon : to use words so loosely that one cannot pin down the content to grammar and alphabet, but can catch the urge and impulse as did primitive man through verbal gestures, the modulations of the voice (suggested by the alignment), and by symbolizing the idea without expressing its name. So here is yet another example of reformers who had to become old in order to seem new.

THE SIGNIFICANCE OF THIS 'CRISIS IN POETRY'

The developments imposed by Doughty, Hopkins, Bridges, Hulme, and their followers amount to a crisis because they are a challenge to our literary habits, a challenge more fundamental than one might suppose. The art or science of criticism used to be justified because it referred our experiences to a centre within ourselves, to a constant element amidst the flux of impressions. We not only enjoyed our enthusiasms, but assessed their worth, and thereby confirmed our identity as thinking beings. The point of reference used to be, not so much an inheritance of literary standards as the common heritage of good sense, proportion, fitness. Discipline, it had been found, leads to insight and elevation. Each new publication should be used as a stepping-stone towards a clearer assurance of our powers of judgement. The 'new poetry' offers no such exercise. It is more or less an effort towards temperamental expansion. It cannot be subject to laws, unless extemporized by itself (e.g., imagism), since each effort is an adventure into the unknown and therefore the unlegalized. Consequently the critic should ask no questions, but try to keep pace with the poet and, if successful, translate the poet's quality into prose. His function was elucidation. Of course every critic has not bowed to this order of the day, but many find it worth their while, and—a sure sign of the times—a number of literary periodicals has arisen to give the elucidator his platform. This encouraging atmosphere may in the end be the best thing for literature. In the meantime it challenges one of the rights of culture, and foments licence in literary taste.

These adventures and controversies reached their climax after 1920, but they are the product of pre-war mentality intensified by post-war confusion.

HAROLD EDWARD MONRO (1879–1932)

The 'new poetry' would have made more enemies within and without except for Monro. After graduating from Cambridge in 1901, it took him ten years to discover that his mission in life was to serve the cause of modern poetry. So in 1911 he began by founding the *Poetry Review*. In 1913 he opened 'The Poetry Bookshop', in which it was possible to obtain the works of any contemporary versifier who had struggled into print, and on the upper floor he instituted weekly readings in recently published verse. In the same year he founded the quarterly *Poetry and Drama*, and after the Four Years War he started the *Chapbook*. These and such other ventures did much to attract public attention, and Monro's unfailing hospitality helped to create the spirit of a fraternity. Thus he became the recognized advertiser, if not prophet, of the movements, and exercised no little influence as an ubiquitous lecturer. Nor could he himself resist writing verse.

These efforts cannot be compared to the best work of his contemporaries, whom he always befriended, sometimes inspired, and, when possible, interpreted. Despite his activities, he was a lonely soul, and is at his best when regretting his isolation among kindred spirits who might mean so much to him, as in 'Hearthstone' and 'Unknown Country'; and contrariwise, when he shakes off his melancholy and indulges his affection for animals. In both these moods he reverts easily and effectively to the traditional style. But at other times he broods on the physical crudities of life and death, or studies his own soul by watching its reactions to outward things (e.g., 'Natural History' and 'The Empty House'), or discards ideals and hopes unconfirmed by science, for instance in 'Earthliness'; and while in this vein he is tempted to sacrifice charm to metrical experiments which he has not quite mastered. He is another of those who cannot live without poetry, but can only help to find it; and he tried to do so by standing between tradition and innovation.

PART II

INTERWAR PHASE

CHAPTER VII

MOVEMENTS BENEATH THE SURFACE

IN the first chapter we glanced at the social and moral atmosphere of the age : the thoughts which people shared, the mood in which they faced the business of existence, their consciousness of the knowledge which leads to pleasure and power, their chances of life, their reliance on progress and culture, their contacts with the publishing world. We saw that existence was full of opportunities, and that the reading public were far from blind to them. But when we turned to the authors who ought to mirror this progress we have noticed that something was missing. There was a hint of frustration because of disunion. The *intelligentzia* could not quite make up its mind. Writers were unable to agree on essentials, so they played with sidelights. In fact the first fourteen years of the twentieth century becomes a period not because its authors wrote alike, but because the same causes made them write differently. We saw at the outset that amongst other causes the reading public had become multitudinous and many-sided, and secondly that however different their ideologies, they all wanted to make the most of civilization in order to make the most of themselves. They wished to play with life rather than meditate on its inner meaning.

We must now consider the less obvious influences which gathered strength during the period and gradually became prominent in the period which followed, not without leaving their mark on the authors we have already studied.

THE ACADEMIC INFLUENCE

It must first be confessed that our Universities all unwittingly added to the instability of letters. By 1915 the best of them had introduced English literature and language as a first-class subject, and every year thousands of students availed themselves of the opportunity. The movement was expected to increase the body of scholarly critics, and inaugurate an age of good taste. But Universities were at that time valued as trustees of learning ; their function was to systematize, elucidate, and transmit to posterity all that was worth remembering. So the authorities rightly insisted on a grounding in our earlier literature and language. Even when exploring the masterpieces of the last two centuries, there was a tendency to keep to the older classics which needed the most elucidation, had stood the test of time, and offered the most attractive material for historical research. Most teachers were inclined to stop at 1850, then at 1875. It was not till after the Four Years War that lecturers, as a rule, ventured as far as 1900.

The system is to be known by its fruits. One of the most representative figures was George Saintsbury (1845–1933), for ten years a schoolmaster, for twenty years a journalist, and for twenty the professor of Rhetoric and English Literature at Edinburgh, a genial master of erudition tempered with common sense. He was an ardent and wide-awake critic of contemporary politics, yet he gave the best years of his life to the production of short histories and primers which cover an immense field of medieval and post-medieval studies and, when middle-aged, he constructed his two monuments of scholarship : *A History of Criticism* (1900–4) and *A History of English Prosody* (1906). He gives you an ordnance map of the Past and leaves you to find your own way through the Present. *The Cambridge History of Literature* (1907–16) is perhaps even more typical. A systematic and continuous survey of the whole panorama was obviously beyond the capacity of any single brain, so contributions were invited from specialists all over the world, including some of the younger and less conspicuous. The outstanding authors were briefly yet adequately discussed, but it was the chief care of the editors (Sir Adolphus Ward and A. R. Waller) to explore the lesser names, and what one might call the background and undergrowth of literary development. They amplified their contributors' generalizations with elaborate bibliographies.

Hundreds of other examples might be quoted to demonstrate that academic influence, at that time, tended towards the training of the intellect—habits of research, organization and insight. Incidentally the treasures of the Past were made public for all who cared to possess them, not forgetting the evolution of language, thought and method. Nevertheless thousands of students were annually being encouraged to look backward for their culture, and to appreciate excellence only after it had been perfected and stereotyped in certain styles, rhythms, myths, and even figures of speech which had acquired the charm and unreality of a vanished world. So the majority could hardly help being prejudiced against novelty. Where their treasure was, there would their heart be also. The more ambitious felt that the great masterpieces—e.g., Shakespearean drama, eighteenth-century prose, nineteenth-century lyrics were by now a frozen perfection, beyond the reach of reproduction or renewal ; or, as H. W. Nevinson put it, as early as 1914, " two into one won't go ". So some ventured to assert that only quite modern literature was worth reading. It is significant that T. S. Eliot is almost the only original writer who has taken an honours degree in literature.

THE DECLINE OF VICTORIAN SCIENCE

For these irreconcilables, science might be expected to supply the most handy and inspiring ideology. The reign of Darwin,

Huxley, and Haeckel had dawned on culture like a second Renaissance. Their doctrines promised certainty, and then led to socialism, politics, the investigation of morality, and religious controversy; and we have already seen that Kipling, Wells, Shaw, Bennett, Hudson, even Bridges, each in his own way, made full use of the opportunity. Meanwhile the reign itself, which began in the 'sixties, was declining in authority from about 1905 onwards. There arose a suspicion that science might continue to explain phenomena, but not existence. It resembled 'a theory of symbols which economizes thought' or 'a statement of coincidences which can be observed under the same conditions by all men', or 'the problem of classifying and interpreting facts, fitting them into patterns called theories and laws'. As early as 1892 Karl Pearson in the first of his many editions of *The Grammar of Science* defined it as 'the classification of facts, the recognition of their sequence and relative significance'. But the facts themselves were becoming too elusive. The evolutionists—for instance W. Bateson, de Vries, and the recently discovered Mendel—were confessing that evolution did not depend solely on environment. Life was an energy, an impulse which transcended circumstances and consequently our comprehension. This impression gained ground because Nietzsche [1] and Butler [1] became known, having just died (1900 and 1902), and Bergson,[1] because he wrote with French lucidity; and in 1907–8 Hans Driesch delivered his Gifford Lectures on *The Science and Philosophy of the Organism.*

Since science was losing faith in its own finality, since evolution was unaccountable, it was felt that man could not fulfil himself through adaptation to environment, even in the social, economic, political, or humanistic senses of the word. On the contrary, he must look into his own heart, and there he would find an urge to resist the vagaries of evolution, an impulse to fulfil aims and ideals which have nothing to do with its frequently ignoble purposes. In the myriad forms of life around us there must be something which corresponds to our deepest intimations, our striving towards self-expression, our instinctive kinship with bird, beast, and clod, our susceptibility to seasonal and astral influences. Our best hopes lay not in adaptation, but integration; not world-knowledge but life-knowledge.

These aspirations had been voiced in the nineteenth century, but the romantic and Victorian poets had offered convictions, not proofs. The twentieth century, though distrustful of science, could not unlearn scientific habits. They wanted to be persuaded logically.

It is a fortunate law of progress that when civilization is in need of an invention or impulse, someone supplies it, as if inspired by the atmosphere. In this case it was Edward Carpenter.

[1] *Ante*, p. 33.

EDWARD CARPENTER (1844–1929) AND BERTRAND RUSSELL (1872–   ) GIVE A LEAD

In the late 'sixties he read mathematics at Cambridge, and for the next ten years studied the physical sciences.   Towards middle age he became discontented with his work, not because his learning was leading him down the wrong road, but because it was not leading him anywhere at all.   It divorced the intellectual part of man from the instinctive and had therefore come to a standstill.   The scientist was merely classifying facts without seeing whither they led.   A perspective was needed.

Carpenter found it in the recently established sciences of anthropology and folklore.   Sir Edward Tyler had published *Primitive Culture* in 1871 and *Anthropology : an Introduction to the Study of Man and Civilization* in 1881 ; Andrew Lang *Custom and Myth* in 1884, and *Myth, Ritual and Religion* in 1887 ; Sir James Frazer had begun his monumental series of *The Golden Bough* in 1890. Carpenter used this knowledge and these conjectures to look at scientific phenomena, not indeed with the eyes of a prehistoric man, but with those of a modern man who had remained true to the best in his prehistoric heritage.   He was much helped by Walt Whitman, Schopenhauer, William James, and R. M. Bucke's *Cosmic Consciousness* (1901).

Viewed from this standpoint, civilization had given us much and deprived us of more.   For untold ages human beings had lived a communal life, spiritually as well as socially, conscious of themselves in everything they saw, induing animals, trees, plants, and even streams and rocks, with the same emotions and habits as they shared with each other.   They did not think in the modern sense of the word ; they acted on instinct and race-memory, each organ contributing its proper impulse, so that a current of subconscious energy pervaded the blood-stream and the nervous systems.   Since then, in the last few thousand years or less—a fleeting moment in the immemorial history—civilization had imposed a wider sense of security, and therewith forethought, the conception of private property, and the institution of class government.   Human beings became conscious that they were individuals, and lost the sense of ' altogetherness '.   They insisted on differences, watched first their interests and then themselves.   Man trusted more to his brain and less to the intimations of his bodily functions.   He raised one organ into governance which conflicted with the others and broke up the unity of his nature.   Hence also the sense of shame and the consciousness of sin, since civilization, even at its best, brings us face to face with our own weaknesses.   Finally, relying on his powers of analysis and synthesis, he obscured knowledge, classifying observed facts objectively, ignoring the human and personal elements in phenomena.

Neither Carpenter nor anyone else would wish to resign our hard-won victories, but he protested against regarding them as final. The civilization-epoch should be viewed as a tentative and not wholly successful period, necessary in order that men could acquire the ' Knowledge of Good and Evil '—that is, self-knowledge. The modern error was wilful persistence in this intermediate stage, blindness to our estrangement from Nature, from our true selves, from our fellow-creatures. We should use our enlightenment to recover the arts of unanimism, to merge our individualities in the ' cosmic-self ', to feel and worship the elemental life coming to us through sex and the influence of the seasons and the heavenly bodies, as in the old nature-religions. To achieve this consummation men of science must unify, not disintegrate, knowledge, merging mechanics into physics, physics into biology and zoology, and these last into sociology and ethics, all culminating in the conception of personality, human and divine. The artist must unlearn self-isolation and realize that he is psychologically a part of all he feels, and that his inspiration wells up from a consciousness diffused through his whole body, the organic functions contributing their flow to the life of the emotions, the nerve-centres playing their proper part no less than the cerebrum.

Carpenter's naturalism is implicit in all he wrote and explicit in *Civilization, its Cause and Cure* (1889) and *The Art of Creation : Essays on the Self and its Powers* (1904). Neither book is fundamentally original. In 1862 Herbert Spencer defined philosophy as ' the unification of knowledge ' (*First Principles*), and as we have seen, the ground was prepared by anthropologists and students of folk-lore ; in fact this modern reactionary might have derived his inspiration from Montaigne's brilliant and paradoxical essay ' Des Cannibales ', published 1580. Carpenter is significant because he applied this knowledge to elucidate the moral, social and artistic perplexities of his age, and thereby demonstrated that it was already possible to start ideas which were later to become conspicuous ; for instance, Bernard Shaw's advocacy of anti-vivisection, vegetarianism, the abolition of capital, the vindication of criminals, D. H. Lawrence's vitalism and unanimism, Somerset Maugham's insistence on self-expression are anticipated in these earlier works. The reader will find much in sympathy with Bridges' *Testament of Beauty* (1929), J. B. Haldane's *The Philosophy of a Biologist* (1935), C. S. Lewis's *The Problem of Pain* (1939). He has prepared the way for the younger poets' claim to write from within, with their whole body ; and for quite recent novelists, like Graham Greene and Frederic Prokosch, to dwell on the primitive streak in modern character. What is most remarkable, he has drawn attention to the ancient Oriental wisdom which has become almost a fashion from the 'thirties onward.

Carpenter startled his readers into thought and showed them where they went wrong. But he did not put them right, except through the most general and controversial assertions. He went no farther than the contention that men and women would recover

I

the old feeling for humanity only through the influence of a reformed society. He asserted but did not explain the principle on which that reformation should be worked.

The explanation was undertaken by Bertrand Russell in *The Principles of Social Reconstruction*. The lectures were written in 1915 and delivered early in 1916. They are affected by the War only so far as they feel in advance the tightening of Government control, and the consequent spirit of irritation. Otherwise they are pre-war.

Russell recognizes that we are imprisoned by civilization, but goes on to argue that only civilization will set us free. The modern man can only be true to himself if he is true to his social institutions. These must, of course, regulate his complex, multitudinous existence, but must also give each individual the power to express the excellence peculiar to his individuality ; the social soil must let him grow as spontaneously as a tree. Every human being has some creative impulse which ends in service to his fellow-creatures, whether through knowledge, art, or goodwill, and neither religion, marriage, education, nationality, nor—worst of all—property must be allowed to serve any other end. This idea of the State is at least as old as Plato ; its direct challenge to our most approved English institutions was new. Russell bequeaths to the younger generation the problem of fusing their social obligations with their right to self-expression.

FREUD'S CONTRIBUTION

Both Carpenter and Russell exclaimed, 'know thyself'. Neither told their contemporaries exactly where to look for the raw material. Anthropologists and their interpreters might suggest the direction, but the inquirer would have to continue where they left off, and use his own eyes. That is why a certain Viennese neurologist was able to give poets, novelists, philosophers and essay-writers something to think about.

Sigmund Freud (1856–1942) was already beginning to explain that our avowed thoughts and reasoned attitudes were the product of education, social conditions and family life. This manufactured mask or garment—the *ego*—concealed and often perverted the universal hormaic man—the *id*—fermenting beneath. Each personality is like a bubble blown up on the surface of a dark, deep stream.[1] This stream is the volume of life-energy with its cross-currents, rhythms and race-memories, perhaps originating in prehuman sources, at any rate common to all humanity. The submerged river permeates our blood-stream, ganglia, and organs, notably the sex-glands, and creeps up into our brains, colouring, though not creating, our thoughts and wishes far more than we suspect.

[1] This simile is borrowed from Herbert Read's *Education through Art*.

Yet the brain, as known to the average man, is not the place in which to examine our 'lower nature', this *id*, as Freud calls it. The mind of man lives a life apart, consciously adapted to environment, intent on its own susceptibilities. Or, at least we must catch our brains in their unguarded moments when instincts, impulses, and fancies rise of their own accord; best of all in sleep, when the reason relaxes its hold and dreams whisper the secrets of the animal, secrets dimly contacted and contraried by the habits of the *ego*.

Freud's influence was indirect and second-hand, but none the less real. He discovered 'the subconscious' to an age eager to know more about itself. In the past, other and greater writers had penetrated with a wider sympathy into that mystery, but as if by accident, dropping hints. The artist's insight was nearly always narrowed by the narrowness of the reader who expected characters to be clear-cut, all compact of unified avowable motives. Freud came with a scientist's authority and reminded us that such sculptured effects were due to artistic simplification. Our sentiments and intentions may seem to spring full-grown out of our heads, but in reality they are each a rearrangement of our unbidden day-dreams, lunatic fears, and unavowable cravings; and heretofore literature had generally suppressed that truth, thus excluding one half of human nature. We now understood more clearly how the outward pose betrays the inner man. Nor need the new knowledge always end in disillusionment. If psycho-analysts began by showing that the functions of the brain or body might suffer because some instinct was twisted out of its course, and a human being become anti-social because inhibited, they also proved that we could sublimate our basest and most scatological impulses into heroism, unselfishness, and art. *Traumdeutung* appeared in 1900 (transl. 1913).

Thus Freud prepared the way for the introspective novel, the internal monologue, impressionism, surrealism, and revealed possibilities in the problem play and autobiography.

We have now seen that the pre-war period was an age of vistas, and that there was necessarily much initial uncertainty about their direction. We have also seen that there was no less uncertainty about the manner and means of exploring them. The most prominent writers kept as closely as they could to nineteenth-century models. The others, who were less effective or popular, nevertheless felt in their bones that their thoughts needed a vivid and unfamiliar presentment either more traditional or more anti-traditional. Both prose-writers and poets have been compared to a man desiring a new suit of clothes, and not quite satisfied with the fashions and materials either of Savile Row or Petticoat Lane.

And all the time an Italian was helping them to make up their minds.

CROCE (1866-   ) AND PURE INTUITION

On the 2nd September 1908, in Heidelberg, Benedetto Croce delivered his lecture on *L'Intuizione Pura e il Carattere Lirico dell'Arte*. He began by discrediting all the established schools of criticism, because they were the work of previous ages. We cannot keep to the Past, simply because it is the Past. With our present-day experience and culture, we must begin again to ask what is poetry, and we shall find that it arose because long-ago human beings opened their eyes and felt by instinct that certain objects impressed them. Such is the meaning of intuition. These primitive observers could not reason or reflect. Their impressions produced a state of mind, not a sentiment. It was *pure* intuition, based on appearances, or the sense of reality, unobscured by after-thoughts. It needed language to become conscious, just as a spirit needs a body, and an impulse needs an action. Such is the origin and quality of poetry—a vision, fantasy, figuration—the first effort towards knowledge, the root out of which culture has branched and flowered, but neither the flower, nor the branch; the naïve and simple gesture of a child's mind, a gesture which continues to accompany the progress of the spirit down the ages, as often as the impressionable, primitive being reappears whom we now call poet.

We recognize his quality by the power of his personality, but it is not the willed personality of the prophet imposing his convictions on his fellows. In that sense all true poetry is impersonal. It is the spontaneous personality of the dreamer realizing his dreams in what he himself sees. The dreams themselves do not matter much; but only the sincerity with which they are dreamt, or rather, the intensity of sensation revealed in the ardour of composition, not the idea evolved; the act of creation, not the ideal created; the flight of the arrow, not the target hit.

Thus, of all human activities, poetry is the earliest, humblest and weakest; and therein lies its value. Without the poet's child-like wonder, our reflections and abstractions would lose much of their meaning, and our lives the sense of continuity. It is true that no impression or desire can be recaptured, because no event can happen more than once. But the poet, by registering not the experience, but what it means to him, can save its significance, enshrine it in the imaginative tradition, and raise it above space and time. Life passes, but art remains.

These views, initiated in the lecture at Heidelberg, were amplified and amended from time to time, notably in *Problemi di Estetica* (1910) and *Breviario di Estetica* (1914). In England they quickly attracted the attention of experts, and gradually penetrated so widely that after the Four Years War many were repeating Croce's idea without having read a word of him, even in Ainsley's translation. His theory may be one-sided, but is not subversive; he applied it to Dante, Aristo, Shakespeare, and Corneille without destructiveness.

But in a restless, transitional period, he was often interpreted as discrediting some of our greatest poets because they were intellectual, and seemed to insist so encouragingly on creativeness that young verse-writers affected spontaneity or sought the sheer and exclusive pleasure of matching an image with exact words, because the image could give no other pleasure.

LITERATURE ACQUIRING A PERSPECTIVE BUT AWAITING AN IMPULSE

So ends a period of efforts, experiments, and divided aims. Moralists, like Julien Benda, looking back on the brilliant beginnings and incomplete endings, have suggested *la trahison des clercs*; rather unjustly, since it resulted not from faithlessness, but perplexity. It is not the function of the *intelligentzia* to put their heads together and construct a philosophy, religion, or social order. They are intermediaries between those who think and those who act or talk—spies trained to explore an unfamiliar country and bring back the information which their own people most need. They turn ideas into ideals and concepts into conduct. Such a synthesis at the best of times is difficult, and in this age was more difficult than ever, partly because culture was no longer united under one harmonious body of knowledge, and partly because cultivated people were otherwise distracted by social disunion, political antagonism and international rivalry.

As far as any agreement could be discerned, culture was beginning to disown the civilization from which it could not escape and to seek wisdom among the emotions we inherit, or are supposed to inherit, from primitive man ; at any rate to admire, though it was impossible to imitate, the vigour, spontaneity, and single-heartedness which had nothing to do with modern sophistication. We have seen that some even revived the diction and style of the uneducated ages, some others protested against capitalism and the slavery of the working classes, yet others dwelt on the pettiness and futility of the well-to-do.

However, in this country public opinion rarely sets itself to choose between the cross-roads until some national event has changed its habits and disturbed its peace of mind. The needful impulse came with a vengeance in 1914.

CHAPTER VIII

IMPACT OF THE FOUR YEARS WAR

THE international catastrophe brought the forces of transition to a crisis, even in the remote valley of the shadow of books. It is significant that no one seemed to remember Zola's *Débâcle* or Stephen Crane's *The Red Badge of Courage*. At first there was something like a return to Victorian idealism. This 'war to end war' would solve our personal entanglements, our social antagonisms, and our political uncertainties. In that spirit the younger generation joined the last volunteer army in English history, and, if endowed with any literary aptitude, found their inspiration ready-made. The prose-writers were not remarkable; the theme was more worthy of poetry; and some 'temporary officers' certainly succeeded in bringing out their sense of strange beauty, their feeling for nature, and the acceptance of death in a great cause. Some descriptive pieces, like R. Nichols' 'The Assault' (1916), Sassoon's *The Rearguard* (1917), are as vivid as dreams. Charles Sorley has, perhaps, succeeded better than any in expressing the charm and gracefulness of his talent on a background of trench warfare. The best single poem is Julian Grenfell's 'Into Action' (1915), though Laurence Binyon's 'For the Fallen' (1916) will live longer.

After the Battle of the Somme the lyrical or romantic spirit mirrored in E. B. Osborn's *The Muse in Arms* (though not published till 1917) passed away. It is true that most of the poets of the mobilization period lost their lives in that 'Push', but as one can see in F. Brereton's *An Anthology of War Poems* (though not published till 1930), there were others at least as talented to take their place. It was simply that the whole nation reawoke to the realities of life; first of all to the bitterest disillusionment that had ever attended the British arms; secondly to the discovery that scientific and social progress could culminate in such a sequence of dreary horrors; thirdly to the tone of civilian life which was beginning to wilt.

The quality of this second group of poets (from about the end of 1916) has been under-estimated. They still believed in human nature, they were alive to unobtrusive heroism, they had a more discerning social sense. Instead of chanting martial commonplaces their patriotism became forethought for the common soldier who shared their life in the trenches. But the spell of sympathy became so unbearably strong that they lost the poet's detachment. What should have been dreams turned into nightmares, soaked in mud and blood. Any sentiment less embittered by protest seemed to be no better than a conspiracy of silence. Their diction and manner were awaiting them in the pre-war neo-realism, for instance, in Conrad without the backgrounds, or Masefield in his 'blackguard' period.[1]

[1] *Ante*, pp. 22, 55.

SASSOON, OWEN, AND BLUNDEN

The extreme example is Siegfried Sassoon, born in 1886 to a social position and opportunities such as favoured Rupert Brooke's tranquil youth, though there was more of Jorrocks in Sassoon's composition. His earliest war pieces do not lack a sober sense of heroism, but in his disillusioned period he felt that literary refinements would mislead both the poet and his audience, whereas violent, foul-mouthed expressions would surprise the public into visualizing life, and especially death, at the Front. So he exposed the bestial and mechanized inhumanities of the trenches with too much technical effectiveness, and thereby missed his full effects. His coarse or silly blasphemies often blind the reader to the deep sympathy they imply.

What Sassoon only implied Wilfred Owen nearly succeeded expressing. He was killed a few days before the Armistice, leaving behind a manuscript which Sassoon edited as *Poems by Wilfred Owen* (1921). These verses are by no means blind to the twentieth-century ' tragedy of blood ', but he is also fully persuaded that the very vileness and humiliation of the soldier's lot can evoke a certain fortitude, even heroism, of which the obscure hero is unconscious. For instance, ' Strange Meeting ' and ' Greater Love ' give curious glimpses of his battered idealism. On the other hand, as an artist, he is not yet quite sure of himself. He relies too much on the academic manner of modern French verse, possibly not uninfluenced by Laurent Tailhade, whom he came to know in 1914. His complete works were published in 1930.

The least exceptionable is Edmund Blunden (1896–   ), who had already served his apprenticeship as a poet of nature, imbuing the pre-war countryside with a pastoral charm, of the earth earthy. He entered the war with his eyes wide open for its inner significance. He too sometimes yields to the sheer clammy horror, and relapses into terrorism (see *Third Ypres. A Reminiscence*). But on the whole he is ready to love everything : the genial warmth of comradeship, the suspense and excitement which keep our spirits alive, even the mystery of desolation.

These three represent a quite numerous group which expressed or tried to express something more than disillusionment. They treat the war as a visitation fresh from hell, or anywhere else outside this planet ; something which desecrated the flower of English poetry. They cared little or nothing for the vast issues at stake, but only for the plight of the common man, who, like themselves, was there because he was there. This touch of denationalized humanitarianism was then unusual, and has since, in the thirties, become a recognized trend of contemporary verse. The war-poets to some degree mark its beginnings. To reach that attitude they had to record a volume of human misery, death and mutilation not easily equalled in literature or history. On both these grounds

they are worth remembering. They also helped to make current
the *anti-God* sentiment already suggested by Housman and Hardy.
As the anonymous atheist declares in *The Diary of a Dead Officer*
(1919), 'if there is a God at all responsible for governing the earth,
I hate and abominate Him—I rather despise Him. But I do not
think there is one.'

After the Armistice there was the inevitable reaction, and war
literature became unpopular, until the boys and girls of 1918 had
grown up, and wanted to know more. So there was a revival, and
the revivalists apparently understood the public taste and supplied
anecdotes, experiences, and impressions, weaving their reminiscences
into autobiographies or novels, of which the centre is themselves.
D. Jones's *In Parenthesis* (1937) is interesting as an imaginative
study in verse as well as prose, and Herbert Read's *In Retreat*
(1925) and *The End of a War* (1933) have all his usual earnestness
and distinction. But the only permanently significant figure is
Manning.

FREDERIC MANNING AND ROBERT NICHOLS

This little-known author epitomizes the transition from the old
order to the new disorder. As an Edwardian, he fully recognized
that man was no more than a man, but that within those limits he
could achieve self-fulfilment, thanks to the union of science, philosophy, and literature. For him religion was 'the contemplation
of the Unknown from the sum of man's experience'. In this spirit
he studied culture and projected his conclusions into vivid and
dramatic episodes (*Scenes and Portraits*, 1909) which represent the
most critical stages in the progress of man's quest for Truth, and
illustrate any thinker's dependence on his own perceptions; for the
human mind can mirror only itself. It sounds abstruse, but rarely
has a scholar mixed so much imagination with his erudition, and
rendered humanism so human. It is noteworthy that his best
'scene', *The King of Uruk*, illuminates primitive mythology.

So with his verses (*Poems*, 1910). Superficially derivative, they
are as clear-headed and clear-sighted as his prose.

These speculations attracted little attention because their author
was too critical to be sympathetic. He trusted no man farther than
the historic environment in which his mind must have been formed.
A similar positivism might again limit his popularity, but would
certainly not impair his judgement, if he ever set himself to handle
contemporary experience. So it was well that Peter Davies offered
to publish his impressions of the Four Years War. The result was
Her Privates We. By 1922 (1930), the story of a ranker who
(unlike Manning) received a commission but was killed before he
discharged it. There is no outraged humanitarianism, pity, or self-
pity, except so far as Manning holds war to be a crime for which the
punishment falls on innocent people; merely an unique record of

lice, trench-feet, bad air, worse champagne, casual companionships, and now and then the most vivid impressions of night raids and shell-fire, varied by visions of sudden death and prolonged stretches of 'fatigue duties'. The prevailing note is friendliness and fatalism projected into half a dozen types so skilfully drawn that they seem to be individuals. The author has apparently lost his culture, though not his perceptiveness and powers of assimilation. On the other hand, he has convinced himself that a civilized man can quickly learn to do without civilization or sentiment, and that in these circumstances it is impossible to feel heroic or, indeed, that one's existence matters to any but oneself; least of all to the nation.

To this record the future historian will add Robert Nichols' *Anthology of War Poetry 1914–18* (1943), not because the collected poems open new vistas, but because the rather long introduction, in the form of a dialogue with Julian Tennyson, is the first attempt to contrast the war psychology of 1914–18 with that of 1939–43. The former was inspired by outraged sensibility, disgust with the attitude of the Home Front, and fear of being called a coward. ' This battle is for the private life. Religion, as Whitehead has pointed out, is what the individual does with his solitariness.'

So far, we have considered the verdict of those who went to the war. Its impact on those who stayed behind is equally important, but less easy to trace. Yet a curious synopsis will be found in the history of ' Barbellion's ' mind.

BRUCE FREDERICK CUMMINGS (1889-1919)

This son of a provincial newspaper reporter had a passion for knowledge, and being a child of his age, turned to science. Being also poor and self-educated, his science was out-of-date. He began by pinning his faith to Huxley and Haeckel, and believed that biology led straight to Truth and self-expression. With difficulty he obtained a foothold in South Kensington Museum, and then learnt that twentieth-century specialization was very different from nineteenth-century vision, and offered little scope for his wider more human curiosity. In reality he was born to be a man of letters, with a poet's sensibilities, a novelist's curiosity, and an artist's eye for the essential. Moreover, he read widely among the authors who unsettle nineteenth-century habits of mind, from Sir Thomas Browne to Bergson. But having learnt from them how to start thinking anew, he did not also assimilate their vision as well as their introspection, and follow the vistas, looking for a faith in something beyond the perception of the senses and the scope of the reason; something that must be sought rather than observed. Scientific scepticism had sunk too deeply. So his restless, acquisitive spirit was turned in on itself. Before 1914 he realized that he had not long to live, and he began to keep off the thought of death by creating a portrait of himself which would survive in a book. Such was his

preoccupation; he made himself familiar with the memoirs, autobiographies, and confessions which perfected the art of self-examination; and tried to 'move about in this ramshackle old curiosity shop
of a world, sampling existence'—especially his own.

The attitude is conspicuously Edwardian. But under the pressure
of the war-atmosphere, he learnt to observe other people as closely
as himself, to see them as they are, some unconsciously heroic,
others eaten up with ignoble desires, others again plain hypocrites.
He came to think the thoughts of the interwar generation. He
perceives that we have each three aspects to our being: the respectable
member of society, the scurrilous, often foul-mouthed commentator,
'the real but unknown I'. He is able to switch himself in and out
of his most cherished emotions, even to exercise his scientific analysis
on the girl he loves best. He notes that lovers are drawn to each
other 'in obedience to a powerful gravitation' far deeper than
consciousness. He foresees a time when obscenity will disappear
because we shall no longer treat the facts of sex as a whispered and
ignoble joke. He is aware that we all continually hold an *internal
dialogue* [1] with ourselves, which is as real as our formal thoughts.

These ideas and ideologies (more might be quoted) were commonplaces among writers who made their mark after Cummings's
death. We should have expected at least one projection of himself
into a novel. Instead, he has left only *The Journal of a Disappointed
Man, by W. N. P. Barbellion* (1919), *'Enjoying Life' and other
Literary Remains* (1919, posthumous), *A Last Diary* (1920, posthumous). And yet these collections of entries, especially the
first, constitute a novel of the new school. The central character,
Barbellion, happens to be the author who leads him through a
sequence of experiences, aimless except so far as they reveal spiritual
contacts through language and the eddying stream of consciousness.
Many novels and poems were to be made out of similar material.

H. G. Wells styled him 'the complete egoist'. He had no time
to get outside himself and range his existence among the many who
were, or hoped that they were, all parts of a super-personal scheme.
Had he lived longer, he might have sought confirmation in some
esoteric cult.[2] In our age an author must achieve detachment
before he can impose his personality on experience.

[1] *Post*, p. 176.   [2] *Post*, p. 141.

CHAPTER IX

THE INTERWAR ATMOSPHERE

BY the end of 1918, the world was supposed to be entering on an age of peace and reconstruction. It was a great opportunity for the artists and intellectuals, as well as for the political and social workers. Many vested interests had disappeared. The ' movements beneath the surface ' discussed in Chapter VII, especially the theories of Carpenter, Russell, Freud, and Croce, had quietly been gaining ground. Educated people were free to try out these values, and if approved, to adjust them to the post-war situation. So much had happened that society seemed now for the moment to be one common body, only divided into those two immemorial classes : the intelligent and the unintelligent. All depended on whether that cleavage could be closed ; whether the vast reading-public would support its leaders. At first it looked as if the nation was in the right mood, and as if the transition would be smooth, as is illustrated by three notable successes which have nothing else in common.

THE DEMOBILIZATION SPIRIT

In 1921 A. S. M. Hutchinson, a journalist and the author of three novels which circulate in lending libraries, published *If Winter Comes*, an ordinary domestic novel, apparently reminiscent of Dickens, but inspired by a good-natured indifference to standards honoured in the pre-war middle-class novel. Its hero, Mark Sabre, is a character too selfless, single-hearted, and amiably tiresome to fit into this pettifogging Georgian circle. The war is not mentioned, but the public recognized the demobilization spirit—Shelley's ' if winter comes can spring be far behind ? '—and the story became the best-seller of the century.

At about the same time, W. R. Inge, an authority on theological ' modernism ', who believed so deeply in the mysticism of the human spirit that he could accept science and disregard ecclesiastical traditionalism, having completed in 1918 his researches into the *Enneads* of Plotinus, produced *Outspoken Essays* (1919, 1922), two series of journalistic discussions on taxation, the value of money, the effacement of culture, and the doubtful future of society. His contentions were provocative, and sometimes ill documented, and he wrote as one of the pre-war generation, righteously outraged by the drift of post-war mismanagement. But he also wrote in a lucid, penetrating style, he handled familiar facts in an imaginative and almost recklessly intimate way ; so his enlightened conservatism was accepted by a generation bent on thinking for itself, and they bought his two volumes by the thousand.

The test example is Strachey.

GILES LYTTON STRACHEY (1880–1932)

He went in 1899 to Cambridge, where he learnt, like E. M. Forster, to value aesthetic emotions and personal relationships as the true end of existence. His intimate friends were like books, and his books like intimate friends, both fascinating illustrations of human character. He first attracted some little attention by *Landmarks in French Literature* (1912), which gives the impression of an Augustan born out of due time, always in love with craftsmanship, wit, and insight into character through art, especially in love with French exquisiteness, lucidity, and humanism, in the cultured epoch of the *Ancien Régime*. In fact he was always a bookman who studied the great wits because they helped him to realize his own sense of form and detachment, and who never admired a dead man without bringing his personality back to life. Such are the qualities of *Books and Characters* (1922), *Portraits in Miniature* (1931), and *Characters and Commentaries* (1933).

No writer seemed less likely to be popular. But by a stroke of genius he once had the idea to portray certain outstanding figures of the nineteenth century as they would have appeared to the eighteenth and as they ought to appear to the twentieth; that is to say, shorn of their borrowed plumes, intensely alive, and therefore unmistakably incomplete, a challenge to our sense of fitness. He was rarely blind to genuine flashes of goodness and grandeur, but he was also maliciously alive to those lapses of character which we note in our best friends and worst enemies, but which our fathers were inclined to overlook in public figures qualifying to survive in history. *Eminent Victorians* (1918) and *Queen Victoria* (1921) were being read when the political consequences of the war convinced us that the old order ought not to be revived and when J. M. Keynes's *The Economic Consequences of the Peace* (1919) convinced us that the old order could not be revived. Strachey's Victorians represented just those institutions which were most open to criticism—for instance, public schools, the Church of England, party government, bureaucratic administration, imperial expansion. Now and then his mockery gets the better of his judgement, but on the whole he leaves us convinced that to master the Present we must acquire the wit and wisdom of the Past—and its classic style.

Many of his readers for the first time perceived the importance of the personal factor in public affairs, even more admired his disposition to criticize without controversy, and all half suspected that humour is the safest criterion of truth.

THE DEMOBILIZATION SPIRIT EVAPORATES

So the interwar period began well. It continued well until about the middle 'twenties. Thereafter, the tone of the nation seemed to change. England was still full of life; if anything too full; but the

atmosphere was not congenial to great literature. So the majority
of talented authors, including (as we have seen) some of the most
prominent, wrote down to their public, and, whether young or
middle-aged, were financially successful. The more original went to
the opposite extreme, as if in self-defence, in order to assert their
artistic freedom ; and this resistance to environment became an
obsession. These strayers from the drove did not make big incomes,
but some made big names.

Such was then the current explanation ; and it is certainly incomplete. At the same time the inevitable reaction had supervened with
unexpected suddenness, like rain-clouds obscuring the sun. The
gloom of disillusionment overspread the reading public and to some
degree influenced the writers who are all members of that same
reading public, even if they refuse to follow its lead. So the dis-
contents of the period must be mentioned.

Many of the younger generation cherished their ideals up to Armistice Day, despite its orgy of neurotic joy-making. Thereafter they
were brought face to face with the difficulties of political, social, and
financial reconstruction and had to realize for the thousandth time
in the world's history that human beings cannot for long be just to
each other. Many young fellows who had risked their lives (as they
claimed) to win the war, and rather naïvely expected a free hand in
winning the peace, now found themselves cold-shouldered out of the
world of administration by experienced politicians, and utterly
ignored by that other unadvertised group of cosmopolitan business
men, whose combines pervaded the social fabric. In fact the
community was far from resolving itself into the single antithesis of
the intelligent and the unintelligent.

As the problems of the first war had not been solved, a second war
seemed inevitable, and this prospect favoured a continuance of war
morality. The burden of the age was insecurity. If public men
made hay while the sun shone, the pleasure-seekers, like soldiers on
leave from the front, followed their example. Why take thought for
the morrow ? It was not an agreeable subject for meditation. It
was quicker and more spectacular to possess a motor-car (then first
becoming fashionable) than to possess oneself. So the Smart Set,
like Galsworthy's white monkey, sucked the orange dry and flung it
away, mocking and jazzing.

This feverish futility was by no means universal, nor bone-
deep. It might have passed almost unnoticed except for Noel
Coward, whose indulgently cynical and technically perfect comedies
advertised the pose and rendered it fashionable, especially in *The
Vortex, Easy Virtue, Fallen Angels, Private Lives* (1922–1930).
Society as a whole was slowly shaping itself. But the new order
with its conflicts and claims, its readjustment of social units and
regrouping of the population, all tended towards an unobtrusive
encroachment on individual liberty and the effacement of
personalities. The old English tradition of unconventionality seemed

likely to disappear. Along with it, there would disappear that other tradition of leisurely rusticity, the nurse of English character in olden times. Nowadays urbanization was inevitable, otherwise civilization could not progress. Yet urbanization either polluted the country-side or lengthened its distance by an interminable wilderness of suburbs. Town and country were still unreconciled, perhaps irre-concilable ; and the divorce was all the more regrettable because city-life isolated the individual among artificial relationships which lacked the sense of permanence or membership.

The author who tried to diagnose the ' body politic ' would come to the conclusion that its temperature was either above or below normal. These symptoms might cause anxiety, but they neither excuse nor explain interwar literature. Genius thrives on opposition. For instance (to take a few chance examples), neither Euripides, Cicero, Dante, Shakespeare, Milton, Shelley, Condorcet, Hugo, nor Dostoevsky could derive much inward peace from outward events. Besides, these years were not only a period of puzzlement and frustration. The duty which England had disowned in her days of opulence was now being discharged almost without friction in her hour of need. That is to say, the national income was so distributed that no human being need die of want, few need fear the degradation of poverty, and all, especially the highest and lowest, could taste at moments the luxury of feeling like everybody else. There was another consolation. If life was less reliable, death was less immi-nent. We have already noted the progress of Victorian surgery and medicine, and its influence on humanism.[1] Since then, the arts of healing had won and are continuing to win astonishing victories over our common enemy and his invidious allies, disablement and deformity. The survival of the unfittest might worry eugenists, but not the humanitarians, nor those who can rejoice that life is more and more like a freehold worth cultivating, and less like a leasehold burdened with restrictions, terminable at a moment's notice. All the while, pure science had advanced so far that it had outstripped positive knowledge. Its discoveries, as we shall see later,[2] were to embarrass alike the rationalists and intuitionists, but it did not fail to remind us that existence is still full of wonders.

And yet the period produced no one able to catch and sculpture human nature in its essential mood and form, under a twentieth-century disguise. The interwar literature is disappointing, and if that disappointment is to be explained we must look farther for the cause.

WHY INTERWAR LITERATURE APPEARS TO BE AN ANOMALY

In the first place we are apt to forget that a literary movement depends on two or three leaders. The English Renaissance would have been quite different if Spenser had been drowned on his first

[1] *Ante*, p. 7.　　　　[2] *Post*, p. 136.

voyage to Ireland, if Shakespeare had been executed for complicity
with Essex, Ben Jonson had lost his life in the Netherlands, and
Bacon had died early of one of the epidemics which visited London
every five or ten years. So now, we cannot tell how much genius
was lost at Loos, La Bassée, Bapaume, and Paschendael ; nor again
how much diverted into business, economics, social studies, or a
political career. Others again, as never before, were compelled by
the sheer cost of living to write only what the million would read in
their leisure hours.

Nevertheless there was still a number of very talented authors—
some competent critics would say men of genius—who had begun to
attract attention in the pre-war period, but had not yet developed
their powers, or had not yet established their reputation. There
were, of course, others who had not taken up their pens till they had
laid down their arms. But it was these slightly older writers, still
young enough to be adaptable, who had the future in their hands.
None quite succeeded in maintaining their grasp on it. They could
not present their idea of human nature in the form (whether verse
or prose) which represented the really heart-felt fundamental
interest of their time. They caught certain facets, and relied on
style to do the rest.

The prevailing note was a new or intensified curiosity, especially
about oneself. As we saw in Chapter VIII, this curiosity was brought
to the surface and sharpened by the ordeals and contacts of the war.
People had become conscious of feelings and thoughts to which they
had formerly been strangers. ' Barbellion ' was a striking example.[1]
And as we also saw, ' Barbellion's ' curiosity was fostered by his
reading and scientific experiences. Most of his interwar contemporaries, those who cared about ideas, had read more widely, if
superficially, than Cummings, and were directly or indirectly aware
of the disturbing theories started just before the war and discussed
in Chapter VII. They had, at any rate, heard of the doctrines of
Carpenter, Croce, Russell, and especially of Freud. In 1920, A. G.
Tansley's *The New Psychology and its Relations to Life,* and in 1922
the publication of *Introductory Lectures on Psycho-Analysis* (translation by J. Riviere) marked the beginning of a vogue which was
bound to prevail because it raised so many questions about one's
inner self. Assuredly a background of ideas was not lacking.

Why was the new knowledge so intractable ? Because it offered
artists their human material in a form which could no longer be
ignored. It touched them too nearly. But it inspired, rather than
satisfied their curiosity ; it classified mysteries without giving them
meaning. It left gaps in their sense of what must be true. It was
so uncongenial to the traditional manner and mood, that it slipped
through the fingers of those who would prefer to practise the traditional technique.

[1] *Ante,* p. 129.

THE PECULIAR INTRACTABILITY OF INTERWAR IDEAS

Most of these ideologies were not so much new, as newly affirmed, presented in a guise which perplexed the serious student of humanity. For instance, Victorian science had imposed the duty of facing facts. ' Logical consequences ', said Huxley, ' are the scarecrows of fools and the beacons of wise men.'   But when the post-Victorian novelist assumed that duty, the new psychology taught him to portray vicious characters not as vicious but mistaken, merely the victims of a situation to which the author would have succumbed, thus effacing the ethical appeal.[1]   Psycho-analysis did, indeed, argue that our hereditary vices could be transformed into social virtues by a mental process ; but neither Freud, Jung, nor Adler even hinted at the inner moral force which accomplished sublimation.   Emergent evolution has already been glanced at ;   the theory apparently influenced Bridges' *Testament of Beauty*.[2]   But when examined, the doctrine (also known as holism, creative synthesis, and epigenesis) seemed to teach that when certain elements combined, quite new qualities emerged, entirely distinct from the component parts.   In the case of human beings, no solid base of character should be looked for, nor inward growth.   The child had ceased to be father to the man. One could count only on a process which eluded the moralist.

These few examples, out of many, help one to realize the inconclusiveness of this new and supposedly positive knowledge.   The *intelligentzia* were asked to renounce rationalism with its axioms and accept ' the nature of things ', thus returning to irrationalism. They would have to follow divergent, ill-marked bridle-paths, leaving certainties behind them, guided not by a definite idea, but by an hypothesis which happened to appeal to this or that man's temperament, and might lead anywhere.   When confronted by discrepancies and conjectures, a human being is liable to take refuge in a nomenclature.   In fact a ' high-brow ' has been defined as one who believes an explanation if labelled with a Greek or Latin name. So now, amid contradictions and inferences, terms tended to lead on to terms by their own affinity.   Even so, they could not always be trusted to keep the thought on its own track.   They threatened to overlap and crystallize the feelings, impose an intellectual tyranny, restrict insight to a connotation ; like railway signals which ought to guide trains but are reverenced as if they ran them.[3]

These many disabilities concerned man's duty to himself, but it was by now recognized that he was not fully a man unless he also discharged his duty to his fellow-creatures.   There were the social sciences to be reckoned with, especially the now fashionable study of Political Economy, all which imposed plans for the re-employment of wealth, the adjustment of machinery to progress, the reorganization of

[1] K. Burke, *Attitudes towards History*.
[2] *Ante*, p. 110.
[3] J. H. Muller, *Science and Criticism*.

industry, the reshaping of public morals based on mutual service, and education for citizenship. These and such-like preoccupations certainly encouraged one's sense of other people, but left the worker just as much a stranger to himself as if the private person had no right to exist as such and was much better without the instinct for self-possession and self-expression. Besides, though the plans for society might produce an ideal state, the state was at present far from ideal. The novel had established itself as the best expression of social life since the eighteenth century, but we have already seen that some novelists could not make the best of their characters in that setting. It had become too money-ridden, disunited, and ignobly competitive.[1] It no longer brought out the best in a man, unless he set himself to reform its abuses, thereby sacrificing those qualities which a novelist loves to depict. So we shall find that the most original masters of fiction—for instance, Maugham, Lawrence, Joyce, and Virginia Woolf, and later E. R. Eddison, Graham Greene, Forrest Reid, and Frederic Prokosch—in their perplexity, tend to stray from the beaten track and portray characters rather than careers. Their plots degenerate into experiments in human contacts, preserving the atmosphere, not the substance of a narrative, just enough to conform to type and hold the reader's attention. Settled society was no longer an inspiration.

Here again, there was disunion. Roughly speaking one might say that some of the older novelists (including Wells, Galsworthy, and Bennett) still interested themselves in their external environment, and inaugurated what might be termed the *photographic period*, a brief and hurried interval of sheer descriptiveness, much of it executed with a trained artist's skilfulness, all of it a joy to those readers who like minding other people's business. They believed that the comedy of life remains the same at heart, though it changes its face every thirty years. The succeeding generation (with exceptions) believed that the comedy had changed not only in semblance but in substance, because we, the observers, had changed. Our environment was within us, in our brains, but also in our bodies. The novel should be an initiation into a more intense order of being, in which the social background is perceived as so many symbols and suggestions of what we could make of ourselves—too often what the novelist could or could not make of his own private self. He then became so absorbed in self-examination that he lost sight of the reader.

The same temptation was even more likely to beset the would-be poet. He, too, must assimilate the inconclusive knowledge of the age and adjust it to his own spiritual needs. He, too, must decide on the most appropriate technique. Ten years earlier Free-verse had been introduced, and by the elderly critics was dismissed as a youthful indiscretion. Now it was accepted as the shortest and simplest means towards spontaneity and self-revelation. Those

[1] *Post*, p. 149.

K

who trusted in freedom were encouraged by noting that Croce [1] had anticipated their ideal of art as a sheer act of creative intuition. The poet should clear his mind of culture, feast his eyes on the object, and then give vent to his emotion, as would a child or a primitive man. At this epoch the object was likely to be himself.

Free-verse, however, suffered from a peculiar disability : freedom to know the worst. As soon as a susceptible man turned his gaze inward, he ran the risk of being distracted by a swarm of conflicting impulses ; emotions jostled one another in his consciousness ; his identity seemed to be broken into facets. The approved prosodies helped the poet to collect his thoughts and imposed the appropriate mood. This modern technique was less amenable to discipline which was all the more needed because writers in this inconclusive experimental age often lacked moral and religious points of reference. So poetry might have taken a somewhat different direction if it had not been for I. A. Richards.

THE INFLUENCE OF ' PRINCIPLES OF LITERARY CRITICISM '

This treatise on aesthetics appeared in 1924. The author was a psychologist as well as an aesthetician, fully alive to the ordinary man's difficulty in co-ordinating his reactions—like bells jangling out of tune. The human being is possessed by impulses which need an outlet in action. Only rarely can each find its appropriate practical outlet, and therefore they obstruct each other ; hence waste of energy. It is the function of literature to supply a sub-stituted outlet. It reconciles and releases these mutual inhibitions inwardly, through some thought or flight of the imagination, and Richards termed the power which touched the spring a *value*. He defined the word as ' capacity for satisfying feeling and desire in various intricate ways '. The poet was the master of the solvent. He achieved this *value* as often as he created and suggested a state of mind in which our inward agitations are harmonized as if on the point of finding their natural vent, suspended but united, on the verge of fulfilment, imagination and mood taking the place of opportunity. These ' imaginal and incipient activities ' were termed *attitudes*.

What exactly are the poetical *values* which produce these *attitudes* ? How does the poet instil this ' inter-inanimation and balancing of impulses ' ? Not indeed by insisting overmuch on the theme which happens to occasion his poem, but by communicating his own serenity through the manipulation of words, images, and rhythms— a substituted poise and stability through the healing power of art. Poetry, then, is a magic spell, practised on the senses, and thence pervading the nervous system, soothing it, bringing its restless promptings to a single point. It induces a subconscious act of self-mastery followed by the enjoyment of release from stifled or mutually destructive impulses.

[1] *Ante*, p. 124.

This integration does not end with the ending of the poetical experience. The after-effects work their way into the structure of the mind ; the attitude becomes a habit ; he who knows how to read poetry knows how to look on life with acquired competence and sanity, and with a deeper insight into its possibilities.

Richards's aesthetic is not remarkably original except in its method of presentment and emphasis. It is obviously adapted to an age doubtful about the older sources of inspiration, and partial to a scientific exposition. The author admitted as much in his short sequel, *Science and Poetry* (1926). But he does not breathe a word against the values of the classic poets, only against our misunderstanding of their influence. Yet *Principles of Literary Criticism* has exercised a wide and deep influence. It has brought the prevailing tendencies to a head ; it has confirmed suspicions ; above all, it has assigned to the poet a duty which no one else can discharge. According to the author, he is not, as Browning said, ' one of God's spies ', on the look-out for touches of perfection in a seemingly imperfect world. He is an artistic psychiatrist, less concerned with man than with his own disordered self, and on that unabashed evidence he cures his fellow-men.

It was only too tempting to infer, perhaps unfairly, that his art consisted solely in the manipulation of words, the juxtaposition of syllables and open vowels, or in the management of incidence, alliteration, broken rhythms, unexpected images, and the shock of surprise. At least such might well be the only avenue of approach in this disconcerted age. The treatment could be so effective that the reader might succumb to his essential charm without fully understanding the import of the poem. Impulse and instinct were the stuff out of which attitudes should be woven into patterns, so Free Verse would continue to be as free as the subconscious.

CLASSICAL *v.* ROMANTIC

There is, of course, no inherent reason why this way of writing should point towards decadence. The released impulses may aim at a higher realization than is possible within the limits of sensuous experience—a gesture of the spirit, impatient of earthly impediments, eager to envisage strange meanings in ordinary things. If so, as Herbert Read suggests in *Annals of Innocence and Experience* (1940), genius may be, as it were, a leap into the dark. Such flights would emphasize the contrast between life as it is and as it could and should be, between our earthly fate and heavenly destiny. The poet has the right to take these liberties. In highly wrought moments he may have to catch at any symbol or secret token—dreams, allegories, mysteries, or even mere phases of feeling—and may claim that his allusiveness expresses the inner structure and rhythm of his being, with which others should be in sympathy ; again, the right of every poet.

But, it can well be objected, the reader also has his rights. Many of them feel in their bones a sense of order and fitness, a fixed intellectual centre to which they can refer their manifold experiences, a standard founded on self-discipline and self-examination ; so much so, that literature loses half its value if one cannot apply this norm and measure. These disciplinarians are averse from science because it tells too little, and from symbolism because it tells too much. It is (they believe) the symbolist's function to see ' more than cool reason ever comprehends ', but his duty to embody his imagination objectively, within the scientist's range of observation, among the things that every enlightened person can know and judge. T. E. Hulme [1] had certainly gone too far when he wished to confine poetry to a succession of clear-cut earthly images ; but, on the other hand, many of the greatest poets had succeeded in breathing their other worldliness into worldly experiences, as a consummate artist should.

These are questions of principle and literary taste, open to discussion, irrespective of any school or epoch, and preferences largely depend on temperament. Unfortunately, the virtues of order, economy, and justness are most conspicuous in the so-called classical and classic authors, and the spirit of adventure, unconventionality, and self-concern are most conspicuous in the so-called Romantic Movement. Consequently professional critics, always on the lookout for a party cry, have revived the nomenclature ; apparently on the ground that the present crisis is the last stage in the divergence, the qualities on both sides having reached their extreme development or decadence. Hulme had given the lead with his ' after a hundred years of Romanticism we are in for a classical revival '. The controversy has produced some able apologists, notably Wyndham Lewis (*Men without Art*) and Herbert Read (Introduction to *Surrealism*) for the romantics, and Norman Foerster, Irving Babbitt, and Elmer More (*Humanism and America*) for the classics ; but on the whole the exchange of ideas is academic and sectarian. It throws down an apple of discord where unity is so much needed and could so easily be won. It is, however, a hopeful sign that T. S. Eliot advocates and practises a fusion of the two manners, and that I. Evans (in *Tradition and Romanticism*, 1940) labours the rather obvious point that most great English poets had already done so.

THE RELIGIOUS REVIVAL

In the sixteenth and seventeenth centuries, an age like ours in its transitions, controversies and disastrous wars, people believed that the devil was more than usually rampant, and besides reviving the Faust-legend, they burnt 100,000 witches, accused of complicity with Satan. Like our forefathers, three hundred years later, we are again beginning to fear the powers of Evil. Wherever the modern man looks—whether into himself with his endocrine glands, sexual

[1] *Ante*, p. 111.

impulses, and inherited animalism, or into society with its rivalries, injustices, and the horror of its devastating wars, or into traditional culture with its old-world sentiments and values—he meets with disillusionment. There may still be much good in the world, but nature and civilization seem to be opposed to goodness. Hulme may have begun to put the idea into the heads of this generation when he became known as a believer in original sin. The war poets and diarists certainly reinforced the impression, and since then C. S. Lewis has openly discussed the principle of Evil, not as an abstraction, but an immanence, in *The Problem of Pain* (1935), and C. E. M. Joad in *God and Evil* (1942), both insisting on its obtrusiveness. This recrudescence of *Satanism* is significant because its effect is very different from that produced at the Renaissance. It is now argued that if the soul is sick and conscious of its sickness, the cure must begin at the source ; the soul must heal itself ; and as if by some instinct of the spirit, it escapes from facts, towards ' something that gives meaning to all that passes and yet eludes apprehension ' (Whitehead).

Some moralists have left the West behind them and consulted the spiritual physicians of the ancient East. They learn from Zoro-astrianism how to distinguish Good from Evil. The Good is the peaceful, laborious life ; Evil is simply *no-life*, the power which destroys. They learn from Buddhism that Evil is nothing else than desire—the cravings which combine in each human being and isolate him from his fellows, condensing (as it were) into a wilful restless personality. This individualism can be effaced through meditation and asceticism, and reabsorbed into the one universal human Self, which partakes of God. From Taoism they learn that there is a divine order or principle to which all things must conform, and from Confucianism how we can convince ourselves of this truth and convert its divine sanctions into human virtues.

The Persian Zarathustra (in Greek Zoroaster), the Hindu Gotama (entitled Buddha the Enlightener), and the three Chinese moralists Lao-tse (founder of Taoism), Confucius, and his disciple Mencius, all flourished about 500 B.C., and all appealed to A.D. 1920, because they taught the inquirer how to simplify and concentrate his idea of himself ; instead of following his nose round the circumference, how to rest in the centre. In that year 1920 Edward Carpenter published, in *Pagan and Christian Creeds*, his two lectures on *The Teaching of the Upanishads*, which were mystical treatises, each attached to one of the four *Vedas*, the ancient sacred books of the Hindus. They do not enjoin the unquestioning receptivity expected from the modern layman, they impose the arduous self-discipline of thought-control and sustained contemplation, and they lead to the enlightened and restful sense of absorption in something infinitely greater than oneself. Man possesses himself by discovering that his spirit is a part of the cosmic whole ; his body does not matter.

Such was the value of Oriental wisdom. It helped the learner to think beyond and beneath the distracting piecemeal theories of his age, to work his own salvation by hard thinking, to trust those age-long intimations which have served mankind since the dawn of culture ; and finally, to transcend thought and reach the Truth in what can only be termed a state of higher consciousness or ' one-pointedness of mind '.

The way for the revival was prepared by Schopenhauer (*passim*), Max Müller (*Sacred Books of the East*), Von Hügel (*The Mystical Element in Religion*), Keyserling (*passim*), A. Waley (*Three Ways of Thought in China*), R. Guénon (*East and West* and *The Crisis of the Modern World*) ; and has since been explained by Charles Gore (*The Philosophy of a Good Life*), Radhakrishnan (*Eastern Religions and Western Thought*), P. D. Ouspensky (*A New Model of the Universe*), C. E. M. Joad (*Guide to Philosophy* and *God and Evil*), and K. Walker's two fascinating volumes, *Diagnosis of Man* and *The Circle of Life*, both in 1942. There are many others ; amongst them Aldous Huxley in *Ends and Means*, 1937, and *The Perennial Philosophy*, 1946. Somerset Maugham has added to his portrait-gallery of eccentrics a more than usually sympathetic study of the young man who was single-hearted enough to live the wisdom of the East (*The Razor's Edge*, 1944).

The way of the ancient Hindus and Chinese was not everyone's way. The Orientals were more concerned with the duty to oneself than the duty to one's neighbour ; they had no ethic ; whereas the Westerner cannot generally possess his soul and heal it unless he shares it with his fellow-creatures. So many erstwhile free-thinkers are beginning to return to Christianity. Some have found what they sought in the Roman Church, and in those cases their conversion influences literature only so far as it steadies their point of view. It is more important to bear in mind that others shrink from dogma and ritual, whether Anglican or Catholic, as uncongenial to the modern mind, symbolisms which have lost significance. These exchange the institution for its founder, instead of a doctrine a moral ideal in the persons of Jesus and St. Paul. Some, as if taking a hint from Strauss's *Leben Jesu* and the other Christologists of the nineteenth century, go so far as to look up to Christ as the myth or symbol of what twentieth-century life should be—not the Galilean prophet who suffered under Pilate, but the ideal personification of Christian society which subsists in Christ.[1] Others are satisfied in the quest of the ' historical Jesus ' as the social Jesus, freed from the complications of socialism—that is, the human being who lived the perfect human life, convinced that good-will was the only necessary passport to salvation, and yet claimed intimacy with God. Yet others still keep to humanity as the One God and believe that every man has within him ' a soul which is spirit and which has a greater

[1] Alfred Loisy, *La Morale Humaine*. See also M. D. Petre : *Alfred Loisy*, 1944.

value than the whole physical universe' (J. Maritain), but nevertheless depends on society for its realization—a reformed society, good in that it aims at the good of each member.

Whether the religionist is Roman, Anglican, or free-lance, his cult is most significant. It represents man's last effort to transcend the limits of ordinary human existence. The twentieth-century Christologist feels that intercourse with the Man-God can be so intimate and spiritual that at moments it is possible to reach the borders of eternity. He resumes in thought the sacred experiences of the New Testament narrative, and feels their influence so deeply that nothing obstructs communion with a Being outside and above mortality—that is, outside and above the Three Dimensions. We can travel backwards and forwards in time, almost in touch with the Eternal Presence.

It sounds like an old story, till one notices the emphasis on the idea of time. That is the only indisputable contribution made by pure science to the life of the spirit. We have seen how the human sciences, whether practical or speculative, were disappointing; but there was still Physics, which studies the mysteries of the Universe and should satisfy man's need of wonder and worship. In the preceding centuries that need had not been fully satisfied because the cosmic miracles had gradually come to be represented as parts of a machine, vast as space. But with the twentieth century, Physics, like the other sciences, advanced into uncertainties. In face of relativity, the quantum theory, and the electron, we were once more moving in 'worlds not realized'. If God were a mathematician, mathematicians should bring us back to God.

It need not be added that this expectation was unfulfilled. Physicists did not handle the materials of direct sense, but the underlying ideas, and rendered them so metaphysical, so *extra*-human and occult, and yet so logically inevitable, that we could not even ' believe because it is impossible to understand '. Nowhere was it more difficult to fit oneself into the scheme of knowledge. The humanist in search of a value would be rewarded only with the artistic pleasure of noting the physicist's constructiveness and presentment—his ' communicable pattern '.[1] The one exception was the idea of Time.

As we saw in Chapter I, the modern man is tempted, almost compelled, to regulate this idea by the face of a clock and the pages of a calendar. This system is indispensable to an age of fixed hours and appointments, but cannot ever satisfy man's consciousness of what passes in his own head. It suggests or confirms the fiction that life is a sequence of continuous yet distinct moments, a perpetual birth of instantaneous impressions, whereas all artistic and imaginative experience insists that life as we perceive it is duration. For example, the first note of a fugue is still present when the last note is struck ; the first scene in a well-constructed drama is as close to us as the episode on which the final curtain descends. All life is fusion

[1] M. Johnson, *Art and Scientific Thought*, 1944.

as well as flux ; so much so, that childhood's impressions become part of the grown man ; and Past combines with Present to form the outlines of the Future. Some visionaries claim the power to relive their own antecedents and to be present at what is going to happen. These persuasions might be, and generally are, dismissed as wishful thinking, though the acceptance of eternity implies the acceptance that all facts are forever present ; but now science was beginning to hint that Time takes place within us.

The man of letters would not trouble to follow the speculations of Aristotle, Isaac Barrow, Newton, Einstein, and Minkowski, though he would probably have heard of them, but if he glanced through Sir Arthur Eddington's *The Nature of the Physical World* (1928) he would gather from Chapter III that we perceive more than what is instantaneous and simultaneous. What seems to be happening now, may really have happened seconds, minutes, hours, days, or even years earlier, or we may be able to see it as if happening later. The mistaken impression of a time-sequence prevails only so far as our perceptions are restricted to the first three Dimensions as revealed in Euclid—that is, the so-called static relationships of matter. It appears quite otherwise when the mind acquires a sense of the Fourth Dimension and learns how to move backward and forward in that 'continuum.' So there may well be scientific truth in the intuitionist's claim that insight transcends our limits of the Present.

From the earliest ages it has been believed that the Past and the Future lie about us, felt but not seen. Now hard-headed thinkers are hinting that the mysterious veil may be of our own making, due to the limitations of our intellect, itself operating within the prison of Time.

These doubts and guesses have been profoundly stimulated by the recent work of psychologists and metaphysicians, notably by S. Alexander (*Space, Time, and Deity*), H. L. Bergson (*Évolution Créatrice* and *La Perception du Changement*), J. E. Boodin (*Time and Reality*), B. Bosanquet (*Value and Destiny of the Individual*), F. H. Bradley (*Appearance and Reality*), J. W. Dunne (*Experiment with Time*, and *The Serial Universe*), J. A. Gunn (*The Problem of Time*), W. R. Inge (*God and the Astronomer*), J. M. E. McTaggart (*Nature of Existence*), Von Hügel (*Eternal Life*).

Those who ignore popular manuals on Physics are not likely to have studied these philosophic treatises, but they all emphasize the recent importance of the problem, and are making their influence felt, even on those who know something of their gist only by hearsay. They all help us to realize more deeply that Time is not a matter of timepieces and almanacks, but of events happening one after another in space ; that sometimes this sequence is so closely knit and the changes operate so slowly that we know them only as persistence or duration—at least, such is their appearance to our perceptions, which are notoriously unreliable. Nevertheless if these impressions can be raised to the level of our super-intellectual experiences, we become conscious that 'going-on-ness' implies a cosmic growth and progress, of a quality to be inferred only through study of the apparent flux around us; perhaps (as Alexander puts it) a *nisus* towards Deity; perhaps (as Bosanquet puts it) a principle of impermanence, novelty, and originativeness which are 'the very source of our freedom and inspiration'. If so, the ancient image of the Womb of Time may be a philosophic truth. Its real nature may be such that we can indeed relive the 'Past' and foretaste the 'Future'. Nay, more, if we examine the phenomenon philosophically, we may possibly be able to deduce, as McTaggart believes, that Time is but an appearance, *mis*-perceived by our senses, and that the only reality is the Eternal Now.

Thus the modern spirit of inquiry is leading us back towards ancient Oriental mysticism and medieval theology. At any rate we have yet another field of sentiment and speculation in which the imagination can wander, and the reason learn to extend its range.[1]

Some poets, especially the Symbolists, are convinced that they can slip into the hidden area, and prose-writers are following them. We have already seen how Hinton, Wells, and Newbolt [2] played with the idea. Henry James laboured on it in *The Sense of the Past*, which he left unfinished. C. A. E. Moberly and E. F. Jourdain presented an intriguing aspect of the problem in *An Adventure* (1911). P. D. Ouspensky in *A New Model of the Universe* (composed 1910–29) speculated on the possibilities. R. A. Wilson worked the idea into *The Miraculous Birth of Language* (1937). We shall see later how Aldous Huxley and T. S. Eliot looked to this hypothesis for an assurance of reality. Had its influence been more penetrating *The Unquiet Grave* (C. Connolly, 1945) might not have been so unquiet, nor even a grave.

[1] For one of the latest discussions, see M. F. Cleugh's *Time* (1937).
[2] *Ante*, pp. 26, 74.

CHAPTER X

LEADING INTERPRETERS OF THE INTERWAR PERIOD

WILLIAM SOMERSET MAUGHAM (1874-   )

To be consulted : P. Dottin, *Somerset Maugham et ses Romans,* 1928 ; F. T. Bason, *A Bibliography of the Writings of William Somerset Maugham,* 1931 ; S. Guéry, *La Philosophie de Somerset Maugham ;* R. H. Ward, *William Somerset Maugham,* 1937.

[*Son of a solicitor attached to the British Embassy in Paris, where he passed his boyhood. At the death of his father, transferred to the guardianship of an old-fashioned and egoistic clergyman in a depressingly provincial parish, and sent to King's School at Canterbury. When his time came to leave, he insisted on spending some months in Germany (mostly at Heidelberg), and enjoyed his personal liberty so much that he thereafter refused to submit to the undergraduate restrictions of Cambridge. So instead of taking the Law Tripos, he entered St. Thomas's as a medical student in 1892. There he escaped from the philistine respectability of his own station in society and acquired a grim impression of life, from which he never escaped. The first fruits of this experience was* Liza of Lambeth *(1897), a piece of descriptive realism, crude and formless, but terribly true to the need of birth-control in the slums.*

Did not take his M.D., and as his first literary effort attracted notice and promised success, he drifted almost at once into writing as a livelihood.

1898–1908, produced eight novels and two farces without much success. 1911–1913, produced eight plays also inconspicuous till in 1907 he employed the Golding Bright agency, and secured in that year three placements which ran concurrently. This unusual success made his reputation.

1913–1920, abandoned the theatre. In 1915 published Of Human Bondage, *an autobiographical narrative, as inconsequential as* Liza of Lambeth, *which nevertheless expressed the contemporary mood and eventually became a household word, in that the author confessed to all the less objectionable frailties of human nature. Thereafter, partly in War service, but also to counteract his own self-consciousness, he took seven long journeys in both hemispheres (including the South Seas and China), in search of more objective material. The result was* The Moon and Sixpence *(1919) and* The Trembling of a Leaf *(1921), his first masterpieces in narrative.*

1920–1924, returned to the theatre, producing eight plays, of which The Circle *(1921) and* Our Betters *(1923) mark the maturing of his dramatic talent. 1925–1928, produced three novels, especially* The Painted Veil *(1925). 1928–1932, produced some of his best work both for the theatre and the book-market, notably* The Breadwinner (1930), For Services Rendered (1932), Sheppey (1933) *for the former;* Cakes and Ale (1930), The Narrow Corner (1932), A Christmas Holiday (1940), The Razor's Edge (1944) *for the latter.*

Though born in the 'seventies and an author in the 'nineties, he acquired neither his style nor his attitude till the interwar period. At his best he is more cosmopolitan than Kipling or Conrad, while his interest in human nature and all its contradictions is perhaps deeper and certainly more expert than theirs.

Out of nearly fifty publications, he will be remembered for about a dozen.]

LITERARY AND IDEOLOGICAL BACKGROUND

As a student at St. Thomas's Hospital Maugham began by acquiring a medical man's attitude to life ; that means a professional familiarity with the defective organization of the body and consequently of the mind. So much so, that creation seemed quite purposeless. He never forgot having once treated a young child who was born simply to die of meningitis ; and with such evidence daily before his eyes, he could not help concluding that conduct is influenced not by principles, but by the impact of desires. As an evolutionist, he was all too conscious of the caveman stirring within us, impatient to break away from the civilization which we had not the intelligence to control and readapt to our best purposes. Yet even in his student days he realized that despite all these futilities and misfortunes, man sometimes rose above himself by producing or perceiving beauty.

His literary biography is a history of these discoveries and rediscoveries, and of the arts by which he projected them into his impressions of conduct and character. But he had first to arrange and unify his ideas, and, if possible, to co-ordinate and interpret his observation of facts. He claims to have dipped into some of the best philosophers, from Berkeley to Whitehead ; but if so, he found little to disprove his pessimism, but something to encourage his artistic instinct : what he called ' the poetry of disciplined thought '.[1] These thinkers had constructed a pattern of spiritual life out of their educated self-consciousness. Could he not similarly impose his personality on experience, using plays and novels to express the result ? If he learnt anything more definite than an attitude, it was Schopenhauer's doctrine of *The Will* as the only reality within the range of human experience, the innate, immanent, and inseparable quality which preserves and asserts the identity of each particular person or thing, and which can be more intelligibly suggested by art than induction.

At any rate our author was led by his temperament and experiences to visualize this aspect of reality in ordinary human beings, including himself—' the need of self-assertion which is in every living thing and which keeps it alive. It is the very essence of man.' [2]

[1] *The Summing Up*, 1928.   [2] *Ibid.*

This philosophy had to be presented in a form which satisfied the author, but also pleased other people. Obviously the bourgeois novel and domestic comedy of the nineteenth century would not leave him a free hand within their conventional limits. In fact he travelled abroad so far and frequently in order to escape the middle-class sameness of Europe. The experiences he sought would sooner be found in a jungle than in a garden. But he had to learn all he could from his predecessors, and it is significant that among English authors he valued Dryden, Swift and Fielding for the lucidity of their style, but modelled his point of view and constructive methods on Voltaire's *Nouvelles* and de Maupassant's *Contes*. He particularly admired their arts of surprise, and the make-believe which, avoiding the detailed documentation of the professed realists, aims at artistic effect.

The portrait is not yet complete. This scientifically minded student of self-assertiveness was not likely to ignore his own need of self-assertion. But he has assured us in *The Summing Up* that he was then poor, infirm, insignificant, nervous and unloved. Not being able to command respect, he was compelled to buy it. He must make a fortune out of best-sellers and plays with long runs, and become a man of importance. So he began his career by cultivating the tastes of his contemporaries rather than his own. Consequently he did not find his true scope till he was verging on middle age. In the meantime he taught himself how to tell a story objectively, with an artist's regard for the economy of effect.

HIS APPRENTICESHIP

The success of Pinero, H. A. Jones, Wilde, Shaw, and Hankin convinced him that the theatre was the quickest and most gentlemanly road to fortune. Inclination led him to believe that the playwright had a better chance, if already known as a novelist. So he began by writing stories such as the English middle-class were accustomed to read. *Mrs. Craddock* (1902) is his most successful effort.

So with his early plays. He acquired the knack of ridiculing the fashions and frivolities of his age with elegance and humour. Now and then he strikes a spark out of human nature as revealed in the Comedy of Manners, taking Congreve as his master. *The Land of Promise* (1913) is the consummation of this phase.

He reached the first turning-point in his career when he temporarily withdrew from the theatre and tried to weave his own experiences and frustrations into a life-pattern. Existence might be a jigsaw puzzle, but the fragments could be worked into a design. It finally appeared as *Of Human Bondage* (1915).

These confessions had an unexpected success because Maugham applied the technique of *Candide*. Voltaire had invented an *ingenu* whom he dragged through the cruelty, injustice, and false sentiment of the eighteenth century. Our author invents a child of nature with a club foot (instead of his own stammer), and trails him through the futile routine of our overcrowded middle-class occupations, riddled with cant, economic slavery, and the sexual instincts which civilization excites and perverts. Maugham is just as detached as Voltaire. Yet his narrative is even more devastating because he feels the sting of writing about somebody very like himself. At the same time Philip Carey is too much the scapegoat of his age to be a reliable self-portrait. He has no mind of his own, self-control, or spiritual refinement. Lacking any talent or aptitude, he drifts. In the course of his vagaries he meets other drifters, as futile as himself, but more tragic because more self-deceived. The author had intended to entitle his novel ' Beauty out of Ashes '. There are ashes in plenty, but no beauty. The narrative is prolix and ill constructed, and the ending is an anti-climax.

Nevertheless, *Of Human Bondage* is a remarkable achievement. Maugham may be solely concerned with the telling of the story, but the reader closes the volume with two other impressions which ought to unsettle everyone's habit of mind. First, one perceives that Philip, and indeed the other characters, are not their own true selves. Modern society seems to insist on the collectivization of the entire human personality. Even the study of art and of science is vitiated by its encroachments. So the irreconcilable individualist can no longer maintain his inward freedom ; he can only escape, with burnt wings, into some factitious egoism.[1] In the next place, this enslavement may concern a social thinker, but offers little scope to a novelist. If the European civilization of safe-careers and salaried specializations gives no elbow-room to the inner man, it also gives none to the creative writer—at least not for novelists like Maugham.

HIS MATURITY

When *Of Human Bondage* appeared, Maugham was already abroad. Intermittently he wandered East and West for several years, picking up copy. Henceforth he is to be ranked with the fraternity of cosmopolitan authors. He certainly returned to his art a new man, having observed decivilized human nature. His mind gained freedom while studying those who were free. Though he subsequently revived the themes of his first period, he seldom forgot the insight learnt through travel. Many younger novelists[2] for the same reason have searched far afield, including Forrest Reid, E. R. Eddison, Graham Greene, and Frederic Prokosch.

Maugham lost no time in applying his lesson, drawing as always on facts, sometimes to excess. Paris was beginning to ' discover ' Gauguin, and was impressed, somewhat superficially, by his deep burning colours, strange savage faces, naked bodies, and luxuriant vegetation, which glows and palpitates. Here was beauty imposed

---

[1] Cf. Nicholas Berdyaev, *Slavery and Freedom* (1944), whom Maugham to some degree anticipates.   [2] Cf. *ante*, p. 91.

on wildness, and the artist set himself to do with his pen what the painter had done with his brush. So *The Moon and Sixpence* was published in 1919, the story of a second victim of collectivization, who revolted just in time at the dangerous age; like Gauguin surrendered himself to the artist's ferocious egoism; became a veritable bear without a ring in his nose; and died of leprosy at Tahiti, where Gauguin had died of syphilis. The theme is unusual; the treatment even more so. Its resemblance to Conrad is superficial because Charles Strickland, the erstwhile suburban stockbroker, is not haunted by his past. His character is conceived on the principle that a man is not tied to his own identity. We can always and at any time die and be reborn, or as T. S. Eliot would say, 'In my end is my beginning'. Nor could this kind of transformation be developed by the older novelistic method as an inner biography or autobiography, because the transformed character is himself unaware of the stages through which he has passed; or so we are led to suppose. So Maugham borrowed from the technique of a stage-play and recorded the death and rebirth through their influence on other people's thoughts and conduct. Strickland's altered personality lives in broken reflections spread over the perplexity and amazement of his circle, including the author. We glimpse a fresh aspect as often as we glimpse the sayings and sentiments of the secondary characters, who do not alter, though they are portrayed with admirable insight and humour.

Within the same period Maugham produced other fiction in a similar vein, especially *The Trembling of a Leaf* (1921), a collection of short stories on characters observed in the South Sea Islands. All depict the erratic will-power of Europeans seeking their true primitive selves stupidly, recklessly, or tragically, amid the languorous beauty of tropical scenery.

Maugham was still barely fifty years old, and with this widened horizon before him, one might have expected more discoveries of eccentricity hidden in human nature, since he knew where to look for them. But fiction rarely brings in money as quickly as the theatre, and is more difficult to write. Besides, an audience, in Maugham's experience, is comparatively easy to satisfy. It is susceptible to mass suggestion, and therefore enjoys recognizing familiar notions in an unfamiliar form. So within these lucrative limits our playwright-novelist was well advised not to spring psychological surprises on his patrons. It was safer to play on current sentiments, relying on his craftsmanship to keep his ' houses ' together. These precautions, of course, did not exclude oriental backgrounds and the humours of character.

The result is notable. Maugham now appears as the masterly technician in stage-sense, and also as the mirror of interwar sentiments and sensationalism. He swung from the comedy of manners to that of morals, or rather of immorality. His protagonists are not sordid or subhuman, but apparently insensible to any motive but their own inclinations and otherwise as good as you and I. Nor does he conceal that his adventurers, sensualists, and law-breakers are playing with fire. One feels that the ghost of tragedy is lurking somewhere behind the scenes, waiting for the cue, which does not come, because there is no eternal law to vindicate. There is only the artist's ability to manoeuvre events and sustain interest through craftsmanship. His best examples are *The Circle* (1921), *The Letter* (1925), *The Sacred Flame* (1928). It is wonderful what tactical concentration can do.

HIS LAST PHASE

Before Maugham was sixty he at last began to feel sympathy with our frailty, and a sense of human goodness. This change of heart is unmistakable in *Cakes and Ale or The Skeleton in the Cupboard* (1930), his greatest or second greatest novel. It is not a satire on Hardy (as at first supposed), but on the humbug surrounding an author of Hardy's eminence. The ' skeleton ' is that in all our cupboards : our real and original selves, a wraith which goes its solitary way, squeezed between the public character we put on, wherewith to face the world, and the more private but equally artificial character we absorb out of our domestic and personal habits. Lawrence had for some years been writing much about this ' original self ' as a matter of the diaphragm and thoracic ganglia, revealed in the anomalies of sex attraction. Maugham reveals it in petty subterfuges and affectations, and refers to it as ' a jest in the eternal mind '. This cosmic farce is not a complete success, because the author makes too much of the puzzlements, surprises, and humorous mistakes of the secondary characters. But no reader can mistake ' Rosie ', the eternal lover, incidentally a nymphomaniac and adultress, yet sublime in her tranquil beauty and kindness of heart, untamed by the parochialism which the others cannot escape.

What Maugham just failed to engrave on his novel, he could only suggest in his next two plays. *For Services Rendered* (1932) is a drama of post-war misery, of which the plot is keenly pointed and the histrionic opportunities are admirable. There is an unmistakable note of deep pity and indignation, but the pathos is depressing without being impressive. *Sheppey* (1933) is a tragi-comedy touched with farce. The hero has a heart of gold and also the oddities of a stage fool. Unfortunately angels in disguise are not easily naturalized in stage-land. The novel was the only medium for this erstwhile cynic's humanitarianism. After some more attempts, notably the vivid *The Narrow Corner* (1932), he achieved complete and characteristic expression in *A Christmas Holiday* (1940). It is an experiment in a character which can be felt without being seen. Berger is the mainspring of the neatly adjusted mechanism, an attractive, artistic and humorous beast of prey who cares nothing for the human species, least of all when embodied in himself. We never meet him in person, but we do meet those affected by his personality, and they introduce us to the heartaches, false values, desperate expedients, grinding poverty, and, above all, heroism gone to waste in a world-capital. Still true to Voltaire's technique, he develops this study in futility through the eyes of an ingenuous young Englishman who knows nothing of life outside the well-bred, leisurely comfort of the upper middle-class. Charlie, and perhaps the reader, is left wondering, at odd moments, whether existence must be always nothing but a painful mystery.

That question is partly answered in *The Razor's Edge* (1944), which presents a circle of well-nourished, well-salaried, and well-mannered Americans—interwar civilization at its best. And yet they are not truly civilized. Had their circumstances been less comfortable, their characters would not have stood the strain. As it is, their worldly preoccupations render them self-centred, superficial, and at times ridiculous. All except the young Irish airman, who knows something of the mystery of death, and has resolved to know more of the mystery of life. He gets nearest to the revelation through the paths of Hindu mysticism, and thereby learns how to ignore all the commercialized values and creature comforts of his environment, absorbed in union with the Universal Spirit, and therefore in love with his fellow-creatures. Maugham, as a story-teller, is judiciously vague about Larry's researches and convictions, but he is the only character whom his creator respects. So do we. Apart from these moral implications, the student will find in this last novel the most complete example of Maugham's technique. Assuredly the old craftsman has lost none of his cunning.

MAUGHAM'S FUTURE

As regards his comedies, the best will hold the stage (after the usual post-mortem interval) because their author understands the mass-psychology of the theatre, and knows how to relieve a situation with touches of humour which are all his own. So he gives the cast ample opportunity to do justice to his ideas.

His novels are better than his plays, but their position is less assured. At first Maugham impresses us as a most accomplished representative of the old objective school, a disciple of Voltaire and de Maupassant. Then we notice that he has added to his skill in narrative the technique of the playwright; his protagonists become vivid through their effect on the 'feeding' characters; again a tradition, much honoured by Molière. By these means his studies in eccentricity dawn on the reader with a shock of surprise, all the more real because astonishing, and with a unique comic flavour. In his first two periods he presents life as a disappointing business, offering the sole consolation of insight through art. With advancing years he perceives that human oddities may be so, chiefly because they are more earnest and less self-seeking than conventional people, and therefore worthier members of society, though still just as comic. His work has a progressive quality, without which an author seldom survives. If England is about to undergo a period of State administration in which social service will be coupled with intellectual conformity, Maugham may be honoured as a champion of individuality. But posterity, already overburdened with its literary heritage, is likely to overlook one who neither founded nor followed a school, especially as certain contemporaries are more conspicuously original.

DAVID HERBERT LAWRENCE (1885–1930)

To be consulted : Letters of D. H. Lawrence, with Introduction by A. Huxley, 1932; J. M. Murry, *Son of Woman* (1931); H. Kingsmill: *D. H. Lawrence*, 1938.

[*Son of a miner and a talented woman with middle-class aspirations. 1901, began as shop assistant, then qualified for his teaching certificate at Nottingham, and taught for five years at Croydon. 1910, his mother, who had restrained and possibly absorbed his sexual impulses, died, and her son began to develop rapidly. In 1911 published* The White Peacock, *and after a severe attack of pneumonia quitted teaching and lived precariously by his pen. In 1912 seduced and in 1914 married Frieda Weekley (née von Richthofen), and under her influence, living much of the time in Switzerland or Italy, produced* Love Poems and Others *and* Sons and Lovers *in 1913,* The Rainbow *in 1915, and* Women in Love *in 1916 (not published till 1920). Though not a pacifist, he was an indiscreet individualist, and 1916–18 fell under public suspicion amounting almost to persecution. In 1919 he tried living abroad, mostly in Mediterranean countries, convinced that postwar England was exhausted as a source of culture. Not finding what he sought except as revealed in* Aaron's Rod (1922), *he returned in 1923 to his own country. Then resumed his wanderings, this time in search of the primitive, chiefly in Australia, which he soon quitted, and New Mexico, which inspired some of his best prose and poetry. To this period belong* Birds, Beasts and Flowers (1923), The Kangaroo (1923), The Plumed Serpent (1926), Lady Chatterley's Lover (1928), Pornography and Obscenity (1929). *1930, died of consumption at Venice.*

His troubled, restless career is one of the most remarkable records of man's effort at self-realization. He made many enemies, and few authors of genius have had more reason to complain that the worst of them was himself.]

LITERARY AND IDEOLOGICAL BACKGROUND

Among gifted authors, Lawrence is the one self-made Englishman, who did not even try to assimilate middle-class customs and

L

culture. To his dying day he remained a plebeian well read but ill bred; too talented, of course, to associate with his own people; too morbidly eccentric to mix with the better educated, except a group of friends, with whom he generally quarrelled. So he stood alone, impatient of literary standards and traditions, starting with a working-man's sense of life, and an artist's passion for self-expression.

Self-development begins with self-knowledge, and he began by trying to extricate his instincts from the muddle of lower-class existence, mostly passed in a stuffy miner's cottage, and that is why he dwells more than is just on his mother's influence. In the next place, as the son of a miner, he had ample opportunity of undervaluing the industrialism and mechanization which are the life of democracy, and of overvaluing the life of the soil, among the farms which encircle the colliery belt. He went 'back to the land', at heart a child of nature, using his education to regain this birthright of which civilization had dispossessed him. His love and understanding of animals have won him many admirers.

So has his sense of natural surroundings. But he was less concerned with their effect on his readers than on himself. That effect became tremendous. When writing on Hardy he speaks of ' the vast uncomprehended and uncomprehensible morality of nature or of life itself, surpassing human consciousness ',[1] and he was gradually convinced that if this ' waste enormity ' and ' terrific action ' could be reconciled with society's modes and manners, a ' supreme art ' would result. So he surrendered himself to these mysterious forces, never shrinking from what he imagined to be their influence and impulse. F. R. Leavis talks of his ' terrifying honesty '; Vernon Lee declares that ' he sees more than a human being ought to see '. Such is the rhetoric of contemporary criticism. In reality, Lawrence reveals nothing at which to close one's eyes or stop one's ears. Many have tasted his experiences, though few have externalized them and used them to create a deeper, more satisfying sense of their own personality. Lawrence is unique because he tried to do so. Each novel or poem was one step more towards a complete self-portrait. Nevertheless it is undeniable that nature seemed to penetrate and trouble his being in some mysterious way, and he could not help trying to realize how and why he was part of the mystery.

Hence his impatience with Victorian traditions, whether literary or social. His artistic ideal was spontaneity—the expression of his original, uncontaminated selfhood retraced to the vital sources of universal being. To a poet the revelation might come on the wind-swept downs, in the silence of a forest, amid the liveliness of a farmyard, or when struck by the beauty and strength of animals. To a novelist it would come with human contacts, especially the

[1] *Phoenix, The Posthumous Papers of D. H. Lawrence,* edited by E. D. McDonald, 1936.

attractions and distractions of love. Lawrence most certainly had
the perceptiveness of a poet, but even more the sympathies of a
novelist, because his sexual problem was his most urgent preoccupation.

He was born and bred in the class familiar with love as a physical
act, undisguised by prudery. On the other hand, he began to think
and observe in a cottage surprisingly well supplied with books (if
Sons and Lovers is a true picture), and dominated by his mother's
insistence on proprieties. As a student at Nottingham, and teacher
at Croydon, he had little opportunity to know himself till he fell in
love with Frieda Weekley. He describes their association as ' a
wonderful, naked intimacy, all kindled with warmth which I know
at last is love '. The experience made him an artist, but it was not
complete, because the relationship was not complete. Though the
undercurrents of their being brought them together, the overcurrents
kept them apart. She was the daughter of a German Freiherr, and
he the son of a drunken miner. The tension pervaded their married
life, and consequently the husband's writing. He was unable to
think of love except as sexual attraction or repulsion.

It is obvious that Lawrence, more than confident in his unaided
genius, was little beholden to the culture of his time, except so far as
it encouraged or enlarged his intuitions. E. Seillière [1] connects him
with the neo-naturalism inaugurated by Schelling's *Ideas towards
a Philosophy of Nature* (1797) and developed by Rudolph Steiner
and Ludwig Klages. Lawrence does not allude to these or any
other such pseudo-Oriental doctrinaires. In his letters he alludes
to his interest in Frazer and Tylor,[2] and affects an indifference to
Freud, whom he must at least have discussed. The basic articles
of his philosophy can severally be found either in Carpenter's
Civilization ; its Cause and Cure [3] or Cummings's *Diary of a Disappointed Man.*[4] His inspiration and expressiveness owe very little
to books and very much to life.

HIS PRE-WAR PERIOD

The White Peacock (1911), his first important work, composed
easily and spontaneously while he was still a teacher at Croydon, is
his most natural though not naturalistic novel. His manner has
been compared to Hardy's, but the resemblance is superficial. In
the first place, the innumerable conversations seem pointless till
one notes that they all dally with the outer fringe of sex attraction
and repulsion, and secondly, Cyril, the self-effacing observer, is
homosexual in so far that he needs another man to lean upon and
is disappointed in George Saxton, the virile, well-favoured young
farmer who fades away into drunkenness and death, because he has

---

[1] *David-Herbert Lawrence et les Récentes Idéologies Allemandes*, 1936.
[2] *Ante*, p. 120.   [3] *Ante*, pp. 120–1.   [4] *Ante*, pp. 129 ff.

no true sense of life and its spiritual possibilities. The country atmosphere and touches of animal life are the book's abiding charm.

Lawrence had learnt much by the time he published *Sons and Lovers*, his most autobiographical novel, in 1913. It tells how a family of boys are so dominated by their mother's affection that when they grow up they cannot love, but only lust. That was the fate which the author had just escaped. Nevertheless the interest in the Morel family, especially in Paul the artist, is admirably sustained; and this achievement is all the more remarkable because, though the characters are always doing or saying something, our attention is fascinated by their underlying thoughts. Lawrence now knows how to let his personages go their own way, according to their own lights, quite indifferent to the social framework in which they are supposed to move. However, the novel is too much of a confession. ' One sheds one's sicknesses in books.' [1] But if so, like any other invalid, whether physical or moral, he makes too much of his ailments. He has not yet learnt to efface himself in the many-sided spectacle of human nature. Nor did he ever learn.

Lawrence must himself have realized this limitation, for his next effort, *The Rainbow* (1915), is much deeper and more varied. He may have learnt something from Balzac's, Zola's, or Proust's studies in domestic ramifications, for this ' novel of the family tree ' covers the destinies of a numerous and ill-assorted kinship spread over many pursuits and two generations. There are pictures of contemporary society, farm life, existence in suburban villas, and the activities of University students; above all, the primitive, pagan magic of the land, with the rhythm of the seasons, and the uncanny, sensual power of nightfall in summer heat. Some of these passages are as good as any in twentieth-century literature.

So it would seem that the artist had acquired a wider, more externalized sense of character and destiny, and thereby achieved his own integration. Yet in reality the advance had left him in a veritable wilderness of self-discovery. Some of the most vivid pages describe prurient marriage-bed antagonisms, and even more impulsive and surreptitious adulteries, all ending in the humiliation of the male and the dehumanizing of the female. He is already bringing into his fiction the emotional tensions of his married life; and the strain has uncovered his naked, prehuman self. In the first place, he tends to blur the outlines of his men and women, and to merge their individualities in the universal sex instinct. In the next place, he tends to diffuse not only the characterization, but the structure of his novel in a pervading sense of atmosphere. Such is the weakness of the composition according to academic standards, such is its strength according to D. H. Lawrence. He feels that he is at last penetrating to the heart of nature, outside time, a part of the earth and skies, in harmony with the vague impulses and influences which must for countless ages have swayed human beings.

[1] To A. D. McLeod, 27 Oct., 1913.

Consequently intellect, will-power, and the tricks of personality are mere accretions which encrust the dark, deep stream of life; mere superficialities hiding the essential truth. He compared his study to the rainbow, a mysterious and immemorial symbol which seems to rise from the earth, traverse the skies, and descend again to the earth. The novel is an original and disturbing adventure among ideas; and was banned by the censor.

A similar story is reflected in *Love Poems and Others* (1913), *Amores* (1916), *Look We have Come Through* (1917). These verses explore every family quarrel and every lascivious secret, so that he can let his imagination loose among the subterranean currents of his being and indulge them without sacrificing his artistic consciousness. Almost every poem can be attached to some experience. They are born of passion, but not of 'passion recollected in tranquillity'. Each is an effort to isolate the passing mood and fix it for what it is worth at the moment. 'Life, the ever present,' he asserted five years later,[1] 'knows no finality, no finished crystallization.' On the other hand, as D. S. Savage has pointed out,[2] this fixation of the 'instant present' has not the collected meditative power of experiences matured and fused into new and significant combinations. It is outside the tradition of authentic poetry. Lawrence would agree and add that 'free verse' is not meant to be like 'restricted verse'. It aims at catching the impulse in its flight, flashes of lightning which the great masters have never been able to photograph, a revelation which transcends the established methods. As such, these experiments are not completely successful —if success is possible—but an impartial critic must recognize the poet's sense of rhythm adapted to the mood, his alertness, his sincerity, and the vigour and directness of his symbolism.

Both in prose and poetry Lawrence had developed a genius for expressiveness, but his mind, which seemed to be prospecting everywhere for truth, had crept into a narrow, tortuous channel.

HIS INTERWAR PERIOD

Up to this point the tendency of Lawrence's art was unpremeditated. He simply followed his feelings. But the outbreak of war brought many troubles and trials to him and his German wife, and gave an embittered and aggressive turn to his ideas. He now began to believe with Otto Spengler that European culture had run its course and was sinking down into a second Dark Age. That was yet another reason why artists, if any were left, would have to begin their quest all over again, starting as if from the Bronze Age. He now turned of set purpose to the current ideas mooted in folklore and anthropology. He persuaded himself that evolution is a word without meaning, for there is no development of new faculties out of primordial energy. The life-force contained all our powers

[1] Pref. to American ed. of *New Poems*, 1920.
[2] *The Personal Principle*, 1944.

in their full vigour from the very beginning, and if they now decay it is due to the desiccating blight of civilization. All should be convinced that our only hope is to explore ' the warm creative stir ' at the basis of life, then follow the instincts, exercising our acquired intelligence, and thus find our way to the realization of the spirit, to ' pure relationship and living truth '.

The first step towards self-rescue is made in *Women in Love* (written in 1916, published 1920). At first glance it reads like his pre-war work; and in the end the story brings two pairs of men and women together. But the upshot leaves a different impression. Gerald and Gudrun cannot escape their mental consciousness and fail to unite. Ursula and Birkin complete each other because their love is ' mindless sensuality '. Through sheer physical contact they realize ' the immemorial magnificence of mystic, palpable, real otherness '. The novel is not one more record of disappointment or frustration.

Meanwhile, like so many of his contemporaries, Lawrence was seeking inspiration outside England. His novels become wider in scope. He fills them with the manners and customs of foreigners, and his backgrounds are often chosen from the wildest, darkest, and most primitive landscapes. He was particularly impressed by Australia, its prehistoric gloom contrasting with the dreamlike, mechanical existence of its inhabitants; or Mexico, abounding in filth, sordid sensuality, and the cults of aboriginal gods, on a background of blazing colours. His characters also become more adventurous.

At the same time he writes like a prophet with a mission, exhorting us to new gestures, embraces, and emotions. In *Aaron's Rod* (1922) and *The Kangaroo* (1923) he preaches a society founded not on the family, but on what Whitman would call ' the love of comrades ', and Lawrence calls ' mate-love ' or ' mate-trust ', the intercommunion between an heroic leader and an enthusiastic disciple, a bond of mutual dependence and aspiration without which the human being is not complete. The homosexual ideal, which he touched on and abandoned in *The White Peacock*, has at last found its proper setting. It is also implied in *The Plumed Serpent* (1926). This is one of his most remarkable novels. He pictures the ancient Mexican community, sullen, bitter, and apathetic because it cannot catch up with civilization, and still prolific in men who do not think through their brains, but through the impulses of their bodies— ' pure sensuality with a powerful purity of its own '—or as if the body were ' the flame of the soul '. There are some strikingly original portraits, and Lawrence tries to weave his story round them, so as to convince us that natural women and especially men will unite and co-operate, not so much for a ' reciprocity of power ' as a ' reciprocity of tenderness '. He does not succeed; though his experience has widened, he is still burdened by his haunting indecision and sense of impotence.

the surface.   Literary tradition means permanence in change.   We have now to see how far this philosophy could justify itself in the light of poetry.

HE CLIMBS PUBLICITY HILL

His verse and prose had already begun to appear in periodicals when he first challenged the attention of the wider public with a reprint in book form, *Prufrock and Other Observations* (1917).   This volume of satires on subjects not worth satirizing—sordid episodes, and characters without character—was mostly conceived, if not composed, before he left America, about 1910.   At any rate it applies to the pre-war world.   Its apparent freakishness, inconsequence, and clipped visions would have been unforgivable except for the individuality of its style.   There is something so compelling and concentrated in the succession of images that one reads on to see what it is all about.   Besides, though the themes are unedifying, the author is not so.   He writes with a cold contempt, utterly uncontaminated by his subject, worthy of the best traditions of satire ; and if his manner is provocative, it is studied.   Then it began to be noted that though his sketches reminded one of an impressionist picture, they had unity of tone ; the details were in keeping with the composition.   Very few perceived, despite the introductory quotation, that, like Dante, this seeming modernist was taking a preliminary trip into the colourless, ignoble Inferno of our days, and trying to reproduce his impressions as graphically and unconventionally ; revealing without sharing the attitudes of his victims.

At any rate it was soon to be realized that this new and challenging author had no intention of overwriting himself.   His next slim volume, *Poems* (1920), was as carefully studied as the first and in much the same tone.   *Gerontion* was accepted as an obscure and allusive monologue fanciful in its expressiveness but unmistakable in its intention ; reproducing the confusion in the speaker's head—not the author's.

HIS INTERWAR PERIOD

Verses which are easy to read may sometimes for that very reason be left unread.   The public occasionally likes to be put on its mettle, and provoked into looking for significance hidden behind a sequence of images, ' the word within a word, unable to speak a word '.   Moreover, Eliot had already shown that, even if satirizing vice and futility, he could nevertheless probe here and there among his dreary scenes for moments of true poetic feeling.   *Waste Land* (1922) is the consummation of these principles.   He no longer confines himself to the absurdities and abuses of modern civilization, but strikes to its roots, or rather its lack of roots.   In his judgement we have lost touch with the scheme of life.   For instance, primitive people were wiser than we are.   They realized that human nature was rooted in procreation, and kept before their eyes the powers of life and death, and symbolized these influences in fertility rites, folk-lore, and magic. Hence the myths and allegories rediscovered in Frazer's *Golden Bough* and Weston's *From Ritual to Romance*. We have lost the discipline of such visions, partly because science has imposed a materialistic, hand-to-mouth civilization, partly because we have unlearnt the ancient oriental art of contemplation, and possibly because our older, saner culture has run its term and is dry, like a land wasting for want of water.

This theme is presented to our ' poetic sense ' in a short series of graphic and startling examples, enriched with the symbolic expressiveness of Biblical, Classical, and Renaissance poets. The allusions are so frequent and recondite that the author feels compelled to add a commentary on his own text, after the manner of Todd on Milton. Many readers merely glance at the notes, but their neglect does not matter, for the poem, despite its erudition, is essentially superficial. Eliot not only overlooks the undercurrent of inventiveness and humanity, which is struggling against the curse of Adam, but he trifles with the symptoms of our alleged demoralization, adducing a few fornicators, unscrupulous financiers, pubcrawlers, workers before dawn, and urban uncleanliness; blemishes which always have and always will disgrace society even at its best, even in Elizabethan London or Periclean Athens. The moralist is still the unreclaimed satirist.

Nevertheless, his cinematographic fugue of impressions, with their abrupt transitions, disconcerting strangeness and puzzlements, all so skilfully blended and dramatically suggested, create an unforgettable idea of aridity and inconsequence. Here at last is a poet who makes you *feel* his intensity. The theme was fashionable in the 'twenties, and *Waste Land* was hailed as the most convincing presentment of social aimlessness.

The versification is noticeable. In his previous poems he most often preferred a rhythmic rhetoric peculiarly his own, with rhymes, inter-rhymes, and assonances which hold attention and complete the music of the words. Sometimes he created a very effective parody of ballad metres. In and after *Waste Land* he makes more use of free verse in such a way as to conceal the economy of expression and convey the sense of unrestrained movement. *The Hollow Men* (1925) is an excellent example of this technique, and the symbolism is more simple and astringent.

The poem is also remarkable because of its change of mood. Its imagery suggests impotence, frustration, and the valley of the shadow of Death. The figures remind one of the phrases a Hebrew prophet might have used, and the poet writes as if he were conscious of a decline in his own powers. The suggestion of gloom and the sense of annihilation recur in *Ash-Wednesday* (1930), but the imagery is far from simple. Eliot seems to be calling in the help of medieval mysticism and allegory in order to produce the right atmosphere. The general import is unmistakable. It is the confession of a spirit which has looked too long on folly and futility; till it fears to become as unspiritual as they, blind to the higher influences just within reach—if the heart can be cleansed of hatred and disgust which are exhalations of the waste-land. Possibly the author feels that like Dante ' in the midway of our life ', he had lost his way in a gloomy wood. At any rate, the poem, despite its obscurities, speaks clearly of repentance and the dimness of advancing years. But if he has lost his masterly self-confidence, he has also abandoned his vigorous, mordant phraseology and the vivacity which rendered his previous work unique.

HIS LATEST PHASE

So it was to be expected that there would be a pause in the poet's progress. It lasted from 1930 to 1940. The only significant production is *Murder in the Cathedral* (1935), the drama of Becket's death retold on the theme that true martyrdom is the sacrifice of one's will, not one's life, to the will of God. Much of his criticism was published during this period, and though his best essays discuss older literature (notably Dante, Seneca, and Pascal), this body of prose-work is an indispensable introduction to his poetry. Quite in the manner of his epoch, he writes as if breaking ground for the first time, explaining what nobody had previously thought of, though in reality most of his views were commonplaces of nineteenth-century criticism. His pronouncement on the ' objective correlative ' is an example. He delivers his views with the calm confidence of an authority whom only fools would dispute. As so many of his younger contemporaries knew nothing about nineteenth-century criticism (except that Arnold was supposed to be out of date), his doctrines and judgements have opened their minds; especially because, compared with his verse, his prose is lucidity itself. Few can say so much so simply in so few words.

Meanwhile his spiritual crisis must have resolved itself; for after confessing and evincing a decline of power he began the 'forties with a series of contemplative poems, to a certain degree foreshadowed in *Ash-Wednesday* but more mellow and much wiser: *East Coker* (1940), *Burnt Norton* (1941), *The Dry Salvages* (1941), *Little Gidding* (1942).

This series reminds one of a man recapturing in retrospect some early impulse or inspiration which had been entangled and obscured among the pursuits of middle life, and must now be extricated and resumed in order to complete his development, thus making a fresh start in life. ' In my end is my beginning.'

The rebirth was to be effected partly through suffering (as also suggested in C. S. Lewis's *The Problem of Pain*), and partly through contemplation and self-discipline, somewhat after the model of oriental devotionalism. Its aim was to look beyond the instant, pressing moment and think of oneself as belonging to what was best in the Past and may be prolonged into the Future. In this chastened and impersonal mood we might come to perceive what ancient sages had taught (and modern science was confirming) that possibly we have not broken with the Past, nor renounced our own future, because the spirit exists in one eternal Now, in which Past, Present, and Future are blended. We mortals can seldom recapture the exact semblance of a past experience, because we look into our own consciousness, seeking of set purpose some particular memory of our own. But if we can unlearn this preoccupation with self and relax into a mood of humble receptivity, we may absorb the fleeting moment in such a way as to feel around us the scheme of existence, now purged of our resentment, vanity, or prejudice. It may be while listening to music ' heard so deeply that it is not heard at all ', or sympathizing with another's pain without thinking of our own, or gazing on some ancient river transfigured to serve modern needs, yet still harbouring the earliest forms of life, or noting the overlapping seasons, or meditating on ancient fertility rites at nightfall in some out-of-the-way corner of rural England, or, best of all, letting one's thoughts go free amid the ruined chapel at Little Gidding from which all recollection of conflict and effort has vanished, but where the intensity of spiritual prayer can still be felt. Perhaps our fears or hopes for the future are like a lavender spray ' pressed between the yellow leaves of a book which has never been opened '.

Such seems to be the import of these four poems. The ideas are not particularly original. As before, Eliot has availed himself of what was floating in the atmosphere, and rendered it a personal expression of his own erudite self. No one, except perhaps Donne, Vaughan, Blake, Wordsworth, or Shelley, had tried to unite so many subtle and complex strains of feeling into four short elegies ; and to shed over the combination an air of earnestness and intimacy— to be utterly unworldly and yet in touch with the world. The poet himself, more than once, confesses to the difficulty of expressing what he feels ; ' the intolerable wrestle with words and meanings '. Unfortunately the reader also has to wrestle ; not, indeed, with the ' imprecision of feelings ', for Eliot is always precise, but with the intrusion of images which baffle the sequence of ideas. Moreover, his style has lost the sting and stab of his earlier manner, of the phrase which kindles the imagination.

IS HE RIPE FOR POSTERITY ?

If Eliot writes no more he will be remembered, not very distinctly, as one of the very few interwar poets who knew what he wanted to say, and said it more pointedly than anybody else. So he exercised much influence on the interwar generation, especially from 1920 to 1930. He picked out the features of the shadowy landscape with unnatural clearness, according to his own lights. While impressing his artistic personality on every line he wrote, he cultivated the impersonality which Croce [1] advocated—that is to say, he did not impose his views; his figures, images, symbols, and transitions were assumed to be self-explanatory; and though always vivid and startling, they sometimes leave the explanation to the reader. Like all great poets, he seemed to be making us think for ourselves; hence his immediate ascendancy. But, unlike all great poets, he relied too much on puzzlement; and many of his admirers were betrayed into believing that they had found all they wanted, when they had found the explanation of this or that poem. They were satisfied to guess the riddle without making sure that the answer really was poetry. Consequently a reaction was bound to come.

He appears to have realized that the exposure of what is wrong, whether in one's epoch or oneself, is only the first and second steps towards spiritual integration, even though enlightened by the wisdom of the ages. As we have seen, the *East Coker–Little Gidding* series is a notable advance.. There is a high seriousness worthy of the best traditions, a restrained emotionalism, and a call to religious meditation. It is as if the poet were on the borders of an unexplored consciousness; as if he was on the point of discovering his true bearings in Space and Time, and owed a responsibility more to God than to his publishers. Unfortunately, his verse is still almost as difficult to read as his prose is easy—unsettling but inconclusive.

So much depends on his next development. If he can ' beat his music out ', he will be the most conspicuous figure of the period. Our age is not ready to interpret the universe; it must first interpret itself—in other words, experiment in its own reactions. It needs and therefore values a poet in prose or verse who seeks what h cannot find, and goes on seeking, his instability of outlook steadi by continuity of effort. That is why Yeats attracts more attent than de la Mare, and why Masefield attracts any attention at That is why Eliot will surpass them all if and when he work way out of the maze.

The perfect masterpieces will be produced afterwards by body else.

JAMES AUGUSTIN ALOYSIUS JOYCE (1882–19

To be consulted : Stuart Gilbert, *James Joyce's Ulyss* E. Dujardin, *Le Monologue intérieur Son Apparition, Ses* *Sa Place dans l'Oeuvre de James Joyce*, 1931 ; H. Gorm *Joyce, a Definitive Biography*, 1941 ; H. Levin, *James* *Critical Introduction*, 1941 (U.S.A.), 1944 (England).

[*Born in Dublin ; his father a middle-class but otherwise* *able Irishman ; the son marked out for the priesthood.* *the Jesuits, he resented their influence for the rest of his l*

[1] *Ante*, pp. 124–5.

a religious crisis, devoted himself to self-culture leading to self-expres-
sion. In 1904 *left Ireland a blasphemous atheist, to become a European*
cosmopolitan. Studied first medicine and then singing in Paris ; then
for ten years taught languages in Trieste and Switzerland. In 1907
published his first volume of poems (Chamber Music) *and completed*
Dubliners *(serialized by Ezra Pound in* Egoist, 14 *Feb.–15 Sept.).*
In 1916 A Portrait of the Artist as a Young Man *(probably begun*
1904 *and rewritten till* 1914) *established his position as a new personality*
in the development of the subjective or introspective novel. In 1922
Ulysses *(begun in Trieste* 1914, *serialized in* The Little Review
(N.Y.) 18 *March–20 Aug., then suppressed and subsequently banned*
in England and U.S.A.) rendered him a topic of conversation wherever
the problems of contemporary literature are discussed. Work in
Progress *began to appear sectionally in* 1927, *and was finally incor-*
porated in Finnigans Wake *and published in* 1939.

Though so astonishingly outspoken and aggressive on paper, he lived
in retirement, mostly in Paris, devoting years of continuous labour to
each MS., struggling against illness and overwork ; the publication
of his works accompanied by friction and obstruction, especially in
Ireland.]

LITERARY AND IDEOLOGICAL BACKGROUND

As an exile in Europe, Joyce changed his skies, but not his heart.
Dublin followed him wherever he went.

Nature made him an artist, but mixed her gifts. He was acutely
responsive to observed details—a gesture, tone, phrase, or outline—
but he could not make the best of them unless they gave sudden
meaning to the thoughts he had acquired elsewhere through intellectual contacts. He must and could detect the whole in the otherwise negligible part. As H. Levin [1] explains, he was by temperament both a realist and a symbolist. These talents could not be
satisfied unless he were conversant with sights and sounds that
moved him, and only then if his mind was busy with ideas and
inferences which favoured the inspirations. Joyce was denied both
these necessities. His Dublin gave him a religion and philosophy
wedded to the Jesuistic discipline (mostly Aristotle as re-edited
by Thomas Aquinas), and even the freer exercise of modern
imposed on artists the duty of living for Ireland, not for the
When he turned from books to the daily impressions of
the town, whether in the streets or his own home, he met
that sphere of frustration, aimlessness, and disintegration which
seem to haunt Irish catholic cities.

outside Ireland were conscious of this blight. Everywhere
community was (or seemed to be) becoming an aggregation,
mechanism. We have seen how some of the most independent
for instance, Yeats, George Moore, Maugham, Lawrence,
were trying to work on a more fundamental idea of

[1] *James Joyce,* 1944.

humanity, each in his own way.   Joyce needed a reorientation more
than any, and while struggling in vain with the old materials and
casting about for some new vista, he became aware of an unexplored
approach to the elements of human nature.   Remy de Gourmont
had pointed out that language is not to be confused with the comparatively modern art of writing.   It is of primitive antiquity, a
fact of life like motility, pervading all the processes of consciousness, a phenomenon of biological significance.   These opinions were
broached in 1908, in *Promenades Philosophiques* (2ᵉ· Série), and since
then psychologists had supplemented biology by proving that the
faculty of speech occupies the dominant ' association area ' in the
cerebrum.   It is the centre in which our impulses and reflexes
cross, serving as a telegraphic exchange, verbalizing what we experience and hope or fear to experience.   Already a school of
neo-linguists was springing up to study word formations and associations, convinced that the human voice is the broadest and most
penetrating approach to the human psyche.   Joyce was a born
linguist, all the more because his eyes were weak and his hearing
acute, and it gradually dawned on him that here was the artist's
opportunity.   Language was a sixth sense, the machinery through
which the human organism revealed its inner processes, an instinctive
and therefore truthful comment on experience ; and like a machine
it obeyed its own laws, and could be set working by the creative
writer.   This unconscious record of our psychic and psychological
adjustments is equally the expression of our lower and higher
nature, the one reliable link between our animal and super-animal
functions, the one aspect through which the futilities, inconsis-
tencies and aspirations of our species can be viewed in their proper
perspective as necessary parts of an intelligible scheme.   This
scheme has nothing to do with literary traditions ; it applies to all
humanity, past, present and future ; and yet its genuineness can be
tested in any special nook and corner of our social existence, and
become the object of the closest observation ; even in dirty, dis-
orderly Dublin which Joyce hated and could not forget.   So here
was a new world for the artist to conquer, leaving his contemporaries
far behind, a challenge to his as yet unrecognized genius.

HIS APPRENTICESHIP

Before creating his medium he had to create his idea of himself,
and externalize his reactions amid the life he led.   This first step
in self-mastery is accomplished in *The Dubliners* (1914) and *A Portrait of the Artist as a Young Man* (1916), though both books were
composed years before.   The former is a tentative study in environment, the latter a searching study in autobiography.   We watch
Stephen Daedalus rescuing his artistic selfhood not only from the
muddle and misrule of his father's household, but also, by contrast,
from the austere discipline of the priesthood with its promise of

M

peaceful poverty and spiritual power. Then, while he wrestles with his adolescence, we watch his efforts at self-assertion, his rehandling of his intellectual resources so that he may look out on the world with his own eyes and master its significance by his own lights. As a youth, Joyce had been an enthusiastic student of Newman, Pater, and Ibsen, whom he imitated in *Exiles* (1918). Since then he had caught up with the ideas stirring in the twentieth century consciousness. Like Eliot, he understands that remembered passages in classical and scholastic lore jump into the mind and illustrate our casual impressions. Like Edith Sitwell and I. A. Richards, he appreciates the psychological value of sheer prosody—'a soft liquid joy flowed through words in which soft long vowels hurtled noiselessly and fell away'. Like Herbert Read, he notes the meaning of rhythm in aesthetic enjoyment. There are hints of surrealism in his daydreams and of the 'internal monologue' in his meditations. Above all, he penetrates below the ordinary indetermination and indecision of youth to an over-sensitized apprehension of difficulties—'a malevolent reality behind the things I say I fear'. One would say that he was well equipped to assert his quality as an artist. Yet one thing he lacked: the sense of fellowship with the spirit of humanity. Obviously there would have to be a sequel in which Stephen (that is, the author) had merged his egoism in the More-than-himself.

' ULYSSES '

The sequel was completed after six to eight years of unremitting labour and experience as a polyglot teacher of languages. The artist is now at one with humanity through insight into the psychology of speech, our most intimate faculty, in which all men share and have shared. In order to assert the timelessness and universality of his apparently modern and specialized work, he has the boldness to present it as an epic, and what is more, the counterpart to the *Odyssey*, the most ancient of epics. He expects us to bear in mind each successive adventure of the old Achaean hero, because they are paralleled by his episodes, and the correspondence makes his meaning more clear. This relativity, he would admit, may seem obscure, but only because the presentment is adapted to the modern mind. Homer dwells on the adventures, and has very little to say about the reactions of the adventurer; generally a single line is enough. That is why his myth seems to be so localized and dated. Since then we are beginning to learn that speech, not action, is the token of humanity; our nature reveals itself in linguistic meanderings. Time and place do not matter; twenty-four hours are enough for the demonstration; and Dublin may serve quite well for the scene. The mind moves on its own plane.

Such seems to be Joyce's design. The result gives free play to the academic critic, and very little to the unacademic reader. It does not much matter that the parallelism with Greek epic breaks down, nor that the theme itself does not fulfil the promise of being a sequel. The Stephen of *A Portrait* was an attractive character, and we should have enjoyed following his progress towards self-fulfilment. Nevertheless the author may have found it more effective to present that consummation in his own perfected artistry and originality of view. But it does matter that the first place has been given to such a couple as Mr. and Mrs. Bloom, and that they are allowed to ruminate with a most decidedly un-Greek prolixity. Joyce might reply that he could not truthfully do otherwise ; Dublin, or any other community, is no place for an artist like Daedalus, or for the qualities in other people which an artist admires. A city man was sure to be ignoble, even in his vices. Unhappily Leopold and his wife are something much worse than the degenerate descendants of the original Ulysses and Penelope. The artist devotes his genius to exposing two soulless souls. The result is alternatively comic and devastating ; an anatomy of evil. For the Blooms are hardly more than the villains of the lower middle class. There is nothing in them even sub-epic, only the fancies and self-indulgences of a primitive being born out of due time and transferred to the safe and sordid viciousness of twentieth century routine. Joyce hovers over the edge of the cesspool intent on the reptiles wriggling below. The other characters who stray into our ken are just as discouraging. This is not truth to life. In order to appreciate Chartres Cathedral we do not examine the beetles in the crypt.

Ulysses, then, is a magnificent and unmistakable failure ; yet it deserves the fullest consideration. Though prolix, disconnected, often unintelligible or blank with stretches of sheer boredom, the author has succeeded in fascinating the reader who thinks. It is done by the technique. Apparently Joyce finally despaired of everything except craftsmanship, and staked his reputation on manner instead of matter ; and thanks to this preoccupation has encouraged, in fact represented, a movement full of possibilities. He is essentially a novelist's novelist. He has shown his fellow-writers how to vivify what was formerly hidden and dehumanized in scientific treatises— for instance, aphasia, synaesthesia, paramnesia, and semasiology. By the sheer force of his apparently inexhaustible imagination he has created the impression of quivering, all-pervading restlessness, and kept up the tension through more than a thousand pages. By virtue of his philological and psychological intuition he has here and there created scenes which are both uncanny and disconcerting in their realism. He has helped to encourage artists, though *Ulysses* is a questionable work of art.

HIS PLACE IN THE FUTURE OF THE NOVEL

It depends on the future value of the internal monologue which is discussed below.[1] Joyce has used this device with an almost reckless

[1] *Post*, p. 176.

originality, and it is quite conceivable that his accumulation of research and insight may eventually be welcomed by the neo-philologists as a source-book. Nor is it unlikely that his most adventurous effusions—for instance, Mrs. Bloom's concluding rumi-nations—will always delight as an example of what the human brain can accomplish. Moreover, his virtuosity and technical dex-terity ought to secure him, at the very least, an 'honourable mention' in the proper quarters. But he allowed himself to become an expert in sub-humanity, and was so obsessed by his technique that he sacrificed the principles of his art to its preciosity ; a monomaniac like the hero of Balzac's *Chef d'Oeuvre Inconnu.* So humanists will value him as a whetstone which sharpens razors, itself unable to cut.

VIRGINIA WOOLF (1882–1941)

To be consulted : M. Delattre, *Le Roman Psychologique de Virginia Woolf,* 1932 ; W. Holtby, *Virginia Woolf,* 1932 ; E. M. Forster, *Virginia Woolf, Rede Lecture,* 1942 ; Joan Bennett, *Virginia Woolf. Her Art as a Novelist,* 1945 ; D. Daiches, *Virginia Woolf,* 1945; J. Bennett, *Virginia Woolf,* 1946.

[*Daughter of Sir Leslie Stephen. Born into one of the most dis-tinguished literary circles of her time, and brought up partly in London, partly by the sea, in Cornwall. Engaged in higher journalism until marriage with Leonard Woolf in* 1912. *Thereafter plunged in politics, especially the feminist movement, and collaborated with her husband in the publication of controversial and modernist literature through the Hogarth Press. In* 1922 *made her reputation with* Jacob's Room. *Thereafter continued to experiment in the technique of the novel, as far as it can represent ' the stream of consciousness ', producing* Mrs. Dalloway (1925), To the Lighthouse (1927), Orlando (1928), The Waves (1931), Between the Acts (1941, *posthumous*), *each rumination amounting to a tentative but studied research into the sensibilities of family life and society. Her characteristic essays on the less obvious aspects of culture include* The Common Reader (1925 *and* 1932), A Room of One's Own (1929), Roger Fry (1940), The Death of the Moth (1942, *posthumous*).]

LITERARY AND IDEOLOGICAL BACKGROUND

Mrs. Woolf inherited as her birthright the artistic privileges for which most authors have to struggle. This environment directed but also circumscribed the growth of her mind, for she derived her ideas from upper-class people, as polished as jewelry. She had no taste for rough diamonds. On the other hand, innovation was in her blood and her environment. So within her limits, anything she wrote would have to be an adventure in style and thought. Those limits confined her to a class, often misnamed the Bloomsbury set, a community of restless intellectuals who changed their habits, ideas and acquaintances so often, and engaged in so many chattering speculations, that they had little time to inquire into the sources of each other's identity, or their own. Their human contacts tended to evaporate after the exchange of opinions. Being one of those who never accept the world on its surface value, Mrs. Woolf was inquisitive enough to look through personality to the selfhood which ought to be found at its core. Such is her significance in the history of literature.

This, the most intimate problem of her own age, was by no means unknown to Victorian moralists. Amongst others, Browning in *Dramatic Monologues* and Arnold in *Empedocles* might have authorized her curiosity. But since their epoch, people had begun to take interest in Time as an aspect of Duration,[1] and Virginia Woolf must have been influenced (directly of indirectly) by Bergson's *Essai sur les Données immédiates de la Conscience* (1889), in which it is argued that past experiences keep pace with every progressive moment we call the present, a constant comparison which colours our accumulating perceptions and is coloured by them, always adding to the volume of our consciousness. The mind is a snowball gathering weight as it rolls along.

The snowball is in danger of wearing thin through friction, and if so, we begin to lose our sense of ourselves ; like railway passengers who have mislaid their luggage and tickets. So thought Proust, who must have exercised a more direct influence than Bergson. This valetudinarian, who despaired of his health and of his social caste, nevertheless retrieved his selfhood while searching for the early impressions which still dimly haunted his passing thoughts. Thereby he perfected, or elaborated the art of writing a novel backwards. He began with *Du Côté de Chez Swann* (1913) when Virginia Woolf had just entered on womanhood ; and his last and twelfth volume of the series, *À la Recherche du Temps Perdu*, was published in 1922 (posthumous), when she had just begun to mature her talent and set out on a similar quest.

HER DEVELOPMENT

Her besetting difficulty was the creation of a plot which would concentrate but not confine her researches. She first saw daylight in *Jacob's Room* (1922), the biography of an impressionable, volatile young man of the pre-war type, his career a series of breezy, fleeting contacts, his actions mirrored in his own consciousness, his character mirrored in the consciousness of other people.

That book was the end of her apprenticeship. Within three years, she had invented the kind of setting she required with *Mrs. Dalloway* (1925). In this adventure she succeeds in distilling the essence of six lives into a cross-section of Time, a single day spent in the neighbourhood of Bond Street. The personages stray into our ken as if by accident, a queer junction of lives, each glimpsed by the process of instantaneous photography, and each trailing threads

---

[1] *Ante*, pp. 143 ff.

of his or her history, whereby we divine how the Past survives into the Present. Such is reality in the Dalloway set; momentary contacts bringing their own atmosphere of tragedy, comedy and satire intermixed.

The reader is intrigued, but not satisfied, because Mrs. Dalloway is not her true self, but a shadow, flitting among the responsibilities of her social position, and the preoccupations of a day's shopping. The next experiment, *To the Lighthouse* (1927), has a closer texture and more firmness. The occasion appears to be just as trifling—a seaside resort, the proposed visit to a lighthouse (weather permitting) —and the personages are no less futile than their pastime. But the group is now a family, and this groupment gives a more intimate opportunity to the play of temperaments, children as well as parents. There is a guest, a detached observer, and we see much through his eyes. As in *Mrs. Dalloway*, the reader gathers up stray threads of their separate though contiguous histories, thanks to their thoughts, spoken and unspoken. But in *To the Lighthouse* we have the stimulating illusion of looking forward, as well as backward. Ten years divide the discussion of this pleasure-trip in Part I and its accomplishment in Part II. Having jumped the interval, we again gather up the threads, and we are at first surprised at the changes, both outward and inward. Then we realize that we might have foreseen the outcome; it was all, or nearly all, implicit in the first of the two acts. We ought to be confirming and correcting our expectations, especially the void which Mrs. Ramsay has left by her death, and the progress of James and Cam, whose childishness has grown to adolescence with its burden of desires and aversions.

By now the authoress was appreciated, but not famous; almost the centre of a cult but still ignored by the general public because her characters seemed to be bloodless; the world-forgetting and therefore by the world forgot. Partly for this reason, she tried to be less subjective, and to enrich her background with an historical pageant. *Orlando, a Biography* (1928) presents an androgynous protagonist, who begins life under Queen Elizabeth as a young man, and continues as a full-grown woman from the age of Addison to the age of motor-cars. But the book loses in depth what it gains in spaciousness. Her Orlando gradually becomes a stage character and his or her environments wear as thin as canvas scenery. The second object of the romance, her contention that there is more similarity than difference between the sexes, was more effectively expounded as an essay, in *A Room of One's Own* (1929).

So she inevitably returned to her proper theme : the groupment of temperaments which always offset and sometimes complete each other. The last of these experiments, *The Waves* (1931), is certainly her most ambitious adventure into ideas. The reader is not required to look backward or forward. He accompanies the characters through their careers, a privileged confidant of their secrets. Six children are gathered together, each burdened with a temperament which spells destiny, their mutual differences all the more sharply defined because they begin life under the same roof. They grow up, pass out of their several schools into the world, and separate to face its favours or frowns, and to skirt its tragedies. Yet she touches on their external contacts only lightly, using them to emphasize the essential inwardness of existence, even in the busy routines of modern civilization. To enhance the contrast they are all reunited at four stages in their progress, which symbolically synchronize with the four stages of the year. This recurrence is suggested to us by the surge of the sea—spring, summer, autumn, and winter tides— suggesting that humanity is a part of nature's rhythm, and we contemplate the currents of life not through the crystal of the intellect, but through a submarine vision, apparently an attempt to suggest the dream-like mystery which encircles humanity.

That final touch (possibly inspired by *The Tempest*) is not effective, except as a triumph of sheer writing. But in the meantime, from *Mrs. Dalloway* onwards, she had gradually acquired the art of inducing her readers to remind themselves that death, like an impalpable shadow, haunts the drift of their being. Its presence may have fastened onto her own consciousness, and clouded her imagination. At any rate she produced nothing more of note. *Between the Acts* (1941, posthumous), despite the guesses which have been made at a hidden meaning, can most safely be read as a piece of genial, local satire.

WILL HER MEMORY SURVIVE?

For some generations at least Virginia Woolf ought to be remembered in histories of the novel, because she did so much to develop the Internal Monologue. Whereas Joyce's achievement is to be associated with word-psychology, hers is to be associated with clairvoyance. She looks into other people's souls, of the complex self-deceiving class, and sees more than they themselves can see. She reads their Past, Present, and sometimes Future from chance utterances and stray thoughts, which are the lines of character, much as a palmist tries to do from the lines of the hand. She should also command attention as one whose life-work was unified in the pursuit of an ideal. Though she never gave us a perfect work, she gave something as good or better: an object-lesson in the quest of perfection, each experiment a further step towards a goal which continued to recede. Her career is a single study in creative continuity, and possibly that is the best that our age can offer.

But because she did not reach her goal she may never become a favourite author—an old friend. She has been compared to Miss Austen, and it is true that both women portray more or less the same kind of people: chiefly nonentities who have not kept pace with the times; and both authoresses are about equally on terms of intimacy with their subjects. But we are not so. Miss Austen lets us know them from the outside inward, as we know our acquaintances, with their oddities and insignificant poses, and we end by liking them. We try to know Mrs. Woolf's characters from the inside outward, and rarely arrive at a satisfying impression of their vital, conscious presence, streaked with unconscious failings.

She may, for some time, survive as an original stylist. Her quality has been described as 'a delicate, flitting, feminine fancy of extraordinary sensitivity'. In this age, when so many were writing verse to be presented as emotional prose, or prose to convey the emotions of poetry, she has succeeded better than any in the art of writing prose-poetry.

THE INTERNAL MONOLOGUE

This technical device has become one of the characteristic features of interwar literature. Its need must often have been felt before, since we find something very like its method in the first English novel, Lyly's *Euphues*, published in 1579. Yet it was not avowedly put into practice till 1887 by Edouard Dujardin in *Les Lauriers sont Coupés*, and explained as late as 1931 by the same author in *Le Monologue Intérieur* as unspoken speech by which a character expresses his inmost thoughts as inconsequentially as they enter his mind. Dujardin's novel is negligible—merely the random moods of a young man who takes an actress out to dinner—nor did it attract much more attention. The average reader in that age had lost interest in his own Subconscious; he had too many other things to think about; and what does not interest us in ourselves, rarely interests us in a book. The experiment was made after and before its time.

Its opportunity came twenty or thirty years later with the decay of the old-fashioned objective novel of episode.[1] The younger generation were beginning to wonder whether human nature could be simplified so artfully and artificially—whether you and I really acted and thought with such logical deliberation, always following motives of which we could render an account—and if not, then objective characterization was one-sided. However, such considerations were only preparing the ground. Any critic could see that subjective characterization ran an equal risk of one-sidedness, and that the two aspects should be combined.

It was psycho-analysis [2] which confirmed the practice. This habit of mind created an interest not so much in the submerged self as in the suppressed self; and then the internal monologue came to hand, a new and searching instrument; not a monologue, but a one-party dialogue between two halves of the same person, each at variance with the other, the intelligence wrestling with circumstances, the impulses wrestling with the intelligence, the mono-dialoguist only aware that his mind has lost its thread. In fact, the speaker is not speaking; he is caught napping. The author and

---

[1] *Ante*, p. 137.　　　　[2] *Ante*, pp. 122 ff.

reader are each enjoying the luxury of being a spy. Spies can discover a great deal; but it must not be forgotten that they are prying into secrets of their own making. Like a conjuror, they supply the objects they seem to produce out of the silk hat. We are not nearer the truth because we approve the avenue of approach. For instance, the modern man need not be so typically sub-moral as Joyce imagines, or so purposeless as Virginia Woolf would have us believe.

For these reasons, the internal monologue might have met with a colder reception, except that it suited the humour of the age. Quite apart from Freud, Adler, Jung, and Ernest Jones, we like to remind ourselves that our psychic stability depends on movement. The cinema does so. Of course it presents an organized plot, but conveys it in a flux of impressions with the *fade-out*, the *close-up*, and the *flash-back*. Impressionist paintings present a single composition, but the effect is not static; the colours and shapes have to arrange themselves in the schematic sense; often they suggest qualities which have no imitative function and merely arouse a corresponding sensation. Something similar has crept into poetry, reaching its consummation in surrealism, in which the apparent chaos of dreams are left to collect their outlines according to the morphology of art.

We may conclude, then, that the internal monologue is of value because it introduces us to an unfamiliar aspect of ourselves; at any rate for the time being. Even when we have all returned to the older ideal of man the master of his thoughts as well as of his destiny, it may still survive, for it provides the shortest and most intimate pathway to our irrepressible interest in other people's least interesting experiences. As examples one might quote Katherine Mansfield's 'The Tiredness of Isabel' (1908, reprinted in *Something Childish*, 1924) and D. A. Richardson's *The Tunnel* (1919).

But it is more likely that when once the novelty has evaporated—but not the difficulties—the story-teller will revert to the model and manners of *Tristram Shandy*, in which Sterne holds his own internal monologue, ruminating inconsequentially on his own private prepossessions and prejudices, in order to interest his readers in himself while interesting them in 'My Father' and 'Uncle Toby'.

CHAPTER XI

THE LAST PHASE. ITS FAILURES AND BIDS FOR SUCCESS

IN the pre-war period both poets and prose-writers, in the main, kept as close as they could to tradition, and tried to restate in a contemporary guise the sympathies and interests common to humanity. Sometimes they invoked the diction and atmosphere of an early age. The writers of the interwar period may or may not have intended to continue or begin in this spirit, but in either case the most noteworthy soon caught sight of a life philosophy, a religion, a principle, or a theory of conduct, and consistently pursued the vision or practised the method. Whether or no they convinced the reader, they surprised him, claimed his attention, and were much discussed. They seem to have acquired their disturbing point of view without much hesitation. But there were others less temperamentally adaptable, or more diffident, or more artistically conscientious ; and these were too perplexed and disappointed to find the right way, and join those ' who never turned their backs, but marched breast forward '. They also claim attention because we must understand their difficulties and discouragements.

EZRA LOOMIS POUND (1885-   )

This American went to Europe as soon as he had left the University of Pennsylvania in 1908, and saturated himself in the culture of the old world. In 1909 his first two volumes of poetry, *Personae* and *Exultations*, were welcomed by discerning critics because their author seemed to be genuinely in search of freedom, and to be finding it among the traditions and aspirations of the Past. As time went on, and he produced among other volumes *Canzoni* (1911), *Ripostes* (1912), and *Cathay* (1915), it became evident that he had won not to the genuine freedom of the artist, but the spurious freedom of the experimentalist, inventing every kind of novelty, but not achieving strangeness. At the same time he plunged into the leadership of literary movements (notably Imagism [1]), which promised to give poetic form to modern consciousness ; he cultivated imitations and paraphrases of Chinese, Latin, and Italian literatures. He wrote with vigour and intensity, but he rarely caught and fixed the pregnant moment in himself ; apparently bent on recapturing the magic of the storied Past, because he had none of his own.

The test came at the conclusion of the Four Years War. Up till then there was still hope that culture would thrive on traditional sympathies and allegiances and leave the artist free to practise clarity of thought. Thereafter the spirit of continuity was temporarily

[1] *Ante*, pp. 122 ff.

lost in the confusion, and the writer had to grope till he extracted out of the chaos some value which he could serve. Pound was unequal to this discipline. It only intensified his sense of frustration. So he wasted his talents in regrets, protesting that the times were out of joint and could not be associated with any poetic principle. His disillusionment finds most forcible expression in *Hugh Selwyn Mauberley* (1920). Since then he has continued to make bricks without straw, free from a moral or social purpose, and therefore enslaved to his own aptitude for craftsmanship, casting images on the visual imagination, offering us not the adventures of the spirit among ideas, but the dance of the intellect among words. He has been compared to a ropemaker weaving strands of culture with strands of himself, but never finding the strands he needed.

It should not be forgotten that he is a writer of vigorous and inspiring prose, and that the best statement of his position is to be found in his series ' On Books ' in the *New York Herald*, and reprinted in *Polite Essays* (1937).

THE SITWELLS. EDITH (1887–   ), SIR OSBERT (1892–   ), SACHEVERELL (1897–   )

A similar burden of frustration and nostalgia seems to weigh upon this remarkable family. The most remarkable, the eldest, has described herself as ' a spiritual adventurer, never a spiritual *parvenu* ', and the future historian will agree. He will have to add that few have judged their epoch more bitterly and more vivaciously. She has dismissed it as ' a thin matchboard flooring spread over a shallow hell ', and fears that we can escape from the pit only by a perpetual ' can-can ', most appropriately represented by the Russian ballet, in which ' the music, harsh crackling rags of laughter, shrieks at us '.[1]

At first it seemed as if her own verses were vitiated with a no less brittle artificiality, for she began by apparently playing with the fanciful and often grotesque imaginings of childhood, presented in outlandish rhymes ; for instance in *Clown's House* (1918), *The Wooden Pegasus* (1920), *Bucolic Comedies* (1923). Then it was realized that she was seeking a direct approach to our inner selves, trying to recreate not so much the nonsense-verses of children, as the moods of childhood, the only core of sanity left in this light-witted world—life viewed as fairyland deepened by adult sensibilities. Thus she hoped to awaken our drugged perceptions.

Moreover, these nonsense verses were far from being nonsense. In *Poetry and Criticism* (1925) Miss Sitwell quotes Blake to the effect that in this modern age the five senses are the chief inlets to the soul, and she would agree with I. A. Richards [2] that those inlets could best be entered by word-formations and combinations. In fact she went farther, and claimed to be addressing a sixth sense which

[1] Preface to *Twentieth-Century Harlequinade*, 1916.   [2] *Ante*, p. 138.

interprets and controls the other five, so that when the speech accommodated to one sense is insufficient, the poet can use the language of another conveying a quality to that sense which can best receive it; for instance, he can speak of ' the *music* of falling snow ', ' the *blunt* rain ', ' the *purring* fire ', ' a *pig-snouted* breeze '. Such combinations (termed sense confusion or transfusion) had, of course, often been practised by the greatest poets, as if on the inspiration of the moment, but Miss Sitwell established the practice as a consistent principle. She condensed imagism into single words.

It sounds as if the technique might be immensely effective, producing again and again a shock of surprise and a sting to the imagination. The reader, thoroughly alert, waits for the echo of a deeper creative note; and waits in vain. Often the picturesque manipulations amount to no more than dashes of colour and sound. Even when most effective, they convey only the impression of two or more streams of consciousness blending in a single current which does not reach the sea. Yet the talented poetess has sincerity, a sense of beauty, and the love of children—qualities of great price in the twentieth century. Nevertheless, though she prepares the way, she cannot follow her own lead. In her latest phase (from *Gold Coast Customs* (1929) to *The Shadow of Cain* (1947)) her outraged humanity speaks as if from a violent dream.

It seems that she lacks not self-reliance nor responsiveness, but depth of feeling. The surface of experience is too much for her personal creativeness; as if all life were as unsubstantial as it appears to be. Her later prose gives a similar impression. For instance, *Edith Sitwell's Anthology* (1940) is a treasury no less golden than the best. With the finest tact, she incorporates the passages which everybody knows, and also many which everybody ought to know but does not, including nursery rhymes and modern French. Yet in the lively introduction there is an almost desolating insistence on the virtues of open vowels, texture, rhythm, and vocables, as if poetry had nothing more to say. So with *A Poet's Notebook* (1943). In the spirit of its selection it is European. In its concentration on ' the necessities of poetry ' it is indispensable to the student and writer of modern poetry. Yet again that touch of perverse restrictiveness—for instance, the value placed on Cocteau, and the implication that music and poetry are different but contiguous aspects of the same art.

Her two brothers seem to be equally disheartened. Sir Osbert's verse, of which the bulk appeared in the 'twenties, is just as subtle and as conscious of the eighteenth-century picturesqueness and refinement which we have lost, but more superficially aggressive. His fascinating series of autobiographies, since 1944, seem touched with the melancholy of middle-age. Sacheverell is also a poet out of tune with his age, but much more notable for his prose, of which *Sacred and Profane Love* (1940) and *Splendours and Miseries* (1943) are perhaps the most characteristic. These original travel books breathe

the spirit of interwar cosmopolitanism. The author seems to be searching the whole world for something on which to expend and realize himself, picking up here, there, and everywhere the discoveries which are most significant, each experience a symbol of the best or worst that can befall human nature. The sequence of incongruous impressions somehow weaves itself into a tapestry presenting the author's mind. Yet, like Byron in *Childe Harold* and Heine in *Reisebilder*, he seems to be looking abroad for what he cannot find in himself.

The Sitwells are unable to focus their talents on some life-giving principle either within or without. The younger Huxley succeeded, and the result is even more disconcerting.

ALDOUS LEONARD HUXLEY (1894–   )

He received his full share of literary and artistic culture acquired in an atmosphere tinged with science and its illuminating ideas, and more than his full share of suffering. Few have had a better chance of reaching wisdom through knowledge.

He first appeared as a poet in *The Burning Wheel* (1916), *The Defeat of Youth* (1918), and *Leda* (1920), and his manner reminds one of the orthodox Georgian school, though now and then we meet touches of wistfulness, as if he were on the brink of a new development, a spiritual keenness and vision. At times he relapses into a mood of pure contemplation, almost Oriental, seeking contact with the Universal Intelligence, ' like a pure angel, thinking colour and form '. And then, unlike an Oriental mystic and very like a Western scientist, he tests both aesthetic enjoyment and mystic experience by what he sees in conduct and character, first in himself and then in the world around him. Both within and without he ends by finding the same half results : an aspiration, even an assurance, let slip by our recurring dullness or perversity. On one occasion he compares the human being to a mole tunnelling through solid blackness (Huxley had been threatened with blindness) till he strikes daylight and sees men as trees. Meanwhile life fades away, like pipe-smoke on top of a 'bus.

So this poet, gifted with fine perceptions and a sense of form, ends his first phase haunted by the horror of dualism, unless it were rather the power of Evil to resist Good. His subsequent development followed the same bent.

Obviously he could not persist in the poetic tradition ; it was too ready to celebrate the triumph of the Good ; so he turned to prose, which in this age meant novel-writing. He was a humorist, a collector of human curiosities, as he liked to confess ; interwar manners were a fashionable subject and earned money. So he seized his opportunity and rapidly rose to fame.

Crome Yellow (1921), *Antic Hay* (1923), *Those Barren Leaves* (1925) and *Point Counter Point* (1928) commanded immediate success because they were witty, accomplished, lucid, and topical. Few at once appreciated their significance. In the first place, Huxley succeeded in fusing the objective and the subjective styles of novel-writing. There are no internal monologues; the incidence of his narrative falls on externals; but only on those peculiarly intimate and unobtrusive mannerisms—conversation, appearance, gait, gesture, pose—which betray not the plans and prospects of the actors, but their inner life. As in the new novel, the characters come and go as if by accident. As in the old novel, their vagaries are interwoven by surprising but credible coincidences; for instance, in *Point Counter Point*, of which the title exactly indicates the artistic purpose. In the next place, this clever technician perfected his method because he was also a moralist. This was the way to expose the self-expression of the interwar intellectuals, those who believe they have brains because they have money, and flatter themselves that they belong to a tradition which no longer exists. Once upon a time men like Mill, Arnold, and Pater had to work hard before they could talk, and their pronouncements were the fruit of their learning. Nowadays pure science had provided an easy answer, at second hand, to our searchings of heart, and applied science had provided comfort and the illusion of power. So these imitators could talk even though they could not think; or could indulge in pleasures, but not understand the meaning of life which these pleasures disguise. Huxley understood and hated the narrowness of this class, having suffered from its influence. The critic is sometimes tempted to complain of the narrowness of Huxley himself. He invites us to contemplate characters which do not matter, except so far as they illustrate futility or frustration. Even in 'The Young Archimedes' (*Little Mexican*, 1924), his most pathetically human document, the father's stupidity stands out as an object-lesson. Even in the cleverly constructed 'The Gioconda Smile' (*Mortal Coils* (1922)) the story ends in a 'commédie macabre', so alarmingly and convincingly circumstantial that vice seems to be as dangerous as unobtrusive. All this skill and literary tact are dedicated to the evils of educated perversity. So ends his second phase.

Then in 1932 he published *Brave New World*, a work of cosmopolitan scope. To understand its significance, one must bear in mind the progress and applications of science. In *Conditioned Reflexes* (translation 1927) Pavlov demonstrated that dogs (and if so, why not humans?) can acquire almost any habits under the pressure of organized stimuli, 'subjecting voluntary behaviour to scientific law'. In *The Nature of Living Matter* (1930) Lancelot Hogben had reminded us that motives and actions may be so cleverly manipulated that new reflexes are brought into being. Or Huxley may simply have glanced through Bertrand Russell's *The Scientific Outlook* (1931), which discusses the future of societies managed by a scientifically minded bureaucracy. Any of these and other such books would, at that time, be read on the background of the Soviet

Five-Years' Plan, which confined the constructive energies of a whole nation to the problem of economic balance and productive efficiency, all depending on the technique of propaganda, and cold-blooded, calculating legislation. If such is the trend of civilization, the old-fashioned science of knowledge is yielding to the new science of power—power over nature, and especially over human nature—and we may gradually accept a standard of utilitarian and machine-like efficiency, to the exclusion of human values.

Such is the inspiration of *Brave New World*, which he styles a novel. As such, the book is poor. Its plot is tedious, its characters uninteresting. They could not be otherwise under the social system he depicts with mordant and vivid satire. Few took the book seriously. It is a protest against the menace of evil as an active force in governments, evil made easy by the study of politics, psycho-analysis, and biology.

In this mood he returned to his proper subject, the waywardness and obtusity of individuals as they now are. He was over forty years of age, and had become more thoughtful though not less censorious. He brings in the verdict that if contemporary civiliza-tion has bestowed new comforts and conveniences, it has also beset us with new temptations which we are unwilling or unable to resist. We can do much more than our ancestors could, and for that reason we shall have to know much more, especially about the physiology of our bodies and their psychic reactions. The principle of evil must be raised and redirected, not by totalitarian administration, but by an enlightened code of self-discipline. This philosophy is explored over a wide field and expounded in essays, sketches, and stories, for instance, in *Eyeless in Gaza* (1936) and *The Olive Tree* (1936), and is implicit in his delightful travel books. Those who would know England must nowadays know the world; and Huxley, like Kipling, Forster, Maugham, Lawrence, Sir Osbert and Sach-everell Sitwell, was an inveterate globe-trotter. Release from England, in fact Europe, widens his sympathies and deepens his insight, and one realizes how much more he might have discovered in human nature. In his visit to the ruins at Copan (*Beyond the Mexique Bay* (1934)) and in *Ends and Means* (1937) he ventures to wonder whether the flux of time, which we try to arrest, is not after all an illusion, due to preoccupation with our personal perishable affairs, and whether by force of contemplation, after the manner of Oriental mystics, we might merge our transitory selves in the timelessness of reality.[1]

It began to look as if he would outgrow his cynicism, and achieve some sort of reconciliation between scientific empiricism and philo-sophic intuition. Then came the Second Great War. Its effect was two-fold. It confirmed his worst fears concerning the psycho-logy of human beings, and inspired his imagination with indirect but none the less startling symbolizations of his horror. He began

[1] *Ante*, pp. 141 ff.

with *Grey Eminence* (1941), an historical biography of a seventeenth-century Capuchin who began as a mystic devoted to the contemplation of heavenly beatitudes, and ended, in all good faith, as Richelieu's accomplice in the destruction of Europe and the horrors of the Thirty Years War. Such is the outcome of ideologies working upon a one-pointed mind. The application is obvious, and its significance is staggering because presented in a remote story which happens to be true, then as now.

As the war progressed, it seemed more and more to revert to primitive brutality. Meanwhile observers began to recall the hypothesis that evolution may possibly overstep itself and reach a stage which is biologically insecure. This premature development may be further endangered by inventions, whether destructive or therapeutic, which spring up to gratify some perverse desire and are not in the course of nature. There are a hundred ways in which the novelist might exemplify this reversion. Huxley's parable is all the more devastating because indirect. The war is not mentioned ; the scene is the corrupt and vitiated circle of a rather contemptible and pathetic millionaire who fears death. His private physician invents a disgusting treatment wherewith to prolong his employer's life. But while arresting the natural course of decay, he inadvertently arrests the course of evolution ; the attributes of humanity die at their proper time ; the patient reverts to the anthropoid ape from which his forbears evolved. The final scene is as powerful as nauseating. Such is *After Many a Summer* (1944). To appreciate its bitterness, the reader must remember the preceding cult of old age. Goethe, in 1828, told Eckermann that age brought its own revival of youth ; in 1853 R. Parise's *La Vieillesse* argued that a man did not even reach full development till at least seventy years old ; Browning believed that the spirit of progress passed from one worker to another, enlivening their faculties till their extreme end, if not beyond ; even Tithonus, in Tennyson's poem (from which Huxley borrows his title), grew wiser as well as sadder with the endless procession of years. In the twentieth century, histologists were suggesting the probability that human tissue, if kept under the proper conditions, need never die, and we have seen what Shaw [1] made of the hypothesis in *Back to Methuselah*. And then Huxley, in a very graphic and well-constructed novel, invokes a counter-hypothesis to dash the dream, and bring us back to the Tenth Chapter of *Ecclesiastes*.

Huxley is a morbidly exacting critic of his age, and what most impresses the critic of Huxley is the ferret-like pertinacity and searchfulness of his strictures. He has developed an insatiable curiosity in the waywardness of his fellow-creatures. Hugh Kingsmill described him as ' a lean and mournful Don Quixote without dreams '. But he had nightmares. That is the penalty of judging others by the rigorous and restricted standards one ought to apply to oneself.

[1] *Ante*, p. 37.

JOHN BOYNTON PRIESTLEY (1894-   )

This student of middle-class character and destiny is in one sense quite distinct from the restless and questioning authors we have just discussed. He first made a decided appearance as a literary critic and commentator (1924–9), and then suddenly became famous as a novelist with *The Good Companions* (1929) and *Angel Pavement* (1930), both parables of moral slavery, under our social system. The first tells of those who have slipped their chain and in the fellow-ship of the open road are free to be good-natured and independent. The second presents the stuffiness of a business office, the inmates, each according to his or her degree, debased by the vice of systema-tized money-making which works like an evil spell on the prisoners in the cage. He stands aloof, half quizzical and half sympathetic, and tells his story in a manner reminiscent of Dickens. The spirit of the twentieth century left-wing reformer is clearly to be felt. We realize what ought to be by realizing what ought not. Yet he lacks vision ; there is no glimpse of the opportunities which our generation has missed ; his common folk are so circumscribed and ordinary, and so convincingly portrayed, that they never seem likely to change, however much the world was changed for them. Since then, he seems to have been searching for the quality of strangeness through plays, sketches, poems, and a book of travels (1932–5). He has not tired of arguing and advocating social reform, and what is more significant, he has begun to show that real life may have its own spiritual revelations. In *Time and the Conways* (1937), *I Have Been There Before* (1937) and *Music at Night* (1938) he has ventured to suggest that our consciousness may become more mystic and metaphysical through contact with the supposedly dead. He sustains interest in his theme, and his characters are as much alive as ever. But nevertheless they do not draw us out of the circle of commonplace observation.

CHARLES LANGBRIDGE MORGAN (1894-   )

Whereas Priestley seems to breathe the atmosphere of the Midlands wherever he goes, Morgan lives among the cosmopolitan or leisured classes who enjoy life's social privileges. He reminds one of Thackeray or Trollope without their humour and irony ; but he writes in their old-world leisurely manner, though rather pedestrian in style. In each novel he gathers together a domestic circle of serious-minded, orderly people, living settled lives, such as most of us would be glad enough to live ; and they are all interesting and seem real, though they take up much space in saying and doing very little to the point. Each of these quiet, self-contained fraternities produces or admits a man of genius, an irreconcilable, who influences the others and is influenced by them, an idealist, an enemy of routine, seeking escape through art, philosophy, or action, always impeded

N

by the network of his attachments, generally forced to choose between going his own way, or that of the woman he loves. Of these novels (1925–41) *The Fountain* (1932) is certainly the best, but all have delighted thousands because each reminds the reader that (for the privileged classes) existence is a matter of temperaments, ideals and adventures in experience, such as all should approve though few imitate. Like Galsworthy, he has also attracted many readers on the continent because he makes the English upper class seem eccentric and intelligible. Yet these brilliant eccentrics are not really convincing for the Englishman. Their thoughts are less dynamic than their words and actions. The author cannot get inside their skins, because they are too full of his own complexities.

HOWARD SPRING (1889–   )

The spiritual hollowness of these two gifted writers will also be found in Spring, who has produced in his later middle-age two very successful novels which contain his verdict on life. He was well equipped for the task, having sympathy with the troubles and temperaments of his fellow-creatures, and an unusually wide range of social experience. Consequently he has no illusions concerning the alleged goodness of human nature. But he has an unmistakable gift for the portrayal of character and personality; and as he is a self-made man who has devoted his strenuous manhood to journalism, he knows much about the intricate windings of this mortal life. Both his novels—*My Son, My Son* (1938), *Fame is the Spur* (1940)—create pictures of working-class life which are all his own, and which the reader does not forget, because they live in his imagination and haunt his thoughts. These humble folk really do labour, aspire, and err. But when he leads us on to those who rise to the surface, and become 'gentlemen', they also become stage-figures, melodramatic or farcical, rightly objects of his pity, contempt, or sardonic amusement, examples of the perversity and freakishness of social life. So he ends by pointing a moral as old as the centuries.

So here is yet another talented author who tells us the truth, but not the whole truth, not that part of it we ought to ask for.

THE INSURGENCE OF THE 'THIRTIES

Pound, the Sitwells, Huxley, Priestley, Morgan, and Spring, seem to be masters of themselves and their art. They have established their attitude, and have done justice to their ideas, as far as they can see. If we are to summarize our disappointment in a phrase, we might borrow Jules de Gaultier's *mot* : *le pouvoir départi à l'homme de se concevoir autre qu'il n'est.* The same is true of other less effective poets, for instance John Freeman (1880–1929) and Robert Nichols (1893–1944), who felt deeply, but could not speak out.

Meanwhile a younger generation fully aware of the disabilities under which their elders were labouring began to look elsewhere for the power which makes all things new.

The novelists look for it in a second hidden realism, suggesting what can be symbolized but not photographed. They are far from ignoring facts; they follow the logic of events; and yet, unlike the Victorian and Georgian novel, their stories flicker or flare with touches of grace or grimness, to show that even prosaic experience has romance in store. De la Mare may have given them many a hint. One of the most outspoken is the American Frederic Prokosch (1908–). On the surface he is grimly realistic, reminding us of the impulses and agonies which may anywhere at this moment be active, but removing then to a safe distance, amid arid, Oriental scenery, cosmopolitan cities festering with intrigues, or a hobo's wanderings in America, so that stay-at-homes may savour the spiritual adventurousness of travel without its human risks, and learn the wider significance of life. Graham Greene (1904–) and E. R. Eddison (1882–) are less harsh and arresting, and both begin unpretentiously, and then lead their readers into an unreal, or unrealizable world which lies within reach of the imagination. Greene develops a rather unnerving forecast of what might await the unwary. Eddison rises to a peculiar quality of imaginative richness. Perhaps the most estimable and under-estimated is the eldest, Forrest Reid (1876–). At his best he keeps to nothing more abstruse than the domestic and perceptive experiences of boyhood, or the family and friendly contacts of youth and age, though in some of his happiest moments he has revived the glamour and glow of ancient mythical Hellas. But in either case he suggests the deepest sympathies, the most delightful surprises, or even dramatic suspense. As a contrast we might note the latest effort of the youngest of the group : Alex Comfort's *The Power House* (1944). Despite the novel's irritating prolixity, he succeeds in making the reader appreciate the awful helplessness of the individualist of our time, isolated and defeated by the machine, thrown back on his subconscious self.

The younger school of poets (if they can be so classified) have attracted more attention.[1] Cecil Day Lewis (1904–) has broken away from the culture to which he has been bred in order to multiply his personality and make himself a poet. He looks for his human contacts among the millions who bear the burden of life without sharing in its privileges (*The Magnetic Mountain*). The cult of the under-privileged may open the heart and broaden the sympathies, but is not enough to complete the man. The poet has himself to reckon with ; and Lewis is trying to fulfil his personality in a somewhat mystic cult of sex and scenery, as he makes clear in *Transitional Poem*, and *Feathers from Iron*.

Stephen Spender (1909–) also aims at beating out his music amid the social and cultural tangle into which he feels that he is

[1] Vide J. G. Southworth, *Sowing the Spring*, 1940.

born, and also seeks that other inward fulfilment in the cult of nature and love (not forgetting homosexuality, much less that wider impersonal affection for all God's creatures). He is on a surer but more ambitious path in his confidence that poetry can inspire the courage to reform the world—a poetry which should express only what the writer experiences and yet hints at a deeper truth beyond. Partly for this reason, he still sometimes fails to convey his meaning.

Louis Macneice (1907–) writes more simply, and is less absorbed in socialism. In *Autumn Journal* (1939) he is as ready as Joyce to abhor the vices and helplessness of city life, but he equally abhors the other's defeatism ; and, indeed, the apathy, resignation, and egocentricity of the 'thirties. It is a less hopeful sign that he is still involved in metrical experiments, of which one cannot yet see the issue.

Wystan Hugh Auden [1] (1907–) is perhaps the most prominent of this generation, because his interests are more varied, his view is wider, and his versification more incisive and penetrating, notably in his poem *Spain*. He, too, is a politician, even a Marxist, and also a Freudian. The drift of his inspiration is towards freedom from self-absorption, partly through socialism and partly through sexual freedom, all leading to the triumph over fear, desire, self-contempt and reticence. So he is not backward in meditating on his own youthful errors and frustrations, even homosexuality. He has tried his hand at drama, social and moral propaganda in prose, and destructive criticism (*Letters from Iceland*, 1937, with Macneice). But if he lives, it will be as a poet who returns to natural scenery for his images and symbols.

If Auden voices the more complex difficulties which the individual has to face, Christopher Murray Grieve (Hugh Macdiarmid), an insatiable fighter, gives the most outspoken if not the best idea of contemporary restlessness and conflict, and the clash of opposing ideas in this disputatious age. He, too, is an inveterate and frequently unsuccessful experimenter in verse and prose styles, too often in the Scots dialect. So he is most likely to be remembered for his autobiography, *Lucky Poet : A Self-Study in Literature and Ideas* (1943), which gives an absorbing, though tiresomely verbose account of the personalities and preachments which are now making and unmaking public opinion.

It is, of course, already well known that this younger generation, of which a few representatives have just been noted, are part of a reaction from the 'Ivory Tower' and 'Axel's Castle' of the 'twenties. These latter, so well discussed by Edmund Wilson,[2] finding the twentieth-century atmosphere too complex or too crude, contented themselves (so their juniors allege) with verbal technicalities or archaisms of thought and expression. Or else they discarded these links with the storied Past, relied on their own untutored creative-

[1] For criticism see S. Spender, *The Destructive Element*, 1935.
[2] *Axel's Castle. A Study in the Imaginative Literature of 1870–1930* (1932).

ness, and satisfied that necessity by spinning, as it were, a web out of their own as yet unexplored subconscious, convinced that they would awake a kindred spontaneity in their fellows. Their successors refuse to be resigned, they cultivate the poor and the lowly partly because they are determined to learn what the world has to teach and partly to hasten the reconstruction of society. In this communal atmosphere they feel more able to explore their intimate selves. These social and spiritual reformers, or rather, would-be reformers, distrust the traditional culture they have learnt at school and college, with good reason, as far as literature, art, and science are an academic, even pedantic imposition on one's own natural impulse to create. Such is false culture. Many have therefore refused the true culture, which shows how the greatest minds of the Past have resisted these same impositions.

The newcomers seem bent on denying themselves this aid without which they can hardly make the most of themselves.[1] Perhaps the omens are more gloomy than the result may prove to be, for the most hopeful feature of the last twenty years is the courage, initiative and industry with which so many young men and women write. Much can be hoped from an age which is not tongue-tied.

REORIENTATION

The rapidity of transition in the twentieth century is now a commonplace, nevertheless it has taken our literary leaders by surprise; and for that reason each may have quickly arrived at his or her opinion on the principles of composition, but they have not had time to study and compare the prevailing theories, and work towards a synthesis. But before the end of the 'thirties the tendencies began to emerge more clearly. Herbert Read (1893–) in *The Politics of the Unpolitical* (1943) divides art into realism, expressionism, constructivism, and superrealism, which Derek Stanford, looking back from 1944, in *New Road* defines as ' the art of the world as the eye sees it, as the heart feels it, as the mind knows it, as the being dreams it '. The last is the most important, because dreams are voyages of discovery into one's own unrealized self—' shapes of prophecy '— intimations of what might become, whatever the means. R. H. Wilenski (1887–) in *The Modern Movement in Art* (1927) quotes Einstein on the need for ' a simplified synoptic view of the world conformable to our own nature, overcoming the world by replacing it with this picture '. Such seems to be the principle at which literature is at present aiming, and it is significant that direction is sought from two kindred though distinct lines of culture. These stages in the movement overlap, and we shall see in the next and final chapter that some progressives have begun to present a more precise and pointed terminology. However, the whole adventure is big with possibilities, but its advocates and practitioners, though surprisingly able, may forget that they are talking to others, as well as to themselves.

[1] Cf. *Poems from New Writing*, 1936–1946. Foreword by J. Lehmann.

CHAPTER XII

THE TENDENCIES OF TWENTIETH-CENTURY LITERA-
TURE AND THEIR CHANCES IN THE FUTURE

A CRITICAL study in literature is generally expected to reveal lines of development, and the rise or fall of schools, and it may be objected that in this case no such attempt has been made. This objection is natural, because we are all accustomed to the study of earlier periods in which the circle has already been completed, whereas the twentieth century is so far only a segment, already thrice interrupted, in 1914, 1919, and 1939. So one cannot do more than emphasize the broken beginnings, and dwell on the impulses that have not yet been crystallized into their most effective forms.

But the impulses are certainly there; they can be felt though not formularized; and this tendentious undercurrent implies a distinct development, a movement along an inward track.

In order to appreciate its significance, the reader is invited to imagine himself back in the sixteenth century, somewhere between 1550 and 1590. He would find an atmosphere of conflicts, cross-currents and tentative experiments, as confusing and indecisive as our own, and a very similar tension between the Old and the New. He would note that many people still enjoyed moralities, interludes, old-fashioned jest-books, and silly farces, all reminiscent of the Middle Ages. They were only just beginning to appreciate historical pageants, presented very much as their ancestors presented the Bible-story. On the other hand, he would find the young men about town, and the university wits already trying their hand at drama modelled on the newly revived Ancients, and scholars like Puttenham and Webbe arguing over the art and craft of literature, as they imagined it ought to be.

He would find that the younger generation were much intrigued by renaissance morals and manners, and were cultivating a fantastic and almost ludicrous prose style and he would observe that their euphuisms were a bid for self-discovery which more or less missed the mark. At the same time older and none the less able men were still writing in natural and incisive English, after the manner of Caxton, Latymer, Ascham, Stubbes, and Gosson, were genuinely alarmed at the spirit of irresponsible novelty around them, and were bent on reaffirming that what was good enough for their fathers was good enough for them.

The nation was already divided over the superstitions and anti-superstitions of the witch-controversy (so ably discussed and illustrated by Reginald Scot), and it had good reason to believe that the

Powers of Evil had broken loose. The country was distracted by heresies and schisms which might any day plunge the community into the savagery of a civil war. The rift between the gentlemen and commoners, soon to be styled cavaliers and round-heads, was already wide enough for Robert Greene to write *A Quaint Dispute between Velvet Breeches and Cloth Breeches*; and the curse of unemployment was filling the town with thieves and impostors and the country with hordes of vagabonds. The unrest was further complicated by the Tudor succession, which then seemed incapable of settlement, and by the ferment of conspiracies which it engendered. Foreign politics intensified the gloom at home. The massacre of St. Bartholomew was perpetrated in the same year in which the Dutch rose in revolt, apparently hopeless, against the tyranny of Spain; and the dread of a like fate did not leave England till after 1588.

If we are to believe E. M. Tillyard's *The Elizabethan World Picture*, educated people still accepted the old cosmology and believed man to be the centre of creation round whom the sun and stars dutifully revolved, though Pythagoras had declared the earth to be a ball floating in space, five centuries before the birth of Christ; Nicolas Koppernik had demonstrated before Henry VIII came to the throne that the sun stood still, and the earth and stars moved round it.

Altogether, that period bears some striking resemblance to our own. Yet no one doubts that in the sixteenth century a steady purpose ran through these conflicts and confusions and was gradually taking possession of the artistic and literary sense. This tendency might be described as the determination to make the best of life with the aid of classical intelligence and the sense of human personality—to observe facts inside and outside oneself, and reason about them on the background of ancient knowledge, using the inexhaustible resources of the Greek and especially Latin languages to clarify one's own indistinct thoughts and to raise vague intuitions to a vivid consciousness.

Every critic and historian recognizes this purposiveness. Yet it did not culminate in the perfection of forms, as in Italy and France. Its most immortal exponent is to be remembered by a collection of stage-plays, a mixture of medieval pageantry and superstitions, Senecan rhetoric, farce, fiction, and tragedy, jumbled together, with flashes of unstudied poetry, none the less technically inappropriate because inexpressibly beautiful and revealing.

Something analogous may be going to happen to the present generation. At least we can point to a similar progress, equally tendentious and contentious, muddling along a similar path, though it may never end in so glorious a realization. In our case, the dominant motive power is not classical humanism—that influence has been discarded no less ungratefully than the Elizabethans discarded gothic art—but observation, clear-sightedness and curiosity inspired by modern science.

This interpretation will be disputed, because when literary men talk about science, they generally think of an edifice of knowledge built on nomenclatures and generalizations, achieved by induction and deduction, concerned only with facts which repeat themselves —or else they remember the dismal history of the liver-fluke and the tsetse fly. These misconceptions ought to have vanished with Haeckel and Huxley. As has been noted, scientists themselves now disclaim certitude. Sir Arthur Eddington, perhaps the most success-ful popularizer as well as *savant*, always insists that what we think we learn from phenomena is something we have ourselves put there.

But that something does not come out the same as it went in. Whoever takes an interest, even at second hand, in scientific research, does not only sharpen his imagination on his external environment ; he begins to realize that his internal environment has acquired a new meaning. One cannot study geology, the structure of society and of the body, or again epistemology and the prehistory of the human animal without meeting a challenge to self-experience. There come reminders that many aspects of one's personality, or place in the social economy, have been left unexplored, or unexemplified. We recall memories, impulses, affinities, the stirring of fresh powers, spiritual as well as sensuous, which at the time passed unnoticed, because not picked out into *relief* by a terminology, or because their end and object were not visualized. Such is the nerve-centre of twentieth century culture, no less than classical-mindedness was that of Tudor times.

But only the nerve-centre. Its significance would have been more clearly recognized, except that no imaginative writer has yet discovered the appropriate technique : the art by which to humanize these and other such stark facts. The ideas have grown and pro-gressed, but their spiritual organization and presentment have lagged behind. No one has yet taught himself how to blend the warmth and enlightenment of personal contacts with the revelations of the bio-chemist, the psycho-analyst, and the authorities on folk-lore and ethnology ; to convince the world that scientific truth is an enlargement, not a restriction of the spirit. As Bergson says in his *Introduction to Metaphysics* : ' A true empiricism is that which pro-poses to get as near to the original Self as possible, to search deeply into its life, and so by a kind of intellectual auscultation, to feel the throbbings of its soul. . . . *It is true that the task is an extremely difficult one, for none of the ready-made conceptions which thought employs in its daily operations can be of any use.*'[1]

Nevertheless the spirit of the age has moved unsteadily forward and has reached the point when authors, despite their irreconcilable idiosyncrasies, seem to be conscious of a common purpose. This unifying idea might be described as the interdependence and inter-

[1] Quoted from M. F. Cleugh's *Time*. Italics our own.

penetration of the social and the psychological man; each of the two aspects enlarged and deepened by the consideration of the other.

In the previous chapters we have noted many unco-ordinated efforts towards some such synthesis, and recently the United States have produced two outspoken manifestoes. In 1943 N. E. Monroe in *The Novel of Society* complained that notable novelists, for instance Virginia Woolf, express nothing but themselves, a subject hardly worth expressing, whereas they would discover a much deeper illumination if they expressed themselves only as a part of essential humanity, an exemplification of Eternal Law, a revelation of man's ancient and unconquerable grandeur, even amid the disintegration of modern society. In 1944, Lewis Mumford, in *The Condition of Man*, reviews the whole history of Western culture and humanism to prove that civilization has now lost its way, frozen in fixed systems, mechanical adjustments, and non-human processes; a routine adapted to our external environment and the multiplication of wealth, but unelastic, tyrannous, uncongenial to the many-sidedness of human nature, constraining each of us to become functions not self-hoods. The future humanism must aim at 'a more perfectly harmonized, a more finely attuned, a more complexly balanced expression of both personality and community'.

England has produced nothing quite so provocative and dogmatic during the last few years, but we have seen that many poets and prose-writers are convinced that these dreams could and should become realities. It is now to be noted that some have given their hopes and faiths a name, thus transforming their ideals into a movement.[1]

These publicists, often dismissed as 'neo-symbolists', or 'post-surrealist romantics', leaving T. S. Eliot, W. H. Auden, C. Day Lewis, L. Macneice, and S. Spender behind, claim to be *Apocalyptics* or *Personalists*. The former believe that man should be a revelation to himself, limited only by his own vision, certainly not by environment, mass-thinking, or conformity to collectivism. The Personalists likewise hold to the supreme duty of understanding and thereby healing oneself; 'the person [is] the key to the meaning of the universe'; but lest such inwardness should limit their aspiration, they widen it to embrace all human activities, especially social responsibility. They not only seek, but share the pursuit of beauty and truth in all its most accessible and communal forms; and also by sympathetic contacts with the humbler, less sophisticated members of society, because these live simpler lives, and do more honest work with less show. In *Transformation* (1944) the editors have gone so far as to devote most of the volume to a definite scheme of education through art, religion, and poetry, which should create a free environment for the adventures of the spirit.

[1] Vide *New Road* (A. Comfort and J. Bayliss). *Transformation* (S. Schernanski and H. Treece). *Kingdom Come* (A. Rook, S. Schernanski, and H. Treece). *The Crown and the Sickle* (J. F. Hendry, H. Treece).

So far, so good ; a war-cry generally implies a united effort. But the reader will not be slow to observe that these aims are not new. They have been proclaimed again and again during the past centuries, sometimes by humanists too well known to be named ; and one fears that these young reformers sincerely believe themselves to be original because they are not aware of the wisdom and experience which ought to complete their ideas and direct their speculations. When they look into their own hearts, they may, perhaps, find less than they expect. When they plan for their fellow-creatures, they may fail to learn from the success and failure of older, but not less enlightened experiments. We have had occasion to note this mushroom culture during the last thirty years. Will it again fail them in face of post-war difficulties ?

They will certainly need all the help they can get, for they will be beset with problems more formidable than those which beset the generation which was entering on life in 1590. Our epoch has been styled the age of the common man, and even if his social sense and status are raised, his intellect may remain just as *common*. We are promised an immediate and satisfying reconstruction of the most ancient and essential institutions characteristic of humanity. It is all to be effected in a few years. Education, financial security, and recreation are to be supplied for all. Such benefits are indeed requisite. But they threaten to stop short at a managed culture, bureaucratically administered, and guaranteed by the lavish expenditure of the national resources. So there is a risk that the movement may again be hampered by rivalries, jealousies, and frustrated hopes, and may relapse into the competition for creature comforts and the acquiescence in routine instruction.

The war has certainly inspired an earnest desire for progress, a generous spirit of philanthropy, and a sense of mutual service, if not of human equality ; and despite maladjustments and disappointments the nation may well create a better life. But will it create a better literature ? An author is only half an author unless his ideas live in the heads of his fellow-creatures. He must feel at home in the atmosphere of his time. There will certainly be a tension between those who want to give everybody the same chance, and those who want to communicate the incommunicable, to reveal to the imagination a new flexibility and freedom. If culture settles down into a uniform, preconceived level, the adventurers and irreconcilables will not meet the response which feeds their genius. In that case they will dwindle into a cult, consoling each other with the appreciation they cannot win from the reading public.

And yet the prospect may not be so bleak. The post-war generation may be like an instrument sharpened in the uses of adversity. The community must by now have realized that democracy cannot survive unless every member understands for himself the tendency of thoughts as well as of events, and while criticizing social and political ideologies, the majority may also have acquired, almost unconsciously, an eye for human relationships, an at present undefined sense of the individual's spiritual needs, probably an aptitude for religious experience, certainly an inclination to discriminate between true and false values. In that case no man of genius will be too great to collaborate with his public.

This renascence will undoubtedly come. We have seen all through this review that the materials for great literature are not lacking; the atmosphere is crowded with expansive ideas, waiting to be symbolized in art; but over-zealous and uninspired reorganization, together with the other disillusionments of Peace, may delay its advent for more years than I wish to contemplate.

INDEX

PRINTED IN GREAT BRITAIN BY RICHARD CLAY AND COMPANY, LTD.,
BUNGAY, SUFFOLK.

Too much will melt it. Boiling water is sufficient. Zinc has a good resistance to corrosion and is used to make a protective coating over steel. Galvanized iron is actually mild steel coated with zinc. That method leaves a rather rough surface and a smoother finish is obtained by smooth zinc plating.

BRASS

Brass is one of the most used non-ferrous metals or alloys. It is an alloy of copper and zinc and proportions vary. The type alloyed for good machining qualities cannot satisfactorily be annealed, but the rolled forms of strip, sheet, bar and rod can be heated to redness and left to cool. Quenching quickly can cause cracks. It does not anneal to be as soft as copper, but it can be shaped in a similar way and work hardened by hammering. Brass has a good resistance to corrosion, but in a salty atmosphere the zinc in the alloy could be eaten away and the metal disintegrates. Brass will melt at temperatures obtainable at a smith's hearth, so it is just possible to use it for casting with simple equipment.

Another form of brass is sometimes called spelter and is used in brazing. The alloy is melted with a flame and fused to the surfaces being joined. This process can also be called hard soldering, but hard soldering is really the use of silver solder, which is a copper/zinc alloy with a little silver added. The effect is to lower the melting point. The melting temperature can be varied according to the proportions of the alloy. It is possible to make one joint, using an alloy of a lower temperature near another without fear of the first parting.

TIN

Pure tin is an expensive metal, so it is not used alone. It has been used as a coating for iron and steel sheet to make the tinplate familiar for cans and similar things. Tin is a safe metal to use with food and it has a good resistance to corrosion. Before plastics took over in many domestic applications, tinplate was used for many kitchen items. A tinsmith (a tinner) was a worker in tinplate, not pure tin.

BRONZE

Tin can be alloyed with copper—much like zinc. The result is very similar. But the color is usually a rich golden shade, depending on the proportions. In sheet form, it can be shaped into bowls and similar things like copper, but with greater trength. Like brass, it can be annealed with heat and hardened by hammering. That form of copper/tin alloy is called gilding metal. In rod or bar form it is called gunmetal. The old "brass cannons" were actually copper/tin alloys, usually with small quantities of other metals added. Many modern bronze items are basically copper and tin with small quantities of rarer metals included to give special qualities. While still known as bronze they can be prefixed by the name of an important added metal, such as *phosphor bronze*. Special types of bronze are mostly cast and can be machined, but they are not intended to be bent or otherwise shaped. Most bronze has a very good resistance to corrosion.

LEAD

Lead is the heaviest of the common metals and many of its uses are connected with its weight. It is an unattractive soft grey metal which is not strong enough to retain much detail. Its melting point is low enough for it to flow at temperatures that can be obtained with a gas flame or fire. Consequently, it can be used for casting, particularly for weights to give stability to something made from a lighter material. Lead alloys easily with many other metals and some, such an antimony, can be used with it to lower the melting point and make a stronger casting. Lead is also alloyed with tin to make soft solder, which is the common joining material in electrical work and other assemblies. The melting point is lower than that of either metal independently, with enough heat coming from a copper bit, heated electrically or by a flame.

ALUMINUM

Aluminum is very light in weight and silvery white in color. It is easily melted and can be cast with simple equip-ment. Pure aluminum is soft, although it is possible to spec the degree of relative hardness required. Resistance to co rosion is good and the metal is safe to use with food, as can seen in the drink cans made form it. Much aluminum availa is actually alloyed with other metals to give special qualiti particularly strength and hardness, which might not adequate in the pure metal for many purposes.

Aluminum anneals with heat and can be work harden but the annealing temperature of 350 degrees is much lov than that of other metals. Too much heat will ruin it. One sl method of getting the right metal annealing temperature i rub the metal with soap and heat only until the soap tu black. Aluminum is the one common metal that cannot joined with lead/tin soft solder. There are special alumin solders, but in general it is better to design aluminum structions so rivets or other fastenings are used instea solder.

Measuring And Holding

14

Accuracy of finished work depends on careful marking out in a way that can be seen and does not allow mistakes to occur due to misreading. Usually, marks are the best made with a scriber the smith can make. Its scratched line cannot be accidentally erased. The only place a scriber is not advisable is on a surface that will be polished or would otherwise be marred by the scratch.

A measurement from an edge is most easily made accurately by using a steel rule with the measurement on the rule over the edge and the scriber drawn across the end of the rule (Fig. 14-1A). If a series of measurements have to be taken, make them all from one mark rather than from each other. This wil reduce the possibility of making an overall error. For instance, a series of marks at 2 inch intervals are better made at 2 inches, 4 inches and 6 inches etc. from one point rather than at 2 inches from each other. However, spacing from one to the other could be used as a check.

Dividers are also useful for stepping off equal spacings (Fig. 14-1B). If a length has to be divided into a number of equal parts and it is not a length easy to divide arithmetically, making a series of steps with the dividers at experimental settings until they are right will get a perfect result. The exact spots are located by swinging the dividers to make short arcs across the base line (Fig. 14-1C).

A fine center punch, often called a dot punch, can be used lightly to make a small impression at any point that has to be marked. If the cone of the punch point is no more than one-sixteenth inch across and the angle a little more acute than the usual 60 degrees, exact location is easy to see and accuracy ensured. If the same location will also be drilled, the dot should be enlarged with an ordinary center punch. If a position has to be marked, locate it with crossing scriber marks and use the dot punch at the crossing (Fig. 14-1D). If a shaped outline has to be followed, a series of light dots is a good guide (Fig. 14-1E). If circles have to be drawn, use the divider . But have a dot punched for the center leg or it might wander.

Mark right angles to an edge with a try square (Fig. 14-1F). Use the try square to check a finished angle. Look toward light, otherwise you might assume that the angle it is accurate when it is not.

Odd-leg or hermaphrodite calipers are marking instruments. The pointed leg is a scriber. If you want to draw a line at a particular distance from an edge, set the caliper and pull it along (Fig. 14-1G). If you want to draw a line along the center of a bar, use the caliper from both edges. If two lines appear, the distance is wrong. Quite often the two lines are a sufficient guide (Fig. 14-1H) for locating a series of center punch dots for screw holes or something else where utmost precision is unnecessary.

Calipers are tools for comparing measurements. They are particularly useful for round objects, where it might be difficult to use a rule directly in position. The calipers depend on a friction joint or have a screw adjustment similar to the dividers. Outside calipers (Fig. 14-2A) can be set to span an external measurement, such as the outside of a cylinder. Inside calipers have their ends outward (Fig. 14-2B) and are used for internal measurements. Settings then have to be

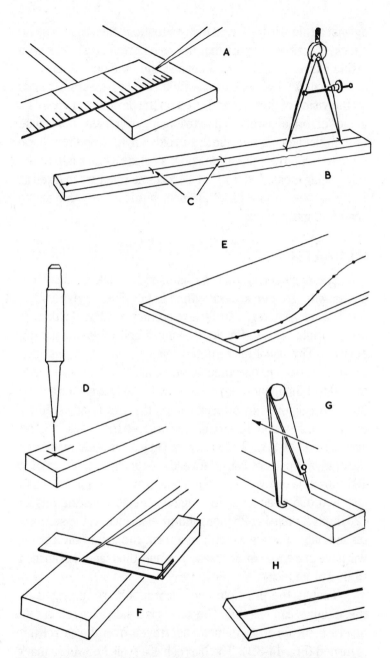

Fig. 14-1. Use a steel rule (A) to measure, step off with dividers (B,C) and mark positions with a center punch (D). Use dots as a guide (E), mark right angles (F), set the calipers (G) and use two lines as a guide (H).

321

against a rule. However, in many situations the caliper can be checked against the part that has to be fitted or a check with inside calipers can be tried against the outside calipers.

Accuracy by measuring with a rule or calipers depends on the vision of the user and even on the direction of view. To avoid "errors of parallax" due to looking diagonally or because of the thickness of the rule are avoided by having the rule on edge to bring the calibrations on it as close as possible to the thing being measured (Fig. 14-2C). Some rules are marked as finely as one-hundredth of an inch, but it is very difficult to read fine graduations.

MICROMETER

The engineering tool that is used for making measurements with greater accuracy than is possible by eye with a rule is a micrometer, usually a micrometer caliper, although the principle is used for depth gauges and other measuring devices. The usual micrometer caliper works in a one-inch range and reads to one-thousandth of an inch. One tool reads from 0 to 1 inch, another reads from 1 inch to 2 inches and so on. The caliper is in a form where the gap is adjusted by turning a screw and the size is read on the barrel enclosing the screw (Fig. 14-3A). The screw is very accurately made and the standard pattern has 40 threads per inch, so if it is turned 40 times it has moved 1 inch and one turn of one-fortieth of an inch is 0.025 of an inch. An engineer might describe this as "25 thous", meaning 25 thousandths of an inch. If the screw is turned only one-twenty-fifth of a turn, the gap in the caliper will have increased or decreased by one-thousandth of an inch (0.001 of an inch).

That is the principle and calibrations are arranged so these things can be read. The screw is inside a barrel, but its head is in the form of a thimble that travels over the barrel as it is turned (Fig. 14-3B). The barrel has a scale showing a mark at each one-fortieth of an inch, or each complete turn of the thimble, with a figure at each fourth mark (1/10 inch or 0.100

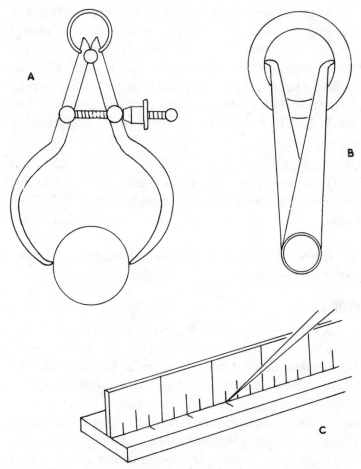

Fig. 14-2. Calipers measure outside (A) or inside (B) curves. Avoid errors by using a rule on edge (C).

inch). So each numbered mark is 0.025 of an inch (Fig. 14-3C).

The thimble has 25 equally spaced marks around its edge. When the caliper is closed, the one marked 0 is level with the line along the barrel. When the thimble is turned to that the next mark is level with the line, the gap is 0.001 of an inch. At one more mark, it is 0.002 of an inch or two-thousandths of an inch (Fig. 14-3D). That is about the thickness of one of your hairs.

As can be seen, the actual measurement is not read as a single figure. A simple sum is necessary and it is usually mentally calculated. There are three things to add: the number of figured line exposed (each 0.100 of an inch), the number of unfigured lines beyond that (each 0.025 of an inch) and the number of marks around the thimble edge (each 0.001 of an inch). The example in Fig. 14-3E can be interpreted as follows:

One numbered turn (tenth)	0.100 inch
Two more unnumbered turns (fortieths)	0.050 inch
Seventeen thimble divisions (thousandths)	0.017 inch
Total	0.167 inch

Other examples can be seen to be computed in the same way (Fig. 14-3F).

VERNIER

A vernier is a different method of making fine measurements and it is not limited to 1 inch steps like a micrometer. The principle is used in many instruments, but a common type serves as inside and outside calipers with a sliding head on a calibrated stem (Fig. 14.4A). The ends of the jaws are a known thickness (often 0.25 of an inch) so their total can be added to the reading obtained on the scale when you use the tool as an inside caliper. Outside measurements are read directly.

The marks on a vernier scale are read from one small scale sliding alongside another where marks that coincide indicate the measurement. A simple vernier to read to hundredths of an inch will show the principle. The main scale along the stem is calibrated in inches and one-tenths of an inch (Fig. 14-4B). This can be any length. On the sliding jaw there is another scale. When zero on one jaw is against zero on one jaw is against zero on the other scale, the jaws are touching.

The vernier scale on the sliding head is nine-tenths of an inch long, but is divided into ten equal divisions. Each of these

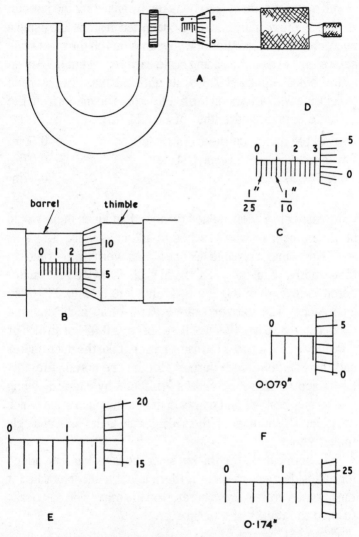

Fig. 14-3. A micrometer has its barrel and thimble calibrated to read to one-thousandth of an inch: (A) the gap is adjustable; (B) the thimble travels over the barrel (C) each numbered mark is 0.100 of an inch; (D) 0.001 of an inch; (E,F) see text for explanation.

divisions is 0.09 of an inch (Fig. 14-4C). This means that a division on the sliding scale is 0.01 of an inch less than a division on the main scale. It is this fact that allows the particular vernier to be read to one-hundredth of an inch.

If a measurement is to be taken by adjusting the jaws on an object, the reading has to be computed in steps like using a micrometer. The number of whole divisions on the main scale before the zero on the sliding scale each represent 0.10 of an inch. Look along the sliding scale until one mark can be seen to coincide with a mark on the fixed scale. The marks from the zero are in one-hundredths. In Fig. 14-4D:

Five whole marks on the fixed scale	0.50in.
Seven marks on the vernier scale	0.07in.
Total	0.57in.

If the caliper has been opened to more than 1 inch there would be the number of whole inches to add in as well.

The same principle is used in a vernier to read to thousandths of an inch. The main scale is divided into numbered tenths, then these are divided into four (0.025 of an inch each). The vernier scale is 0.60 of an inch long and divided into 25 parts. Each of these parts is 0.024 of an inch or 0.001 of an inch less than a main division. Like the micrometer and the one-hundredth vernier, tenths are noted. Any fortieths and further thousandths are found by checking along the vernier scale to find marks on it and the main scale which coincide. The number on the sliding scale is the total of single thousandths.

In both cases, the thickness of the jaws must be added for an inside measurement if there is not a second scale for this. Some verniers are calibrated on the other side metrically to read to fiftieths of a millimeter.

VISES

The blacksmith's leg vise can be used for general metalwork. Precision work, particularly over different thickness ranges, is more easily done with a parallel-action machinist's vise. It need not be as large as the leg vise, which can be up to 6 inches or more across the jaws. A parallel-action machinist's vise with 3 inch or 4 inch jaws will be large enough for most

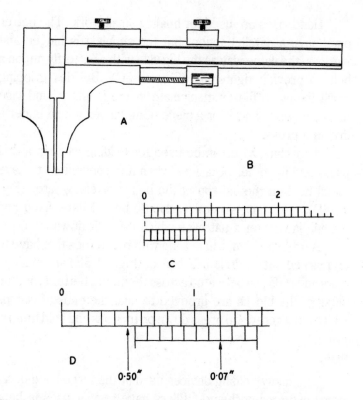

Fig. 14-4. A vernier gauge (A) uses two scales (B,C) sliding against each other.

benchwork. This bolts to the top of the bench and should be arranged to overhang enough for the fixed jaw face to come a little further out than the edge of the bench (Fig. 14-5A). Have the bench top thick (as much as 2 inches) and bolt through. Wood screws would soon loosen. A modern machinist's vise will withstand fairly heavy hitting, but if it is to remain accurate it is better to do all hammering on the leg vise.

A machinist's vise has hardened steel jaws with teeth cut in them. Make vise clamps from brass or other soft metal to protect polished metal from the teeth (Fig. 14-5B). Some vises have a quick-release action by pulling a lever to open a split nut. This is a convenience, but it does not improve the use of the vise.

Hand vises are used for holding small work. The better ones have a parallel action, but the simplest is hinged and works in the same way as the leg vise with a butterfly nut on a bolt to provide tightening (Fig. 14-5C). Besides gripping small things to file or manipulate in the hand, a hand vise makes a good handle for a piece of metal being held under a drill in a press.

A machine vise can be used for holding work in a drill press and for other occasions when it is convenient to have metal held on the flat top of the bench or elsewhere. (Fig. 14-5D). Ther are several versions, but all have fixed and moving jaws over a flat base which can bolt down.

A problem comes in dealing with round rods that have to be marked out or drilled. V-blocks (Fig. 14-5E) are made in pairs and rods can be rested across them. In a better type, the sides of the blocks are grooved to take the ends of clamps which have screws to press down on the rods and hold them in place.

PLIERS

The many holding devices used at the forge have occasional use for benchwork. Pliers have regular uses in benchwork. Examination of a tool catalog will show that there is an enormous range of pliers available. Of most use are those with broad flat jaws and stout enough not to flex when gripped tightly. These will do many things, from picking up small items to closing folded sheet metal and pushing rivets through holes. Many pliers have cutters in the jaws nearer their pivots and there might be wire cutters at the side. Occasionally there are uses for thin-nosed pliers for getting into awkward places, while round-nosed pliers are useful for twisting loops in wire.

Gas pliers have jaws hollowed across with teeth pointing inward—using two sizes of hollow in one pair of jaws. They are useful for gripping and turning round objects. The type of plier or wrench that can be adjusted and then locked on with a lever can be used as a hand vise as well as pliers.

328

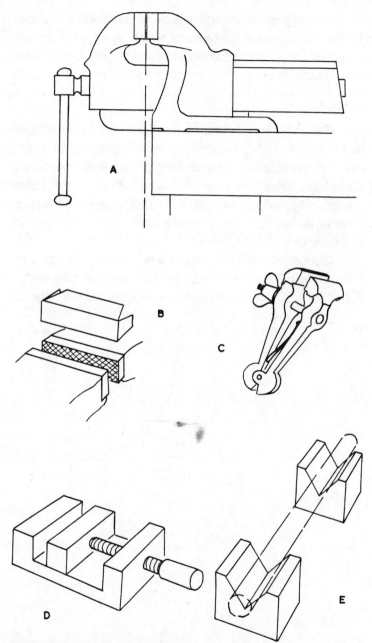

Fig. 14-5. A vise overhangs the edge of a bench (A) and can be fitted with clamps (B). Hand vises (C), bench vises (D) and V-blocks (E) will hold work for machining.

Sizes of pliers to choose depend on the work to be done. There are some delicate ones for watch repairs, but for the usual benchwork an overall length of about 8 inches should be satisfactory.

CLAMPS

Woodworkers' C-clamps have occasional uses in holding metal parts together for drilling or during assembly. However, there are few uses for engineers' clamps. A toolmaker's clamp has two jaws and two crews across them. The one near the gripping end pulls in and the other pushes out with a levering action. This design is to a clamp commonly made in wood for general woodwork.

Much clamping is done in a vise or by using bolts through holes in the parts. Where there are no holes, two bars can be drilled for bolts and the parts drawn together between them.

Cutting And Shaping

If benchwork is being done in the same place as the forge, some pieces can be cut to length on the anvil with the hardie and sets. Most general metalwork cutting and shaping will have to be done to the cold metal with hand tools on the bench. Work on the anvil would be inappropriate to most of the non-ferrous metals in any case.

The basic cutting and shaping tools are saws and files. Thinner metals are cut with a scissor action by snips and cold chisels.

SAWING

Unlike woodworking saws, metalworking saws have disposable blades and these are discarded when blunt or broken. Metalworking saws are not resharpened. Hacksaws are the general purpose metalworking saws. Blades are mostly about one-half inch wide with teeth on one edge and holes at the ends to engage with pegs in a hacksaw frame (Fig. 15-1A). The teeth are designed to cut on the push stroke and they are set alternate ways to make a cut wider than the thickness of the blade so that it does not bind in a deep cut. Instead of setting individual teeth, some of the finest teeth are in blades with the edge made wavy to give the same effect.

Hacksaw blades are made in several lengths, but for most purposes, 10 inches or 12 inches are a good choice. Teeth coarseness is described by the number of teeth per inch—18, 24 and 32 are commonly available. Hacksaw blades are made of high carbon steel, but makers also supply blades made of special alloy steels to give special qualities. Blades described as *high speed* steel are not necessarily for using fast, but this indicates a hard, long wearing steel. However, some of these steels are brittle and an unintentional twist during sawing could shatter a blade. Better high-speed steel blades have graduated hardness, softening towards the back, giving flexibility and toughness. Other blades are described as unbreakable or flexible, which should be regarded as relative terms only. Keep a stock of blades as they do not have a very long life.

The simplest hacksaw frame has a bowed rigid back and a straight handle to a rod with a peg for one end of the blade. At the other end, the rod is screwed with a butterfly nut to tension the blade (Fig. 15-1B). This is the basic frame and one would not be difficult to make. A straight handle is not the most natural way to control a saw. Most manufacturers produce frames with piston-grip handles, usually on a frame that can be adjusted in length to accomodate different sizes of blades (Fig. 15-1C). Details vary. Usually a butterfly nut at the handle end tensions the blade and the rods are square section to turn into any of four positions. The blade can be set across the frame as well as in line with it.

In woodworking, it would be considered wrong to put your second hand on the far end of the saw. But in cutting metal, it is usual to hold the far end of the frame to provide extra control and put on pressure (Fig. 15-1D). To position a cut accurately, start by making a small groove with the edge of a file. Metal is best cut with a slow heavy stroke going the full length of the blade. Keep enough pressure on for the teeth to be always cutting. If they merely slide over the metal, they will quickly blunt. Fast light cuts are not as effective as steady

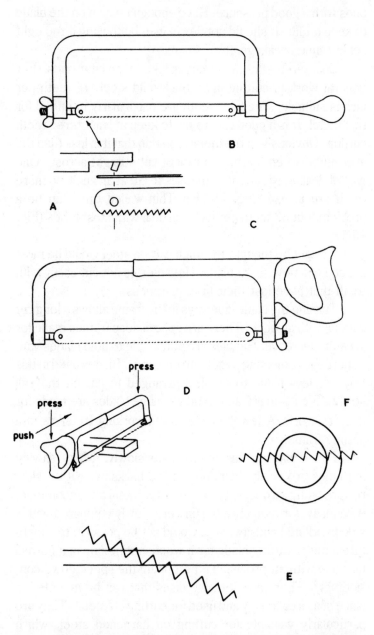

Fig. 15-1. A hacksaw cuts on the forward stroke. Teeth size have to be chosen to suit the work: (A) the peg engages a hacksaw frame; (B) the blade is held by a butterfly nut; (C) piston-grip handle; (D) apply pressure and push; (E) cut at an angle; (F) most tube can be cut with a hacksaw.

ones with a good pressure. Have enough tension on the blade to keep it taut. It should not flex in use, but pulling it too tight could cause breakages.

Coarser teeth should cut quicker than fine ones. For general work in cutting fairly thick mild steel, 18 teeth per inch is suitable. The finer teeth are particularly intended for thin metal. It is a good rule to try to keep at least three teeth cutting. Obviously, if the metal is so thin that it is less than the spacing between teeth, you cannot cut straight across. One way of dealing with thinner metal is to cut at an angle so more teeth are in use (Fig. 15-1E). Thin-walled tube can be a problem, but 32 teeth per inch will deal with most tubes (Fig. 15-1F).

It might be thought that high carbon steel would be most in need of a new sharp blade. However, is not cut easily with teeth that have lost their first sharpness.

Turning the blade sideways in the frame allows a long cut parallel with an edge. There are special deep frames made for greater clearance. Handles are obtainable to hold blades with a short end projecting to get into openings. Blades used in this way are less liable to break if arranged to cut on the pull stroke. Some small frames and very fine blades are made for delicate work. A jeweller uses metalworking fretsaws in a sprung frame.

Power sawing has to be done slowly. Many sawing machines are really adaptions of the hacksaw, with a slow reciprocating stroke. Circular saws for metal are uncommon. A bandsaw for metal has to run very slowly compared with a woodworking bandsaw, so it would not be possible to substitute a metal cutting blade for a wood cutting one in a normal machine without provision for stepping the speed down considerably. There are abrasive discs that can be mounted in place of a circular saw and used for cutting off metal. They are particularly valuable for cutting off hardened steel, which would not respond to any saw blade. Hardened steel can be held against the edge of a grinding wheel to cut notches around it. Then it is snapped off.

SHEARING

Much sheet metal can be cut in a similar way to scissors cutting cloth. An example is the use of a cold chisel across a vise, where the vise jaw acts as one shearing blade and the chisel is the other (Fig. 15-2A). It is possible to cut through quite thick and hard metal in this way and moderate curves can be followed by altering the position of the metal in the vise between cuts.

For thinner and softer metals, it is more common to use snips. They are usually sold as tinner's or tinman's snips, from their common employment when tinplate was more generally used. Snips have short blades and long handles to provide leverage. The handles can be straight (Fig. 15-2B) or given eyes like scissors (Fig. 15-2C).

Straight blades will cut large sweeping curves as well as straight lines. For tighter curves, there are snips with curved blades. The best choice, if only one pair is obtained, are combination snips which are narrow and suitable for curves or straight lines. Overall lengths are from 8 inches to 13 inches and there are small versions for delicate work. Some snips are made with alloy steel blades for cutting hard metals and there are others with toggle action for greater leverage.

When using hand shears or snips, a long cut is made by opening it as the cut progresses and tilting the snips slightly. Both sides of the cut will have to be bent slightly to give clearance for the snips. The newly-cut edge is often sharp, so be careful you do not cut your hand. One side of the cut—that over the lower blade—will remain true, but the other will buckle slightly. It is possible to get snips hinged opposite ways to allow a choice of which is to be the good edge, but it is usually sufficient to arrange the important part to the left when using the normal right-handed snips.

A bench shearing machine is useful for cutting across large sheets, although it will also deal with smaller work. It will also cut thicker material than can be cut by hand snips and it can have a hole through the jaws so rod can be cut off. There are several versions, but basically the machine has a straight jaw to the left and a curved jaw to the right to pivot over it when pressure is put on with a lever (Fig. 15-2D).

For cutting wire and thin rod, many pliers have notches in the side so the wire can be laid across with the pliers open and a squeeze on the handle cuts it. Another arrangement has the cutting edges meeting. This is seen in top cutters (Fig. 15-2E) where the blades are not far from the pivot point and considerable leverage is provided. The cutters extend wider than the body of the tool so wire can pass along the side. Side cutters (Fig. 15-2F) are a similar tool, but with the cut angled. Both types can be used for cutting off the ends of rivets and similar things as well as for cutting wire.

FILING

After metal has been cut, the edges have to be brought to exact size and this is usually done by filing. A file is to metalwork what a plane is to woodwork. A file is a piece of hardened steel with grooves cut across it so as to raise cutting edges. With a set of single cuts the tool is called a mill file. It is more usual for a second set of cuts to cross the first, so the intersections form teeth instead of broad cutting edges. If teeth are raised individually, the tool is a rasp and not a file. Rasps are used on wood and horses' hooves and are unsuitable for metal.

The length is quoted as the size of a file, but this excludes the tapered tang that goes into a handle. There are a great many sizes of files and most types range from 4 inches up to 18 inches or more. For general use 10 inches is a reasonable choice.

Files are given different *cuts*, meaning coarseness of teeth. From coarse to fine the cuts are: rough, bastard, second, smooth and dead smooth. However, many files are only commonly available as bastard and smooth and these cuts serve most purposes. "Cut" is relative to length. For instance, a bastard 12 inch file is actually much coarser than a bastard 6 inch file.

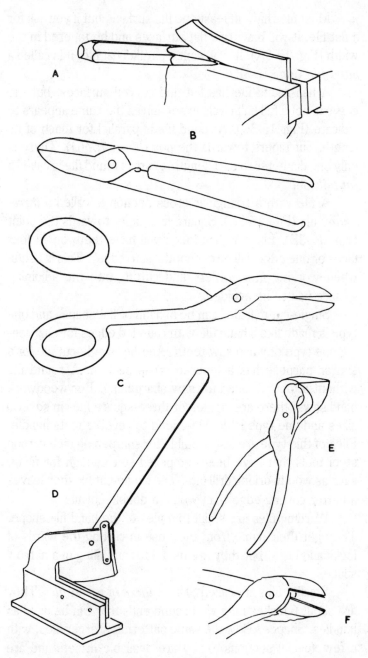

Fig. 15-2. Sheet metal can be cut with a chisel across a vise (A) or with snips (B,C,E,F) or shears (D).

337

Most files have at least one flat surface, but if you ask for a flat file, it will have two flat surfaces and be tapered in the width (Fig. 15-3A). If you want a parallel flat file, it is called a *hand file* (Fig. 15-3B).

A half-round file has flat and curved surfaces, but the curve is not a full half circle in section as the name appears to indicate (Fig. 15-3C). A round file is parallel for much of its length, but tapers towards the point (Fig. 15-3D). There is only one diameter to each length. A small round file is called a *rat tail* file.

A file with a triangular cross section is called a *three-square* file (Fig. 15-3E). Square files taper towards the point (Fig. 15-3F). Flat and hand files will have teeth on all four faces or one edge will be a smooth "safe edge". This is useful when working into corners and cutting into the adjoining surface has to be avoided.

Single-cut mill files can be in hand or flat shapes and one type is made like a hand file with rounded edges for sharpening one type of wood saw teeth. Another single-cut file for a similar purpose has a tapered cross section. A round file without a taper is used for saw sharpening. For woodwork hand saws, there are single-cut three-square files in several sizes and one type is double-ended to reverse in its handle. Files of this type are also suitable for sharpening high carbon steel tools that have been tempered soft enough for filing, such as woodworking drill bits. The single-cut file then leaves a better cutting edge than would a double-cut file.

Warding files are small thin files of the hand file shape. They get their name from their use in cutting the wards of locks and keys, but they are useful for any filing in a narrow space.

Smaller files are called *Swiss pattern* or *needle files*. They are about 6 inches long with round ends that can be used as handles. Shapes follow the same patterns as larger files, with a few special sections. They are available in sets and are intended for watchmakers and other fine metalworkers, but they are useful for small cuts in general work.

Files tend to clog in use. This can be reduced by rubbing the cutting surface with talc (French chalk). But there are

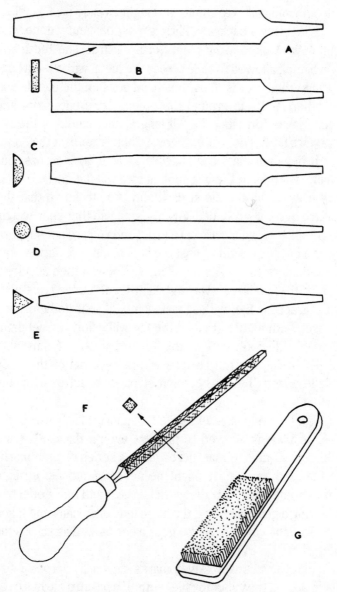

Fig. 15-3. Files are made in many sections (A, B, C, D, E) and can be cleaned with a wire brush (F, G).

occasions when the space between teeth will have to be cleared. This is best done with a file card (Fig. 15-3G) pulled across the lines of cut. It is a wire brush, that can be brought by length and nailed to wood, or bought already on a handle.

Like using a hacksaw, filing is most efficiently done with long slow strokes using plenty of pressure. The teeth will soon blunt if allowed to slide across the metal without cutting. In all but the shortest files, one hand goes on the handle and the other is closed around the other end. Apart from any other reason for using the full length, the middle of the file gets worn first. Therefore, there are better teeth at the ends.

It does not matter if a saw rocks as it goes across, but usually when filing the intention is to get a flat surface. It is very easy to dip the file at each end of a stroke so that the surface becomes rounded. Always stand so that your weight is on your feet, which are spread out and you are not supporting part of your weight against the bench. Use your arms from the shoulders as well as the elbows. You will then acquire a rhythm that involves swaying slightly on your legs as your arms direct the file, with all main joints of your body forming linkage. With a little practice the file will follow a level path. Although a file only cuts on the forward stroke, it is usual to slide it back over the surface with a reversal of the body linkage action. Lifting between strokes would destroy the rhythm.

If a long edge has to be filed, support it fairly low in the vise. If much is allowed to project, even a thick piece will judder or vibrate so that there will be a series of jump marks on the filed surface. It might be necessary to file straight across some parts, but the work is easier and more effective in getting a good surface if the file is held diagonally and taken across so the cutting surface goes along as well as across the edge (Fig. 15-4A).

Filing in this way leaves marks diagonally across a size that matches the cut of the file teeth. If a bastard file has been used to remove metal quickly, it should be followed by one with a smooth cut—preferably at a different angle to the first strokes so that a smoother surface results. There is another way of getting an even smoother surface by *draw filing*. Hold the file straight across the metal edge with a hand at each end and move it sideways along the edge (Fig. 15-4B). Using a smooth file in this way leaves very fine lines along the edge in place of those diagonally across.

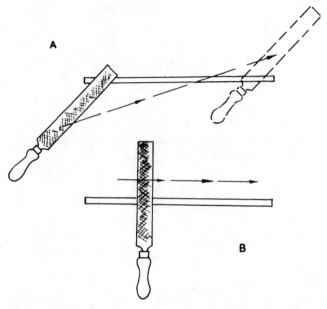

Fig. 15-4. The full file should be used along an edge (A). The edge is then finished by draw filing (B).

If there is a turned-over edge, that can be rubbed off with the tip of a file. If further smoothing is needed, use abrasive paper wrapped around a flat piece of metal or wood. The traditional abrasive for use on metal is emery. But there are other abrasives just as suitable.

Double-cut files serve for nearly all metals. For hard steel, as in saw sharpening, single-cut mill files work better. Lead and other soft metals and alloys quickly clog ordinary files. Single-cut files with quite coarse teeth in curves across the face are made for use on lead.

Drilling And Screwing

16

Throughout the time that man has worked metals, he has mastered most techniques. However, the weakest technique for a long time was making holes, particularly in the harder metals. The blacksmith punched holes and worked them to shape with drifts. But these were not precision things that would give an exact fit on a cylindrical rod as required for an axle running in a bearing. The alternative, until comparatively recent times, was the use of a flat drill which cut mainly by a scraping action and required considerable force to get it through any thickness of metal.

Flat drills can be made with simple equipment. That is an advantage, since they can be made to special sizes. However, the only continuing use for flat drills in a modern shop is for countersinking. To make a flat drill, flatten the end of the rod of high carbon steel. See that the flattened part is central with the rod and thick enough to provide strength. It should be about one-eighth of an inch for drills and one-half inch to 1 inch in diameter. It is proportionally less for smaller ones. Grind the two faces and grind the two cutting edges (Fig. 16-1A). The point where the cutting edges meet must be central. Rotate the rod to see if this is so and regrind until it is right.

Not only must this be central, but the cutting edges must be at the same angle to the centerline of the rod. For countersinking, the included angle is usually 60 degrees. However, it could be between 60 degrees and 90 degrees (Fig. 16-1B).

Although the cutting edges could continue to the outside made by flattening if it is only intended for countersinking, the edges should be ground parallel if the drill is to be a particular size (Fig. 16-1C). This also looks better for a countersink drill. Leave the grinding of the cutting angle to last. For brass, this should be about 12 degrees (Fig. 16-1D). The scraping action produced by the vertical leading edge works well on brass, but on steel and most other metals there should be some relief on the front. This can be made by grinding a groove across the edge (Fig. 16-1E). Harden and temper the end.

TWIST DRILLS

The flat drill was followed by a straight-fluted type, usually with three flutes to do something to prevent the tendency to drill slightly eccentrically when cutting edges are opposite. Otherwise the cutting action was the same as a flat drill. Improvements came when Henry Morse twisted the flutes to make what has become the universally used twist drill. For nearly all drilling of metal, twist drills are the choice. Twist drills are made in all the sizes likely to be needed. In the smaller sizes, there are drills that differ only by thousandths of an inch. Sizes go up to much larger than could be used in a small shop.

A twist drill has two cutting edges from which the flutes twist back to carry away the swarf (metal cuttings). The outside of the drill is parallel so that it is guided to cut straight when drilling deeply.

The important part is the cutting end. This has to be ground to angles which combine to make the drill cut (Fig. 16-2A). A new drill comes correctly ground, but when it becomes blunt it has to be ground on an abrasive wheel. With

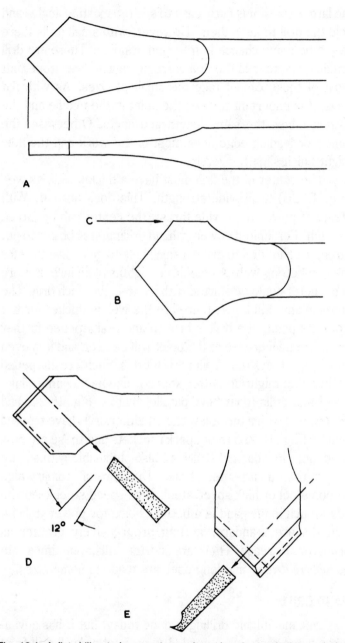

Fig. 16-1. A flat drill cuts by scraping and can be given a better angle by grooving: (A,B,C) grind the cutting edges to angle; (D) use this angle for brass; (E) grind a groove.

the larger sizes, it is fairly easy to see the existing angles and hold the drill to keep them. However, with small drills there has to be some chance in freehand grinding. There are drill grinding jigs to hold the drill correctly against the stone, but most of these cannot take the smallest sizes. As with flat drills, it is important to keep the point in the middle and the cutting edges the same length and angle. Otherwise, the longer or leading edge does most of the work and the hole might finish slightly oversize.

The center of the drill must have a thickness in its web (Fig. 16-2B) to provide strength. This does not cut. With plenty of power to provide thrust, the center can be forced through. For limited power or hand drilling, it is better to put through a pilot drill to make a small hole to give clearance for the non-cutting web. A hole three-eighths of an inch or more in diameter could be started with a one-eighth inch drill. The flutes in any drill taper, therefore the web is thicker further from the point. If a drill is broken and resharpened further back, the thicker web at the point will be seen and it is even more important to use a pilot drill for this. Such a resharpened broken drill might be better kept for use as a countersink.

Most drills today have parallel shanks (Fig. 16-2C) and are gripped with a three-jaw chuck. Other drills have tapered shanks (Fig. 16-2D) to fit special sockets and these are now used more in industry. Drills are also obtainable with square shanks to fit a carpenter's brace. Drills are of ordinary high carbon steel or high speed steel. High speed steel keeps its edge much longer and is a better choice for power drilling. Lengths are standard, getting progressively greater as diameters increase. There are shorter drills, sometimes called *jobbers drills*, and long ones are made in some sizes.

HAND DRILL

Not much hand drilling is done today, but it has advantages when restraint is needed to prevent a small drill from going too far. The slow speed of hand work makes a countersink drill cut better. A carpenter's brace can be used with a countersink bit. For other hand drilling, there is a drill that is sometimes called a *wheel brace* (Fig. 16-2E). It can hold drills up to one-fourth of an inch or larger if it is designed with a handle to lean against and provide pressure.

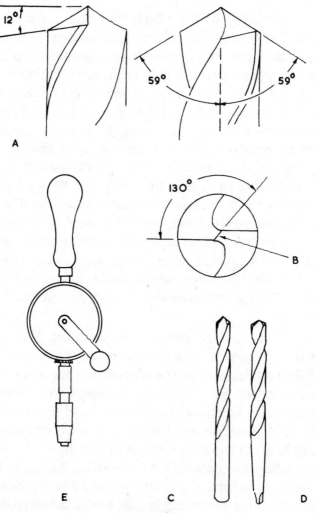

Fig. 16-2. A twist drill has to be sharpened correctly. Small sizes can be used in a hand drill: (A) cut; (B) center must be thick; (C) parallel shanks; (D) tapered shanks.

It is better for most purposes to have an electric drill, preferably with a capacity to at least three-eighths of an inch and with speed variations. This can be used freehand for much drilling. For accuracy, particularly in keeping a hole at right angles to a surface, the electric hand drill should be mounted in a stand or a more ambitious drill press should be used.

Fortunately, drills are fairly tolerant of differences in speed. The work is more efficient if the speed can be adjusted to suit the diameter. It is the peripheral speed that counts. A point on a large diameter drill travels much further in one revolution than a point on a small drill, so the revolutions of the large drill should be less than those of the small one. A three-speed drill gives enough range, so drills near the chuck capacity should be driven at the slowest speed, small drills at the high speed and others at the intermediate speed. As the actual speed of an electric drill varies with the load, actual cutting speeds are usually lower than that indicated by the electric drill maker. Using too low a speed is better than having it too high. A little experience will show when a drill is cutting at its optimum speed. As an approximate guide, a one-half inch high speed steel drill in mild steel should revolve at about 500 rpm and a one-eighth inch drill should revolve at 2000 rpm.

Drills are started with a center punch dot. Make sure this is large enough to take the non-cutting web of the drill so that the point stays on the starting point and does not wander before it enters. Sheet metal should be supported, either on another piece of metal or a piece of hard wood. It is unwise to hold metal being drilled by hand. If precision is important, it would be better to hold the work in a bench vise, V-blocks or other appropriate manner. If it is something that can be held by hand, use a hand vise or the type of pliers that lock on. When a drill breaks through the far side of the metal it can snatch and jerk lightly held metal from your hand. The point of snatch also shows if the drill chuck has not been tightened sufficiently since the drill grips the metal and slips in the chuck. The chuck jaws will then damage the drill so that it will be difficult to mount accurately another time. Use the chuck key tightly. If there are several positions for it, using it in each will help to get maximum grip.

Drilling generates heat. If the drill is allowed to get too hot, its temper will be drawn and it becomes useless. There is no satisfactory way of heat-treating highspeed steel drills in a small shop. To keep the temperature down, any drilling more than the occasional hole should be accompanied by lubrication. There are special soluble oils used in production work, usually running continuously on the drill, but in a small shop a brush could be used to apply a little at a time from a container. Soapy water is also suitable for mild steel. Cast iron cuts without generating enough heat to matter. Kerosene can be used on brass and aluminum. Light lubricating oil can be squirted on from an oil can for occasional drilling.

SCREW THREADS

The principle of the screw thread has been known for a very long time. Archimedes in ancient Greece knew all about it. The practical problems associated with cutting internal and external screw threads to match prevented much use of such things as nuts and bolts until quite recent times. Blacksmiths and engineers of only a century or so ago avoided screw threads if they could. If they had to use them, matching internal and external threads were made and these bore no relationship to other threads. A nut would only fit the bolt it was made for. The Industrial Revolution brought standardization as the quantity production of screw threads became possible. Unfortunately, the users of screw threads never agreed on common standards. Far too many standard screw threads became established. Some of these are still in use. There is agreement on threads for most purposes, but there are still exceptions. Obviously, metric threads differ from those based on inches. Bicycle parts, for instance, are still made with different threads than other things.

Most thread forms are triangular, but these do not all have the same angles. There are other forms, mainly in larger sizes. For general use, there are triangular threads that suit most purposes and screwing tackle to cut them. Threads are mostly known by diameter and a number indicating threads per inch. The diameter is that of the rod on which an external thread is cut. A thread described as one-fourth by 20 means one cut on a one-fourth inch rod with 20 threads in one inch of length. The hole in which a matching thread would be cut would have to start smaller (Fig. 16-3A). This is the tapping size. For the one-fourth inch thread, the tapping size in most metals should be thirteen-sixty-fourths of an inch. It might have to be slightly larger in hard steel and could be slightly smaller in softer metals. A table is usually provided with screwing tackle, indicating the size drill to use.

DIES

Screw threads on rod or bolts are cut with a die. At one time dies were in two parts, but now the common type is solid (Fig. 16-3B). There is a screw thread through a central hole and three or four holes that break into it provide cutting edges. The threaded part is ground away to provide a tapered entry for the rod to be screwed. The die is turned with a wrench, called a die stock. A round die is fitted in and prevented from turning with pegs or screws (Fig. 16-3C). Alternatively, the die can have a hexagonal shape and the stock has a matching recess. That type of die can be turned with a wrench like a nut for cleaning damaged threads or getting into places where there is no space for the stock. A split die gives limited adjustment (Fig. 16-3D). A pointed screw into the split can expand the dies slightly so a finished thread can be tighter in its nut.

The die is put in the stock with the tapered part of the thread outward. It helps to bevel around the end of the rod to help it enter the die. Have the rod pointing upward in the vise. Start the die on it with firm downward pressure and see that it

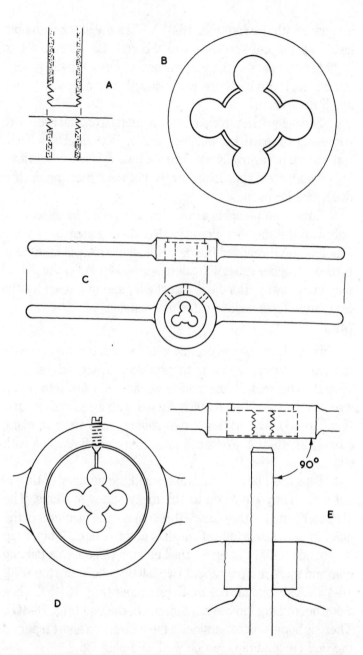

Fig. 16-3. External threads are cut with a die in a die stock: (A) the hole starts smaller; (B) solid die; (C) pegs or screws prevent turning; (D) a split die; (E) hold the rod in a vise.

is square with the rod (Fig. 16-3E). Turn the stock with both hands so the die screws on to the rod. Be careful not to wobble or threads at the end will brake. Once the die is seen to be true, it can be screwed down with a turning action only and little pressure.

The die will remove particles of metal from the rod. With some metals, particles will clear easily. With others, a backward move occasionally will free the swarf. Use thin lubricating oil on a steel rod. Brass might not need lubrication. If it does, use kerosene.

Cutting and shaping a thread is partly done by the cutting edges of the die, but there is also some squeezing by the shape of the threads in the die. Not all metals will take clean threads. Copper rod is difficult to screw as parts of the thread may break away. If a die is adjustable, spring it open for the first cuts. Then reduce it for final cuts.

TAPS

Threads in holes are made with taps. A tap is a screwed rod with grooves along it to produce cutting edges (Fig. 16-4A). The end of the rod is square and fits into a tap wrench. The simplest wrench is a bar with a square hole in it (Fig. 16-4B). Others have two sliding parts to take many sizes (Fig. 16-4C). For small taps, there are wrenches with chucks (Fig. 16-4D).

Taps are known by diameter and the number of thread per inch. They are made to suit many screw systems. The diameter is that of the outside threads, not the diameter of the hole. In each size a full set consists of three taps. A taper tap is ground so that the tip is small enough to go into a tapping hole and there are only about two full threads at the top (Fig. 16-4E). A second tap has much less taper (Fig. 16-4F), while a bottom or plug tap has full threads to the end (Fig. 16-4G). There is some confusion since a tap with only a short taper on the end (second tap) can be sold as a plug tap.

Precautions are needed when starting dies. Be certain to have the tap square to the surface and in line with the hole.

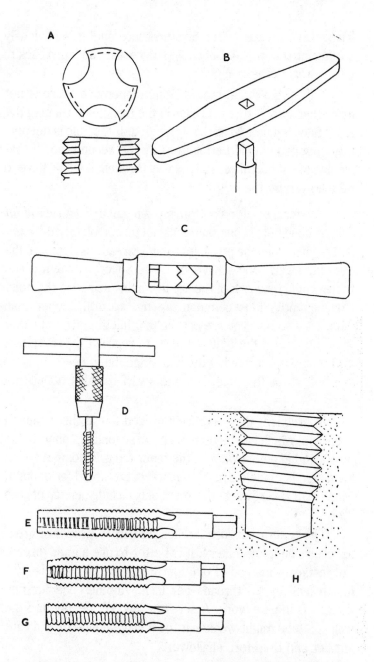

Fig. 16-4. A tap wrench is used to cut an internal thread: (A) grooves produce cutting edges; (B) a bar with a square hole; (C) sliding parts take many sizes; (D) wrench with a chuck; (E) a taper tap; (F) a tap with less taper; (G) plug tap.

Then make it start with a firm pressure until it is obviously cutting into the metal. Lubricate if necessary and turn back to clear swarf occasionally.

If it is thin metal that is being tapped and there is not more than two or three threads in the thickness, running the taper fully in might be all that is needed. If the hole is deeper, the taper tap should be followed by the second tap. If that would not cut full threads all the way through, it would have to be followed by the bottom tap.

The main use for a bottom tap is to cut a thread in a *blind hole*. A blind hole is one that does not go completely through. Although it would be possible to cut a thread absolutely to the bottom, swarf would have to be removed frequently and there would be a risk of the tap becoming seized in the hole. Consequently, it is common practice to drill deeper than necessary so that you are certain that full threads go further than the end of the bolt will have to reach (Fig. 16-4H). A bottom tap is still used as the final stage, but it need not go to the bottom of the hole. If some swarf remains, it will not matter.

In practice, there is rarely a need for all three taps in each size. Much can be done with the second tap only. It can be started in a hole without the taper tap preceding it an if a blind hole is made extra deep it will cut a thread far enough. Many sets of screwing equipment only include one tap of each size.

The general purpose threads are fairly coarse. For greater precision in machinery, it is better to use a finer thread. For instance, instead of one-fourth inch by 20 there is one-fourth inch by 28 threads per inch. Another use for fine threads is in pipe work. A screw thread cut deeply into the wall of a tube might weaken it too much, so pipe threads are smaller and therefore shallower.

All normal screw threads are right-handed. They tighten when turned clockwise. Taps and dies to cut lefthand threads are available. If the action of a part would tend to loosen a righthand thread, it can be made lefthanded.

NUTS AND BOLTS

There is no need for a mechanic to make standard nuts and bolts and other screwed parts since they are available as stock items. However, you might want to screw special parts or lengthen threads on standard parts. Modern production is such that standards are close enough for a screwed part made in one place to fit the same made in another. This applies to other sizes, such as heads and the outside of nuts. Wrenches and other equipment for dealing with nuts and bolts have

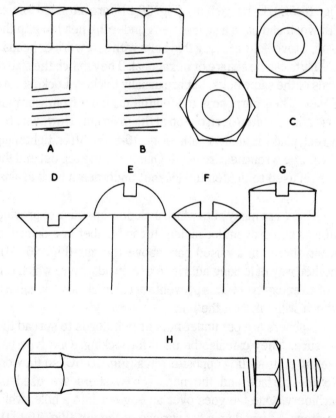

Fig. 16-5. Bolts and nuts can be square or hexagonal (A,B,C) and screws can have various heads (D,E,F,G) intended for use with a screwdriver. A coach bolt has a square neck to pull into wood (H).

become standardized. Because there are still several standards in use, a mechanic needs to have a large number of wrenches.

It is correct to refer to a bolt only if it is threaded part of its length (Fig. 16-5A) and call it a machine screw if it is threaded to the head (Fig. 16-5B). Nuts and bolt heads intended to be turned with a wrench are square or hexagonal (Fig. 16-5C). If a head has a screwdriver slot, it is flat when countersunk level with the surface (Fig. 16-5D), round if it is curved above the surface (Fig. 16-5E) and oval if it is slightly domed above a countesunk part (Fig. 16-5F). If the head stands above the surface cylindrically, it is fillister or cheese (Fig. 16-5G). Carriage bolts (Fig. 16-5H) are intended for use with wood and have a square neck under the head to grip the wood. Stove bolts are long thin bolts with screwdriver heads.

Nuts can be square or hexagonal. They match the size of heads of the same bolts, but are usually thicker. Locknuts are thinner. Their purpose is to stop the main nut from vibrating loose and are often seen on top of the main nut. However, the correct place is underneath (Fig. 16-6A). After tightening down, two wrenches are used. One holds the top nut and the other is used to tighten the locknut underneath back against it.

There are many nuts which include something to provide stiffness and prevent loosening. It can be fiber or a distorted sprung thread in a raised part above the nut (Fig. 16-6B). Another way of locking nuts is to use an adhesive, which can be of an epoxy type. This prevents accidental loosening, but a wrench will still turn the nut.

Washers are put under nuts or bolt heads to spread the pressure. They can also be used for locking. One type has meeting ends sprung opposite ways (Fig. 16-6C) so they dig into the surface and the nut. Tab washers are used on machinery. One tab goes over an edge or into a hole, while the other is turned up a flat surface of the nut (Fig. 16-6D).

Castellated nuts are not so common now, but they are a

positive way of locking a nut. They are used with a split pin (cotter pin) through a hole drilled in the bolt (Fig. 16-6E). This is a useful way of locking a nut to a bolt when there are moving parts being held and a nut locked by other means would possibly loosen. Withdrawing the pin allows disassembly.

WRENCHES

As with nuts and bolts, there has been some standardization of wrenches. Experience has shown what length is most

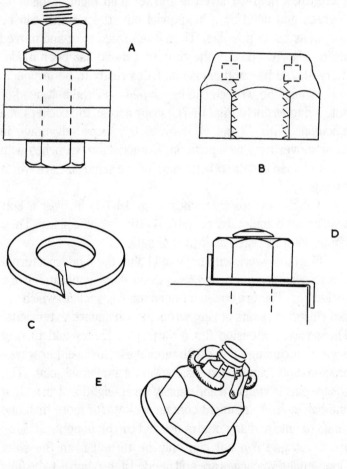

Fig. 16-6. A nut can be locked with another nut (A), with friction material (B), a spring washer (C), a tab washer (D) or a split pin (E).

suitable for particular sizes. A reasonable length is needed to provide enough leverage, but too much might shear off a bolt or strip a thread. Too short a wrench might not get the nut tight enough.

The blacksmith who made individually matching nuts and bolts usually made an open-ended wrench to suit. That type has continued as the common pattern of wrench, usually double-ended, either two sizes or the same size at different angles (Fig. 16-7A). When there is only limited space to move a wrench, it helps to have the end set at an angle. If this is 15 degrees and used on a hexagonal nut, the wrench can be moved as far as possible. Then it is turned over and moved again (Fig. 16-7B). By the time that move has been made, there should be another pair of faces ready to be gripped.

Where the wrench can be slipped over the bolt head or nut, a ring wrench (Fig. 16-7C) grips across the corners of a hexagon. With 12 points it gives the same advantage in turning over for a new position. Combination wrenches with one end open and the other a ring for the same size are worth having.

Tubular or box wrenches (Fig. 16-7D) fit over a bolt head or nut completely, so there is little risk of slipping. They can be long to reach awkward situations.

For most work with nuts and bolts, the modern alternative to separate wrenches for a great many applications is a socket set. This is a boxed outfit containing sockets which are like closed versions of ring wrenches on square extensions. The square extension fits a variety of levers and turning devices, including a lever with ratchet that turns either way, a brace-action handle, extensions and a universal joint. The square part is standard and usually three-eighths of an inch or one-half inch. A set might contain sockets for more than one range of nuts and any others needed can be bought. Sockets are of no use if a nut can only be turned from the side. Open-ended wrenches are still needed if the shop is to be fully equipped.

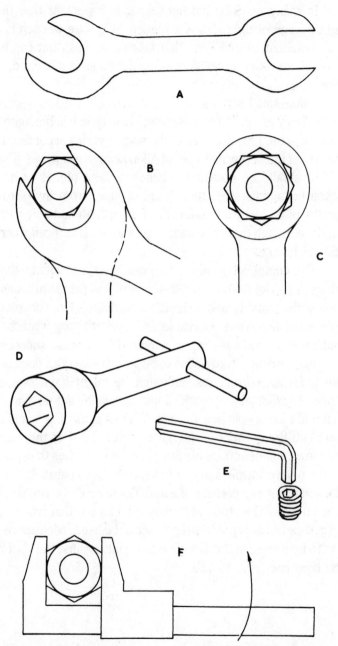

Fig. 16-7. A wrench can be open-ended (A,B), ring (C) or box (D). A screw can be turned with an Allen key (E) or an adjustable wrench can be used (F).

In many machine assemblies, it is important that the right degree of tightness is achieved. A torque wrench is a self-contained wrench (one that takes a socket) that can be adjusted so when a set degree of tightness is obtained, it slips.

Some small screws without heads are used to secure parts. They are called grub screws. One type has hexagonal sockets in the top. The size of the socket varies according to the size of the screw and a set of Allen keys or wrenches (Fig. 16-7E) should be obtained. These are bent pieces of hardened hexagonal steel rod. A set of nine, from five-sixth-fourths of an inch to one-fourth of an inch should suit most needs, although there are metric sizes as well for foreign cars and machinery.

The complexities of modern machinery, including such things as refrigerators and dish washers, call for maintenance tools with cranked and bent handles. Such tools from obsolete equipment are often obtainable and a great many wrenches that have general uses can be acquired from these sources.

Any engineer who claims to be proud of his craft does not like adjustable wrenches, although he might have one or more. An adjustable wrench cannot usually be set so exactly that it fits like a one-size wrench. When it is used, it tends to round off the corners of the nut or bolt head. For the same reason an engineer does not like pliers or wrenches that work on the plier principle and do not keep the jaws parallel. They slip and round the corners of a nut. There might be occasions when none of the stock wrenches will fit a nut that has to be turned and an adjustable wrench has to be used. Make sure it has to be turned in the direction that pulls against the root of the rigid jaw (Fig. 16-7F).

Soldering And Brazing

17

The best method of joining two pieces of iron and steel, when the method is appropriate, is a blacksmith's weld. If the two pieces are being worked on the anvil at red heat, a higher heating so that they can be hammered together is the obvious way of joining them. The ability to make a blacksmith's weld is an important accomplishment and anyone who considers himself a metalworking craftsman should not use any other method when that is the technique that will get the best results.

However, there are many situations where steel parts have to be joined and it would be unsatisfactory to raise them to welding temperature. There are also the problems of joining other metals to themselves and to each other. Blacksmith's welds are only appropriate to iron and steel.

In some assemblies, it is satisfactory to rivet or bolt parts together through drilled holes. But there are other joining methods that actually fuse the metals together in a manner related to the smith's weld. These methods use a lower and more localized temperature and a filler metal that is run into the joint and bonded to the surfaces.

There are two methods, also known as welding, which can be done with an oxy-acetylene flame or by using electricity. Both methods produce a very high temperature heat in a very small space. A filler rod and the surface to be joined can be melted together without the adjoining parts becoming very hot. However, both methods require fairly elaborate equipment and the occasional user might not be justified in obtaining it.

Other methods are called soldering and brazing. They are done at lower temperatures and use much simpler equipment. The simplest method is soldering, often described as "soft" soldering to distinguish it from the method described next. The joint is not very strong, but there is ample strength for many purposes and it is particularly good for electrical work. A soldered joint makes a through route for electricity that cannot be affected by corrosion, as a screwed or sprung joint might. "Hard" soldering and brazing are similar techniques to each other and the names may sometimes be transposed. Brazing uses a higher temperature and makes the strongest joint—sometimes as strong as welding. Hard soldering can also be called silver soldering. It is done in the same way, but temperature and strength are less than brazing.

The melting points of the metals being joined have to be considered. Brass will melt at brazing temperatures. Some metals are more amenable to one method than another. Of the common metals and alloys, aluminum does not lend itself to the methods which are easy with other metals.

Soft solder is an alloy of lead and tin. Sometimes there are small quantities of other metals, but a lead/tin alloy is all that is needed for normal joints. The melting point of the alloy is considerably lower than that of either of the metals alone. This applies to nearly all alloys. The proportions of lead and tin affect the melting point and the characteristics of the solder. A high proportion of lead allows the solder to remain plastic much longer. This property was used when much plumbing was done with lead pipes and the plumber "wiped" a joint while the solder was soft enough to be moulded into shape. That sort of solder is unsuitable for general joints and the appropriate type for most work is sold as tinman's tinner's solder or electrician's solder. It might be in a bar up one-fourth of an inch thick or more like a wire about one-sixteenth of an inch in diameter. The lowest melting point is made with proportions of two parts tin to one part lead (181-⅛ degrees C). A small amount of bismuth added will make the melting point even lower. General-purpose solder has about equal parts of lead and tin.

Soldering is done by heating the solder and the surfaces to be joined. Heat causes oxidization and this prevents a proper flow of the solder. It stays in little globules instead of spreading over the metal. The surfaces have to be kept from the air by melting flux over them and the flux also assists the flow of the solder.

FLUX

At one time, the recommended flux for soldering most metals was *killed spirits*, which was zinc dissolved in dilute hydrochloric acid to make zinc chloride. This is corrosive and is not recommended any more. Prepared fluxes can be bought, either as pastes or liquids, which are more effective and less dangerous to the user or the metal. Where practicable, fluxes should be washed off. For electrical work, this is usually impossible and the flux has to be left on the work. Electrician's flux is a resin, which does not corrode, so it does no harm if left in place.

Other fluxes include tallow, used on lead and sal ammoniac (ammonium chloride), once the usual flux for copper. A paste manufactured flux is more convenient for small joints and a liquid manufactured flux is better for large areas. One type of electrician's solder is supplied as a tube with resin flux inside. This melts when heat is applied. There is no need to apply flux separately to small joints, such as the end of a wire to a contact point.

The comparatively low temperature needed to melt soft solder can be obtained with a gas flame or from a heated metal rod. Copper has a particular affinity for soft solder and the tool used for heating small joints is a soldering bit (Fig. 17-1A). The traditional type is heated with a flame. But most soldering bits today, particularly for electrical and other fine work, have electric heating elements enclosed (Fig. 17-1B). However, for stouter metal parts that will take away heat rapidly, more heat is required and a soldering bit of considerable bulk to hold enough heat is still needed. That is better heated with a gas flame.

The alternative is to use a flame directly. This is described as sweating a joint. Direct heating of the work over a gas ring or a bunsen burner will melt solder, but it is better to have the flame under control so it can be directed where needed. A propane torch, burning gas and air, is convenient (Fig. 17-1C). For fine work, a mouth blowlamp can be used. In a simple form, the flame is produced by alcohol soaked in batting in a metal tubular container and the blowpipe diverts the flame where needed (Fig. 17-1D). The flame from a torch or other device should be controllable so it can be anything from a little needle-like flame to a full blast.

Surfaces to be joined should be both mechanically and chemically clean. They can be scraped just before soldering to remove corrosion and get them bright. Flux will deal with chemical cleaning. Solder will not flow on and bond to dirty surfaces. The stick of solder should also be clean and this is achieved by dipping it into flux just before using. If a soldering bit is being used, its end must also be cleaned and already *tinned* (coated with solder). To tin a bit, heat it with its own element or with a flame until solder melts when touched on the end. With a little practice the correct amount of heat can be judged by holding the bit a few inches from your cheek—which is a very heat-sensitive part of your body.

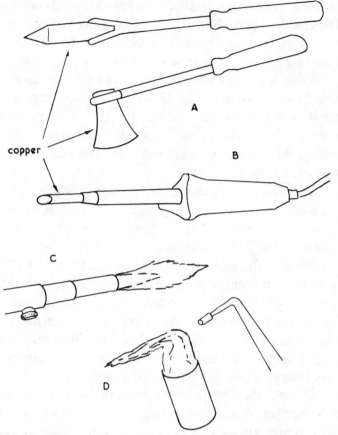

copper

A

B

C

D

Fig. 17-1. Soldering can be done with a copper bit (A,B) or a torch flame (C,D).

USING A BIT

Merely touching solder on the bit will result in gobules being formed. Quickly rub the end of the bit on all faces with a file and dip its end in flux. Then touch the stick of solder on it. Solder will flow over the bit faces. It might help to put the solder on a piece of clean scrap metal and rub the bit on it. Once the bit has been tinned, further treatment should not be needed for a long time—unless the bit is very much overheated.

Each time the bit is heated, dip it very briefly into flux before use so that it comes clean to the work. If much soldering is to be done, it is better to keep a second container of flux for dipping the bit and the stick of solder in. Otherwise the working flux might become contaminated with dirt. Use a brush or a pointed piece of wood to apply flux to a joint.

As an example, a piece of sheet metal can have another flanged part joined to it (Fig. 17-2A). With brass, copper or mild steel, rub the meeting surfaces bright with emery paper or scrape them with a knife blade. With tinplate, scraping would go through the very thin layer of tin. Therefore, merely wipe and let the flux clean it.

Heat the soldering bit sufficiently, dip it in flux and melt a little solder on its end. "Tin" both surfaces. Have flux on them and slowly move the bit along them (Fig. 17-2B). As heat flows from the bit into the metal, solder will melt and flow from the bit. The metal has to get heat from the bit and be raised to the melting point of solder. If you hold the metal in a vise, that will take heat away rapidly. Wood is a poor conductor, so if you want to grip the metal, put wood pads in the jaws (Fig. 17-2C). You can probably work with the metal resting on wood. Feed more solder on to the bit as you tin the surfaces. If necessary, reheat the bit to complete tinning.

To make the joint, put more flux in the joint and hold the parts together. A small piece of work can be held with pliers, although wiring is a good way of temporarily holding without the risk of clamps or other masses of metal taking heat away. Soft iron wire can be twisted (Fig. 17-2D). A second loop allows easier tensioning with pliers.

Run the hot bit along one side of the joint and feed more solder on to it (Fig. 17-2E). Be careful not to melt too much. You will see when the solder has melted right through the joint by brightness on the other side. There is a shine or gloss to melted solder that is distinct from its solidified appearance. Watch this brightness as you move the bit along. Be careful not to move the parts while the solder is molten. After the heat has been withdrawn watch the surface of the solder. The brightness will suddenly disappear. When this happens, the

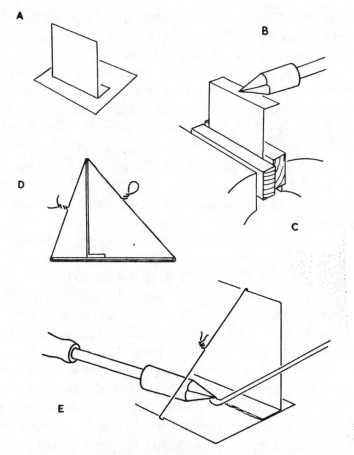

Fig. 17-2. Parts to be soldered are tinned with solder and wired together: (A) flange; (B) use flux and slowly move the bit; (C) use wood pads in the jaws; (D) twist the iron wire; (E) run the bit along the joint.

solder has set and the joint will not move. Leave it to cool, although it can be cooled quickly with water without affecting strength.

USING A FLAME

Melted solder will flow towards the hottest point. This property is used to sweat a joint. The solder is put on one side and the heat is applied to the other side of the joint. The effect is to draw the solder through. As an example, a tube can be mounted on a flat piece of sheet metal. If the finished article is to be a closed bowl, the bottom is made oversize and the surplus metal filed level after soldering.

For this sort of joint, there is no need for the surfaces to be tinned. But if larger areas are to be joined, tinning first is advisable. However, the surfaces should be mechanically clean, so rub them bright before assembly. Put the tube on the base and secure it with iron wire (Fig. 17-3A). Apply flux. It is possible to add solder by touching with the end of a bar of solder, but it is very easy to let too much melt then. A safer way of getting the right amount is to put small pieces of solder in place before heating.

Solder is very ductile and the end of a bar can be hammered to spread and thin it. Hammer the end so pieces can be cut off with snips (Fig. 17-3B). Put these around the inside of the joint (Fig. 17-3C). A useful tool for doing this is a spatula made from wire about one-eighth of an inch in diameter that is flattened at the end (Fig. 17-3D). For soldering with a flame, it helps to stand the work on a piece of asbestos.

Adjust a torch flame quite small and play it around the outside of the work. Keep the flame moving so that heating is fairly even. It is the end of the blue cone in the flame that is the hot part. Keep this in contact with the metal. The solder inside will be seen to melt and run into the joint. Once this happens, there will probably be enough heat in the metal to complete the joint. Hold the flame to one side, ready to apply it briefly if needed. Excessively overheating will burn off the flux and badly oxidize the metal so the solder does not flow. If the silvery line of solder does not show through the outside of the joint all round, dab a little flux on with a brush. That should draw it through. If not, a quick heat might do it. Do not disturb the work until the solder has set.

Spelter

Brazing is done with brass, although the particular mixture of copper and zinc intended for the work is called *spelter*.

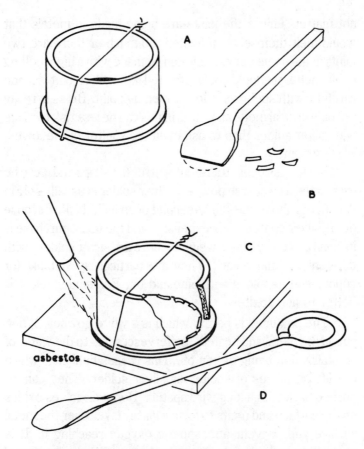

Fig. 17-3. Pieces of solder can be melted and drawn through a joint with a flame: (A) secure with wire; (B) hammer and cut pieces with snips; (C) position pieces on inside of the joint; (D) use a spatula made from wire.

Silver solder is a mixture of copper, zinc and a small amount of silver. The addition of silver lowers the melting point. Except for this, the joints are made in the same way. Spelter can be bought with different proportions of copper and zinc. Equal parts gives a melting point of about 550 degrees C, three parts copper to two parts zinc gives about 620 degrees C and two parts copper to one part zinc melts at 700 degrees C. Oddments of scrap brass can be used for brazing, but the melting point will not be known without a test. All of the heats are red hot in any case. The differences in melting points do not matter, unless the joints are being made in metals that would melt themselves if heated too much or there are two joints in the same thing. If one can be made with a high melting point spelter it should not be affected if the other joint is made carefully with spelter of a lower melting point. Brass is really the only critical metal and joints in this can be less risk to make with silver solder than to use even the spelter of the lowest melting point.

Spelter is supplied as stout wire or flat strips and it can be granulated as a coarse powder. Silver solder is usually sold in flat sheets about one-thirty-second of an inch thick. Because of the silver content, it is expensive and the usual purchase is in small pieces by ounce weight. There are silver solders with different melting points. They are particularly suitable for copper and its alloys with zinc and tin. For mild steel, it is better to use spelter.

The flux used is borax, which is a white powder. When put on the metal and heated, it effervesces due to the water of crystallization being driven off. This causes bubbling, which can lift off pieces of spelter or silver solder. They can be pushed back with a long wire spatula. Borax dissolves oxides on the surface and melts to form a glassy layer over the metal surface and prevent atmospheric oxygen reaching it. It is possible to get rid of the moisture by roasting the borax and then pounding it to a powder. It can be made into a paste with a little water, as well as granulated spelter, if that is how the spelter is to be applied.

Liquid brazing fluxes are obtainable. These are basically borax, but they do not bubble when heated. The hard glassy flux can be chipped off after the joint has cooled. It can also be dissolved in a hot alum solution or it can be removed in an acid pickle (see Chapter 18).

A typical joint is along a seam when sheet metal is rolled into a cylinder (Fig. 17-4A). It helps to file the joint so that it is slightly open on the inside (Fig. 17-4B). Use soft iron wire to tie the cylinder in shape. It will be heated to redness and there

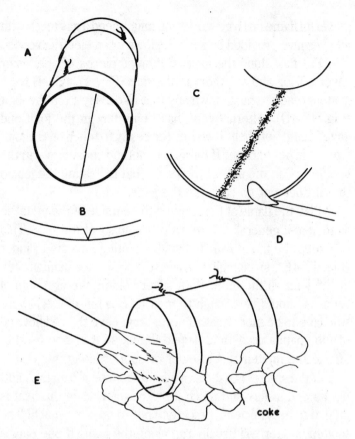

Fig. 17-4. For hard soldering a seam (A,B,C,D) the metal is wired (E) and supported with coke.

will be no opportunity to adjust or alter things once brazing has been started. Therefore, get the assembly secure with wire that will not melt.

Support the piece with the joint downward. Small coke can be put under and around so as to reflect heat inwards as well as support the work. Pieces of asbestos can be used in a similar way. The best place is on the smith's hearth or in a metal tray of coke so that the flame is prevented from doing damage to anything nearby.

Use a gas torch. A self-contained propane torch is most convenient. A kerosene torch could be used. For a more powerful flame on large work, you might need a gas torch with air pressure provided by a foot bellows or an electric blower.

Put flux along the joint. Cut small pieces of spelter or silver solder and put them in the flux (Fig. 17-4C). Have a spatula ready to push down any that rise away from the joint (Fig. 17-4D). Alternatively, have only flux in the joint and have a length of spelter wire or rod ready to touch on the joint when it is hot enough. If this is the method chosen, warm the spelter rod in the side of the flame that is heating the job so that it does not go cold into the joint.

Play the flame at first around the outside of the metal so as to heat it generally. Direct it occasionally at the joint. This will keep the flux down. Follow by heating into the cylinder (Fig. 17-4E), swinging from side to side, rather than directly at the joint all the time. With silver solder, the first sign of redness should be enough to melt it. But for spelter, there will have to be more heat. If necessary, have the red hot end of the spatula ready and dipped in flux so it can be used to stroke the molten silver solder or spelter along the joint.

If the spelter is used as a wire to be touched on the joint, dip its end in flux and touch it on the joint when the heat is judged to be sufficient. Be careful not to melt too much. The molten spelter will usually run along the joint. If one part is obviously hotter than another, touch the cooler part of the joint.

In either case, leave the work in place to cool until it is well below red heat—then it can be cooled in water. Quenching at red heat might crack spelter. If the work is dipped in an acid pickle to clean it and remove flux, remove any iron wire first. Otherwise it will cause discoloring of copper or brass.

When dealing with mild steel or anything or much bulk, there might be difficulty in raising enough heat. Metal away from the joint can draw away so much heat that it might be difficult to get the joint hot enough. Conserve heat as much as possible. Have the joint level and accessible, but support and surround the work with coke. The coke will get red hot during heating. This will be reflected back to the metal, preventing heat being dispersed and directing it where it is wanted.

Mild steel should be bright. A joint cannot be made in the black condition that is usual with a smith's weld. File and rub with emery cloth or use a scratch brush. In a bad case, grind the surface. Coat joints with borax and braze in the way just described. Lap joints can be made similar to soft soldering

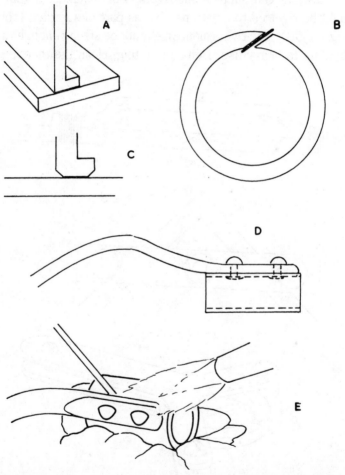

Fig. 17-5. Brazing is done with the metal heated to redness: (A) lap joint; (B) spelter coated with flux is placed between ends; (C) the joint must be open or filed to a V shape; (D) tube rivetted to bar; (E) apply flux before heating and brazing.

373

(Fig. 17-5A). A ring from thicker material might have a piece of spelter coated with flux put between the meeting ends (Fig. 17-5B). There must be a slight space for spelter to flow. Soft solder will creep through an almost tight joint and silver solder does not need much space. But for spelter, the joint must be open or filed to a V shape to give the molten metal an entry (Fig. 17-5C).

Brazing can supplement rivets. For instance, a tube might be rivetted to a flattened bar as part of a garden tool (Fig. 17-5D). The rivets alone might not be strong enough to stand up to heavy use. Before rivetting, clean the meeting

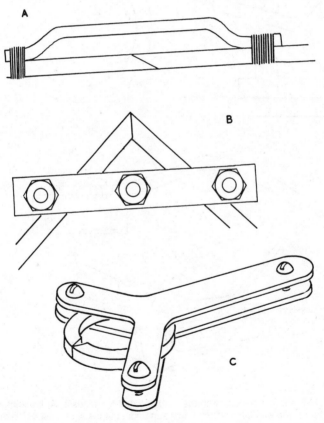

Fig. 17-6. Parts to be brazed have to be held together with improvised devices: (A) wire on a strut; (B) bolt parts; (C) use a Y-clamp.

surfaces bright. Close the rivets, but not quite as tight as you might have done if they were to be the only fastenings.

Support the work with one side upward and horizontal, but apply flux underneath as well as on top (Fig. 17-5E). Heat and braze the parts, using enough spelter to run through. After the joint has lost its redness, pick up the work with tongs and turn it over. The joint will probably be satisfactory on the far side, but if not, support it that way up and heat again with more spelter there.

Keeping parts together so they will not move or distort when heated to redness is sometimes a problem. Iron wire is useful. Even if it becomes brazed on, it can be filed off. Various clamping devices can be made, but the must stand up to heat. It is possible to wire on a strut to parts away from the flame (Fig. 17-6A). Strips of metal can be used with bolts through holes to hold parts together (Fig. 17-6B). For joining the ends of rings, which tend to open as they expand with heat, a Y-shaped clamping piece can be made (Fig. 17-6C). There could be nuts and bolts or screws into a tapped part.

Hollowing And Raising

18

The internal particles of metal can be made to flow. This is shown by many operations in blacksmithing, where hammering will make steel longer and thinner or shorter and thicker. The whole mass of steel is still the same in total amount, but its shape is different. A blacksmith can work sheet steel to a compound curve while it is hot, but it is too rigid to permit this when it is cold. Many other metals and alloys are sufficiently ductile when cold to allow compound curvature without heating. The metal is made to flow so some of the content of a part is made by moving some to another part that will accept it, because that part is made by moving some to another part that will accept it, because that part has to be increased in size.

Most of the non-ferrous metals and alloys can be shaped in this way, although some intended mainly for machining will be too crystaline and brittle. Metals and alloys that have been produced by rolling into sheet form can be worked to compound curves. The process is called *raising* by some craftsmen, whatever the method of shaping. Others talk of *hollowing* when the shape is obtained by deepening the middle

377

of a disc and *raising* when it is obtained by stretching its rim. Much shaping is a combination of the two processes.

Bowls and cups of most elaborate design have been made in gold and silver, but the cost of materials prohibits their use by the average craftsman. Similar work can be done with less valuable metals.

Copper is particularly suitable since it can be made into quite deep compound shapes and its finished appearance when polished is quite attractive. Sheet brass is less ductile, but brass with a high copper content can be made into bowls and similar things. The copper and tin alloy, called *gilding metal* in sheet form, will shape almost as much and as easily as copper alone. It polishes to a rich golden color and can be made harder than copper. Aluminum can also be shaped, but not to the same extent as copper and the fact that it cannot be brazed or hard soldered limits what can be made of it.

Copper and its alloys can be plated, so the finished work can be coated with nickel, chromium or silver to prevent corrosion and give a rich appearance.

All of these non-ferrous metals work harden. As the process of raising involves a considerable amount of heavy hammering, it might be necessary to anneal a piece of work many times before the shape you want is obtained. Consequently, a propane torch or something similar should be available. The metal could be put on the coke in a blacksmith's hearth or there could be a special hearth for annealing. A suitable form is a sheet steel box about 18 inch square and a least 4 inches deep. This should be almost full of coke or pieces of asbestos could be used. What is needed is something that will not allow heat through, but will conserve it around the metal so that heats quickly.

The annealed metal can be cooled in water and then scoured clean with a damp cloth and pumice or domestic scouring powder. Dry it before continuing work. If much beaten work is to be done, it is better to cool the metal in an acid pickle. This will quench and clean at one time. Acid baths have been mentioned, but for frequent use while annealing copper, brass and gilding metal during raising, a sulfuric acid pickle made in the following way is suitable.

Use an earthenware container. Have a wooden lid that is kept on except when metal is being dipped. Locate it in the open air or in a well-ventilated place. Do not breathe the fumes when metal is dipped and do not let the fumes reach tools, as they will become corroded. Use a proportion of one part sulfuric acid to six or seven parts of water and always pour the acid slowly into the water. **Never pour water into acid**. It will spurt dangerously.

Do not let iron or steel go into the acid. This means that smith's tongs or pliers cannot be used for dipping. Apart from corroding them, the steel affects the acid so stains occur on the metal being dipped and these are difficult to scour off. It is possible to buy brass tongs or they can be made from copper rod, worked cold, otherwise they are similar to smith's tongs made from steel.

Another way of making them is to use brass sheet that is about one-eighth of an inch thick. Cut two similar parts (Fig. 18-1A) and silver solder jaws to them (Fig. 18-1B). Use a copper brass rivet. After dipping metal in acid, wash the tongs

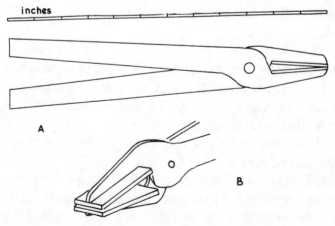

Fig. 18-1. Brass tongs (A,B) for dipping acid can be made from sheet.

as well as the metal in water. Use plenty of water on spilled acid. Avoid getting acid on skin or clothes. If there is an accident, dilute quickly with plenty of water.

There are two broad divisions of the work. In the first stage, the metal has to be kept as soft as possible for as long as possible during shaping. The number of times work has to stop for annealing is kept to a minimum. In the second stage, work hardening is deliberate to strengthen the finished article. Wooden tools are considered to work harden less than steel ones, so most craftsmen prefer to do the early work with mallets and keep steel hammers for the final work, called planishing. However, it is possible to hollow and raise with steel hammers and special ones are made. The difference in the degree of work hardening between wood and steel is slight.

TOOLS

The main wooden hollowing tool is a bossing or doming mallet (Fig. 18-2A). The head is close-grained heavy hardwood and the handle is usually cane, although it could be an ordinary hammer handle. For flat work, there is a similarly-made tinman's or tinner's mallet (Fig. 18-2B). For raising, one end of the tinman's mallet head can be given a shape similar to a cross peen on a hammer (Fig. 18-2C) or a special mallet could be made from flat-sectioned wood (Fig. 18-2D).

If hollowing is to be done with a steel hammer, the special hammer is made with two ball peens on a head longer than a normal hammer. It is sold as a hollowing hammer, in weights between 1 pound and 3 pounds but much hollowing can be done with an ordinary ball peen hammer.

Hollowing can be done over a sandbag. This is leather or stout canvas, filled with fine sand (Fig. 18-2E). Stout stitching is needed to stand up to heavy pounding. Much hollowing can be done on wood. For a small hollow, such as a spoon, all that is needed is a hole in the end grain of a piece of wood (Fig. 18-2F). For a larger bowl shape, a hollow can be gouged out of

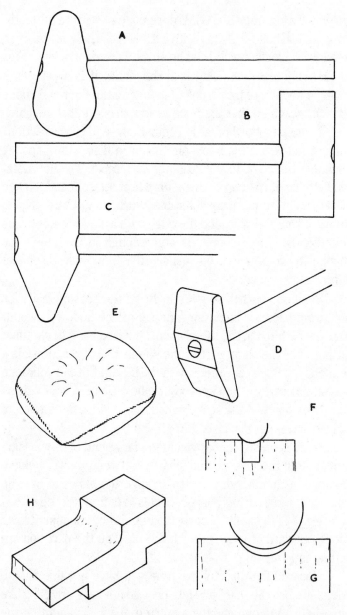

Fig. 18-2. Sheet metal is hollowed with mallets. The material is held on wood blocks or a sandbag: (A) doming mallet; (B) tinner's mallet; (C) shaped tinner's mallet; (D) mallet made from flat-sectioned wood; (E) canvas filled with fine sand; (F) hole used for hollowing; (G) a log is used for hollowing; (H) a shaped block of wood.

the end of a log (Fig. 18-2G). It does not have to be a perfectly symmetrical hollow. A tray with a flat rim can be worked over an edge. A block of wood can be shaped to grip in a vise (Fig. 18-2H). If much hollowing is to be done, it is worthwhile having a section of tree trunk standing on the floor and about 30 inches high so that the hollows in it are at bench height.

To make a bowl of fairly regular curve in cross-section, but not necessarily a hemisphere, cut a disc with snips. A thickness between 16 and 20 gauge is suitable. Thinner metal can be difficult to keep in shape for a first attempt and thicker metal might require considerable work to get the shape. Remove sharpness around the edge with a file so as not to cut your hands. Some copper is soft enough in the sheet for shaping to commence, but usually it is advisable to anneal before starting work.

Position yourself so you can swing the bossing mallet or hollowing hammer over the sandbag or the hollowed wood. You will be moving the metal about, but you have to continue hitting over the same part of the support. At first, there is a tendency to follow the metal with the blows. Spread your legs so you do not sway and keep your elbow close to your side as the pivot point. At first it might help to draw a number of pencil circles on the disc (Fig. 18-3A).

Start near the center, using the large end of the bossing mallet. Pull the disc around slightly between blows, holding its edge at the far side. Try to arrange the blows to overlap and follow increasingly large circles. At first the edge will wrinkle, but this will be corrected as the overlapping blows move outwards to the rim. Tilt the bowl so the part you are hitting is level (Fig. 18-3B).

You will find that by the time you have got this far the metal will be quite hard and hits on it do not have anything like the effect they did when you started. This is a sign that the metal should be annealed again. Immediately after annealing copper, in particular, it is very ductile and that is when you can get the greatest effect.

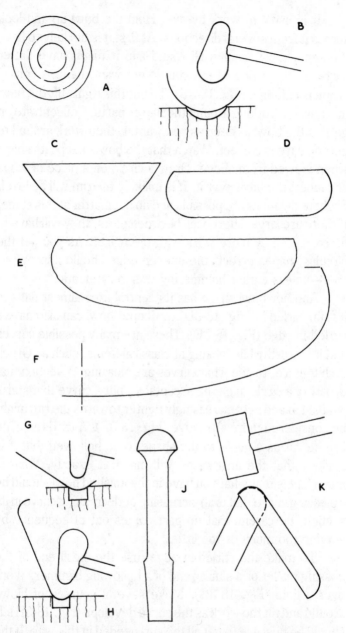

Fig. 18-3. The edge of a hollowed bowl can be turned in over a stake: (A) pencil drawn circles; (B) tilt the bowl; (C) a conical shape; (D) curled rim; (E) a deeper bowl; (F) a flat curve; (G) use a bossing mallet; (H) develop the curve; (J) at the bottom might fit into a hardie hole; (K) use a tinman's mallet.

It is usual to work by eye. Hold the bowl up and look across it from several directions. At first it is unlikely to have the same cross-section all round and it might have flatter parts of the section where you do not want them. A conical shape is common (Fig. 18-3C). To put this right, tilt the bowl more when working around the flatter parts. Concentrate on getting the bowl as deep as you want it, then work around to get the curves correct. Watch that the bowls keeps its shape when viewed from above. Draw a circle on a piece of wood and invert the bowl over it. It is unlikely the rim will be level. Slight undulations are possible and do not matter at this stage. If there are large differences between parts, they will have to be corrected by more work with the mallet. As you get the circular shape correct, the uneven edge should improve as well—unless earlier hammering was very erratic.

Another bowl shape has its central area almost flat and its rim curled in (Fig. 18-3D). A deeper bowl can also have a curled-in edge (Fig. 18-3E). There are many possible curves and it is worthwhile looking at classical items, such as Greek architecture, to see what curves are pleasing. A section that is part of a circle might be acceptable, but a curve that starts almost flat and gets increasingly tighter towards the rim might be considered more attractive (Fig. 18-3F). A card template can be cut as a guide to the shape to be hollowed, but it is unlikely that the final shape will match it exactly. What is important is that what you have in the finished bowl should be a pleasing curve. If it is an increasing or decreasing curve in its section, be careful that no part comes out of sequence by curving too much or too little.

To make the curled-in edge, use the small end of the bossing mallet or a similar end of a hollowing hammer. Work over a hole (Fig. 18-3G). Make several courses of blows around and tilt the work as the curve develops (Fig. 18-3H). It should be possible to get all the curl needed in this way. If the edge wrinkles, finish it on a sandbag or on a shallow hollow in the wood instead of a hole. If the curl is to turn in much, final shaping might have to be over a round stake.

This is a steel rod with a rounded top. A bought one might have a head larger than the stem and be something like a ball peen. Its bottom either fits in the hardie hole of the anvil, into a hole in a tree trunk or can be held in a vise (Fig. 18-3J). The end of a round rod could be ground to shape. In both cases, the part on which the bowl will rest should be finsihed smooth. Any marks on it would be reproduced in the bowl. Use a tinman's mallet to close the rim over this mushroom stake, working around a little at a time to get an even shape (Fig. 18-3K).

A bowl or tray with a flat rim is something like a curled edge inside a border. Draw the circle where the hollow is to come. If the rim is to be round, it is helpful to drive in two nails as guides—whether hollowing is to be over the edge of a piece of wood or a shaped block (Fig. 18-4A). If the outer edge is not to be parallel with the hollow, you will have to estimate the hollowing position in relation to the wooden edge. After the first course of blows, the angle can be seen and corrected in further series of hits. A round hollow in an octagonal or other polygonal rim looks attractive.

Start hollowing with light blows (Fig. 18-4B). The first time round you are mainly feeling the accuracy of the positioning of the blows. Follow with more blows that bring the angle to near the marked circle (Fig. 18-4C). When the outline is established, make more courses from this toward the flat bottom to get a sufficient depth. There will have to be some flattening blows on the bottom to maintain shape (Fig. 18-4D). When doing this, check the flatness of the rim and the regular height all round (Fig. 18-4E).

Anneal as necessary when you find your blows are having little effect. Continuing far too long could crack the metal, which becomes crystaline and brittle as it also becomes hard.

PLANISHING

After a bowl or tray has been hollowed to a satisfactory shape, it might be hard from hammering or it might be soft if

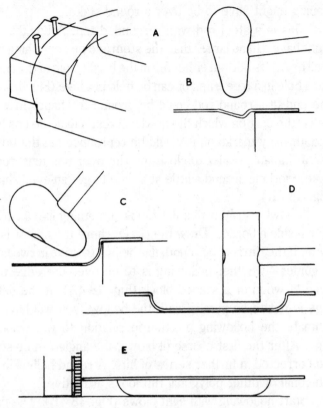

Fig. 18-4. A tray with a rim is shaped over a wood edge (A,B,C) and its base flattened level (D,E).

the final work came just after annealing. This has to be followed by planishing, which is careful hammering all over. It is done to get the metal uniformly hard and strong and to decorate it. The work finishes with little overlapping facets that polish to reflect the light and give the work the characteristic hammered hand-wrought appearance.

Planishing hammers are mostly light, one-half pound to one and one-half pound and with long springy handles. Most work is done with a flat-faced hammer head on a curved surface (Fig. 18-5A). But for a flat or near flat surface the face is domed (Fig. 18-5B). The faces or peens can be round or square. The hammer face must be absolutely smooth and

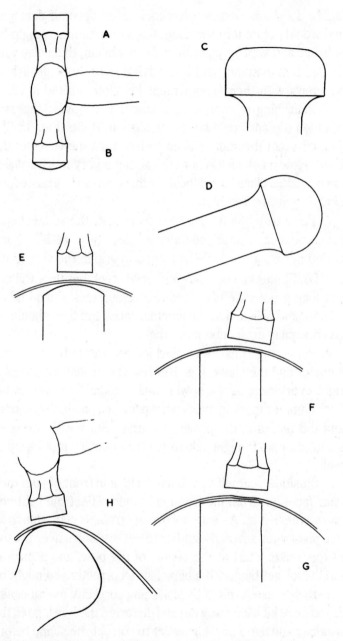

Fig. 18-5. Planishing is done with polished hammers and stakes: (A) flat-faced hammer; (B) this face is domed; (C) rounded edges; (D) curled-in rim; (E) pinch the metal; (F) bowl curve; (G) flattened; (H) tilt the stake.

highly polished. Ordinary hammer faces become damaged and would not do for planishing, but a new hammer might be polished and kept for planishing. Do not hit anything else with a planishing hammer and it is advisable to store planishing hammers with their faces wrapped in cloth soaked in oil.

Planishing is done over a stake. For bowls, this is a rounded top and could be the mushroom stake (Fig. 18-3J). The curve of the stake should be less than the curve of the bowl. How much less is not critical, but a very much smaller curve makes planishing difficult as there is less tolerance for a slightly misdirected blow.

For a tray or anything else nearly flat, the stake should have a near-flat center and rounded edges (Fig. 18-5C). For a curled-in rim, a rod could be forged to grip in the vise (Fig. 18-5D). Stakes can be made with mild steel, but they will not last long if not case hardened. Stake surfaces should be as smooth and polished as the hammer faces and they should be given similar protection in storage.

Planishing consists of pinching the metal between the hammer and the stake (Fig. 18-5E). The problem is to get it right every time as the bowl is pulled round just enough for each hammer mark to overlap the previous one in that course and the marks in the previous course. Start with the bowl scoured clean. It might help to see the effect if it is polished as well.

Position yourself so you have a light in front of you, then each facet left from the hammer should reflect the light and show where it is. As with hollowing, arrange your stance so you pivot your arm and hammer to get the blows over the top of the stake. Start at the center of the bowl and planish in circle that get bigger. If a blow falls incorrectly you might be able to disguise its mark by planishing correctly over it again. If you have hit a long way out and distorted the bowl, go to the sandbag and use a bossing mallet to correct the shape before you continue planishing.

As you continue on a bowl that has a tighter curve

towards the rim, you will have to tilt the stake. Inside the bowl, the stake is marking the metal with every blow outside. If the curve of the top of the stake conforms to the bowl curve, there will be no mark (Fig. 18-5F). Even worse, if the stake curve is flatter than that of the bowl, you will flatten the shape (Fig. 18-5G). Tilting the stake allows you to planish over a suitable curve (Fig. 18-5H).

With a flat-bottomed tray the central area is planished with a domed hammer (Fig. 18-6A). As the curve is reached, change to a flat-faced hammer and tilt the stake so you work on its curved edge (Fig. 18-6B). Some planishing hammers have one square face and this is easier to use close to the angle (Fig. 18-6C). For the flat rim, use a domed hammer over a flat straight-edged stake (Fig. 18-6D). This could be a piece of flat polished bar extending from one side of the vise.

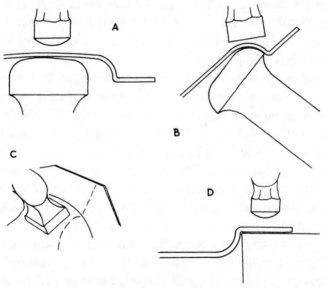

Fig. 18-6. The metal has to be trapped between hammer and stake (A,B) for correct planishing (C,D).

When any piece of work has been planished, its edge will almost certainly have to be trued. If it is a tray with a flat rim, the outer edges can be filed straight, cleaned with emery cloth and then polished with the surfaces. The edge of a bowl can have exceptional high spots rubbed level with a file, but levelling the edge is best done by inverting the bowl on a piece of coarse emery paper attached to a flat board. Rub the bowl on this until it can be seen to have levelled all round. Follow with a finer grit and then round the edge with the emery paper in your hand.

ASSEMBLY

A flat-bottomed tray or bowl will stand without any support, but a bowl with a rounded bottom needs feet or some other base so it will stand level. Some silverware designs have quite elaborate supports and these designs can be reproduced in copper or its alloys. A simple ring shows how a base can be added.

The base ring can be made from a solid bar. For a bowl about 4 inches across it might be one-fourth of an inch by one-eighth of an inch section, or proportionately bigger for a larger bowl (Fig. 18-7A. To match the curve without the need to file the top of the ring, it should slope outward, so that the first step after annealing the bar is to bend it to the curve of the bowl at the point it will touch. A piece of card or scrap metal can be made into a template (Fig. 18-7B. The theoretical length of bar needed is π d, or about 3.14 times the diameter. If you cut it to a little more than three times the diameter, that will do. The ring will stretch slightly during making up. Bend the bar edgewise to the template. The beak of the anvil is convenient to work on with a mallet. Otherwise, have a thick round rod in the vise (Fig. 18-7C).

Having got the shape in that direction, wrap the bar in a circle around the beak or rod. File the meeting ends slightly open on the inside (Fig. 18-7D) and braze or silver solder them. True shape of the ring with a mallet over the beak or a rod. Try it on the bowl. If necessary, use a half-round file to correct any unevenness of the top edge. Stand the bowl on the ring and move it about until the rim is level all round. Mark where the ring comes with scratches from a scriber.

Tie the ring on with iron wire, then sweat it on with soft solder. Be careful not to overheat. Sufficient heat to melt soft solder will not be enough to anneal the copper and undo the hardening achieved by planishing. Put flux around the joint

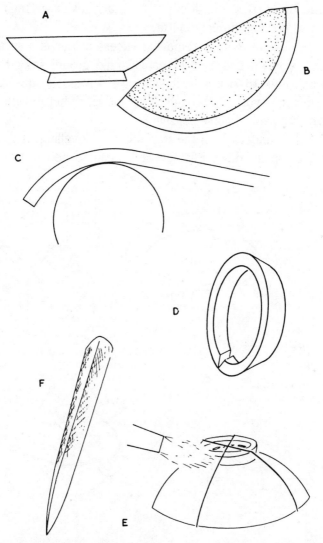

Fig. 18-7. A base for a bowl can be made from a strip brazed and soldered on: (A) bowl; (B) template; (C) bend the bar edgewise; (D) file the ends; (E) heat gently; (F) scraper.

and have small pieces of solder inside the ring while heating gently outside (Fig. 18-7E). Stop heating as soon as the solder melts. If it does not run everywhere in the joint, touch the gaps with a brush dipped in flux. If there is obviously not enough solder, touch the end of a stick on the inside of the joint. But do this very briefly or too much solder will melt and run where you do not want it.

A useful tool for removing excess solder is a scraper made from the end of an old triangular file, ground smooth to a point (Fig. 18-7F). Use it sideways across the unwanted solder until you are through to the metal, then rub with fine abrasive paper before polishing.

The underside of the ring will need levelling. It can be rubbed up and down a flat file while being turned or it can be

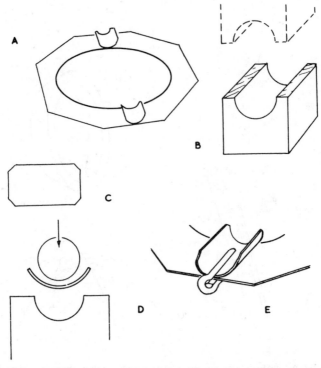

Fig. 18-8. Cigarette holders can be soldered to the rim of a tray: (A) tray; (B) mold; (C) cigarette holders; (D) tap the holders in the molds; (E) clamps.

rubbed with a circular action on a piece of emery paper on a flat surface.

A small tray with a flat rim can have pieces put on to make it into an ashtray (Fig. 18-8A). A suitable mold for shaping the pieces can be made by drilling a hole about three-fourths on an inch in diameter across a piece of hardwood, then cut it in half (Fig. 18-8B).

Cut the cigarette holders (Fig. 18-8C) with rounded or bevelled corners. They could be left smooth or planished while flat with a domed hammer on a flat stake. Smooth the edges and shape the pieces by using a piece of wood rod to tap them into the mold (Fig. 8-18D) with the planished side on top.

Sweat the holders to the tray rim with soft solder. Split pins sprung open make suitable clamps (Fig. 18-8E). Very little solder is needed. Put a small piece of flux at one side and heat the other side gently until the solder runs through.

All of the shaping described so far is hollowing, done mostly from the inside. Raising is stretching the metal mostly from the outside and is used to make a much deeper thing than a bowl. By careful work, it is possible to start with a disc and finish with a cup or vase much deeper than it is across (Fig. 18-9A).

The first step is to hollow the disc in the same way as if making a bowl, except the center area can be left flat if that is what you want (Fig. 18-9B). Work the bowl to a reasonable depth, but there is no need to go more than the metal wants to go by this method.

Raising is done with the mallet shaped like a cross peen or with a raising hammer, which is like a cross peen hammer, but with a longer head to give sufficient reach. The hammer can make more progress with each blow, but it rapidly hardens the metal. The mallet might be slower, but annealing stops should be less frequent.

Use a stake with a domed top and tilt it in the vise. Start by working around just above what will be the base (Fig.

18-9C). Make a course above this, but not closely adjoining it (Fig. 18-9D). Make one or more courses above this until you are hitting around the rim (Fig. 18-9E). On the way, it is probable that the edge will start wrinkling. Keep this in check. Have a piece of leather on the bench and use a bossing mallet to knock out any wrinkles over this (Fig. 18-9F).

Anneal the work and go back to the start again. Make courses around the metal. Work between the previous courses and be careful to deal with wrinkles as they occur. What you are doing is stretching the metal upward, but at the same time you have to reduce the circumference of the rim considerably in the process. The lower part will get to shape first, but you will have to work progressively upward with many annealings to get the top to the shape you want. A flaired vase looks good and curving the section outwards toward the rim simplifies the final stages of raising.

BUILT-UP WORK

Raising is a slow process, although the results are very satisfying to the maker. A very similar result can be attained by building up the work. This also allows the making of some shapes that would be impossible by raising, such as a vase with a narrower top than bottom (Fig. 18-10A). The body is made from flat sheet rolled around and brazed or silver soldered. Then the bottom is added. The techniques are described in Chapter 17.

Draw a fullsize side view of the vase. Extend the side lines until they meet. Use this as the center for compasses to get the developed shape needed to make the conical body. Step off three times around the curve and allow a little extra (Fig. 18-10B).

Cut a piece of copper or gliding metal to this shape. Anneal it and wrap it around the beak of the anvil or a rod in the vise. File the meeting edges straight and slightly open on the inside. Wire the cone and braze the joint, then the bottom can be silver soldered. Alternatively, silver solder this joint

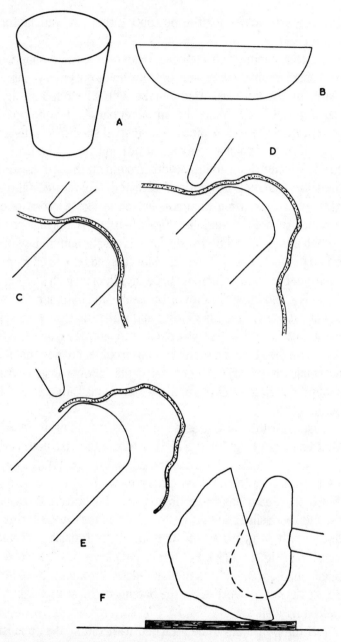

Fig. 18-9. Use a hammer or mallet to make a deep shape: (A) hollow the disc; (B) the center area is left flat; (C) work just above the base; (D) make a course; (E) make a course until you are hitting against the rim; (F) use a bossing mallet.

and use soft solder for the bottom. Either are satisfactory (Fig. 17-4).

After joining and cleaning true the circular shape, if necessary, rub the top and bottom level on emery paper. Flare the top outward. Use a stake with a rounded straight top (Fig. 18-10C). Make it from steel bar. Grind and polish the curve of the top. A piece of mild steel should be satisfactory for occasional use. An old flat or hand file can be broken to a few inches long and the teeth ground off toward the end, then the rounding ground and polished. This little stake is used with a creasing hammer, which is like a cross peen hammer in both directions (Fig. 18-10D). A normal cross peen hammer could be used, but a creasing hammer with a broad flatter curve is more suitable. It could be forged from a length of bar about 1 inch by three-eighth of an inch section.

Hold the vase tilted over the stake and hammer around to flare the top. Use light blows and watch that the flaring is even (Fig. 18-10E). The silver soldered or brazed joint should flare with the adjoining metal without trouble, but see that it is not built up thickly. If necessary, file it level inside. Any avount of flaring should be possible, but a small amount should be adequate.

At the other end, use a stake with rounding to match what you want (Fig. 18-10F). Have this in the vise and work around with a mallet to turn in the edge (Fig. 18-10G). Level the bottom by rubbing it on emery paper.

If the seam has been brazed and the bottom is to be attached with silver solder, go ahead and make the joint. Cut a disc slightly larger than the bottom of the tubular part and wire it on (Fig. 18-11A). Put borax and pieces of silver solder inside and heat outside to melt and draw through the solder. Be careful not to overheat or the brazing of the seam might be melted as well.

If the bottom is to be attached with soft solder, planish the conical part now. Deal with the turned-in bottom over the stake it was shaped on and the body of the vase over the

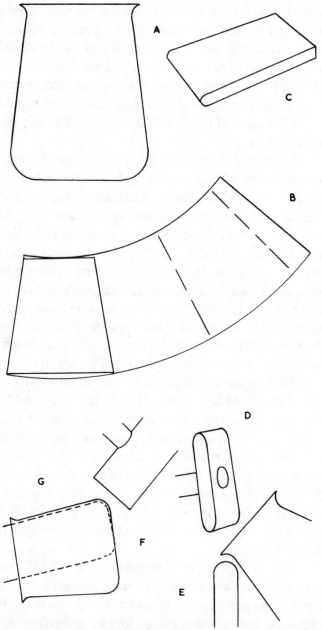

Fig. 18-10. Instead of raising, a deep shape can be built up: (A) vase; (B) step off three times; (C) round straight top; (D) creasing hammer; (E) flare evenly; (F) use a stake to round; (G) use a mallet to turn in the edge.

smooth top (Fig. 18-11B). Use a domed planishing hammer. Take care to make the planishing marks overlap and go close to the flared top without getting so close as to damage it. When this has been done, wire on the base disc and sweat the joint with soft solder—using no more heat than necessary.

In either case, go around filing the edge of the disc to match the curve of the vase (Fig. 18-11C). Rub this smooth and polish the joint.

There could be punched decoration around the top. The pattern shown in Fig. 18-11D is made with two punches. One is a piece of steel rod filed to a half-moon shape on the end (Fig. 18-11E). The other is made by drilling a small shallow hole in the end of the rod, then filing around to make almost a knife edge around it (Fig. 18-11F). Draw a pencil line around the vase as a guide. Punch the overlapping half-moon marks about three-fourths of the way around, working over a supporting rod in the vise. Then check the remaining space and adjust the last few marks accordingly. A variation, using the same two punches and another straightline one, has a continuous line with leaves and berries (Fig. 18-11G).

Another form of decoration is a ring of twisted wire, often put around the top of a bowl or cup (Fig. 18-12A). A doubled piece of wire somewhat more than twice the distance around the object should be annealed just before twisting. Grip the two ends in a vise and hold the loop with a hook in the chuck of a hand drill. Pull back on the hand drill while turning the handle to twist the wire (Fig. 18-12B). The action of twisting hardens the metal rapidly. If a tight twist is to be obtained, it might be necessary to anneal the wire again to get the closest twist.

Cut the meeting ends diagonally (Fig. 18-12C) so that the joint is less obvious than if it was cut straight across. Make the ring too small, as it is easily stretched. If it is too big, it cannot be made smaller, except by cutting a section out and joining again. Silver solder the ends. Lightly tap around the ring with a mallet over the beak or a rod until it has stretched almost enough to press into position. It is unwise to stretch it absolutely to size and then try it in place. This might be enough to further stretch it oversize before fitting. A varia-

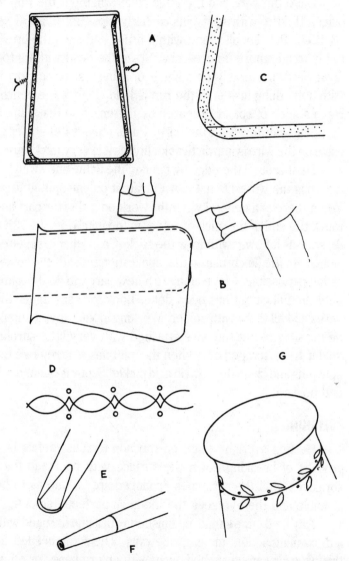

Fig. 18-11. The bottom is soldered to a vase which can be decorated by punching: (A) wire the disc; (B) shape over a stake; (C) file to match the disc; (D) punched decoration; (E) file to shape; (F) drill a shallow hole; (G) leave and berry decoration.

tion on leaving the wire round in section is to use a hammer on the wire so the outside is flattened to give a different appearance.

Have the wire and the edge clean, then put the ring in place. Hold it with split pins at fairly close intervals (Fig. 18-12D). Put flux all round with a brush and have the brush ready to add more if necessary. Stand the bowl with its top downward, preferably on a sheet of asbestos, or support it with something inside so the rim is held clear of the bench. Have a stick of solder prepared by flattening so that quite a thin edge can touch on the wire. Putting pieces of solder in place on the wire is impracticable, unless it is very thick wire.

Heat around the edge by fanning the flame and swinging it across the wire. Do not concentrate it on one spot at first. When there is a general warmth, work on a shorter part and touch the end of the stick of solder in the joint (Fig. 18-12E). As soon as it flows, withdraw the stick. Coax what has melted along with the flux brush so that application spreads the solder as far as possible. Move along to a new part and do the same until the full circuit has been done. Look for gaps under the wires and fill them with solder. Working in this way, it should be possible to get the wire attached with very little surplus solder to be scraped off. When the joint has set, remove the split pins and clean the bowl in acid pickle. Scour it clean, dry it and polish it.

POLISHING

Getting a bright shine on the non-ferrous metals is a process of breaking down the surface with finer and finer abrasives until the scratches produced are so fine as to be invisible and the eye sees the metal as perfectly smooth.

Any filed edge should be finished with a fine file used with a draw filing action, moving sideways. The scratches left by this process can be rubbed away with emery paper or other abrasive. Two grades should be enough, but make sure the coarser grade really does remove file marks and the finer

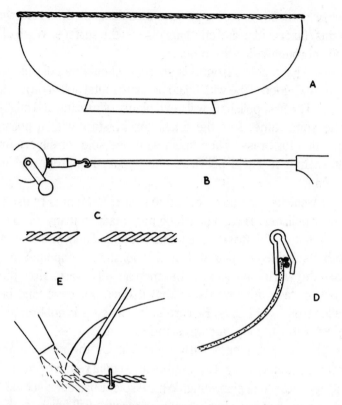

Fig. 18-12. Twisted wire makes a decoration around the edge of a bowl: (A) bowl; (B) pull and twist the wire; (C) cut ends diagonally; (D) hold with split pins; (E) heat by fanning the flame.

grade removes the marks of the coarser grade. Do not let the emery paper rub the planished surface.

Spelter and silver solder will polish with the metal and silver solder will finish almost the same color as gilding metal and not show much on copper. The brass color of spelter is slightly more obvious. However, make sure there are no projections at the joints since polishing will highlight them. Rub them down with the tip of a file, followed by emery paper. Soft solder will not polish. Any that has gone where it should not must be scraped away to expose the metal underneath.

A planished surface is already fairly smooth, due to the compacting action with hammer and stake. Use pumice powder or domestic scouring powder on a damp cloth to remove stains, flux residue and anything else on the surface. Wash off and thoroughly dry the metal.

To hand polish from this stage, it should be possible to bring up a good shine with liquid or paste metal polish on a soft cloth. The first polishing will need plenty of rubbing and might take some time. For the finest finish, start with a polish intended for brass. Then finish with one sold for silver. An alternative to liquid polish is one supplied impregnated in batting.

A quicker and more effective first treatment is to use a power polisher. Have a polishing mop made of many discs of cloth that can be driven at a sufficient speed and well charge with a suitable compound. It is the polishing compound that does the work, so recharge the mop as necessary. Hold the bowl or vase downwards so that it does not catch and be pulled from your hands. Be careful that an edge is not brought upward to the mop, for the same reason.

Power polishing is fairly powerful. On the main areas, treat the metal lightly. Heavy pressure could remove much of the appearance of planishing. Where solder has been scraped or an edge has been filed, heavier pressure will finish off the effect of scraping and remove abrasive marks or small particles of solder. Final polishing is best done with a mop without polishing compound on it. Do not use a mop that has been used on steel or the softer metal may be scratched.

Although an initial polish on a power mop gets a good finish, too much of it later would reduce the planishing effect. Upkeep of the finish is better done by hand polishing. A suitable protective treatment is a spray with transparent lacquer.

Casting

19

An alternative to forging and fabricating metal is to melt it and run it into a mold. When metal is extracted from ore it is run into molds. Then the blocks are further worked during manufacture to form the bars and sheets we use. If sufficient heat is available, most metals and alloys can be melted again and poured into molds of any shape. It is the amount of heat necessary that limits the choice of metals which can be cast in a small shop.

If some decorative ironwork is examined, much of it will be found to be a combination of forged and cast iron. Castings are used where an animal or human face has to be included or where there are floral representations too complicated for forging. The gate to a medieval castle might have the coat of arms of the owner as a center piece cast to shape. Many small decorations, such as a cast iron flower finial come at the end of a forged bar. Cast iron of this type is rather brittle, but used for decoration without fine detail, this does not matter. In the industrial production of cast iron and steel, there are techniques that overcome any tendency to brittleness and other faults. Many steel tools start as castings. Casting is also valuable where weight is important. Anything bulky, and therefore heavy, is almost certainly cast. Even if it is machined extensively after casting.

Unfortunately, the heat required to melt iron and steel is more than can be achieved in a blacksmith's shop. The end of a bar might be heated enough to melt away, but what is required is enough heat to melt a quantity of metal in a container to a state where it is fully liquid and can be poured. The heat limit restricts what casting can be done in a small shop to those metals alnd alloys with low melting points.

Lead is the metal in general use with the lowest melting point. This is a good choice for practice castings. It does not cast with very sharp angles, but if it is alloyed with antimony it becomes printers' type metal and will cast sharply. Proportions are four parts lead to one part antimony. Old printing type could be used. Aluminum has about twice the melting temperature of lead, but that heat should just be possible using a blacksmith's hearth. Some fires may just melt brass. Zinc is not readily available, but if it can be obtained, it can be alloyed with lead and antimony to make a good casting metal within the heat range of a smith's shop. A suitable proportion is 14 parts lead, five parts zinc and one part antimony. Typical melting points are shown in Table 19-1.

Most metals and alloys shrink as they cool. This will have to be allowed for in making a casting. A shrinkage of about one-eighth of an inch per 1 foot is probable. An alloy containing antimony keeps its size or expands slightly on cooling.

Lead and type metal can be melted in an iron container. For a small quantity this could be a ladle, but a handled iron pot with a spout is needed for larger quantities. Metals that require a higher temperature should only be melted in a crucible, which is made of fireclay or plumbago. Special long tongs with jaws to embrace the crucible are used with it. Obviously, molten metal has to be handled with great care and early experience is best gained with lead or its alloys melted in a ladle. If a metal runs where it should not, smother it with sand. Never pour water on it.

Table 19-1. Melting Points.

Metal	Degrees Fahrenheit	Degrees Celcius
Lead	621	327
Zinc	787	419
Antimony	1166	630
Aluminim	1214	660
Brass	1650	900
Iron	2768	1520

Metal can be melted repeatedly. Old castings can be melted to make new things. Cutting or breaking into small pieces will speed melting. Once there is some molten metal, anything solid lowered into it will soon melt. Impurities will rise to the surface and this *dross* should be skimmed off with a small ladle before pouring. When metal is poured, do not break the flow.

Casting is done in a mold and sometimes the whole process is described as molding. For metal casting, the mold is usually made of sand. Sea sand or builders' sand is not really suitable, although there can be experiments with available sand. The best material is sold as foundry sand or green sand, which has the right proportions of clay and silica to give a good bond combined with ventilation. It is used slightly damp. Having it too wet could be dangerous when the moisture comes into contact with the hot metal. A mixture with five percent water is about right. To test the right amount of moisture, squeeze a handful of sand tightly. It should keep the shape of the hand when released. If much sand is left adhering to the hand it is too wet.

SINGLE MOLD

For most casting, the mold has to be in two parts. But some simple things that have a flat part pointing upward can be made in a single mold. An example is a lead block to be used as a weight (Fig. 19-1A). In a simple example, the hole is not cast, but is drilled or punched afterward.

Use any wooden box that is big enough to hold enough sand and stout enough not to burst when the sand is rammed tight. Put sand in the box and ram it down a little at a time with a flat-ended piece of wood (Fig. 19-1B) or even the handle of a hammer.

Make a wooden pattern of the weight. It must be tapered so that it can be withdrawn from the sand. This applies to the narrow part for the hole as well as the main body. It could be cut from solid wood or built up (Fig. 19-1C). If a lathe is available, a round pattern can be turned. Finish the surface smooth. It does not matter what wood is used. For general patternmaking in industry, pine and mahogany are used. For this weight, the wood can be used as it is. When a pattern is to be used many times, it is usual to seal its surface with shellac or varnish.

Scoop out some sand from the middle of the box and press the pattern in. It helps to put a screw eye in its base so it can be withdrawn (Fig. 19-1D). Ram the sand tight around the pattern and level its top. When you are certain it is closely packed, withdraw the pattern and examine the mold. Pour lead in until it is level and let it cool. Then remove some sand so that you can lift it out. Punch or drill the hole. File or hammer the bottom level.

That shows the principle and is a method that can be used for the simplest castings. For most casting, the mold is made in two parts even when one surface of the finished work is to be flat.

FLAT-FACED CASTINGS

Molding is done in flasks, which are boxes open top and bottom and arranged to fit against each other. In production work, the flasks are cast iron. However, small work can be done in wooden flasks. The lower one is called a drag and the other is the cope or top part.

Wooden boxes can be made in identical sizes (Fig. 19-2A). Pieces across the end act as handles and provide positions for locating dowels that stand up from the drag and

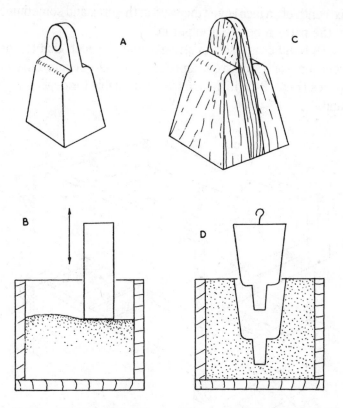

Fig. 19-1. A weight (A) can be cast from a wooden mold (C) in a box of sand (B, D).

engage easily in holes in the top part (Fig. 19-2B). So that the parts cannot be reversed in relation to each other, have the dowels off-center so that they will not match the other way. It will help to have grooves on the insides of the box to provide a key to grip the sand (Fig. 19-2C). Sizes will depend on the work to be done, but the wood should be thick enough to remain stiff and the corner joints should be strong.

Although green sand is used in the flask, there has to be another sand to sprinkle between the meeting surfaces to prevent them bonding together. The parting sand is used dry and can be bought as such, but brick dust can be used. It is sprinkled through a fine sieve or riddle (mesh about one-sixteenth of an inch) over the sand in the drag and sometimes on the pattern before it is put in.

A rammer is a sort of straight-ended mallet, that can be wood or iron. A narrow tapered end will get into smaller spaces (Fig. 19-2D). Have a trowel available for dealing with sand.

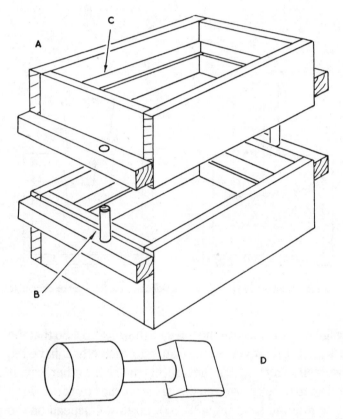

Fig. 19-2. A wooden flask for casting can be made as two open boxes: (A) identical size boxes; (B) dowels; (C) grooves; (D) a narrow tapered end.

If the object to be made has a flat face and the rest of the shape can be tapered to withdraw from the sand, the whole shape can be arranged in one half of the flask. The weight just described could be made in this way or a stepped pedestal would be an example. Make a pattern and include a slight

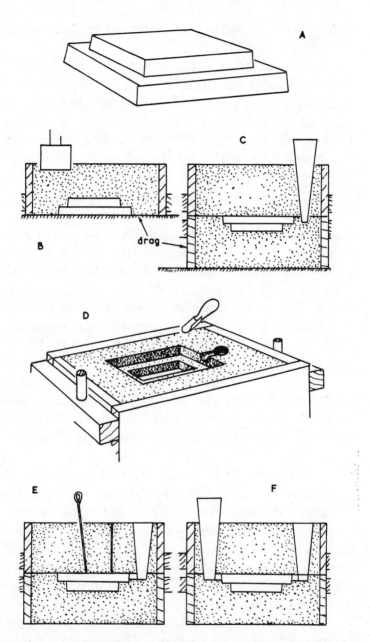

Fig. 19-3. A flat pattern (A) goes into one part and is covered with sand in the other part (B). Then the sand is cut to allow pouring molten metal (C). A deep scoop (D) will cut the metal. A pointed wire (E) allows air to escape or you can use a riser (F).

409

taper to all edges. Surfaces can be flat as they do not affect withdrawal (Fig. 19-3A).

Put the pattern on a flat board and have the drag face downward around it. Sprinkle facing sand through the sieve on the board and pattern. Put in green sand with the trowel and press it down at intervals with the rammer (Fig. 19-3B). Make sure the whole box is filled. See that sand is forced into the corners. Fill to overflowing, then scrape the surface level with a straight-edged piece of wood.

Lift and turn the drag over. Put the top part in place. Sprinkle facing sand in. So that the metal can be poured in, stand a a tapered rod slightly to one side of the pattern (Fig. 19-3C). This is called a gate stick and can be wood or metal. It could be round, but a tapered square or octagonal piece of wood will do. Fill the top part with sand, ramming it tight in the same way as the drag, then scrape its top level.

Ease out the gate stick. Tap it gently at the side to loosen it. The top of the hole left can be made into a funnel shape for ease in pouring metal.

Lift away the top part and put it aside, face up. Cut a small channel from the gate stick position to the pattern as a runner for the molten metal when it is poured. A piece of sheet metal folded into a deep scoop or gouge will cut the runner (Fig. 19-3D).

To get the pattern out, enter the point of a screw in it, so that it can be used as a handle. There will almost certainly be a few flaws in the mold where sand has fallen or broken away. Bellows can be used to blow away loose sand. If repairs have to be made there are molders' tools that are used like small trowels for pressing sand into place. They can be made by a smith and are bars with opposite ends formed into small trowel shapes (Fig. 19-4).

If the work is small, all that has to be done now is to put the parts of the flask back together and pour the metal. There will be enough ventilation in the sand to carry the air away, but the pouring metal will put pressure on the whole mold and the

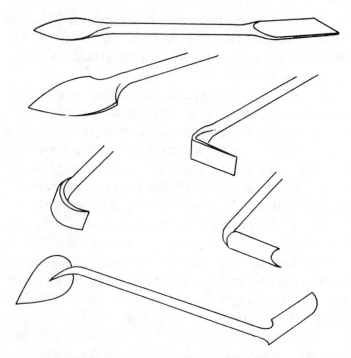

Fig. 19-4. Small steel hand tools are used to correct a mold.

top part should be weighted or attached to the drag to prevent it from lifting. For a clean casting, the inside of the mold can be dusted with graphite.

If the work is larger, it is advisable to provide some escape for air as the metal is poured in. This can be done while the pattern is still in place by pushing in a pointed wire pricker at several places until it is felt pressing against the pattern (Fig. 19-3E). For a very large casting, it might be better to provide a hole called a *riser*. A riser is really a repeat of the gate stick hole at the side remote from it (Fig. 19-3F). Excess metal that has run off that way or into ventilating holes will have to be cut off after the casting is removed.

SYMMETRICAL CASTINGS

Many things that have to be cast could not be made in one half of the flask since it would be impossible to withdraw the pattern. Many castings have a cylindrical form. The only way they can be cast is to have half in each part of the flask so that the curves are into the sand, which should not be disturbed when the pattern is removed.

To get a tight pack of sand in each part when a solid symmetrical pattern is being used, preparation has to start with a temporary filling of the top part of the flask. Place the top part with the side that will be toward the drag upward and fill it with sand. Pack it reasonably tightly and press the pattern halfway into it (Fig. 19-5A). If it is a big pattern, cut out some of the sand first and finish the sand surface level.

Put the drag on. Sprinkle on parting sand. Fill the drag and ram the sand tightly. Scrap it level (Fig. 19-5B). Turn over the flask to bring the drag underneath. Separate the boxes carefully to leave the pattern in the drag. Knock out the sand from the top part. Put it back on the drag, sprinkle in parting sand and repack the top part tightly. Then scrape it level. Having this extra stage is necessary because the first filling of the upper part cannot be done tight enough.

With both parts of the flask properly packed, use the gate stick and make ventilating holes if they are needed. Then separate the parts and remove the pattern (Fig. 19-5C). Cut a runner and clean up the mold if necessary. Dust with graphite. Put the parts back together and pour the metal.

CORED CASTINGS

Many castings have to be made with holes through them. Sometimes holes are drilled, but it is helpful to cast the hole when the metal is poured. For many purposes, that is all that is needed. For more precision, the cast hole can be opened to size. To make a hole, there has to be a core arranged in the mold so that the metal flows around it and the core can be removed from the casting after it has set.

Suppose a cylindrical casting is required with a hole through that will be machined to make a bearing (Fig. 19-6A). A core must be made longer than the final length of the casting

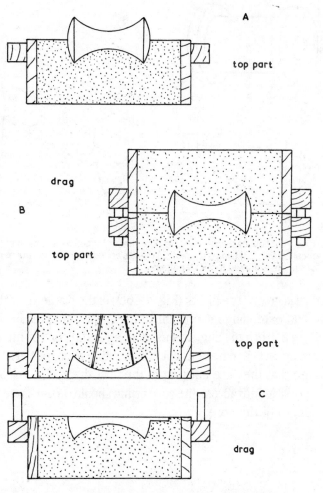

Fig. 19-5. A symmetrical item is arranged in both parts of a flask.

so that it can be supported in the molded sand. This is built up in a core box, which is a two-part mold, into which the sand mixture can be packed (Fig. 19-6B). Make it from wood, with half the diameter gouged from each part. Use dowels or other pegs to keep the two parts correctly located in relation to each other (Fig. 19-6C).

The core will go into the sand so it is supported outside the main hollows left by the pattern. To allow for this, the

413

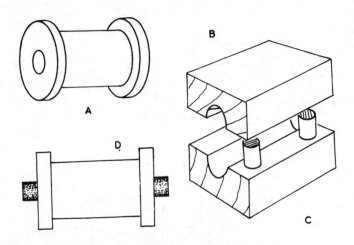

Fig. 19-6. A hollow casting requires a core that is formed in a core box: (A) cylindrical casting; (B) two-part mold; (C) dowels are used to position the parts; (D) core prints are used to make patterns.

pattern is given core prints (Fig. 19-6D) of the diameter of the core and extending far enough to make the recesses in the sand. In pattern making, it is usual to stain the core prints so that they are a different color from the main pattern to indicate that they are not part of the final shape. Of course, the overall length across the core prints should be the same as the length of the core.

Glossary

Glossary

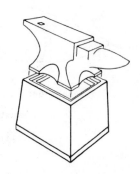

abrasive. A natural or artificial substance used for grinding, polishing, buffing, lapping, or sandblasting. Commonly includes garnet, emery, corundum, diamond, aluminum oxide, and silicon carbide.

aging. In a metal or alloy, a change in properties which takes place slowly at room termperature and more rapidly at higher temperatures.

alloy. A substance having metallic properties, composed of one or more chemical elements, at least one of which is a metallic element.

alumel. A nickel-based alloy frequently used as a component of thermocouples.

angle iron. Now actually mild steel. Bars with 90 degree angle cross-section.

annealing. Heating and holding at a suitable temperature and then cooling at a suitable rate, usually for the purpose of reducing hardness, improving machinability, or achieving other desired properties.

anvil. Any heavy iron or steel device on which work is hammered.

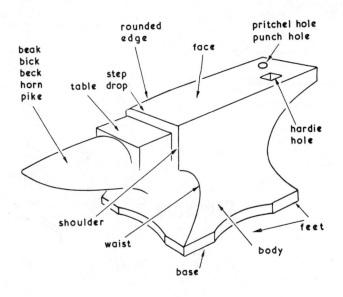

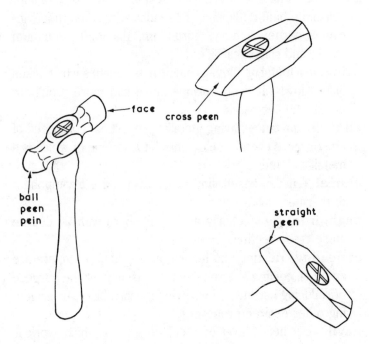

Names of the main parts of the anvil and hammers.

arbor. Round part to hold another being worked on. A rotating shaft.

asbestos. Fire resistant minerial material.

auger. A wood drill bit having its own handle, instead of fitting in a brace.

backing up. Upsetting by hammering end of work.

baking. Heating at a low temperature to remove gases.

base metal. The metal present in the highest proportion in an alloy. Brass, for example, is a copper-base alloy.

bastard. Intermediate—a file with teeth between coarse and fine.

beak or bick. Round conical pointed end of anvil. Also horn.

bell mouth. Spread end of tube.

belt grinding. Grinding with an abrasive belt.

bentonite. A clay-like substance used as an ingredient in molding sands.

bevel. The cutting angle of a tool.

bick iron or bick horn. Light anvil for sheet metalwork.

biner. A material, other than water, added to molding sand to bind the particles together.

bit. Less common name for jaws of tongs.

bit or drill bit. Tool for making holes by cutting and not punching.

blacksmith's vise. Alternative name for leg vise.

blasting. Cleaning or finishing metal by impingement with abrasive particles carried by gas or liquid.

blind riser. A riser which does not extend through the top of the mold.

blowhole. A hole in a casting caused by gas trapped during solidification.

body. Main part of anvil.

bolster. Block with hole to support work being punched.

borax. Chemical used as welding or brazing flux.

boss. Center part of a wheel. In smithing, a locally raised part. Type of punch for raising sheet metal from the reverse side.

bossing mallet. Wooden mallet with egg-shaped head for shaping sheet metal.

bottom board. A flat board used to hold the flask when making molds (usually called molding board).

bottom fuller. Tool to fit in the hardie hole of anvil for drawing or shaping steel.

bottom swage. Tool to fit in hardie hole of anvil, having a grooved top surface.

brass. An alloy consisting mainly of copper (over 50 percent) and zinc, to which smaller amounts of other metals may be added.

brazing. Joining parts by flowing a thin layer of non-ferrous filler metal in the space between them. The term brazing is ordinarily used if the process is carried out above 800°F.; below this temperature it is called soldering.

breeze. Alternative name for coke.

brine. Salt water, used as a cooling bath.

brinell hardness test. A test for the hardness of a material by forcing a hardened steel or carbide ball of specified diameter into it under a specified load.

bronze. A copper-based, tin alloy with or without other elements. Certian alloys without tin are sometimes referred to as bronzes. The term is rather loosely applied.

buffing. Developing a lustrous surface appearance by contacting the work with a rotating buffing wheel.

buffing wheel. Fabric, leather, or paper discs held together, usually by sewing, used to form wheels for grinding, polishing, or buffing.

bumping. Ramming sand into a mold by jarring or jolting.

burin. An engraving tool.

burnt-in sand. A casting defect caused by sand adhering to the surface of the casting.

burr. Turned over edge. Small rotary file.

butt. End to end as in a butt weld.

butterfly nut. Nut to fit on bolt, with projections for hand tightening.

calipers. Tool with hinged curved jaws for checking thicknesses and diameters.

capillary attraction. A combination of forces which causes molten metals or other liquids to flow between closely spaced solid surfaces.

cape chisel. Narrow chisel for cutting grooves in metal.

carbide. A compound of carbon with one or more metallic elements.

carbide tip. Very hard tip to make a cutting edge bonded to a steel tool.

carbonizing. Alternative name for case hardening.

carriage bolt. Bolt with shallow domed head and square neck to prevent turning in wood.

carriage screw. Similar to wood screw end.

case hardening. Applying a high carbon surface to mild steel.

casting. (noun) An object obtained by solidification of a substance in a mold. (verb) Pouring into a mold to obtain an object of the desired shape.

casting shrinkage. The reduction in volume of a metal as it solidifies and cools.

casting stresses. Stresses set up in a casting primarily caused by shrinkage.

catalyst. A substance which changes the rate of a reaction without itself undergoing any net change.

center punch. Pointed punch to make a dot in metal.

centrifugal casting. A casting made by pouring metal into a rotating mold.

chaplet. A metal support for holding cores in place in sand molds.

cheek. An intermediate section of a flask used between the cope and the drag when molding a shape requiring more than one parting line.

chill. A metal insert placed in a sand mold to increase the cooling rate at that point.

chisel. A tool for cutting wood or stone.

chromel. A nickel-chromium alloy used for thermocouples and heating elements.

clay. An earthy substance consisting mainly of hydrous aluminum silicate and used often in molding sands as a binder.

clinker. Waste product from burned coal.

coke. Substance resulting from heating coal to drive out elements producing yellow flame and smoke. Coke is smokeless and burns with a blue flame.

cold chisel. Tool which is hammered for cutting cold metal.

cold sett or sate. Handled chisel for cutting cold steel.

cold shut. A discontinuity in the surface of a casting as a result of two streams of molten metal failing to unite.

collar. Loop joining parts of scroll work.

cope. The upper or topmost section of a flask, mold, or pattern.

core. A formed section inserted inside a mold to shape the interior of a casting.

core blower. A machine for making foundry cores.

corrosion. Oxidation of surface of meral, such as rust on iron.

countersink. Bevelled edge of hole. Tool for producing this.

coupler. Ring to slide on handles of tongs to lock them.

croning process. A shell molding process.

cross-cut chisel. Alternative name for cape chisel.

crowbar. Steel lever, usually with curved notched end.

crucible. A pot or vessel used for melting metal or other substances.

crush. A casting defect caused by partial displacement of the sand in a mold before the metal is poured.

cupping tool. Punching tool with hollowed end for forming a round head rivet. A lower one is a rivet set.

cut-off tools. Upper and lower tools for shearing rod with a hammer blow.

cut-off wheel. Thin rotating abrasive wheel for cutting hard steel.

cutting saddle. Plate to put over an anvil face to protect it when the part to be cut is too large for the table.

defect. A condition that impairs the usefulness of an object.

degasser. (or **degasifier**) A material added to molten metal to remove dissolved gases which otherwise might be trapped when the metal solidifies.

degassing. The act of removing dissolved gases from molten metals.

dendrite. A crystal with a branching tree-like pattern often seen in castings which have been very slowly cooled.

deoxidizer. A substance added to molten metal to remove dissolved oxygen.

die. Tool for cutting a screw thread on a rod or a tool for forming steel.

die casting. A casting process whereby molten metal is forced under pressure into the cavity of a metal mold.

dividers. Hinged pair of points for scratching a circle or comparing distances.

dowel. In smithing, a projecting locating part to fit into a hole in another piece.

draft. Taper on the surfaces of a pattern to allow it to be withdrawn from the mold.

drag. The bottom section of a mold, flask, or pattern.

drawing. The action of hammering to make iron longer and thinner.

drift. Tapered pin to drive through holes to pull them into line.

drill bit. Tool for making holes by cutting and not by punching. Also drill or bit.

drill press. A machine which uses bits to drill holes.

drop. A casting defect caused by sand dropping from the cope.

dross. The scum that forms on the surface of a molten metal due to oxidation or impurities rising to the surface.

dry sand mold. A mold made of sand and then dried.

ductility. The ability of a material to deform without fracturing.

dusting. Applying a powder such as graphite to a mold surface.

elasticity. The property of a material allowing it to regain its original shape after deformation.

emboss. Raise sheet metal with hammer, punch or boss from reverse side.

emery. An impure form of aluminum oxide used as an abrasive.

erosion. A casting defect caused by the scouring action of flowing metal.

etching. Eating into steel with acid, usually to mark a name.

eye. Ring shaped in the end of a rod.

eye bolt. Bolt with a flattened or shaped end with a hole through.

face. Working surface of anvil. Level machine part. The action of making a surface flat.

facing. Special sand placed in direct contact with the pattern to improve the surface finish of a casting.

faggot weld. End of rod turned back and welded close to itself.

ferrule. A tube or cap on a wooden handle to prevent it from splitting.

file. Tool with teeth made with grooves cut across it.

fines. Sand grains substantially smaller than the predominate size in a sand mixture.

finish. In a metal, surface condition, quality, or appearance.

firebrick. Brick that withstands high temperatures.

fireclay. Clay that will not crack when fired.

fireplace tongs. For picking up coal.

flairing. Spreading the end of a tube.

flask. A metal or wood frame for making a sand mold.

flatter or flattie. Handled tool with broad flat face that can be put over an uneven hot surface and hammered to flatten it.

flux. Liquid or powder used to aid metal flow in welding, brazing and soldering.

forge. A furnace for heating iron and steel.

forge, rivetting. Portable forge with fan blower, originally intended for heating rivets for structural steelwork.

foundry. A place where castings are made.

fuller, bottom. Tol to fit in hardie hole of anvil for drawing or shaping steel.

fuller, top. A similar handled tool used with it.

gagger. A piece of metal used to reinforce or support the sand in a mold.

galvanized iron. Iron coated with zinc as protection against rust.

gas pocket. A cavity in a casting caused by trapped gas.

gassing. Evolution of gasses from a metal during solidification.

gate. The portion of the runner where molten metal enters the mold cavity.

gated pattern. A pattern which includes the gate in the mold.

gauge. Size, particularly thicknesses and sizes of rods, by number or letter to a recognized scheme or code.

grain refiner. A substance added to molten metal to attain a finer grain structure in the casting.

green coal. Unburned coal.

grinding. Removing stock from work by use of a grinding wheel.

grinding wheel. A circular cutting tool made of abrasive grains bonded together.

grit size. The nominal size of abrasive particles according to the number of openings per lineal inch in a screen through which the particles will pass.

hacksaw. Metal-cutting hand saw with blade tensioned in a frame.

hardie or hardy. Tool that fits in the hardie hole of the anvil with an edge for cutting steel.

hardie hole. Square hole in heel of anvil.

heading plate. Thick steel plate with tapered holes to take rods on which thickened heads can be formed.

heat treatment. Heating steel to alter its character, including annealing, hardening, tempering and normalizing.

heel. Opposite end of anvil to beak. Also tail.

high carbon steel. Steel with sufficient carbon to permit hardening and tempering. Steel with 0.2 percent carbon.

hold-down or hold-fast. Device of angular form driven into an anvil hole so its other arm holds down work on the anvil face.

holding furnace. A small furnace in which molten metal is transferred and held until ready to pour.

hollow ground. A concave bevel on a cutting tool.

honing. Sharpening or smoothing with a fine abrasive stone.

hook rule. Rule for measuring from a hooked end over the edge of hot steel.

horn. Alternative name for beak of anvil.

horse power. Unit for stating power produced or needed.

hot chisel. Tool which is hammered to cut hot metal.

hot sett or state. Handled chisel for cutting hot steel.

hot tear. A fracture formed in a casting during solidification because the casting is restrained from shrinking for some reason.

ingate. Same as gate.

ingot. A casting used for remelting.

insert. A removable portion of a mold.

investing casting. Casting metal into a mold made by surrounding (investing) an expendable pattern (usually wax with a refractory slurry which sets, after which the pattern is melted out. Also called "lost wax" casting.

investment compound. A mixture of refractory filler, binder, and liquid used to make molds for investment casting.

jacket. A wood or metal form slipped over a sand mold for support, especially during pouring.

jaws. Gripping surfaces of tongs or vise.

jig. A deviceto guide tools, particularly in repetition work.

joggle. An offset double bend in a bar.

ladle. A receptacle for transferring or pouring metal.

lapping. Using a grinding compound between two surfaces to rub them to match each other.

lathe. Machine for revolving wood or metal so a tool can make it round.

leaf spring. Flat steel long spring usually in graduated sets, as used in automobile suspensions.

leg vise. Vise to attach to bench with leg to floor.

loam. A molding material consisting of sand, silt, and clay used for making very large castings.

lost wax process. Investment casting in which a wax pattern is used.

low-carbon steel. Steel that cannot be tempered. Carbon content less than 0.2 percent.

machinist's vise. Vise to mount on top of bench.

mall or maul. Large mallet.

malleable. Capable of being shaped.

mallet. Type of hammer with wood, rawhide or plastic head.

mallet, bossing. With eggshaped wooden head for shaping sheet metal.

mallet, tinman's. With cylindrical wooden head for sheet metal work.

mandril or manrel. Iron block on which parts are shaped, particularly a round cone for shaping rings.

match plate. A plate of metal or other material on which are mounted patterns to facilitate molding operations.

melting point. The temperature at which a pure metal, compound, or eutectic changes from a solid to a liquid.

metallurgy. The science and technology of metals.

mild steel. Low carbon steel, which cannot be tempered.

milling tool. Rotating cutter.

misrun. A defective casting not fully formed caused by solidification of the metal before the mold cavity is filled.

mold. A form of sand, metal, or other material which contains a cavity into which molten metal is poured to form a casting.

molding machine. A machine used for making molds by mechanically compacting sand around a pattern.

mold wash. An emulsion of various materials used to coat the surfaces of a mold cavity.

mulling. Mixing sand and clay by a rubbing or rolling action.

nail beader. Heading tool with a raised face.

nail set or sett. Punch with flat end for driving nail head below surface.

neutral flame. A gas flame in which there is neither an excess of fuel nor air.

normalize. Reduce internal stresses after working by heating and allowing to cool slowly, in the same way as annealing.

offset. Double bend to alter alignment of bar.

oxidation or oxidization. Colored spectrum that forms on polished steel as it heats. Used as a guide for tempering heats of tool steel.

oxidizing flame. A flame with an excess of air (or oxygen).

parting dust. A composition used to facilitate the separation of the pattern in sand molding and prevent sticking of the sand at the junction of the cope and drag.

parting line. A plane on a pattern corresponding to the separation between the cope and drag.

patina. Colored oxidation on metal surfaces, due to long exposure to air, particularly on bronze. It can be simulated by chemical action.

pattern. A form of wood, metal, or other material around which molding material is places to make a mold.

peen or pein or pane. The shaped end of a hammer head.

peen, ball. Hemispherical knob.

peen, cross. Narrow rounded wedge shape across the head.

peen, straight. Similar, but in line with handle.

peening. Hollowing with ball peen hammer.

permanent mold. A metal mold which is used repeatedly for the production of castings.

pickling. Removing surface oxides from metals by chemical action.

pig. An ingot.

pintle. Single fixed hinge pin.

pipe. A central cavity formed in a casting during solidification.

plaster molding. Molding where a slurry of gypsum (Plaster of Paris) is formed around a pattern, allowed to harden, and thoroughly dried.

pliers. Small gripping tool with tongs action.

plumbago. A high qualtiy graphite powder.

poker. Tool for moving coal in fire.

porosity. In a metal, fine holes or pores; in a sand, degree of permeability to gases.

post vise. Alternative name for leg vise.

pouring. Transferring molten metal from a ladle or crucible to a mold.

pouring basin. A basin or funnel on top of a mold to receive the molten metal.

precision casting. A metal casting of accurate, reproducible dinmensions.

precoat. A special refractory coating applied to wax patterns in investment casting.

pressure casting. Making castings with pressure on the molten metal as in die casting.

pritchel hole. Round hole in the tail of an anvil.

punch. Tool intended to be hit with a hammer to make a dent or hole.

pyrometer. A device for measuring temperatures above the range of thermometers.

quench. To cool hot steel in a liquid.

quenching bath. The liquid into which hot steel is dipped to cool it quickly.

rabbling. Stirring molten metal with a tool.

rake. Poker with bent flattened end for pulling coal in fire.

ramming. Packing sand into a compact mass.

rasp. A coarse file-type tool with teeth individually raised.

reducing flame. A gas flame produced with excess fuel.

refining. Light hammering to finish a surface.

refractory. A material with a very high melting point suitable for use in molds and furnace linings.

reins. Handles of tongs.

resinoid wheel. A grinding wheel bonded with synthetic resins.

riddle. A sand sieve used in a foundry.

riser. A reservoir of molten metal attached to a casting to provide additional metal required as a result of shrinkage during solidification.

riveting forge. Small protable forge.

rivet set or sett. Tool with hollow for supporting or forming a round-head rivet. An upper one is called a cupping tool.

rout. Cut grooves or hollows.

router. Hand or power tool for cutting grooves and hollows.

rule. Measuring tool. Not "ruler". Can be brass.

rule, hook. Handled measuring rule with hooked end.

runner. A channel through which molten metal flows, usually the portion connecting the sprue with the gate.

runout. The accidental escape of molten metal from a mold.

rust. Corrosion on iron or steel.

saddle, cutting. Plate to put over an anvil face to protect it when the part to be cut is too large for the table. Shaped piece over which steel is curved.

sag. A casting defect caused by insufficient strength of the sand.

sand. A grandular material from the disintegration of rocks. Foundry sands are mostly pure silicon dioxide. Molding sands contain clay.

sate. Alternative name for sett.

scab. A casting defect where a thin layer of metal separates from the casting.

scarf. Bevelled end ready for welding.

scarf collar. Loop used to hold parts of scroll work together.

scrap. Discarded metal which may be reclaimed by melting.

scribe or scriber. Hard sharp steel point for scratching metal.

scroll. Decorative spiral bend.

scroll forks. Double pinned tools for pulling curves around.

scroll iron or tool. Pattern around which a scroll is shaped.

scroll wrench. Double pronged hand tool for curving.

sea coal. Finely divided coal sometimes added to molding sands.

semipermanent mold. A metal mold in which sand cores are used.

seating. Preparing a surface on to which another has to fit.

second man. Support for long work.

set. A hammer-like head on a wood handle, hit with a hammer to shape steel.

set screw. Screw used to draw parts together.

shank. The neck or part of the tool between the handle and the blade.

shell molding. Croning process. Forming molds from thermosetting resin-bonded sand mixtures brought into contact with a hot pattern.

shift. Casting defect caused by mismatch of the cope and drag.

shot. Small spherical pieces of metal.

shoulder. A thickened part of a rod, against which another part may rest. On an anvil, the side of the face next to the table.

shovel. Scoop for coal.

shrinkage cavity. A void left in a casting as a result of shrinkage.

shrinkage cracks. Hot tears in a casting due to shrinkage.

shrinkage rule. A measuring rule with expanded graduations to compensate for shrinkage of a casting as it cools.

shrinkhead. Same as riser.

silver brazing. Brazing with silver-based alloys.

skim gate. A gate designed to prevent passage of slag into the mold.

skimmer. A spoon-shaped tool for removing dross from the surface of a molten metal.

skull. The solidified metal or dross left on walls of a cruicible when the molten metal is poured out.

slag. Non-burning waste from coal.

slag inclusion. Slag or dross trapped in a solidified casting.

sledge. A large two-handed hammer.

slush casting. A hollow casting, usually made of low melting metal. After the desired thickness has solidified on the walls of the mold, the balance of the molten metal is poured out.

snagging. Free hand grinding of castings to remove flashings, etc.

snap flask. A flask hinged at one corner so that it can be quickly separated from the mold.

solidification shrinkage. The decrease in volume of a metal when it solidifies.

spatula. A bar with a flattened end, for use with plaster, paint etc.

spectrum. The rainbow range of colored oxides on heated polished steel.

spring steel. High-carbon steel, similar to tool steel.

spring swage. Top and bottom swages linked with a spring handle.

sprue. The channel that connects the pouring basin with the runner. Sometimes the definition includes all gates, risers, and runners.

stainless steel. Steel alloyed with other metals to resist corrosion.

stake. Shaped block used as an anvil for sheet metalwork.

stake vise. Alternative name for leg vise.

steel. Alloy of iron and carbon.

steel plate. Sheet metal over about three-sixteenths of an inch thick.

steel sheet. Thinner steel sheets.

step. Top edge of face next to table.

stock. Supply of steel. The body of a tool. One head of a lathe.

stress raiser or stress riser. Changes in contour of a part which introduce localization of stress.

strop. Leather strap used in final stages of tool sharpening.

swage block. Large block with many hollows and holes.

swage, bottom. Grooved tool that fits into hardie hole of anvil.

swage, spring. Top and bottom swages linked with a spring handle.

swage, top. Handled grooved tool used over the bottom swage.

table. On an anvil, the flat part between the face and the beak.

tail. Opposite end of anvil to beak. Also heel.

tang. Part of a tool that is driven into a handle.

tap. Tool for cutting a screw thread in a hole.

tarnish. Surface discoloration of a metal caused by formation of an oxide film.

temper. Reduce fully hardened steel to a suitable hardness for a particular use.

template. Pattern used for marking around to transfer an outline.

tenon. Projecting lug on one part to fit into a hole in another part.

tensile strength. The ratio of the maximum load a bar of metal can withstand to the original cross-sectional area.

thermocouple. A device for measuring temperature consisting of two dissimilar metals which produce a voltage or current roughly proportional to the differences in temperature of the hot and cold ends.

tines. Prongs, as on fork.

tinman's mallet. Mallet with wooden cylindrical head for sheet metalwork.

tinplate. Thin sheet steel coated with tin, a used for cans.

tinsnips. Shears for cutting sheet metal.

tolerance. The permissible variation in size of a part.

tongs. Long-handled plier-type tool for holding metal.

tongs, bow. With gap in jaws behind meeting points.

tongs, close-mouthed. With jaws that meet when closed.

tongs, fireplace. For picking up coal.

tongs, flat-jawed. With flat gripping surfaces.

tongs, open-mouthed. With jaws that do not meet when closed.

top fuller. Handled tool, used with bottom fuller for drawing or shaping steel.

top swage. Handled tool with grooved surface to match bottom swage.

traveler. Handled wheel to measure curves by counting revolutions.

tripoli. Abrasive compound used for buffing.

tumbling. Turning work piece, as when making square end on rod.

tuyere or twee iron. Nozzle through which blast of air enters fire.

uphand sledge. Sledge hammer of moderate weight, not used with a full swing.

upsetting. Making steel shorter and thicker. Reverse of drawing down.

veiner or veining tool. V-shaped wood carving tool.

vent. A small opening in a mold for the escape of gases.

vise or vice. Two-jawed device with tightening screw. Fixed to bench and used for holding work.

vise, blacksmith's. Vise with leg, post or stake to floor.

visegrip pliers. Self-locking pliers.

vise, machinists. Vise to mount on top of bench.

waist. Narrow part of anvil body.

wash. A coating sometimes applied to the cavity of a mold.

weld. Fuse two pieces of meta together with heat.

wildness. A condition whereby molten metal relea es so much gas that it becomes violently agitated.

wing nut. Alternative name for butterfly nut.

wrench. Any tool for levering or twisting.

wrought iron. Iron with little or no carbon, produced by a puddling process.

Index

Index